STUART ENGLAND

STUART ENGLAND

Edited by Blair Worden

PHAIDON · OXFORD

Acknowledgements

The publishers have endeavoured to credit all known persons holding copyright or reproduction rights for illustrations in this book, and wish to thank all the public, private and commercial owners, and institutions concerned, and the photographers and librarians. Numbers refer to plate numbers; page numbers refer to Picture Essays.

p141(3) By kind permission of His Grace the Duke of Northumberland; 175 Rijksmuseum Paleis Het Loo, Apeldoorn; 57 By kind permission of His Grace the Duke of Norfolk; p82(2) MAS, Barcelona; 174 Central Library, Birmingham; 181, p258(2) Walter Scott (Bradford) Ltd; 25 Fitzwilliam Museum, Cambridge; p88(2) By permission of the Master and Fellows of St John's College, Cambridge; 108, 198 By permission of the Master and Fellows, Magdalene College, Cambridge; p60(1) (2), p61(3) (4) (5), p212(2) Photos Courtauld Institute of Art, reproduced by permission of the Chatsworth Settlement Trustees; 102 Reproduced by permission of the Chatsworth Settlement Trustees; 29 Reproduced by Courtesy of the Essex Record Office; 38, 90 National Galleries of Scotland, Edinburgh; 39 By Courtesy of the Trustees of the National Museums of Scotland; p54(3) By kind permission of the Marquess of Salisbury; p34(2) The University of Hull Photographic Service; 69, 141, p205(4) BBC Hulton Picture Library; 19, 20 and frontispiece, 23, 64, 85, p141(3), 110, 111, 112, 118, 131, 138, 179 Bridgeman Art Library; 7, 30, 97, 98, 99, 112 British Library; 16, 17, 31, 41, 44, 68, 76, 148, 160, 161, 195, 197 Reproduced by Courtesy of the Trustees of the British Museum; p101(3) British Tourist Authority Picture Library; 33, 50, 119, 132, 137, 139, 182, 183, 189 Christie's Colour Library; p212(1) (4) (5) Country Life Magazine; 42 Department of the Environment; p236(1) E.T. Archive Ltd; 114, 165, 194 The Fotomas Index; 12, 13, 28, 35, p54(1), p55(5), 54, 96, 117, 121, 146, 147, 164, 168, 170, 171, 178 Anthony Kersting; p89(6) Lund Humphries Publishers Ltd; 2, 5, 46, 49, 63, 78, 79, 82, 91, 94, 124, 125, 128, 149, 166, 173 Mansell Collection; 187(3) Pitkin Pictorials Ltd; p66(1), 59, 60, 71, p83(4), 86, 150, 159, p227(4) Reproduced by gracious permission of Her Majesty the Queen; 6, 32, p89(4) (5), p109(4), p186(2), p187(5), p259(4), 192, 193 Royal Commission on Historical Monuments of England; p187(4), 145, 196 Society of Antiquaries; 92 Sotheby's; 37 Thames and Hudson Archives; 1, p141(4) (5), p162(1) (2) (3), p163(4) (5), 131, 135 (Theatre Museum), p226(3) Reproduced by Courtesy of the Board of Trustees of the Victoria and Albert Museum; p109(3) Webb & Bower Publishers Ltd; 24, 45, 47, 72, 73, 74, 77, 127, 155, 160, 172 Weidenfeld and Nicolson Archives; 65 Reproduced by permission of the Clerk of Records; p251(5) The Warden and Fellows of All Souls College, Oxford; 4, 11, 26, 27, 34, 40, 51, 62, 70, 75, p101(4), 80, 81, p115(4), 100, 104, 107, 120, 142, 153, 163, p237(2) (4), 187, 188 Bodleian Library, Oxford; p186(1) Thomas Photos, Oxford; 58 Giraudon; p205(3) Musée de l'Armée, Paris; 55 Chomon Perino; 10 Library of Congress, Washington; 87 National Gallery of Art, Washington: Andrew W. Mellon Collection; p67(3) By kind permission of the Provost and Fellows of Eton; p204(1) (2), 154 By kind permission of His Grace the Duke of Marlborough (Photos: Jeremy Whitaker); 129 Photo: Derrick Witty; 169 Mr and Mrs Peter Ainsworth (Photo; Gareth J. Davies); 184 Harry Smith Horticultural Photographic Collection.

Phaidon Press Limited, Littlegate House,
St Ebbe's Street, Oxford OX1 1SQ

First published 1986

British Library Cataloguing in Publication Data
Stuart England
1. Great Britain—History—Stuarts
1603–1714
I. Worden, Blair
942.06 DA375

ISBN 0-7148-2391-0

Designed by Trevor Vincent
Typeset by BAS Printers Limited, Over Wallop, Hampshire.
Printed in Great Britain by Balding + Mansell, Wisbech, Cambridgeshire

FRONTISPIECE
Detail from *The Tichborne Dole* (see Pl. 20)

Contents

The Picture Essays are listed on the next page

Picture Essays MALCOLM OXLEY

The Stuarts and the succession

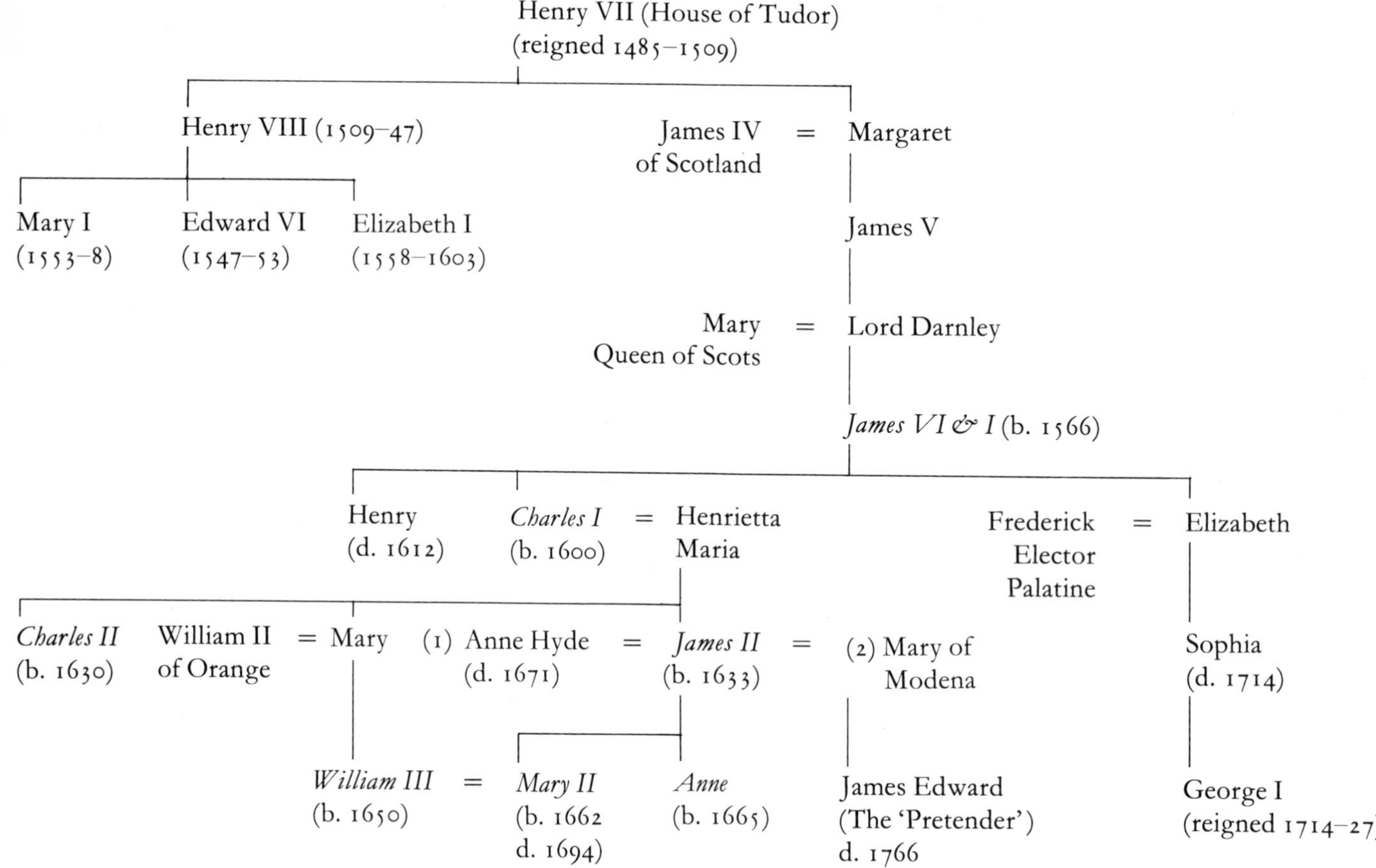

Introduction

Kings and Kingship

No king of England had had a more secure or more enviable inheritance than that to which James VI of Scotland succeeded as James I of England on the death of his distant cousin the childless Queen Elizabeth on 24 March 1603. Over the previous century the Tudors had overcome fundamental opposition to their rule and built a durable system of government. The great baronial families which had fought the Wars of the Roses in the later fifteenth century had been tamed or extinguished, and their military followings abolished. By the end of the sixteenth century a high proportion of noble families owed their eminence not to independent bases of power in the regions where their estates lay, but to the favour of the crown, whose policies they implemented in the localities and at whose court they competed for further rewards. In areas where previously the king's writ had at times seemed scarcely to run, especially Wales and the north of England, the royal machinery of justice had first rivalled and then superseded the power of local magnates as a focus of loyalty. By the time of James I's accession the regional rebellions of 1536–69 belonged to the past.

Under the Tudors, grave problems of religion and foreign policy had been, if not overcome, at least substantially reduced. The Church, hitherto the servant of two masters, had been wrested from papal sovereignty by Henry VIII in the 1530s and subjected to the royal supremacy, first by Henry and then by his daughter Elizabeth. During Elizabeth's long reign the painful process by which Protestant beliefs replaced Catholic ones had advanced sufficiently far to give England that semblance of religious unity on which contemporaries believed political unity to depend. The nation's conversion to Protestantism had brought it close to invasion by Spain, the mightiest power in Europe, but the threat had receded with the defeated Armada of 1588. In Ireland, where Spain had aided the Irish chieftains who were in rebellion against English rule, the back of the resistance had been broken and the way cleared for further English settlement and colonization. Conditions were still more favourable to England in Scotland, for James's acquisition of the English throne closed to England's continental enemies their back door to the southern kingdom. Finally, the long-standing problem of the succession had been solved. Whereas the infertility of the Tudors had prevented them from dispelling fears that renewed civil war would follow their deaths, James I had children. The Stuart dynasty was safe, and the crowning of James's son as Charles I in 1625 was the first straightforward succession for more than a century.

Yet by 1642 Charles was at war with his subjects in England, in Scotland and in Ireland. In 1649 his victorious Puritan enemies executed him on a charge of treason. In 1660, when those enemies had fallen out among themselves, his elder son was restored to the throne as Charles II; and by 1685, when the king's younger brother succeeded as James II, the English monarchy looked stronger than ever. Yet three years later James, like his father before him, lost his three kingdoms. He had wrought in English – and British – politics an insecurity that was to endure through the reigns of his son-in-law, the Dutchman William III, who expelled and replaced him in 1688–9, and of his daughter Anne, who reigned from 1702 to 1714.

How can the recurrent instability of a dynasty that had initially seemed so stable be explained? In the last fifty years many historians, concerned especially with the convulsions of the mid-seventeenth century, have pointed to long-term developments – social, economic and religious – as the causes of the crown's difficulties. Certainly there were social and economic tensions in the background to the political upheavals of the period, and religious conflicts in their foreground. But it took the Stuarts to turn problems into crises.

For to a greater extent than the modern imagination can readily grasp, the course and character of seventeenth-century politics were determined by the policies and personalities of kings. Occasionally a seventeenth-century voice was heard – the voice of a John Milton or an Algernon Sidney – to protest against the deficiencies of the monarchical system of government. Why should the nation's well-being rest with individuals whom heredity, not merit, had elevated? Why should subjects endure the misfortunes attendant upon the rule of minors (whom seventeenth-century England happened to be spared) and of royal favourites (of whom it experienced all too many)? Why should the occupancy of thrones, and the foreign policies of nations, be determined by the marital arrangements of royal families who did not hesitate to keep clauses of the treaties between them secret from their subjects? As they looked at seventeenth-century Europe, the handful of English republicans saw a universal process of political decline. In the Middle Ages, they believed, kings had been kept in order, and their subjects protected from them, by powerful, frugal, war-like barons. Now, in the 'new monarchies' of the Renaissance, kings had been made into demi-gods, indecently flattered by obsequious nobles in luxurious and lascivious courts

1. Isaac Oliver, *Richard Sackville, Third Earl of Dorset*, 1616. Oil on canvas, 9¼ × 6 in. (23.5 × 15 cm.). London, Victoria and Albert Museum.
The rise of Renaissance monarchy in England weakened the independence and softened the manners of the ruling class. What had become of the warlike medieval peerage? In this miniature, Dorset, who inherited his title in 1609, has his armour by him, but he is a 'carpet' noble, his brightly plumed costume calling to mind his contemporary John Donne's description of a courtier as 'glistering, and so painted in many colours that he is hardly discerned from one of the pictures in the arras hangings, his body like an irongirt chest girt in, and thick ribbed with broad gold laces'. Not that Dorset was wholly subservient to James I, for he opposed the further creations with which James I devalued the peerage in the course of the reign.

and absurdly idealized in masques and pageants. As Protestants, Englishmen had learned to reject idolatry in the Church. Why, then, did they practise it so wantonly in the state?

The isolation experienced by republican thinkers indicates the depth to which the principles of kingship had penetrated seventeenth-century thought and imagination. Members of parliament who disliked government policies were careful to criticize only the king's advisers, whose actions had obscured but could not diminish the virtues of their royal masters. In 1643, when parliament to its acute dismay found itself at war with the king, the MP Henry Marten ventured to ask the Commons whether the institution of kingship was necessary; the House's response was unanimously to vote Marten to the Tower. The emotions of war did, it is true, make republicans of some men, especially among the more radical soldiers and supporters of Oliver Cromwell's army, but their republicanism was rarely thought out. The improvised republican constitution of 1649 convinced few even of the Puritans

2. The Coronation Procession of James II in 1685.
Contemporary engraving.
The ritual of this procession of James II and his courtiers in 1685 would have been witnessed at every coronation of an English monarch from the high Middle Ages to the present day. Samuel Pepys helps to carry the canopy (front left).

who introduced it; and the ensuing experience of kingless rule, by identifying republicanism with militarism and with Puritan sectarianism, confirmed the nation in its monarchical preferences. The politicians who deposed James II in 1688–9 acted to preserve monarchy, not to replace it, and quickly vowed their continuing loyalty to hereditary rule.

Monarchy was enjoined on England by God's providence and by the laws and customs of the land. It corresponded to principles of lineage, kinship and heredity that were close to the heart of a society based on family networks, on family trees (not all of them authentic), and on the inheritance of property. In public as in private life, the past was a legacy to be preserved for posterity. Generally the older a law or institution the better it was; 'innovation' was a dirty word. Revering the 'ancient constitution', the term they used to describe the accumulation of custom and medieval statute that defined the powers of king and parliament, Englishmen protested only when novel policies of royal advisers appeared to undermine that constitution. Fundamental change or long-term planning would be an impertinent rebuke to the past. It was also likely to be fruitless; with early death being frequent – so frequent that the very concept of 'life expectancy' was unimaginable – the king might die at any time, and his successor (however strenuously he had been educated in his predecessor's principles) was bound to revise the political map. So there were severe limits to human presumption in politics. How could there not be, for how could 'fallen' man expect perfection on this earth? Admittedly, pessimism and resignation were not universal, and in the course of the Stuart period their hold was to be weakened. Even so, they remained the starting-points of political thought and political behaviour.

If the institution of kingship was sacrosanct, then there were good practical reasons for making kings strong. A monarch whose authority was secure at home could stand up to his counterparts abroad. He would be the better equipped to preserve order and thwart factional interests within his realm. He would be the better equipped too to defend the Church of England from its Catholic enemies at home and abroad, and to champion the laity, who looked to him to preserve the political and economic superiority over the clergy which royal leadership had given them in the Reformation.

The aura of divinity that shrouded kingship was more impressive than – and perhaps was needed to compensate for the limitations of – its institutional base. Although for convenience we shall use the term 'the government' to describe the institutions which formed and implemented policy from one reign to the next, the ambitions of that government were small. There was a civil service, but nothing to compare in size or organization with the bureaucratic apparatus of the modern state, or even to rival the machinery of government that was being developed by the monarchies of France and Spain. James I's principal advisers – his Privy Council and the Secretaries of State – had their own staffs, as did the Royal Household, the Mint, the Ordnance (armaments) Office, the Navy Office and, outside London, the Councils of the North (centred on York) and of the Marches of Wales. So did the law courts, whose legal duties were combined with financial and administrative ones, for royal power was inseparable from its ability to provide justice. But the monarchy of James I had no standing army – only under-equipped and under-trained county militias – and no police force – only the parish constables and their assistants. In most of England there was no professional system of local government. Instead the counties were governed by the landed ruling class. It governed them in accordance with what it took to be the crown's interests, but also with its own. The peers and the leading gentry – their sympathies and beliefs and powers – were the key to the successful government of England: a truth that first Charles I and then James II fatally forgot.

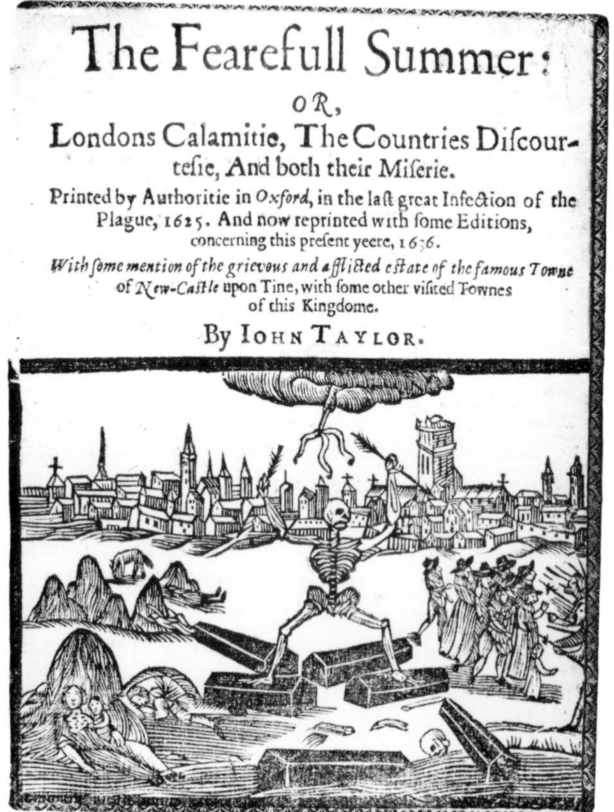

The Fearefull Summer:

OR,

Londons Calamitie, The Countries Diſcourteſie, And both their Miſerie.

Printed by Authoritie in *Oxford*, in the laſt great Infection of the Plague, 1625. And now reprinted with ſome Editions, concerning this preſent yeere, 1636.

With ſome mention of the grievous and afflicted eſtate of the famous Towne of New-Castle upon Tine, with ſome other viſited Townes of this Kingdome.

By IOHN TAYLOR.

3. *The Fearefull Summer*, a pamphlet by John Taylor (1636 edition). *Although the plague of 1665 was especially devastating, plague itself was not an infrequent occurrence. In 1625 Charles I held a parliament at Oxford in order to escape the plague in London, and this reprinted pamphlet appeared in another troubled year, 1636. Plague was normally interpreted as a divine punishment for national sinfulness, and attempts were made to placate God's wrath through fasts and prayers and sermons. But in the seventeenth century medical explanations were growing up beside providentialist ones, and magistrates were learning methods of containing plague. Spread by fleas parasitic on the black rat, plague never began in England, and the adoption of Continental quarantine methods in the ports may explain why plague ceased in England after 1665.*

The landed class was resilient because it was not exclusive. The system of primogeniture encouraged the younger sons of gentry to become civil servants or lawyers or merchants, while newly-wealthy members of those groups would purchase landed estates (although both the frequency and the rapidity of such elevations can be exaggerated). The government was not in a position to pit a landed interest against a mercantile one (as the French monarchy did). Landowners provided capital for colonial and overseas trading ventures, cooperated with merchants to extract iron and copper from their estates, and befriended the towns, which they often represented in parliament. But the basis of their wealth was the land, and that wealth was not always easy to sustain. Many landowners were heavily in debt by the early Stuart period: some because they had failed to adjust to the inflationary pressures which had persisted from the sixteenth century into the early seventeenth; some because, in the reckless competition of conspicuous consumption among the nobility and gentry on either side of 1600, they had heavily overspent, most probably on the building, furnishing or decoration of country houses (or on the houses which more and more of them were acquiring in the capital); some apparently because, wishing to be well-thought of by their tenants, they had given them more employment or better terms of landed tenure than the market required. In this last respect new landowners tended to be more hard-headed than the old, and were often responsible for a ruthless reorganization

4. The Earl of Kingston hawking.
From Richard Blome, *The Gentleman's Recreation* (1686).
The land which provided the wealth and power of England's ruling class also sustained its pleasures. The Nottinghamshire home of the earl's family, Holme Pierrepoint (Picture Essay, p. 42), is visible in the background.

of estate management – although there are signs that by Charles I's reign the long-established landowners were also coming to see that tightened efficiency was necessary for economic survival. The pickings of office at court could be essential for survival too. But even that minority of nobles and gentlemen whom luck or need brought into the service of the king in London or on his progresses were unlikely to leave their estates for long.

Amidst economic anxieties there was time for rural pleasures: for the hawking or hunting or fishing, and the provision of hospitality, through which the connections between landed families were fostered and the advantageous marriages of children contrived. Among many, leisure also took the more earnest form of intellectual and spiritual improvement. While methodically studying their bibles and organizing their sermon notes, exploring the literature of classical antiquity and modern works on theology, law, history and politics, the pre-Civil War ruling class became the most learned, and perhaps the most self-serious, that England had known – and possibly has ever known.

This was not a ruling class to shirk its responsibilities, even when under Elizabeth I and the early Stuarts the administrative burdens of local government mounted. Government rested on the consent of the landowners, and in the main they were eager to provide it. The institution through which consent was formally expressed was parliament, where the Lords (peers and bishops) and the Commons (represented principally by the gentry) gathered to discuss the problems of the realm and, with the king, to pass laws designed to solve them. But parliaments met only occasionally and briefly. Local administration was a permanent requirement; and it was in the counties, as Lords Lieutenants or Deputy Lieutenants of the shires or as the Justices of the Peace who implemented legislation and kept order, that the nobility and gentry made their major contribution – a largely unpaid and largely thankless one – to the government of the country. Their cooperation could not be taken absolutely for granted. They prided themselves on their independence of judgement and believed that they understood local problems better than the central government did. But local office carried a prestige that made them reluctant to risk dismissal. Only under the provocation of a Charles I or a James II would consent be withdrawn and a strong system of government become a weak one.

Conflict and Change

James I's favourable inheritance was impaired by one fundamental problem: the crown's inadequate revenue. In the sixteenth and earlier seventeenth centuries, under the pressures of inflation, the crown sold the bulk of its lands and so lost the income they had yielded. When the House of Commons could be cajoled into voting money, its subsidies fell short of the government's needs, took long to collect, and were reduced in value by the skill of landowners (especially the richer ones) in ensuring that their incomes were under-assessed. Attempts by James I and Charles I to increase extra-parliamentary taxation had some success, but were unable to balance the crown's books and roused fears that the crown intended to reduce parliament's place in the constitution. While the monarchy could expect to remain solvent in peacetime, war was beyond its resources. Conceivably a war with the nation behind

Cancellarij sedes &c.
Lo. Wharton
Lord Willughby
Lord Paget.
Lord North.
Lord Chaundos.
Lo. Compton
Lord Wotton.
Lord Peter.

6. The entrance front, Greenhead, Reedley Hallows, Lancashire.
A minor Lancashire gentleman, John Moore, built this small manor house in 1641. The parish or the county would have been the normal boundaries of Moore's political awareness, although news of national events spread surprisingly quickly and, especially when parliaments met, could arouse keen interest among men of his standing.

it would have enabled the government to revolutionize the financial system, as happened in early seventeenth-century Sweden and as would happen in England during the wars with France after 1688. But Charles I's wars of the 1620s and late 1630s, failing to carry the country with him, quickly emptied his coffers.

The government's financial difficulties were both cause and symptom of social tensions. Since the crown could not afford to pay proper salaries, its civil servants were allowed to make up their incomes either by selling the future tenure of their offices, so that the manning of departments was distanced from the crown's control, or by exacting fees and perquisites from subjects, so

5 (opposite). King Charles I opening parliament in 1625. Contemporary engraving.
Charles follows the custom of calling a parliament early in the reign. The three estates of parliament – king, lords and commons – assemble in the House of Lords. The king, enthroned, is surrounded by his closest councillors; the lay peers and the bishops sit round the Lord Chancellor's woolsack; the commons stand at the bar of the House. The arrangement has changed little to this day.

that the maximization of such rewards almost became the organizing principle of departmental activity. Subjects bore other iniquitous consequences of governmental poverty – an especially grievous example being the sale by the crown of patents of monopoly, which enabled the beneficiaries to sell goods at prices protected from competition.

Early seventeenth-century society seemed full of imbalances. Wealth and influence were being sucked from the regions into the court and the capital. London's trade grew at the expense of the outports and with it grew the massive fortunes of its leading merchants. Landowners, whose properties involved them in interminable legislation, were obliged to pursue it in London. There they endured the notorious delays of a legal system whose prolixities seemed designed to enrich the lawyers rather than to procure justice. The smaller, more provincial gentry envied the more prosperous and more cosmopolitan landowners who collared for themselves and for their clients the court offices whose cost the country bore. They resented too the electoral patronage of magnates which gave many parliamentary seats, and consequently the expression of local grievances at Westminster, to gentry from outside. Tensions within the landowning class did not (as has sometimes been suggested) cause the civil wars, but

7. *The Merchants Mapp of Commerce,* a pamphlet by Lewes Roberts (1638); title-page engraving by Cornelius van Dalen.
Dislocation of the international economy in the second and third decades of the seventeenth century stimulated a growing body of critical literature concerned with the problems of survival and competition in foreign trade. A director of the East India Company, Roberts had literary interests and enjoyed the company of Isaak Walton (for whom see p. 133). One of his sons became sub-governor of the Africa Company, and was knighted by Charles II. Seventeenth-century governments listened carefully to mercantile pressure groups, on whom they depended for news of economic and political developments abroad. In writing for 'gentlemen and others that travel abroad for delight or pleasure', Roberts reminds us of the intermixture of mercantile and landed values.

the wars brought them to the surface; and by 1649 there were smaller gentry willing to abolish the House of Lords and to overhaul the electoral system.

Tensions existed outside the ruling class too. The English economy was precariously dependent on the export of woollen goods to shrinking markets in northern Europe. Wars on the Continent and currency manipulations by its rulers exposed the English cloth trade to violent fluctuations and its manufacturers to periods of sudden poverty. Distress also came from bad harvests; from the enclosure of common land by improving landlords (although this brought less protest in the seventeenth century than in the sixteenth); and from the government's fiscal methods of the 1620s and 1630s, which helped to strengthen the alertness outside the ruling class to events at Whitehall and Westminster. That alertness was to be sharpened by the civil wars; and in the grim economic conditions of the late 1640s, and again in those of 1659, Levellers and other radical groups gave eloquent expression to the grievances of the under-privileged. It was only in the later seventeenth century that the growing diversification of the English economy both at home and abroad reduced the incidence of hardship and the volume of discontent.

Early Stuart government lacked sufficient confidence in economic prescription and state intervention to give decisive support to the many proposals that were aired for the enlargement of the nation's wealth. When it did intervene, as in its backing of the scheme devised in 1614 by Alderman Cockayne to transform the cloth export trade, its want of expertise and its vulnerability to the persuasions of sharp profiteers caused acute economic damage. The monarchy was better informed about the challenge of administrative and fiscal reform, but the reign of the extravagant James I was not a period likely to produce it. Having fought bitterly and expensively for its survival under Elilzabeth, the nation now permitted itself to share the mood of relaxation and display that characterized the leading European courts during the respite from continental war in the early seventeenth century. In the 1620s the mood of Europe changed, and that of England with it. The general European conflict known as the Thirty Years War, which was to prove the most destructive and fanatical of wars, had begun in 1618, and during the opening years of Charles I's reign England was briefly and humiliatingly drawn into it. Naval and military disaster combined with economic hardship and religious and political conflict to scar the minds of the MPs who matured in the 1620s and who were to carry their grim memories of that decade into the civil wars of the 1640s.

Charles was more interested in reform than his father. The challenge before him was to impress upon parliaments the advantages of voting taxes high enough to make it worth the crown's while to summon them. If they would do so, they might enable the government both to remove the administrative abuses of which they complained and to provide the effective national defences and the strong foreign policy for which they called. But the king commanded neither the trust of the rulers of the shires nor the arts of personal and political management required to educate them in that perception. Soon he resolved to dispense with parliaments – an understandable reaction, perhaps, to the parochial perspectives of those MPs who were more concerned with protecting their constituents from taxation than with grasping the nature and extent of the government's difficulties. Yet we need not paint too melancholy a picture of the crown's relations with its more powerful subjects. Many grumbled at Charles I's administrative policies, but for long there were few who actively opposed them. By themselves those policies would never have undermined the nation's basic loyalty to the crown or opened the way to civil war. Even when war came, the king's cause was not predestined to defeat. Had he won the battles which he needlessly lost, posterity might have come to view his pre-war attempts at reform more sympathetically.

The financial and institutional shortcomings which plagued the government between 1603 and 1640 were to be largely overcome before the end of the Stuart period. The principal stimulus to change was war: the civil wars of the 1640s and the foreign wars of William and Anne. It is the irony of the Puritan Revolution of 1640–60 that its consequences ran counter to the intentions of the civil war victors. The parliamentary gentry who, under Charles I, had complained against arbitrary taxation and state interference in the localities found themselves, when they struggled to finance and organize the war effort, imposing on the provinces degrees both of taxation and of central control that were not imagined before 1640. Rulers of the shires who declined to serve on parliament's hated county committees found themselves bullied by radical upstarts appointed in their place. The victors emerged with a standing army and with a navy strong enough to give much-needed protection to merchant shipping. With institutional change came mental change. The civil war, originating as a series of provincial protests and skirmishes, produced national armies and national arguments that helped to broaden provincial outlooks into national ones.

In 1660 most of the institutional alterations of the previous two decades were repudiated. As so often in English history, lasting change was to come not from the replacement of institutions but from a process of adaptation that preserved their continuity. Amidst a profound reaction in favour of traditional forms of rule, Charles II at first seemed happy for the nobility and gentry to resume their control of the counties and for his regime to rest upon the consent which the resurgence of royalism abundantly provided. With institutional restoration came social restoration. The House of Lords returned with the monarchy; royalist landlords recovered the estates which their parliamentary enemies had confiscated; and in the decades ahead – during the agricultural depression of the 1670s and 1680s and then when the French wars after 1688 were financed by a massive land tax – smaller landowners were again less able to adjust than greater ones, whose control over the land and politics of England was if anything greater in 1714 than in 1603. Even so, during the troubles of mid-century, new possibilities of state power had been glimpsed. They were glimpsed too in the example of France, where from the 1660s Louis XIV was building up a formidable machinery of centralized control. Charles II and his brother James were suspected of wishing to emulate him. They scarcely had the resources to do so, but by the 1670s the monarchy was building up an effective standing army that might be used against its subjects; and in the 1680s the crown developed new techniques of purging local government and of disqualifying the government's critics from parliament. The England of James II seemed close to absolutism.

Historians of the seventeenth century have long found their attention pulled to one or other of the great upheavals of the period – the 'Puritan' revolution that thwarted Charles I or the 'Glorious' one that defeated James II. To the great nineteenth-century historian Macaulay, the events of 1640–60 were a mere dress rehearsal for the later and more portentous drama. In the twentieth century scholars have been drawn more towards the protracted mid-century conflicts, whose social and ideological dimensions have seemed broader than those of the swift aristocratic coup of 1688. Yet the importance of the Glorious Revolution remains, even if its moral significance may seem less universal now than it did to Macaulay. Since 1688 parliament, previously so insecure an institution, has met every year, and ministries have had to command majorities in them to survive. William III, having accepted the throne in order to bring England into the Dutch war against France, was driven to yield constitutional powers in order to keep her there. Parliament's new role dismayed even some of its warmest friends, for having previously been the subject's guardian against the state, it became drawn into the executive. A striking expansion of the civil service, largely to meet the needs of war, swelled the government's patronage and gave office to many MPs, whose independence was consequently compromised. It was undermined, too, as leading politicians, scrambling for the votes which the increased stature of parliament made so critical, created the rival party machines of the Whigs and the Tories – although parties were much less regimented than those of the twentieth century. The intermixture of the executive and the legislature strengthened rather than weakened the government, for (as in the 1640s) parliaments were able to mobilize the nation's resources as the crown alone could never do. Parliamentary support for the wars gave the money market the confidence to develop the financial institutions and the techniques of public borrowing on which England's military and naval greatness was built. Just as the civil wars and then the French wars strengthened the domestic resources of the state, so they spectacularly enhanced her standing abroad. England, a minor power at the start of the Stuart period, was a major one at its end.

The Background to Foreign Policy

Foreign affairs were still primarily European affairs, although the spread of European trade and settlement in the wider world over the sixteenth and seventeenth centuries added a dimension to European conflicts. On James I's accession England was at war (mainly a naval war) with Spain. Sixteenth-century Spain had acquired a vast empire in central and southern America; it had annexed Portugal and the large Portuguese maritime empire (although it was to lose them to rebellion in 1640); it had built the mightiest army in Europe; and it had become the military arm of the Counter-Reformation, the movement in which the Catholic Church dedicated itself to the extinction of Protestant heresy throughout Europe. Spain's rulers belonged to the Habsburg family. So did those of the Holy Roman Empire, that vast agglomeration of principalities and cities which, broadly speaking, is now occupied by Germany, Austria and much of eastern Europe. In 1555 the Habsburgs had resolved to separate their Spanish from their German lands. Even so, the two empires remained natural allies: allies against France, a country torn apart by religious wars in the later sixteenth century; allies against Protestantism; and allies against the Turks, whose threats to Christendom both in the Mediterranean and in eastern Europe cast a shadow over European diplomacy of the seventeenth century as it had over the sixteenth.

The division of the Habsburg inheritance allocated to Spain the family's possessions in Flanders and the Netherlands. Her efforts to tighten her control and to crush heresy there provoked the protracted Dutch war of independence. The war spilled into France, and from 1585 it drew in England. Elizabeth's advisers had been divided on the question of aid to the Dutch rebels; and their disagreements set the terms of a debate on foreign policy that profoundly influenced English politics until 1640. The debate was partly about the competing merits of peace and war, but it was an argument, too, about the extent to which foreign policy should be determined by religion. Elizabeth I, James I and Charles I were all conscious that long wars were beyond England's means. They were also alive to the economic profits of peace. James's decision to end the war with Spain (a decision which did not prevent England from retaining a limited military base in the Low Countries) enabled English merchants to expand their trade in the Mediterranean, where with time their exports were to rescue the country from its dependence on the ailing northern cloth market. Later periods of sustained peace, from 1630 and again from the mid-1670s, were to produce trade booms. But there were also arguments for war – arguments vigorously propounded even if not always realistic. The establishment of Protestantism under Elizabeth I and the threat which Spain provided to it bred an aggressive patriotism. To the more zealous Protestants on Elizabeth's Council, the Dutch revolt was merely one branch of a global struggle in which the forces of Protestant light must unite against those of Catholic darkness. The same view was widely held among the councillors and MPs of the early Stuart period, and there was dismay when the Anglo-Spanish peace of 1604 terminated England's naval and piratical exploits in the Atlantic and the Caribbean. There was dismay again when Charles I, having initially fought an inept war with Spain, made peace with her in 1630. In the 1620s the victories of the Habsburg armies in the Thirty Years War seemed to place the very survival of Protestantism in peril. It was rescued by Gustavus Adolphus of Sweden, whose army fulfilled the role that, in the eyes of frustrated Protestants in England, should have been hers.

Sweden fought as an ally of France, a country under Catholic rule, but the friend of European Protestants against the Habsburgs. Initially centred on a struggle between the Habsburgs and the German princes for control of the Holy Roman Empire, the Thirty Years War had been broadened by the renewal of the Dutch War of Independence in 1621. The anti-Habsburg alliance of France and Sweden broadened it still further. In the first half of the seventeenth century the French monarchy, first under Henry IV (assassinated in 1610) and then under Louis XIII, restored and extended its authority at home and once more made France mighty abroad. From the 1660s, under Louis XIV, she was to become mightier still. Her rise was Spain's decline, for Spain was gravely weakened by the Thirty Years War. The peace of 1648 left her in possession of Flanders,

8. Unknown artist, *The Somerset House Conference* (1604).
Oil on canvas, 81 × 105½ in. (205.7 × 268 cm.).
London, National Portrait Gallery.
One of the sessions of the negotiations in the summer of 1604 which reached their conclusion in the Treaty of London between England and Spain. The English delegates are on the right, seated in order of precedence from the window. They are: Thomas Sackville, first Earl of Dorset; Charles Howard, Earl of Nottingham; Charles Blount, Earl of Devonshire; Henry Howard, Earl of Northampton; and Robert Cecil. The picture cannot be quite accurate, for the Spaniard nearest the window, the Constable of Castile, was not present at the treaty. The tapestries are Elizabethan.

but recognized the independence of the northern Netherlands. The weakening of Spain was hastened by the alliance against her of France and Cromwellian England in the 1650s. In that decade, England, whose capacity for making war had earlier been so limited, possessed an army and a navy that were the envy of Europe. Much of the power that the Cromwellian period gained for England was lost after the Restoration, when the religious policies of Charles II and James II drove those kings into alliances with France in which England was, at best, a junior partner. But in 1688 the succession of William III brought about a revolution in foreign as well as domestic politics and aligned England against France. The result was a war effort of unprecedented scale and achievement.

Religion was never the sole determinant of seventeenth-century English diplomacy. Even when the Dutch were fighting for their independence, there were bitter economic rivalries between the two Protestant powers; and when that independence had been achieved, the two nations fought major wars for maritime and commercial supremacy in the 1650s, in the 1660s and in the 1670s. Even England's wars against Catholic powers were never fought for wholly religious reasons. But religious feeling could win support for war as no other political force could. England, which had ended the sixteenth century in a Protestant alliance with the Dutch against the might of Catholic Spain, ended the seventeenth in a Protestant alliance with the Dutch against the might of Catholic France.

Religion

In domestic affairs as in foreign ones the interaction of religion and politics in the seventeenth century was continuous. The Reformation of the sixteenth century had been, among other things, an assertion of national self-sufficiency: the boundaries of the Church had become those of the state. The medieval Church had possessed great lands and wealth and staffed many of the offices of state. In the sixteenth century the nobility and gentry squeezed the clergy out of government, appropriated monastic and other Church lands and acquired with them the right of appointment to a high proportion of Church livings. Parliament had risen in importance well above its clerical counterpart, Convocation. But if the Church's worldly influence had declined, the Church retained strong powers and rights. Its presence was everywhere. The laity were obliged by law not only to attend church, but to pay the tithes with which clergymen were financed; and laymen could

94 *The Parſon's Completeneſſe.*

CHAP. XXIII.

The Parſon's Completeneſſe.

THe Countrey Parſon deſires to be all to his Pariſh, and not onely a Paſtour, but a Lawyer alſo, and a Phiſician. Therefore hee endures not that any of his Flock ſhould go to Law; but in any Controverſie, that they ſhould reſort to him as their Judge. To this end, he hath gotten to himſelf ſome inſight in things ordinarily incident and controverted, by experience, and by reading ſome initiatory treatiſes in the Law, with *Daltons* Juſtice of Peace, and the Abridgements of the Statutes, as alſo by diſcourſe with men of that profeſſion, whom he hath ever ſome caſes to ask, when he meets with them; holding that rule, that to put men

to

9. A page from George Herbert, *A Priest to the Temple, or The Country Parson* (1652).
In this book, apparently completed by 1632, the clergyman and metaphysical poet George Herbert gave advice to his clerical colleagues. Beside their spiritual and consolatory roles, the clergy were expected to help keep the peace of their parishes. Although complaints survive about the inadequacies of many clergymen, there were inconspicuously conscientious ministers too. Herbert's book was published posthumously under Puritan rule.

be punished by Church courts for moral or sexual misdemeanours. The Church retained a share in a system of censorship which imposed severe limits on publishable opinion. Church buildings, substantial and permanent, dominated the skylines; and the parishes were centres of secular as well as ecclesiastical administration. Religion not only belonged to the world: it explained it. Peace and war, wealth and poverty, sickness and health, good harvests and bad ones – all were to be understood as fruits of God's unceasing involvement in the world He had created.

The Church of England established by Elizabeth in 1559 took a unique form. Its theology was radical, its institutions conservative. With the papal supremacy England had rejected essential Catholic teachings; the churches, hitherto ornamental, were made plain; the doctrines of the Swiss reformers (Calvinist and Zwinglian) concerning the sacraments and the eternal predestination of men's souls to heaven or hell were adopted and developed. Yet the system of government of the Church by bishops remained, even though elsewhere in Europe Calvinists had replaced it by a Presbyterian system, in which power rested with elected representatives of congregations and with regional and national assemblies. Most English Protestants accepted the existence of bishops and of traditional institutions. Some, it is true, rejecting all 'dregs of popery', illegally formed 'separatist' congregations outside the Church; and during the civil wars, when the Church of England collapsed, the sects were to make a dramatic impact on English politics. In the same period parliament, partly to secure the alliance of Scottish Presbyterians against the king, introduced Calvinist church government into England, albeit in a modified form. But in 1660 episcopacy was easily restored. In the main, the nobility and gentry would accept any Protestant church that left them in effective control of the parishes.

The spread of Protestant belief under Elizabeth had been slow, especially in the outlying regions of Wales, the north and the west. Protestants of the early seventeenth century were nervously aware that the Reformation was incomplete. They had captured the establishment, but even then there were Catholics at the courts of James I and Charles I. Parliament, local government and the universities (where the clergy were trained and the sons of gentry educated) had been won for the new faith. But the establishment had been converted because the crown had been converted. What would happen to Protestantism – and to the lands and offices which Protestants held – if the crown were reconverted and if consequently the laws enforcing Protestant worship and disqualifying Catholics from

10. *The Double Deliverance,* a cartoon by Samuel Ward, 1621. *This engraving by the stoutly Puritan minister of Ipswich, Samuel Ward, sought to rally anti-popish and anti-Spanish sentiment against the government's proposal for a marriage alliance with Catholic Spain in 1621. The key recent dates of anti-popish mythology, 1588 (the Armada) and 1605 (Gunpowder Plot) are emphasized. In a tent sit the pope, the devil, the King of Spain and other plotters against England. The Spanish ambassador Gondomar complained about Ward's satires to the English government, and he was examined by the Privy Council and briefly imprisoned. Elsewhere he wrote vigorously against the ostentatious decadence of James I's court. 'The glory of Ipswich', Ward was well paid and looked after by the corporation, which under Charles I thwarted the attempts of the Laudian church to unseat him.*

public life were repealed? There were zealous Protestants – 'Puritans' as they were called – among the nobility and gentry; there were Puritan aldermen; there were Puritan merchants and clothworkers. But in all these groups, Puritans felt themselves to be in a minority; and there were few Puritans among the poor, where popery and ignorance and superstition seemed rife.

Fear of popery – of undercover papal and Jesuit agents seducing souls, plotting treason, even winning over kings – was the great anxiety of seventeenth-century politics. In reality the Catholics, like other religious minorities of the period, were mostly anxious to demonstrate the political loyalty that might win them freedom of worship; but that was not the impression created by the Gunpowder Plot of 1605, the memory of which Protestants so assiduously preserved. Within the Church of England of the earlier seventeenth century, it was the Puritans who called most vigorously for action against Catholics at home and abroad. Amidst the political and ecclesiastical difficulties which mounted from the 1620s, the conventional Protestant belief that these were the latter ages of the world assumed increasingly urgent and apocalyptic expression among Puritans, who believed the struggle with popery to be a cosmic battle for the destruction of Antichrist. In 1640–2 anti-popery became a fever which swept the institutions of Church and state before it. There were to be similar fevers after 1660; and in the fall of James II, as of his father, fear of Catholicism was the decisive force.

In order to combat popery and bring God's saving word to the congregations, the Puritans of early Stuart

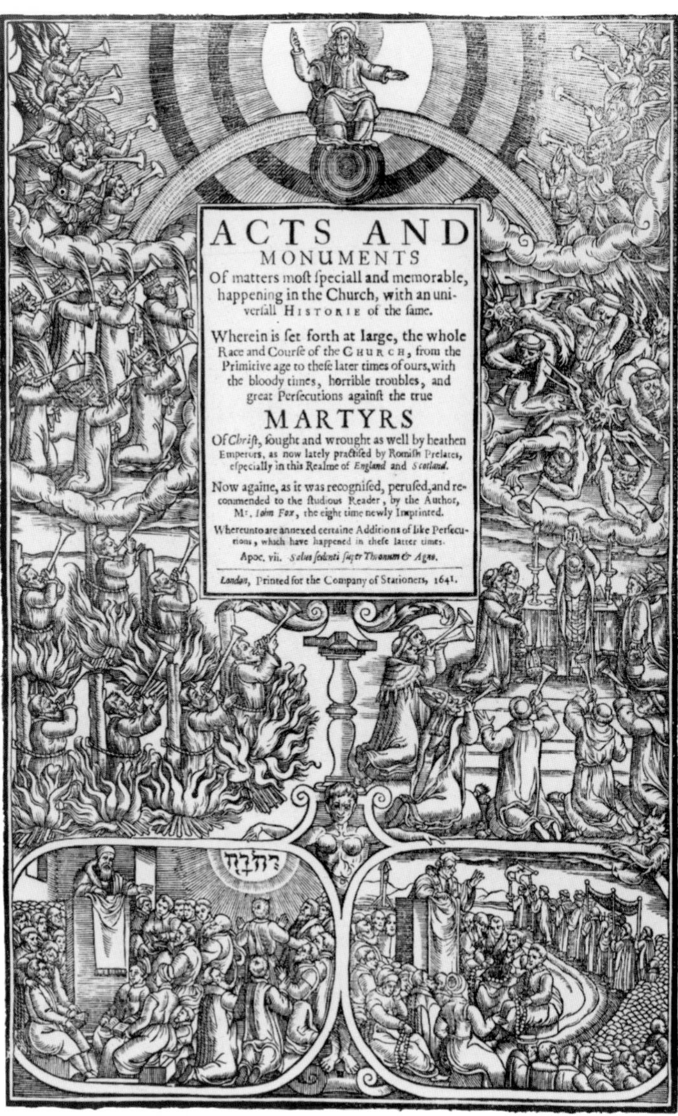

11. John Foxe, *Acts and Monuments* (1641 edition).
The Bible apart, Foxe's Book of Martyrs *was the most influential religious book of the seventeenth century. An Elizabethan production, it supplied a Protestant history of the Church of Christ and of the Church of England. It traced the record of persecution of the righteous from the book of Genesis to the burnings under Queen Mary, and placed that persecution in a millenarian scheme of history which persuaded Englishmen that they were fighting a holy war against the Antichrist. Under Elizabeth (whom Foxe called a second Constantine) and James I, Church and state encouraged the spread of Foxe's views, which helped bind the nation against the external popish threat. But the Church of Charles I drew back from the apocalyptic element in Foxe – an element that became increasingly obvious in the upheavals of the 1640s. In 1641, the year of republication, Puritan zeal for reform of the Church was at its most bold and confident. The frontispiece shows Roman Catholics (on the right), beguiled by priests, rosaries, processions and the mass, being consigned to hell, while on the left God's Protestant Englishmen discuss sermons, read spiritual works, are martyred for their faith and enjoy the bliss of heaven.*

England urged an evangelical programme of teaching and preaching until the nation should become Protestant not only in outward conformity but in inward conviction. The spiritual and educational qualities of the clergy, Puritans argued, needed to be improved so that they could properly instruct their flocks in those glorious truths of the Bible which had been brought to the people through vernacular translation and the printing press since the Reformation. Puritans looked to the clergy for sermons which would smite their listeners with a sense both of their own sinfulness and of the saving power of faith. They also expected the clergy to guide the faithful through the protracted and devastating process by which so many of them found God's grace awakened in their hearts and triumphant over sin and despair. Puritanism can be related to many contemporary developments: to revulsion from the morality and hollow values of the court; to the economic necessity or economic benefits of self-restraint; to the wish to preserve the social order by imposing 'godly' discipline on the poor. Yet the religious experience of Puritans belongs to those mysteries of life of which historians now find socio-economic explanations increasingly inadequate.

Puritanism was a verbal, not a visual religion. It mistrusted images and the play of the senses. In general it was not much interested in the building or repair of churches – of which the period from the Reformation to the civil wars was not the most productive in English history. The power of religion lay in its spirit not its form: in the inner man not outward observance. Yet within the early Stuart Church there was a rival philosophy to that of Puritanism. Since 1559 the Church of England had gained in confidence. Whereas on the Continent the advances of both Calvinism and Counter-Reformation Catholicism had brought destructive civil war, England appeared to have found a middle way between the fanaticisms of Geneva and Rome. If that middle way were to be preserved, then the Church must carry conviction not only to Puritans, whose sense of godliness set them apart from the unregenerate, but to the wider nation. How broad an appeal had plain churches, long sermons, and a theology which predestined most men to eternal perdition? Beside Puritanism there emerged a view that can be called (albeit anachronistically) Anglican: the view that wished to restore aesthetic beauty to churches and services, that emphasized the sacraments rather than preaching, and that urged doctrinal moderation.

Under James I these two strands coexisted, thanks not least to James's management. Under Charles I and his Archbishop of Canterbury William Laud, coexistence turned to confrontation. Laud and his circle were

12. Wadham College, Oxford, quadrangle.
Completed by 1613, Wadham represents the work of the master masons William and Edward Arnold. The college was founded by Nicholas Wadham, a wealthy Somerset landowner, and his wife Dorothy. Since the Reformation more and more gentry families had sent their sons to university, a movement indicative of a growing intellectual curiosity but also of the part which a university education could play in providing the skills, the polish and the connections necessary for a public career. Alongside this lay function, Oxford and Cambridge remained the training grounds of the clergy. In the 1650s Wadham became the centre of a remarkable group of scientists which centered on the Warden, John Wilkins.

called by their Puritan critics 'Arminians' after the Dutch theologian Jacobus Arminius, who had challenged the Calvinist doctrine of predestination. Laud was never the Roman Catholic that his enemies called him, but he and his supporters did believe the Reformation to have gone too far. They restored a compulsory ceremonialism to church services; they claimed for the clergy the sacerdotal office, the political influence and the social and economic status of which the previous century had deprived them; and they appeared to make of Charles I, who supported their programme, an unwitting accomplice in a clericalism which was determined to destroy both the lay basis and the royal supremacy of the Church of England. These were the policies which created so keen a fear of popery by 1640, and which then produced two parliaments alienated from the Church as no parliaments had been before. By that time thousands of Puritans had chosen to leave for the 'howling wilderness' of New England. Those who remained were perplexed to find themselves harassed as enemies of the Church of which they believed themselves to be the most loyal members. But in 1640 they found decisive parliamentary support.

The experience of Puritan rule produced a reaction against Puritan teaching. When it was restored in 1660 the Church was careful not to repeat Laud's mistakes: it respected the influence of the laity and contrived to distance itself from popery in the public mind. Indeed the Church was to play a leading part in the overthrow of the Catholic James II. Even so, the anti-Puritan reaction encouraged its leaders to restore much of Laud's ceremonialism, which the intervening trauma had made more acceptable to England's landlords. The religious divisions of the nation hardened in the 1660s, when Puritans who would not conform to the Church were forbidden to worship outside it or to hold public office. Post-Restoration Puritans – 'nonconformists' or 'Dissenters' – often abandoned political aspirations and turned instead to trade. In their introspective sobriety they sought to preserve the moral strenuousness that the world around them seemed to have abandoned. The Dissenters gained a large measure of religious freedom after 1688, but not of political freedom. Between 1660 and 1714 Anglicanism and Dissent developed as the rival traditions from which those of Church and Chapel were later to emerge. In religion as in politics, the divisions of the seventeenth century left an enduring legacy in the English memory and in English culture.

MUSEUM

CHAPTER ONE

English Society

The Social Structure

The politics of Stuart England were directed by the actions and intentions of that small section of English society which can be identified as a ruling class. But who were the people they ruled: that great mass of the population for whom the political ambitions and decisions of the great must have seemed of little relevance in their daily lives? How was society organized and how did that organization change during the Stuart period?

At the time of the succession of James I in 1603 an ideal description of the social order would have seen it as a series of ranks or degrees, all clearly distinguished from each other and all related to the land, which ultimately provided all degrees of men with a living. At the top of society were the gentlemen, differentiated according to their titles as lords, knights, esquires and 'last of all they that are simply called gentlemen'. These men dominated national politics and local government. They drew their economic strength from their ownership of some two-thirds of all the land in England, relying mainly on a rental income to support a leisured life, though many of the lesser gentlemen farmed their own land.

Below the gentry in the rural hierarchy were the yeomen, a group which comprised the larger tenant-farmers and the owner-occupiers of that part of the land not owned by the aristocracy and gentry, the crown or the Church. Yeomen were commercially-oriented working farmers who had neither the wealth nor often the desire to lead the leisured life of the gentlemen, but who owned or worked sufficient land to live comfortably and, except in adverse circumstances, to save and accumulate capital. Beneath them were the husbandmen, some of whom were owner-occupiers, but most of whom worked land that they held on various types of tenure from their social betters. The husbandmen worked considerably less land than the yeomen, sufficient in a normal year to sustain their families but not enough to give much hope of saving and so improving their fortunes. They were in essence the classic type of peasant farmers who worked self-sufficient farms with family labour. Their lives were hard and not very comfortable but were normally very much more comfortable than those on the lowest rung of the rural social ladder, the cottagers, whose land was not sufficient to support their families and who were therefore forced to increase their income by working as labourers on land owned by the more prosperous members of rural society.

Needless to say, rural social structure was not in reality as simple as this model would suggest. Each group overlapped the next; many men moved from one group to another during their lifetimes; and vanity and ambition ensured that others described themselves as gentlemen when their contemporaries thought of them as yeomen. Many areas did not include all four strata of rural society. In some places there were no gentry and all land was owned by freeholding yeomen. In others, rural society consisted entirely of small, self-sufficient peasant farmers and there were no wage-earning cottagers. The social dividing lines also varied quite considerably in different parts of the country. A poorer man could be considered more a gentleman in the north and west than in the richer south and east. The amount of land necessary to sustain a husbandman in self-sufficiency also varied from place to place depending on the type of soil, the vicinity of markets and, perhaps most of all, the availability of common land on which to graze livestock and gather firewood and building materials. None the less, despite these problems of definition and overlap this fourfold description of rural society was a useful one as long as access to the land was the determining factor of English economic life.

Two features of social and economic change were important in undermining this requirement. The first was the growth of towns and the increasing sophistication of the division of labour. As English society remained predominantly rural, these developments should not be exaggerated. Industries often developed in the countryside, where employers could escape the

13. Abingdon Town Hall (Berks., now Oxon.), built 1678–82. *The civic pride evident in London and the large cities could also be found in a substantial market town such as Abingdon, which, with its river traffic, its cloth trade and its prosperous rural hinterland, could afford this monument. Celia Fiennes (see Picture Essay, p. 42) praised the building as the finest town hall in England. The 'undertaker' or architect was Christopher Kempster of Burford, Christopher Wren's master mason (see Picture Essay, p. 186).*

14. Attr. Paul van Somer, *Robert Carey, First Earl of Monmouth, and his Family*, c. 1617. Oil on canvas, $89\frac{1}{2} \times 85\frac{1}{4}$ in. (227 × 216 cm.). London, National Portrait Gallery.
In 1617 Robert Carey (centre) was made Chamberlain to Prince Charles. The earldom of Monmouth followed early in Charles's reign. On his right is his wife, daughter of Sir Hugh Trevannion of Cornwall and widow of Sir Henry Widdrington of Northumberland. To her right is his heir, the future second earl, who would become a celebrated translator of Italian works into English. On his left is his daughter Philadelphia, who would marry the fourth Lord Wharton (see Pl. 87). To her left is her brother Thomas.

restrictive regulations and the wage protection supplied by the towns and their guilds: only in London were there seventeenth-century industrial suburbs. Yet change did occur. When the urban population was less than ten per cent of the total population, as it probably was for much of the sixteenth century, there was little need for the social analyst to concern himself with this marginal exception to his rural definitions of social structure. Writers noted that there were citizens and

15. Attr. David des Granges, *The Saltonstall Family*, *c.* 1637. Oil on canvas, 78 × 107 in. (198 × 271.5 cm.). London, Tate Gallery.
Sir Richard Saltonstall of Chipping Warden (d. 1650) leads a son and daughter to the bedside of his wife, Elizabeth, who has given birth to the child held in swaddling clothes by her bed.

burgesses who did not fit conveniently into an overwhelmingly rural society, but for the most part they were prepared to leave it at that. Most towns were, in any case, very small and were little more than a focal point of the surrounding countryside, where landowners often dominated their politics. The inhabitants of towns were often farmers themselves who provided marketing facilities and a few specialist manufacturing services for a limited region, in addition to working their own land. By the end of the Stuart period, however, the towns contained nearly a quarter of the whole population. Much of their relative growth was in London which, with a huge population of over half a million, had become the largest city in Europe and housed half of all of England's town-dwellers. Other towns had grown as well, although Norwich, which was the biggest town after London, had only 30,000 inhabitants and only a handful of other towns (Bristol, Newcastle, Exeter, York and perhaps Yarmouth) had populations over 10,000. In the larger towns there was a feeling of civic pride and a generally efficient amateur system of local government.

As towns grew, so did the range of occupations carried on within them become more diversified and sophisticated. Simple marketing and manufacturing functions now became increasingly specialized and subdivided as the urban market itself grew and as the specialist production of one town was traded to a wider national market. This tendency was, of course, most pronounced in London, whose greater population was paralleled by a greater variety in forms of urban economic activity. London was the seat of government and hence the home of most government servants, the main residence of the court, the only banking centre,

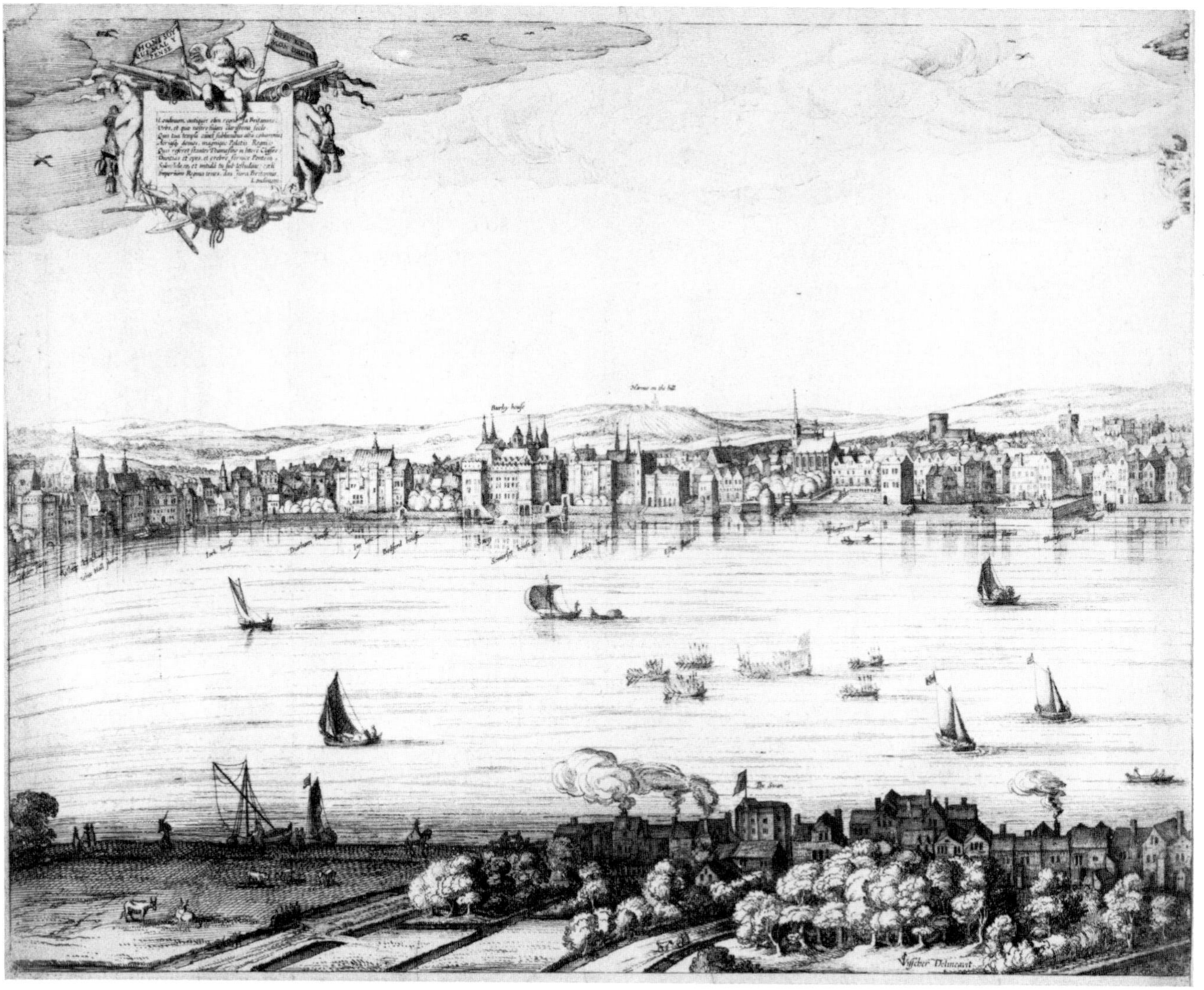

16. C. J. de Visscher, *View of London*, 1616.
Engraving, $15\frac{1}{2} \times 20$ in. (39.5 × 51 cm.).
This engraving shows the eastern approaches to the city of London. On the left, on the north (top) side of the river, are the sprawling buildings of Whitehall Palace which, far from being formally separated from the townscape around them, merge into it. To the right of Whitehall, as we move towards the city, are the town houses and palaces of noblemen and prelates. In the distance is Harrow-on-the-Hill. The south side of the river is still largely rural, although the Swan Theatre (middle-right) belonged to the development of entertainment facilities for Londoners in the late sixteenth and early seventeenth centuries. The appearance of seventeenth-century London was to be transformed by the Great Fire of 1666 and by a huge and rapid increase in population.

virtually the only centre of publishing and the home of a large proportion of all professional people. The metropolis also controlled three-quarters of England's foreign trade, owned nearly half of England's mercantile marine, dominated inland trade and had much the largest concentration of industrial workers in the country, many of them working in industries which could be found only in London or which London dominated in national production.

Such a wide range of occupations and functions, all of which were increasingly subdivided and specialized, posed the social analyst an almost insuperable task. Where and in what order in the social hierarchy did all these people fit? And if one could define an urban hierarchy, how did it relate to the existing rural hierarchy? One attempt to solve such problems resulted in the famous social hierarchy compiled by Gregory King in 1695. King started with the various categories of noblemen and gentlemen and followed them by persons in government office, merchants, lawyers, clergymen, freeholders, farmers, 'persons in liberal arts and sciences', shopkeepers and tradesmen, and artisans and craftsmen, in that order. This order may have been acceptable to him, but it is puzzling now. There were so many ways in which it was possible to assess the worth of a man: which was more important – birth, land-ownership, money, education or the 'gentility' of some particular occupation? Society had become too complicated to be so easily analysed.

The growth of the professions, each with its own hierarchy, was one important complicating factor in such an analysis. At the accession of James I only the Church and the law and, to a lesser extent, schoolteaching provided major opportunities for a man to earn a living (outside agriculture) in a professional rather than in a commercial or industrial career. However, by the end of the Stuart period new opportunities existed through the rapid expansion of the numbers employed in medicine; the monopoly that had been claimed by the small number of exclusive physicians was successfully challenged by the surgeons and even more so by the apothecaries, who had upgraded themselves from mere sellers of drugs to a position approaching that of the modern family doctor. The second half of the seventeenth century also saw the beginnings of a professional civil service whose numbers grew rapidly; and the wars fought during the reigns of William III and Queen Anne introduced for the first time a truly professional officer corps in both the army and the navy.

Every one of these professions claimed for its more successful practitioners a gentility that had little or nothing to do with older concepts of gentility based on the ownership of land. This was an important factor in the development of what can be called the urban gentleman, a rather different and generally more sophisticated character than the country gentleman living in his big house on a landed estate. However, not all urban gentlemen were professional men. Many were simply men of independent means. Some drew their income from the rents of country estates and so fitted the classic pattern of the gentleman even if they did choose to reside for most of the year in London. Other men of leisure, who behaved like gentlemen, got most of their income from urban investments. Since many of the citizens earned their living and behaved in exactly the same way, there was an inevitable blurring of the concept of gentleman in people's minds. The 1730 edition of Nathan Bailey's dictionary simplified the whole matter by defining a gentleman as anyone who had money, but it is doubtful whether many of his contemporaries would have considered this a very satisfactory definition of what was thought to be the most important dividing line in society – the line between those who were gentlemen and those who were not.

The growth of towns and their growing attraction for a leisured class were important reasons for making older descriptions of society less realistic. The other main reason was the growth of something resembling a modern proletariat in both town and country. Even in 1600 there were many people who owned or worked no land at all and relied entirely for their very bare living on occasional farm labour or on the work provided by a widespread rural manufacturing industry. This group of landless workers was to grow continuously throughout the period. Such a life, entirely supported by labour for others, was also to become the lot of the

17. Unknown artist (perhaps Dutch), *The North End of Westminster Hall with the Courts of Chancery and King's Bench in Session*, early seventeenth century. Drawing, $7\frac{3}{4} \times 11\frac{1}{2}$ in. (20 × 29.5 cm.). London, British Museum.
The royal courts of law were still held in the medieval hall of the king's oldest palace where they had begun, even though the day-to-day operation of the law had long since been separated from the monarch's own affairs. The Courts of Chancery and King's Bench are shown in session.

18. Jan Siberechts, *Landscape with Henley-on-Thames*, 1692.
Oil on canvas, 17 × 20 in. (43.2 × 50.8 cm.).
Collection of Lord Middleton.
Even in the later seventeenth century the town merges with and is dominated by the countryside. The market town of Henley, whose importance derived from its position on the Thames, was a port for the supply of timber, corn and malt to London.

majority of urban workers. There had been a time when a young person in a town could expect to move up the ladder, starting as an apprentice, then becoming a journeyman or paid worker and finally opening his own shop as a master. During the Stuart period a much smaller proportion of the work-force was able to make this final progression as the increasing sophistication and capitalization of small urban businesses raised the entry costs for potential aspirants, and as more and more masters ignored the apprenticeship laws and simply took on labour as and when they wanted it.

As a result of these changes, some contemporary writers moved away from the analysis of the social order as a series of ranks or degrees and began to think of society as divided into the three groups or classes that the twentieth century finds familiar. This idea of a tripartite division of society is perhaps most clearly expressed by Daniel Defoe at the very end of the period: at the top of society were 'the upper part of mankind', the gentry and aristocracy – men of independent means, normally but not necessarily landowners, who lived 'on estates and without the mechanism of employment'. Then there were the 'middling sort of people', the equivalent of the modern middle classes – 'tradesmen, such as merchants, shopkeepers of all

19. Claude de Jongh, *London Bridge,* 1630.
Oil on canvas, 20 × 66 in. (50.8 × 167.6 cm.).
London, Kenwood House, The Iveagh Bequest.
This was the only bridge to cross the Thames in London, where the river was most often crossed by boat. The picture is not reliable in detail.

20. Gillis Van Tilborgh, *The Tichborne Dole,* 1670.
46 × 81½ in. (117 × 207 cm.). Private collection.
Sir Henry Tichborne dispenses the hereditary dole of bread before his Hampshire manor house, a sixteenth-century building now demolished. The ideals of English society – its ordered hierarchy, its cohesion, the hospitality of its rulers – are celebrated in this ritualized distribution of charity.

sorts, and employers of others, either in trade or manufactures, farmers of land etc'. And finally there were 'the mechanick part of mankind', what might be called the working class – 'the meer labouring people who depend upon their hands'. Such a division of society poses its own problems; the professional people for instance fall uneasily between the first two groups. However, the fact that it could be made at all clearly suggests that the social structure during the reign of Queen Anne was very much more modern than it had been at the beginning of the Stuart period.

Economic Change

Why had the social structure changed in this way? How had England become a society that, in many ways, was recognizably modern? The answers to such fundamental questions are not simple, but it is possible to provide a framework for explanation by examining England's particular response to a general crisis which affected the whole of Europe in the sixteenth and seventeenth centuries. This can be most simply understood as a Malthusian crisis, a long period in which population growth pushed against the limited and inelastic resources which were available for the production of food. In the course of this crisis the English people were to endure hunger, dearth and the worst material conditions that they had had to experience since the early fourteenth century – worse conditions than they would ever have to experience again. However, the English did not suffer so severely as most other people in Europe, mainly because the crisis in England forced a structural change in its agrarian society which carried with it the possibility of innovation and thus a very substantial increase in the food supply. The cost of this change was what one writer has described as the disappearance of the English peasantry, though this was not fully realized under the Stuarts.

In the course of the sixteenth century the population of England had approximately doubled, from just over two million in 1500 to some four million by 1600. In the Stuart period the population continued to grow, but more slowly, reaching a peak of about five and one-quarter million in 1650 – after which the population declined until about 1675 and then stabilized at around five million. The long period of population growth before 1650 played havoc with the structure of society and with the material conditions of the people. In some European countries population growth led to a continuous subdivision of the land with the result that the peasants became progressively impoverished as they struggled to feed their families with the produce of a decreasing amount of land. In England, by contrast, the final result of population growth was fewer farms, not more, with the result that an increasing proportion of the population was divorced completely from the land, or at the most had only a small cottage garden. The reason for this particular and almost unique response was that population growth offered a commercial challenge to the more prosperous and enterprising members of rural society and in England this challenge was successfully met.

The most obvious aspect of this challenge was a growth in the market for food and, to a lesser extent, for raw materials which were related to agriculture, such as wool and leather. These markets were concentrated in the expanding towns and particularly in London, but there was a growth in the rural market as well. This was provided by the new landless population who were now obliged to buy their food from their commercially-minded and wealthier neighbours. The food markets grew faster than supply in the earlier part of the period with the result that food prices increased rapidly and so provided farmers and landlords with a strong incentive to devote their efforts towards commercial farming. This incentive was made doubly attractive by the fact that an increasing potential work-force had brought real wages down to their lowest level for three centuries by the 1620s. Cheap labour and a rising market formed an attractive proposition for the commercial farmer.

Inertia, incompetence and the rigid nature of existing tenurial relationships delayed the total victory of a commercialized market-oriented agriculture, but change – stimulated and guided by a voluminous pamphlet literature in favour of improved agricultural techniques – was all in the same direction. Gentlemen who worked their own land and yeomen farmers devoted their attention to the market and sought, where possible, to increase the amount of land at their disposal. Meanwhile the aristocracy and those gentlemen who lived off rents sought to benefit from the increasing profitability of agriculture in order to increase their rental incomes. Such a process took a long time, since the conditions of tenure and the rents of much of the land had in the past been fixed on very favourable terms for the tenantry. However, sooner or later long leases came to an end or tenant families died out or were bought out or found that their rights were not so secure in law as they had supposed. The result was that by the last decades of the sixteenth century rents were rising universally and were increasingly being paid by commercially-minded farmers whose growing profits could easily absorb the new level of fixed costs. Those who suffered were the husbandmen and cottagers – farmers with too little land to benefit from the rising market. Some suffered because, through

21. Bassingham enclosure petition, 1629.
Lincolnshire Archives Office.
The River Witham borders the village of Bassingham, Lincolnshire, whose church and farmhouses are clearly illustrated. So are the drainage ditches which flow into the river or towards the fen to the south. The petitioners complain of the 'incommodity of the long way to the cow-pasture': to avoid the wide stretch of cornfields, the cattle have a 'journey every day above six miles long', which 'sore beats their feet and impoverisheth them. . . . besides, the daily trampling of 500 or 600 cattle in our fallow-field and ox-pasture soileth and destroyeth the grass.' Separation of the cornfields by enclosures is the solution favoured by the petitioners; and enclosure did bring much agricultural improvement in the seventeenth century. But in the shorter term the removal of common rights could cause hardship and resentment.

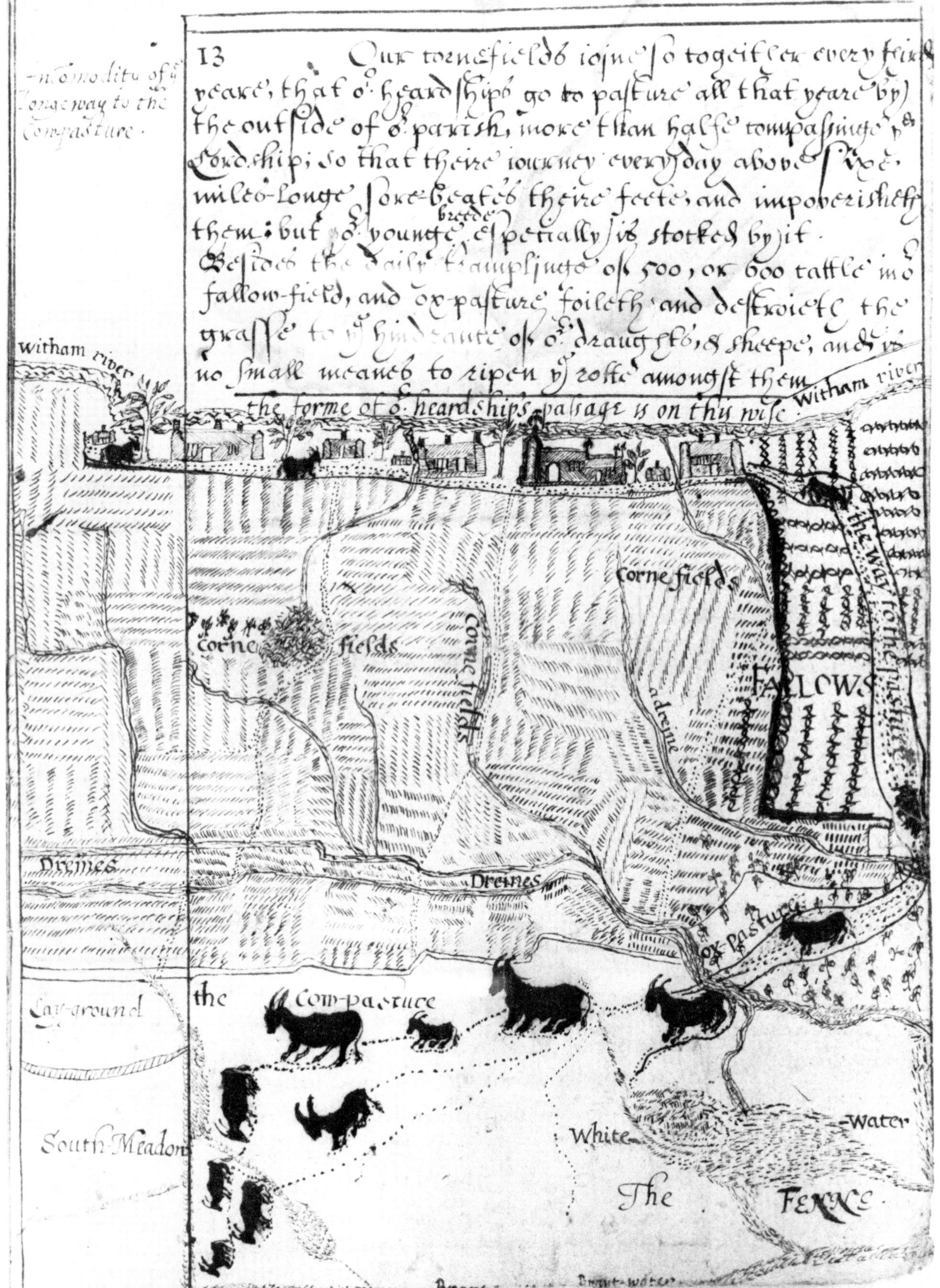
witham river
Witham river
the forme of o' heardships passage is on this wise
corne fields
Corne fields
corne fields
FALLOWS
the way to the pasture
a dreine
Dreines
Dreines
ox-pasture
the Com-pasture
Lay-ground
South-Meadow
White-Water
The FENNE

22 (above). Hertford Borough Charter, 1605. Hertfordshire Record Office.
The ornate borough charter is proudly decorated with an imagined rural scene. With the award of the charter Hertford fulfilled the common aim of towns: to win the formal incorporation that would give it control of its own markets, fairs and courts and free it from the manorial rights of royal or noble landowners. About fifty towns gained charters in the seventeenth century. But the independence thus acquired proved largely illusory. Charters tended to give power to a local élite which excluded humbler men and ruled in deference to the crown; but during the century the crown learned to manipulate charters to extend its power over the towns.

23 (below). Grant of Arms to the 'New' East India Company, 13 October 1698. London, Guildhall Library.
The East India Company, founded in 1600, enjoyed a monopoly of English trade to India and Indonesia, and over the century brought England into a worldwide trading system. As well as the bilateral trade between England and the Indies there was the re-export of East India goods to continental and Mediterranean markets, and a carrying trade in the east. A long-running battle between the company's monopoly and those who wished to break into or open up the trade was resolved in 1698, when the 'old' East India Company was obliged by crown and parliament to make way for a new one.

AUSPICIO·REGIS·ET·SENATUS·ANGLIÆ

To all and Singular to whom these Presents shall come S.r Thomas S.t George Kn.t Garter Principal King of Arms, and S.r Henry S.t George Kn.t Clarenceux King of Arms, Greeting: Whereas his most Sacred Majesty has bin graciously pleased by his Royal Charter, under the Great Seal of England, bearing date the fifth day of September, in the tenth Year of his Ma.ties Reign to Incorporate several of his Loving Subjects (in pursuance of an Act of Parliament) into one Body Politique, and Corporate, by the Name of the English Company Trading to the East Indies in a joint stock, whereby they are Entitled to have a perpetual Succession, and a Common Seal, with many other Priviledges, and Immunities, as by the said Act, and Charter, doth more plainly appear: and Whereas Edward Allen, Abraham Beake, James Bateman John Cary Esq.rs S.r Henry Furnese Kn.t Peter Godfrey, Peter Gott, Gilbert Heathcote, Edmund Harrison Esq.rs S.r Theodore Iansen Kn.t Samuel Lock Edward Littleton, Ioseph Martin, Streynsham Master, Ephraim Mountague, Peter Paggen, Robert Raworth, Benjamin Rokeby, Samuel Shepheard Esq.rs S.r William Scawen Kn.t William Stewart, Thomas Vernon, William Withers, and George White Esquires; Directors of the said English Company Trading to the East Indies in a Joint Stock, have made Application to his Grace HENRY Duke of Norfolke, Earl Marshall of England etc.a That such Ensigns, Viz.t Arms, Crest, and Supporters, may be Devised for, and Assigned to the said Company, as may most eminently manifest his Majesties Princely Favour, and Distinguish the said Corporation by marks of Honor suitable to the Grandeur of the same; the King's most Excellent Majesty, and divers of the Nobility, being Members thereof and Whereas his Grace HENRY Duke of Norfolke Earl Marshall of England, hath by Order, or Warrant under his Hand, and Seal of his Office of Earl Marshall bearing date the Thirtieth of September last Ordered Us to Devise, and Assigne unto the said English Company Trading to the East Indies in a Joint Stock such Arms, Crest, and Supporters, as they, and their Successors may lawfully bear, and use KNOW ye therefore that we the said Garter & Clarenceux, in pursuance of the said Earl Marshalls Order, and consent signified by his said Warrant, and by Authority of the Letters Patents of our Offices to each of us respectively Granted under the Great Seal of England; Have Devised, and Assigned, and do by these Presents, Grant, Assigne, Ratifie, and Confirme to the said English Company Trading to the East Indies in a Joint Stock, and to their Successors forever, the Arms, Crest, & Supporters hereafter mentioned Viz. Argent a Cross Gules, on a Sheild in the Dexter Quarter the Arms of France, and England Quarterly within a Compartment, adorned with an Imperial Crown; and for their Crest, upon a Helme, on a Torse or Wreath Argent, and Gules, a Lyon Rampant Gardant Or, holding between his Paws an Imperial Crown proper, Mantled Gules, Doubled Argent. Supported by two Lyons Gardant Gold, and each of them holding a Banner Argent, charged with a Cross Gules; as in the Margent hereof is more plainly Depicted In Witness whereof we the said Garter, and Clarenceux Kings of Arms, have to these Presents Subscribed our Names, and Affixed the Seals of our respective Offices this Thirteenth day of October, in the Tenth Year of the Reign of our Soveraign Lord WILLIAM the third by the Grace of God King of England Scotland, France, and Ireland, Defender of the Faith etc.a Annoq: Dni: 1698.

custom or inclination, they subdivided their land between their sons and thus created less viable farming units. Others suffered because higher rents brought a burden of debt that could prove fatal in years of bad harvests when normally self-sufficient husbandmen were themselves forced to buy food at inflated prices.

By the early seventeenth century all these developments had considerably polarized the rural population. The great majority of landlords who had been able to raise their rents became increasingly prosperous and self-confident. Yeomen also did very well and many did so well that they were able to swell the ranks of the gentry, a class which grew considerably in numbers, wealth and social and political ambition during this period. But those who were unable to produce for the market did badly. Scholars who have studied landholding at the village level have found a considerable fall in the numbers of the husbandmen or the self-sufficient farmers who had once been the backbone of English rural society. Meanwhile there was a huge increase in the numbers of people at the bottom of the rural hierarchy – cottagers with a few acres of land or just a garden and labourers with no land at all. By the end of the seventeenth century this process of polarization had gone far towards undermining the former structure of rural society. Many peasants survived, particularly in the more pastoral north and west of the country, but much of agriculture had taken on that tripartite division apparent in society as a whole. A new world in which landlord, commercial farmer and labourer formed the three strata of rural society had arrived.

The rise of commercial farming was accompanied by innovation in agriculture which was eventually to free England from the fear of famine. One major feature of innovation was a radical reorganization of the rural landscape. Farms were combined to create larger units for the commercial farmer. Much land that had formerly been farmed under communal rules or used as common land by small farmers was now enclosed – that is to say it was fenced or hedged and farmed as separate units. Fenland was drained, moors reclaimed and woodland cleared to increase the cultivable area. These processes greatly increased the land available for commercial food production, but they also deprived the poor cottagers and other marginal people of their former access to grazing, fuel and raw materials and so made their lives even harder.

Innovation also changed methods of husbandry. Most of these changes involved an increase in production and an improvement in the quality of fodder crops and grasses. This had the double advantage of increasing the number of animals the land could sustain and, simultaneously, providing the much larger supply of animal manure needed to fertilize arable land and so raise the yields of grain crops. It was a gradual process, but by the second half of the seventeenth century English agriculture was making a quite remarkable contribution to the nation's wealth. Now a smaller proportion of the population was producing a much larger and more varied amount of food and this food was being sold on the market at stable or even falling prices. A commercial challenge had been met, perhaps too well for many of the smaller or less efficient farmers who found that the days of bonanza were over and that rising prices were no longer able to conceal their incompetent or old-fashioned methods of farming. Meanwhile the poor at last benefited. The end of population growth improved their competitive position in the labour market and modestly increased their wages – facts that, together with stable or falling food prices, ended the extensive period of falling real wages and gave the poor a modicum of comfort by the end of the Stuart period.

But this is to anticipate. What work existed for the hundreds of thousands of people who were landless, near landless or living in towns? Who paid them the wages that enabled them to survive this harsh period in English history? The growth of commercial agriculture itself created a considerable amount of employment, though much of this was only seasonal and indeed many of the poor could only have been fully employed at harvest time. Nevertheless many of the displaced and landless must have found work on the farms of their yeomen and gentlemen neighbours. Commercial farming also created a large demand for labour in the processing, distribution and marketing of food and raw materials. Poor men, whose fathers and grandfathers had been peasants, might in this new world find employment with millers, maltsters, carters, drovers, tanners, butchers, bakers and the like. However, the jobs created by commercial farming were by no means sufficient to absorb all the newly-created poor.

Another possibility, and one in which England had a great comparative advantage, was in the production of goods for export. For most of this period this essentially meant the production of woollen cloth — England's biggest industry and one that had a large and growing foreign market in the first two decades of the seventeenth century, but that was later to meet difficulties as foreign competition grew. Most woollen cloth was produced in the countryside, the spinners and weavers working up the raw materials in their own cottages. Cloth-making could therefore be combined with a small farm and often was, but it was increasingly the sole occupation of many of the new landless population.

'Points of Good Husbandry'

FARMING WITH HENRY BEST

Elmswell, a manor in Great Driffield Parish in the East Riding of Yorkshire, was bought by Henry Best from his brother in 1618 and farmed by him until his death in 1645. Henry returned to Yorkshire from Braintree in Essex, where he had married the daughter of a leading citizen and had acquired an agricultural expertise based on a reading of Thomas Tusser's famous *500 Points of Good Husbandry*. As Woodward wrote in his edition of Henry Best's *Farming Book*, the Bests were 'workaday gentry supervising closely the exploitation of their estates', yet they were not country bumpkins. They were well-travelled, and Henry's brother was a Cambridge don.

Henry Best's *Farming and Memorandum Books*, written for the agricultural education of his son John, convey a sense of the realities of seventeenth-century farming. The home farm was at least 460 acres and there were usually about eight tenant farmers on the estate. Best was accustomed to the basics of farming. He supervised work on the spot ('You must call to them to stoop and to cut low and round'). The *Memorandum Book* shows in vivid detail his transactions, his hirings, his concern for getting things right, and the methods by which he became a successful commercial farmer on the edge of the Yorkshire Wolds.

Elmswell was a hamlet of less than 100 people, a community tightly controlled by the Bests. Henry was a fair but not a generous man, eager for his pound of flesh. When hiring men 'you are not to commit overmuch to their trust'. Workers' pay was carefully recorded. At the Martinmas hirings it was common to take on eight people for the year – a foreman, three men, two youths and three maidservants. At Martinmas (11 November) 1628, Robert Sandy, presumably the foreman, was hired for £3 per year, the highest paid of the labourers. He also got his 'godspenny', which would be an additional sum of money, or some second-hand clothes or boots. Sometimes there were also benefits such as board and lodging.

Few of Henry's annual workers seem to have applied again for more work at the next Martinmas. But there was certainly no shortage of labour around Elmswell, for Henry had no trouble in hiring day-labourers, men who survived by supplementing their own smallholdings. Harvest brought more labour demands and Henry's barns were full of extra hirelings from the North Yorkshire moors. He was served by a host of local craftsmen, too, again usually part-time husbandmen supplementing their incomes. Before haymaking, 'we send to the wright to come and see that the axle trees and felfes to the wains be sound. Cobblers call for 3d. a day, but leather has gone up and they now get 6d. and their meat.'

Best's commercial farming at Elmswell was compact and tightly controlled. Missed opportunities were noted for future

2 Elmswell Manor House, showing the south side and east gable.
The House, in a poor state, appears to have been little altered. It was substantial, and probably boasted nine hearths.

Of Sheepe.
Sheepe is not onely a common name for both sexes, but is likewise putt and taken for all generally; as when men say a flocke, a keepinge, or a folde of sheepe: all sheepe are eyther Tuppes, i.e. Rammes. Ewes, Weathers: Tuppes are eyther Hunge tuppes: Close tuppes: Riggon tuppes: Hunge tuppes are such as have both the stones in the codde, & they onely are to bee kept for breeders; because of the experimented adage, omne animal generat sibi simile: Close tuppes are such as have both the stones in yt ridge of the backe, & are therefore very difficult to gelde: Riggon tuppes are such as have one stone in the codde, the other in yt ridge of the backe, & therefore ye most danger & difficultie is in geldinge of these, being to bee cutte in two places, before they can bee made cleane weathers.
How to knowe tupps from weathers:
If the tuppe bee eyther a close tuppe or Riggon tuppe you may (if hee bee an horned tuppe) knowe him by ye bignesse & greatnesse of his hornes which in a weather seeme to bee both smaller & shorter; but if hee bee a dodded tuppe you may knowe him also by the breadth of his fore-heade which appeareth high

1 Facsimile of page 1 of the *Farming Book*, Howard Vyse Papers, Humberside County Record Office, Beverley, DDHV/75/50.
'"Of Sheepe". Sheep is not only a common name for both sexes, but is likewise put and taken for all generally; as when men say a flock, a keepinge, or a folde of sheep. All sheep are either: Tuppes, i.e. Rammes, Ewes, Weather, Riggons. Tuppes are either: Hunge tuppes, Close tuppes, Riggon tuppes. Hunge tuppes are such as hath both the stone in the codde, and they onely are to bee kept for breeders . . .'

guidance. 'We sold our wool this year to a Beverley man . . . and had for it viiis a stone besides xiid in earnest; and if we had kept it a fortnight longer, might have had ixs.vid., if not xs. a stone.' The household economy of bacon, beef, cheeses, oatmeal and honey kept in the house was recorded. The production of honey used as a sweetener and for making mead was one of Henry's hobbies.

The Bests lived in a style befitting their social position and as was necessary for the running of a substantial business. The manor house, which still survives, was a large brick dwelling of three stories and nine rooms. In 1635 Henry ordered 400,000 bricks, almost certainly for its construction and for that of the barns, hay-lofts, dovecot and sheds or helms. In the house, 16 people lived including six children and nine servants, while the outbuildings accommodated a fluctuating number of workers. That was the setting for the real business at Elmswell – the farming. It was mixed: wheat, rye, maslin (a mixture of wheat and rye), barley, oats and peas were cultivated, but sheep were the main cash product and they were folded on the arable land; oxen and horses were kept as draught animals, some cows for milk and some farmyard pigs and poultry. However much they wanted to specialize for the market, all farmers were perforce mixed farmers, as animals were necessary for arable, and crops were needed to sustain animals. From late autumn through to spring, tillage dominated, with ploughing, harrowing, rolling and sowing all crammed into these hard months. Henry was typically careful with his seed corn. 'It is no point of good husbandry to lie such barley aside for seed as is either moweburnt [overheated in the stack] or hath much slaine [a black powdered mildew] in it . . . but . . . in wheat if the seed be not changed once in four or five crops, it will slay extremely.'

When considering the best mix with rye, Henry showed an innovatory approach: 'we find experimentally that Kentish wheat is the best or that which thereabouts is called Doddereade'. The benefits of manuring were assessed in relation to furrow depth and a mass of such observations are recorded. Oats was the major Elmswell crop and most of it was used as fodder and not marketed. The same applied to peas and hay. Interestingly, the largest crop was not directly commercial. Barley, the second-largest crop, was marketed in bulk, with wheat and rye grown and sold in smaller quantities. Crops seem to have been sold to the north-east via Bridlington. Some land was left fallow each year for recuperation; but it was not uselsss, for when it was newly ploughed lambing ewes would graze on it, 'where they may get the roots of grass and weeds, which are a great furtherance to milk'.

Harvesting was a time when all hands turned to the sickle and scythe. 'The next good shearer (of corn) is he that taketh a good handful at every cut.' As usual, Henry got his money's worth. 'The mowers come at five in the morning, and then they will sleep an hour at noon.' This was a heavy job for men, but women joined in the reaping.

Livestock farming dominated life at Elmswell and the *Farming Book*. Henry had 310 sheep and in October 1641 'three score and fifteen lambs were greased'. Very detailed instructions are given on sheep care. Henry admired the methods of Lord Finch by which 'there is vid. allowed to a piper for playing to the clippers all the day'. Henry, always anxious not to repeat errors, added: 'we libbed [castrated] our lambs this 6th of June, but it would have been better if they had been libbed the month before . . . We carried also a penknife for the shepherd to libbe them with and a ball of wild tansey, chopped and made up with fresh butter for anointing their codds and keeping the flies away'. Such is his mixture of sage advice and earthy technical description. It takes his readers directly into the farmyard and on to the fields of East Yorkshire.

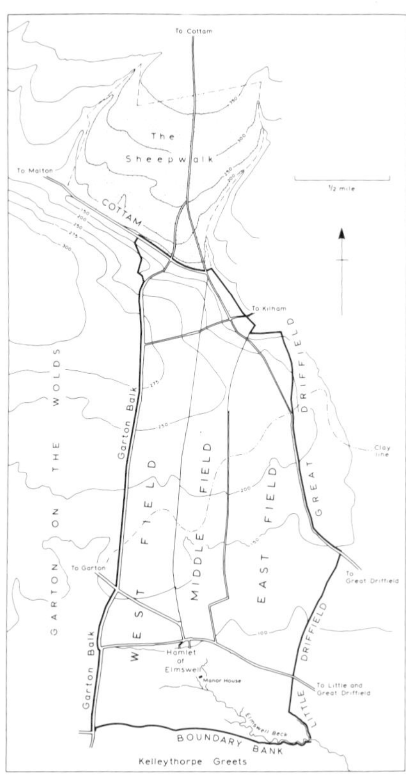

3 Map showing a reconstruction of the Elmswell estate in the seventeenth-century. Reproduced from *The Farming and Memorandum Books of Henry Best of Elmswell, 1642*, ed. D. Woodward, OUP (1984).

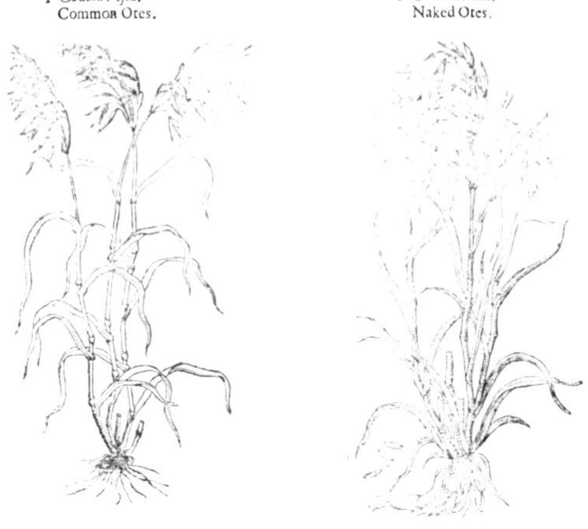
LIB. I. Of the Hiſtorie of Plants. 75

Otemeale is good for to make a faire and wel coloured maid to looke like a cake of tallow, eſpecially if ſhe take next her ſtomacke a good draught of ſtrong vinegre after it. C

Otemeale vſed as a Cataplaſme dries and moderately diſcuſſes, and that without biting; for it hath ſomewhat a coole temper, with ſome aſtriction, ſo that it is good againſt ſcowrings. D

1 *Auena Veſca.* Common Otes.

2 *Auena Nuda.* Naked Otes.

CHAP. 55. *Of Wilde Otes.*

¶ *The Deſcription.*

4 'Common and Naked Oats' from John Gerard, *The Herball or General Historie of Plantes* (1597).

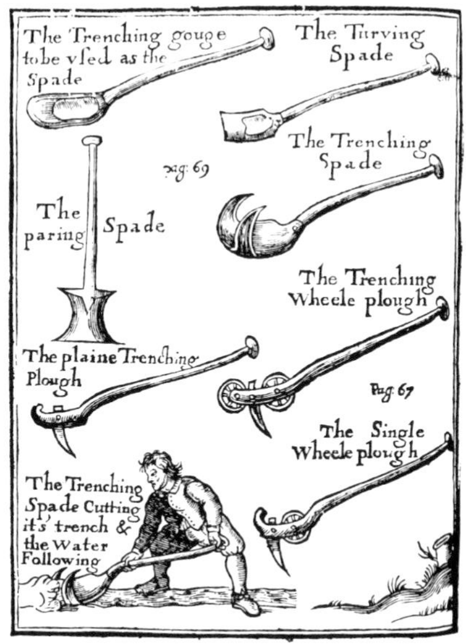

5 Trenching tools.
A page from W. Blith, *The English Farmer Improved* (1642).

At the beginning of the Stuart period most of the cloth that was exported, and indeed most of England's trade, went no further than the short sea route between London and the Low Countries from where it was distributed by foreign merchants to more distant markets. Although this was to remain the most important axis of trade throughout the period there was to be a massive geographical diversification of English overseas trade in the course of the seventeenth century. From the 1570s increasing numbers of English ships had been trading directly to the Mediterranean, and trade with the Ottoman Empire, Italy, Spain and Portugal was to become very important as English cloth could be sold there in exchange for a useful range of wines, foodstuffs and raw materials, such as wool and silk. In 1600 an even more exotic trade was inaugurated with the founding of the East India Company. Settlements were founded at Bombay, Madras and Calcutta, but it was trade rather than territorial expansion that dominated this first century of England's Asian adventure. This trade expanded dramatically, particularly in the 1670s and 1680s when a flood of Indian cotton and silk textiles arrived to transform English and European taste.

The third major development in England's long-distance trade and the most important in terms of its effects on the English people was caused by the growth of the American colonies, a process which started with the settlement of Virginia in the reign of James I. This successful experiment was quickly repeated both in North America and in the West Indies and the process was accelerated by the large-scale emigration of Puritans to New England in the 1630s. The overthrow of the Church of England in the 1640s ended the Puritan emigration, although from 1681 Pennsylvania was to provide a refuge for Quakers. Religion was not the only cause of an exodus to which hardship and over-population also contributed. By the end of the century there were English colonies planted along most of the North American seaboard and in several West Indian islands. Seventeenth-century colonization has been estimated to have absorbed a quarter of a million emigrants from England, itself a major factor in reducing the pressures of population growth (although there was also some immigration from Europe – most notably from Huguenots driven from France in 1685). Colonization did not have merely demographic consequences. The colonies provided a major market for a wide range of industrial goods produced by English workmen as well as for the ships built and sailed by Englishmen and colonists for transporting the goods to America and returning with the bulky cargoes of sugar, tobacco and forest products that Europe bought. Charles II's reign also saw England gaining an important share of the African slave trade. England's expanding overseas horizons had a considerable importance in solving the problems of the English poor, providing some of them with a new home and providing others with work in export industries, shipbuilding or as sailors in a rapidly expanding mercantile marine. The new trades also, of course, brought wealth to merchants and shipowners and so helped to create the expansion of the urban middle classes.

Although production for a foreign or colonial market was increasingly important and tended to dominate the economic policies of European countries, there is no doubt that industrial production for the home market was many times greater and this was the most rapidly growing source of labour for the poor. One major reason for the growth of the home market was the previously-mentioned processes of commercialization and social polarization. Those who got rich in this process, such as gentlemen, yeomen and the growing numbers of 'middling' people who controlled distribution, now had much more money to spend. Some of this money was spent on imports, a fact which helps to explain the diversification in foreign trade as merchants sailed the world, bringing back exotic products for their wealthy customers. But most of this new spending power was translated into goods and services produced by the English poor. New wealth created a rapidly increasing demand for domestic servants, better housing and furniture, metal goods of all sorts, clothing of increasing sophistication and variety, and a host of other insignificant but cumulatively important products – all of which provided labour opportunities for the poor both in towns and in the countryside. This process was cumulative, since each new industrial development created new entrepreneurs, distributors and shopkeepers to swell the numbers of the middling ranks and thereby swell the demand for the same goods and services. By the end of the Stuart period, with the gradual rise of real wages, even the poor provided a marginal addition to the demand. Meanwhile the growth of the market for industrial goods allowed for a much greater division of labour and specialization in their manufacture, thus increasing productivity and allowing manufacturers to cut their prices and to expand their market still further. This process was accelerated by a growing tendency to introduce labour-saving devices, such as the knitting-frame and the ribbon-loom, both of which greatly increased productivity and were Stuart precursors of the more dramatic technological changes of the Industrial Revolution. Indeed it is no exaggeration to say that the process of industrialization that was to usher in the

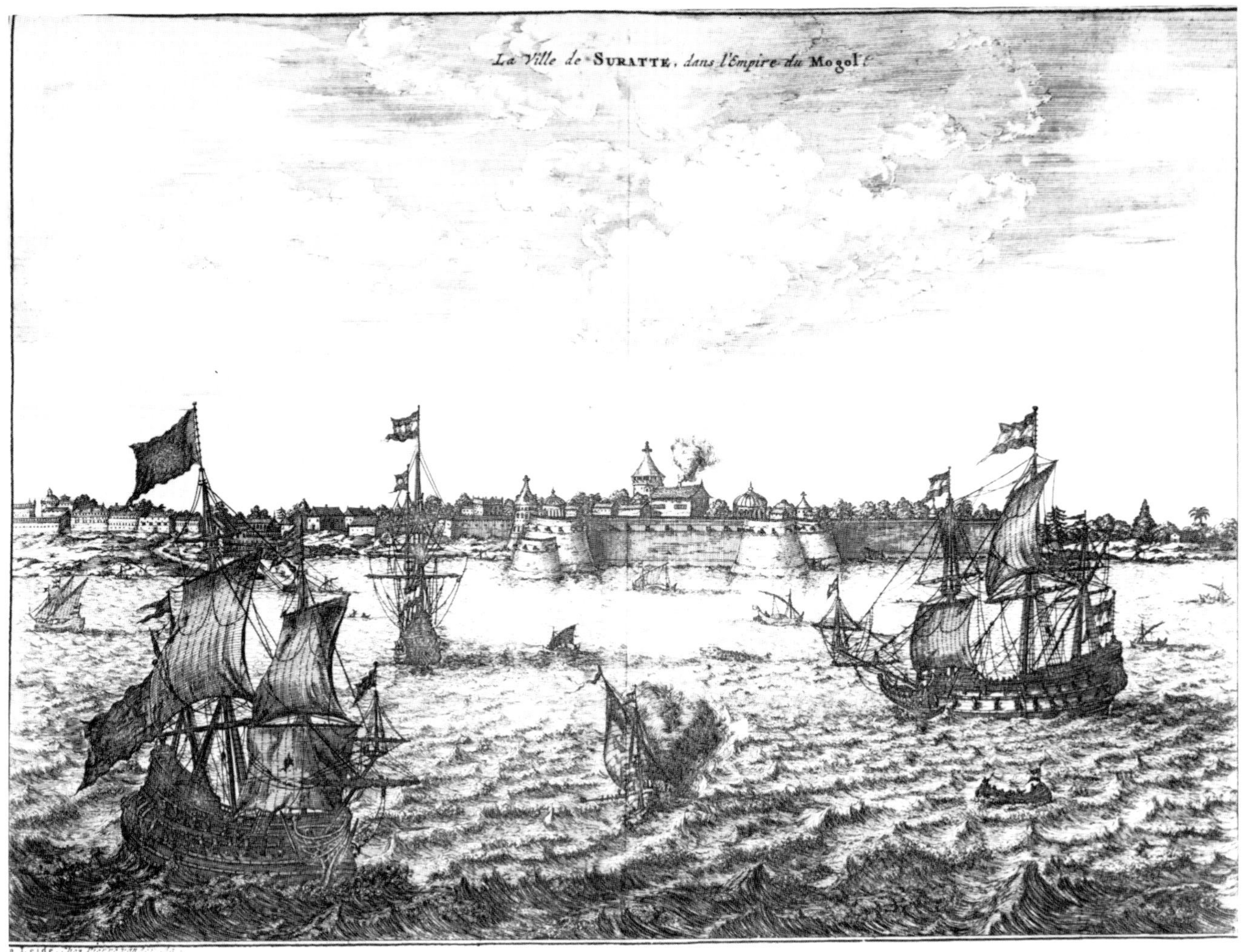

24. Seventeenth-century Surat.
Engraving in the India Office Library.
Surat, in western India, was the seat of the presidency of the English East India Company. In the expanding eastern markets England competed with the declining Portuguese seaborne empire and, less successfully, with the rising one of the Dutch, which thwarted English attempts to dominate the spice trade. Surat was a depot for cotton, saltpetre and indigo from the Indian interior, and a base for privateering ventures against England's European rivals. The English company enjoyed the protection of the local Moghul viceroy, an invaluable asset until 1664 when a raid on the town by a neighbouring Indian power exposed the limits of the viceroy's authority and led the company to look for an alternative base. They found one in Bombay, which came into England's possession under Charles II as part of the marriage portion of Catherine of Braganza.

modern age had already started by the end of this period.

The processes of polarization, urbanization and the growth of rural industries drove many of the English people from their native villages in order to seek a new life elsewhere in the country, quite apart from the large numbers who emigrated to America, the West Indies and to Ireland. Migration on a limited scale had always been common as people travelled in search of a new position as a servant, to take up a new farm or to marry. But during this period people moved longer distances. This migration tended to be in three main directions. Many sought the less densely-populated and less strictly-ruled parts of the country where a living could be made by exploiting extensive common land or by working-up local raw materials into manufactured goods. Such motives drew men and women to the remaining woodlands, to the fenland and, in particular, away from the south and east towards the midlands, north and west, thus slowly changing the geographical balance of population and anticipating the eighteenth and nineteenth-century concentration of people in the Midlands, Yorkshire and Lancashire. Others left their villages to seek employment in nearby towns. By far the biggest urban migration was, of course, to London, lode-star of rich and poor alike. By the end of the period the metropolis was the home of one in nine of the English people and, since it was a very unhealthy place where far more people died than were born each year, it required additional migrants to maintain its growth. One estimate suggests that one in six of all English

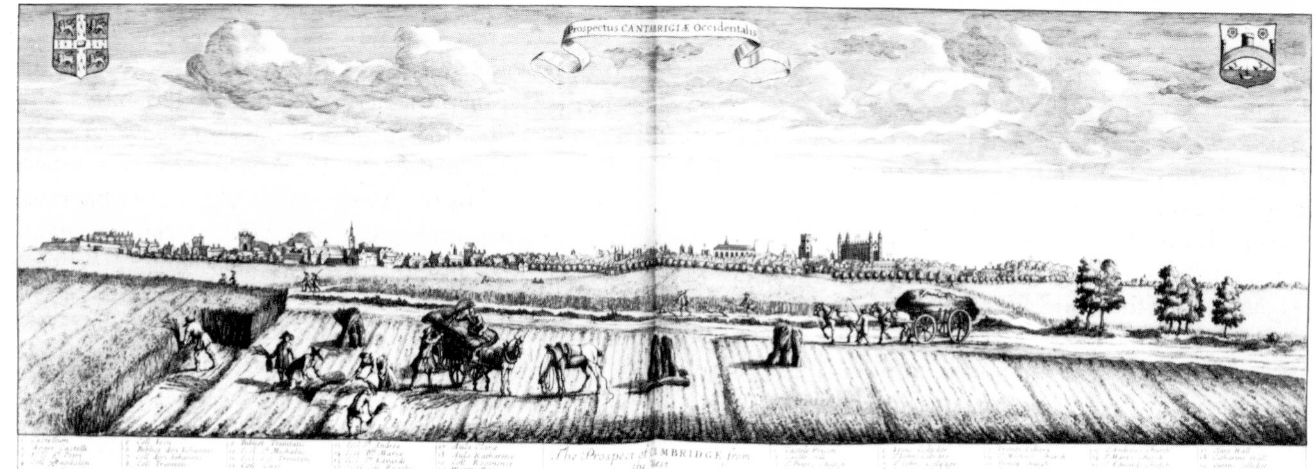

25. David Loggan, *Cantabrigia Illustrata* (1688).
In Loggan's 'Prospect of Cambridge from the West', town lives cheek by jowl with country, the 'backs' of the university with haymaking. Like many of the artists who help to provide the visual legacy of seventeenth-century England, Loggan was a foreigner. Born in Danzig, he appears to have come to England during the Puritan Revolution, and was naturalized in 1675, when his work was becoming well known. His engravings of portraits were celebrated, and he made series of illustrations of the universities of Oxford and Cambridge, both of which appointed him their official engraver.

26. A page from John Evelyn, *Sylva* (1664; repr. 1670, 1679).
Charcoal-burning belonged to the large rural base of English industry, although the high prices of wood and charcoal were making mineral coal an effective competitor for the provision of heat. The burning of charcoal had damaging effects on England's forests and woodlands.

people spent some time in London during their lives. Some stayed there; others returned to their previous homes and carried elements of the much more modern metropolitan culture back to the provinces.

This behaviour, endlessly repeated, played a vital role in breaking down regionalism in every sense. New tastes, new habits, new patterns of spending were transmitted from London throughout the land, as much by migrants and gentry visitors to the capital as by those inland traders and chapmen whose job it was to promote new patterns of expenditure for their own profit. English society retained its provincial and local aspects and the county and the village remained important units of administration and loyalty, but they became increasingly affected by the impact of the metropolitan culture, a process that was to have immense significance for the future.

Rich and Poor

The preceding analysis of economic and social change in Stuart England has been, perhaps, rather optimistic. Change did bring progress and nearly everyone was better off in 1714 than their forefathers had been in 1603. Progress, however, meant only a very marginal improvement to the incomes of the poor and did little to protect them from insecurity. Neither did progress act to reverse the gross inequalities of English life. At the end of the seventeenth century Gregory King estimated that the national income was about £8 per head or £40 per family. Such numbers are almost impossible to convert into modern equivalents, so great has been

27. An illustration from J. A. Comenius, *Orbis Sensualium Pictus* (1672 edition).
Coopers, suppliers of barrels, provided one of the most essential and one of the most skilled service trades of the period.

inflation and the change in relative values. It is sufficient to say that these figures suggest that England was about the wealthiest country in the world in 1688, rivalled only by Holland and the recently-settled English colonies in America, but very poor by twentieth-century standards, with a national income per capita equivalent to the poorer – but not the poorest – countries of the Third World today.

The national income was very unevenly distributed between the different strata of society. Most wage-earners earned five to ten new pence per day, the latter figure being the price of two gallons of strong beer at the end of the Stuart period. Such a wage produced a yearly income of £10 to £15, depending on the number of days on which employment could be found. Skilled artisans could earn considerably more, but few people in this social stratum could expect to leave a personal estate worth more than £5. By contrast people in the middling ranks of society earned incomes from £40 or £50 up to several hundred pounds and might expect to leave estates ranging from £50 in the provinces, £100 in London and up to thousands or even tens of thousands of pounds for the wealthier London manufacturers, shopkeepers, merchants and financiers. The wealth of the richer middling people over-topped that of most of the gentry and aristocracy whose incomes ranged from less than £100 to several thousands of pounds for the greater aristocracy. It was then quite possible for a landlord to have an income one hundred times greater than that of the labourers on his estate, while even a man in the lower-middling ranks of society would typically earn three or four times as much as the workmen he employed.

This juxtaposition of wealth and poverty in society was seen as the natural order of things, and the wealthy went to considerable effort to reinforce and justify it. Whether a man was rich or poor could be explained by the accident of birth or by the fulfilment of God's providence, though there was a tendency in the later Stuart age to explain such matters more in terms of personality and human behaviour. Now wealth could be seen as the product of past labour, application and diligence with the implication that the poor were poor because they deserved to be poor. Whatever its explanation, the existence of poverty created the biggest social problem of the age, especially in the first half of the century.

Since poverty often presented itself as a problem of law and order, it is useful to examine briefly the structure of social control that existed in Stuart England. In the period up to the civil war the main organ of the central government interested in maintaining order was the Privy Council, a role which was left largely to the two Secretaries of State after 1660. One of the Council's main priorities was to control and imbue with a sense of duty the Justices of the Peace who were the effective rulers of the counties. Assistance in this respect was provided by the Assize judges who made a biannual circuit through the counties in order to clear the gaols of persons awaiting trial. At the same time, they were expected to oversee the work of the Justices of the Peace and expound government policy to them.

Attempts to impose a centralized control on the counties must in the long run be deemed a failure. The justices were prepared to take on more and more work as time went on, but they were not prepared to give up their local autonomy. They were therefore selective in their enforcement of the laws, mediating between central government and their neighbours' interests. They did, however, see social control and the supervision of the poor as a major part of both their duty and their interest and such work took up a considerable proportion of their time, both collectively in Quarter Sessions and as individual justices examining complaints brought before them or summarily sentencing offenders. They were also responsible for supervising the work of those who were supposed to exert authority at the village level. Such men were increasingly drawn from a small group of the more prosperous village worthies who generally monopolized the offices of churchwarden, constable and overseer of the poor and constituted the greater part of local juries. Their prime interest was harmony in the village and they were often reluctant to enforce legislation that disturbed it or that might make them offensive in the eyes of their neighbours.

The problem of poverty presented itself to those in authority in two different, but closely related, ways – the maintenance of the poor and the care of their social, physical and moral well-being. Maintenance was seen as a local function. Each parish was responsible for its own poor. In most rural parishes this made good sense and presented little difficulty, though problems of a quite different order existed in city parishes densely packed with near-destitute paupers. Most of the village poor, however, were those whom their contemporaries called 'deserving' – the aged, the sick, widows, abandoned mothers and orphans. Such people had always existed and, if their own relatives were unable to look after them, most parishes could draw on charitable endowments or on the charity of the living to provide them with maintenance in an almshouse or in their own homes. The elderly were sometimes boarded out and children apprenticed, while great efforts were made to discover putative fathers who were brought to bear the cost of raising their bastards. If all else failed, parishes

28. St. Bartholomew's Hospital, Newbury, 1618, with alterations of 1698.
This handsome U-shaped brick building was one of at least three hospitals or almshouse complexes to have been established in the important cloth town of Newbury by the early eighteenth century. Comparable buildings survive in numerous towns and villages of England.

29. Payments by Chamberlains of Maldon, Essex, to paupers and vagrants, 1622.
Maldon Borough Records, Essex County Record Office.
This record of accounts notes the allocation of '3s 4d. paid and allowed unto Robert Camper, one of the constables of the said borough, for sending a poor woman with two children found vagrant within this borough, once to Mundon by cart and twice to Heybridge by foot, another time to Mundon at Mr Bailiff's commandment . . .' In hard times, communities were keen to 'move on' poor people who had wandered from other towns or parishes. In the 1620s hardship was brought to the Maldon area by depressions in the cloth trade, bad harvests and heavy taxation. In 1629 a band of women and children from the region boarded a ship that was being loaded with grain and extracted rye from the crew. Such disorders were the nightmare of local authorities, whose resources for keeping peace and enforcing laws were minimal.

were entitled by the Elizabethan poor laws to raise a local rate to maintain those poor who could not be supported by charity or by their neighbours. The general impression, however, both from contemporary comment and from the gradual rise in poor rates, is that the old-fashioned virtues of charity and hospitality were on the decline – one more sign of a more 'modern' and more materialistic society.

There was certainly little charity shown to those who were called by their contemporaries the 'undeserving' or able-bodied poor (and whom we would call the unemployed), a group whose numbers had expanded rapidly in the late sixteenth and early seventeenth centuries as a result of population growth and economic change. Involuntary unemployment was not a concept that was at all well understood in the seventeenth century and there was a tendency to treat all fit people who were not working as delinquents or idle good-for-nothings or, if they were on the move, as vagabonds or 'sturdy beggars'. Treatment of such people varied, but the law provided for harsh punishment, including whipping and incarceration in a house of correction or a workhouse. Nobody felt that even undesirables such as these should starve, however, and in practice most of the undeserving received the same dole as the deserving. The law also permitted parishes to export the problem by removing vagrants to their parish of birth and much time and effort was spent to these ends.

Despite their failure to understand the general problem of the unemployed, their contemporaries did realize that circumstances could quite suddenly swell the numbers of the poor for reasons beyond the responsibility of any individual. Bad harvests or the collapse of foreign markets were the main causes of such periodic crises. These circumstances could create conditions of terrible dearth and social unrest that were truly frightening for the propertied classes who were only too aware that they were a minority in society. It should be remembered that in the period before the civil war England had no professional armed forces in peacetime and there was no police force. The only permanent force available at the local level was provided by the village constable, whom all able-bodied persons were supposed to assist if asked.

There was, it is true, a militia organized at the county level and officered by the county gentry. The militia was poorly trained and poorly armed and would have posed no threat to any foreign invader, but militiamen were quite capable of checking the riotous ambitions of the poor. Such a force was not, however, always trustworthy since militiamen were drawn from the same social milieu as the rioters and were often sympathetic to their grievances with the result that they were rarely called out unless matters got completely out of control, as in the Midland Rising of 1607. In most cases conciliation rather than force was the preferred policy, particularly in dealing with food riots, which were the most common form of disturbance; there were about forty such outbreaks between 1585 and 1660, the worst occurring in the dearth years of 1630–1. Conciliation took many forms. Attempts were made to compel employers to keep the poor in work and so provide them with an income. Great efforts were made to maximize the supply of food. Exports were banned, alehouses closed to prevent grain being used for brewing and traders in the market-place were forced to sell food at low prices. Town governments kept buffer stocks of grain to sell cheaply to the poor in times of dearth, while wealthy individuals bought grain in the market to sell inexpensively or to give away. Yet there was a price to be paid by the poor for such charity – the price of deference, gratitude and obedience. Such policies were very effective. Few people died of starvation and there were very few riots compared with other countries. There was even less trouble in the later Stuart age when improved agriculture and distribution greatly increased the food supply.

Belief and Learning

In addition to being dependent on their betters for employment in good times and for maintenance or charity in bad, the poor were also subjected to a programme of moral and social reform whose long-term aim was to ensure social control and subordination. Vagrants and mothers of illegitimate children were whipped and placed in houses of correction to dissuade them from behaving in the same way again. A long campaign was conducted to supervise more closely the alehouses, which were seen as alternatives to the church as the focus of village life – an alternative considered to be both disreputable and potentially subversive. Other popular amusements and holidays were discouraged or curtailed on the grounds that they promoted habits of idleness or dissipation.

The most intimate details of life were monitored. Respectable villagers might be encouraged by justices and parsons to peer through their neighbours' windows to discern the evidence of adultery and fornication and to present such matters, as well as cases of swearing, drunkenness, non-attendance at church and other moral or unneighbourly offences, to the relevant secular or ecclesiastical courts. The work of the latter reached a peak in the early decades of the seventeenth century. Much of their jurisdiction concerned cases of moral delinquency and tens of thousands of erring men and women were to find themselves shamed before their neighbours and made to stand in the church or market-place wearing the robe of the penitent with a placard around their necks bearing a description of their offence. Presentment, prosecution and punishment were linked with exhortation and recrimination in this campaign by the 'respectable' people of England to make the poor work hard, behave themselves and give no trouble to their betters.

Such behaviour by laymen was supported from many pulpits. The period from the reign of Elizabeth I to the civil war has been seen as one in which a serious effort was made by the Church to turn a population still influenced by pagan beliefs into one which accepted without question the fundamental tenets of Protestant theology. Church ministers were drawn largely from the younger sons of the gentry, a group who combined a social obligation to reinforce the natural order of society with a spiritual duty to inform their congregations of those finer points of doctrine which they had learned at Oxford or Cambridge. It is doubtful if many could have understood the theology, especially the fundamental doctrine of predestination, but few could have mistaken the exhortations to work, to obey and to serve with which sermons were peppered.

It is difficult to estimate the success of this attempt to make better Christians of the English people. It is certainly true that there was a religious intensity in English life in the first half of the seventeenth century which would be difficult to match in other periods. It is also true that the Church was able to instil into the majority of the English people an ingrained fear and hatred of Catholicism which was to provide a rallying cry for bigotry throughout the Stuart period. However, the Church was never able to achieve a spiritual uniformity. Catholics remained an important minority who were especially well-represented in the upper echelons of society, despite intermittent persecution. And within the Anglican Church itself, religious enthusiasm was often an extremely divisive emotion and thus did not necessarily promote the harmony and order which might have been expected. Some of the most subversive elements in society, who emerged as sectaries in the civil war, drew their inspiration from a new reading of the Bible which overturned the cosy ideas of the social order preached from most Anglican pulpits. Such sectaries were drawn mainly from the middle ranks of society or from the poor in towns or in rural manufacturing areas.

The evidence for deep religious feelings on the part of the great majority of the poor is, however, less clear. Contemporary evidence suggests that many of those who went to church retained no understanding of the

'It is the Travel of Curiosity'

THE CURIOUS TRAVELLER IN STUART ENGLAND

The greatest traveller and travel writer of the seventeenth century was Celia Fiennes. In her preface to the *Journeys*, which relates her extensive English travels from 1682 to 1712, she justified the travel craze by referring to the practical and recreational gains which would result 'if all ladies, and much more gentlemen, would spend some of their time in journeys to visit their native land and be curious to inform themselves and make observations'. Travel within England was essential 'for gentlemen in general service of their country at home and abroad', as well as for curing the 'evil itch of over-valueing foreign parts'. Her visit to Nottinghamshire in 1697 gives the flavour of her curiosity.

Her views as a Dissenter did nothing to put her off the local ale, which 'looked very pale and exceeding clear'. After being ferried over the Trent ('so deep but waggons and horses ford it . . . which is a fine river though not as broad as the Thames at Kingston'), she noted fine riverside rides, the ridge of wooded hills, striking stone buildings en route and Lord Kingston's house at Holme Pierrepoint, 'which looks finely in the woods'. The town of Nottingham 'is the neatest town I have seen'. Its streets were compared favourably with London's, and its broad market place commanded 'two very large streets much like Holborn but the buildings finer, and there is a piazza all along one side of the streets . . .'. In addition there was the castle from which, on a clear day, Wollaton Hall could be seen, and distantly, Belvoir Castle, plus 'a prospect more than 20 miles about showing the diversities of cultivation and produce of the earth. The land is very rich and fruitful . . .' As for

1 The frontispiece to John Ogilby, *Britannia or An Illustration of the Kingdom of England and Dominion of Wales . . . a Geographical and Historical Description of the Principal Roads thereof* (1675).
Celia Fiennes would almost certainly have used this atlas on her journeys. Ogilby, a colourful figure who, besides his interest in dancing, translation and publishing, was also a cartographer, and his survey of the main post roads led to his producing the first practical road atlas.

2 A section of the Nottinghamshire maps from Ogilby's *Atlas*.

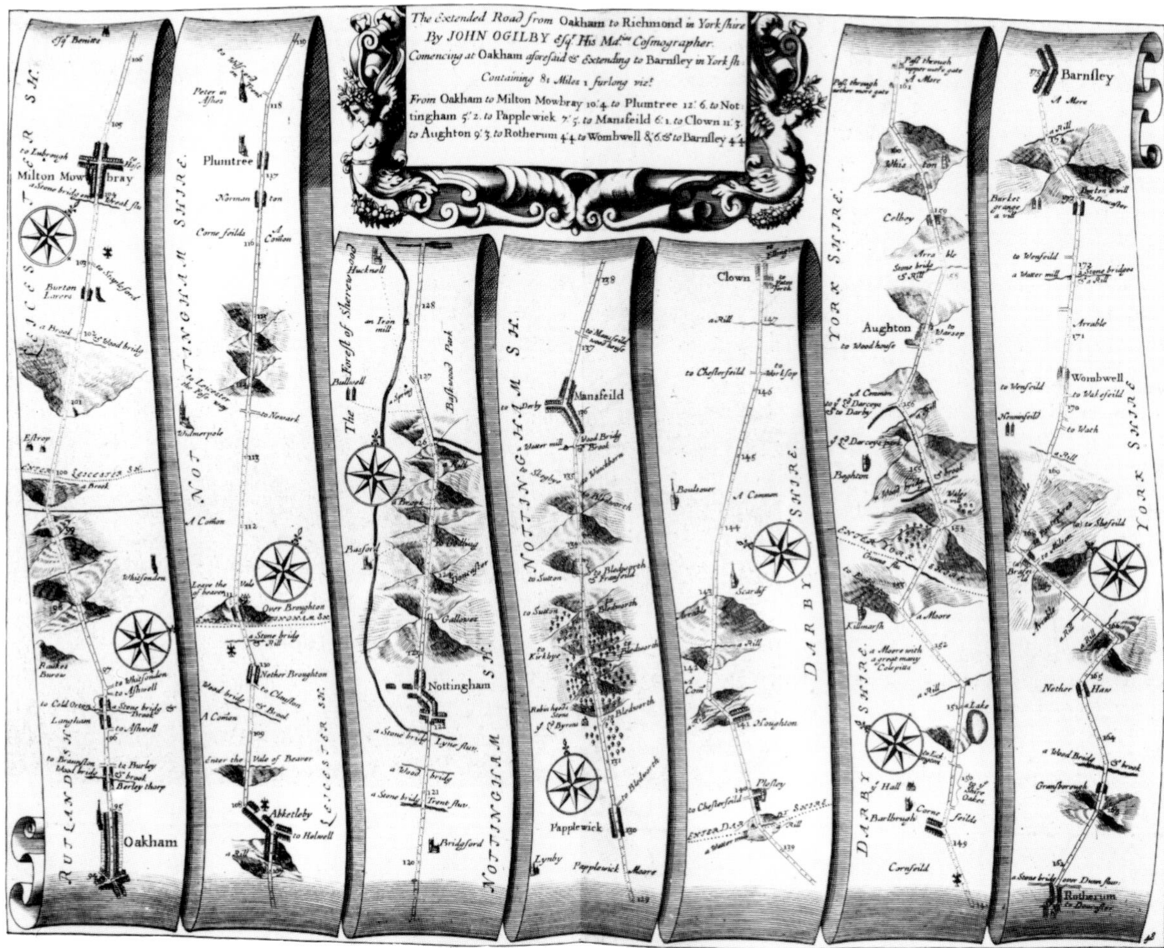

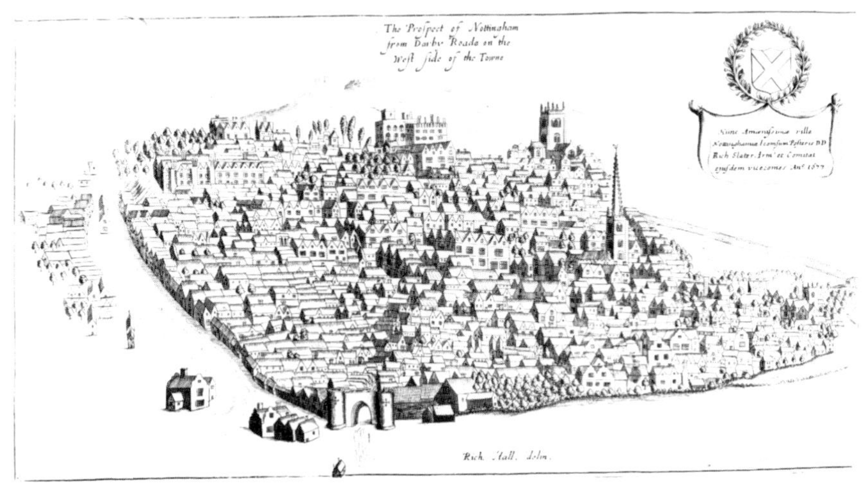

3 View of Nottingham from R. Thoroton, *Antiquities of Nottinghamshire* (1677).

industry, 'they make brick and tile ... There is stocking weaving ... [and] ... there was a man that spun glass'. He made, as well as ornaments, 'buttons which are very strong and will not break'. The visit ended with more ale in the cellar of the Crown Inn and 'we were very well entertained and very reasonably at the Blackmoors Head'.

Celia Fiennes was travelling just to look and learn, showing a new curiosity among the English about their environment. Travel for sheer interest was advocated in the early part of the century: in *The Complete Gentleman* of 1622, Henry Peacham placed travel high on the list of desirable pursuits, preferably to be undertaken on horseback and with a companion, to observe the 'churches, villages and houses of gentlemen and husbandmen, several habits and faces, variety of country labours and exercises'. This was travel for travel's sake and for self-education in topography, natural history and sociology. It was the domestic equivalent of the Grand Tour, but open to a wider income group.

In the 1630s, John Taylor, Thames waterman, bad poet and popular pamphleteer, walked from London to Edinburgh, like Ben Jonson before him. He went, as he recorded in his *Penniless Pilgrimage*, 'not carrying any money, neither begging, borrowing or asking meat, drink and lodging'. Only twice did he have to sleep out, and he never went hungry, for the tradition of hospitality survived. Taylor never accepted money or refused a drink. Crowds frequently gathered, as at Daventry, to look at this indefatigable traveller. His book provided a guide for carriers on business trips, but it also informed curious readers about their native land. So in 1633 did *A Survey of Twenty Six Counties observed in a Seven Week Journey*, supposedly written by three soldiers. The book makes England seem dangerous and unknown, although the Lincoln innkeeper unable to welcome them because he had 'bouz'd it so' sounds familiar.

After the Restoration the fashion for travel spread. In the summer of 1674 the diarist John Evelyn, who had earlier made a Grand Tour abroad, made a 700 mile journey in England. The following year John Ogilby's *Britannia* provided strip maps and other information for tourists. By the end of the century Celia Fiennes was only the most distinguished of a host of 'curious' travellers. In 1724 Daniel Defoe, aiming to persuade a wide audience of the virtues of the middle class and its economic activities, elected to sing their praises in a guide-book, *A Tour Through the Whole Island of Great Britain*.

The hotel and catering trades expanded to meet the needs of travellers, and many inns which survive today came into existence at that time. Even so, travel was not easy. The London to Chester run took six days and a similar 'package tour' between York and Exeter took eight. The one-day Oxford to London run was regarded as reckless. Journeys were always uncomfortable and unhealthy and were suspended from November to spring.

The accounts left by travellers reveal a keen sense of region. A traveller's fare varied according to the local setting, and Cambridge brawn distinguished that county as much as its colleges and fens. Banbury cakes and Cornish pasties can now be bought throughout the land – in the seventeenth century they belonged to their regions. Yet throughout the century, travel and the literature which catered for it were helping to reduce the strength of regionalism as Englishmen came to learn more about England.

4 Jan Siberechts, *Horsemen Crossing a Ford with Wollaton Hall in the Distance*, 1695. Oil on canvas, 43 × $57\frac{1}{2}$ in. (109 × 146 cm.). Collection of Lord Middleton.
'... you have a very fine prospect ... you see Sir Thomas Willoughby's fine house on the other side of the town' (Celia Fiennes).

Christian religion despite the repeated efforts of their ministers. It is clear, too, that despite the penalties, many people did not go to church and that fornication, drinking in the alehouse, idleness or even work provided formidable competition to the correct observation of the Sabbath.

Such indifference was later to be shared by many of the more respectable members of society. After 1660 there are clear signs of a growing disinterest in the more spiritual and enthusiastic aspects of religion as opposed to the social and political, while materialism, hedonism and a growing secular spirit informed the minds of society. The same period saw a considerable relaxation in attempts to reform the poor. The Church courts declined in importance and far fewer moral offences were prosecuted in secular courts, despite an attempt to promote a new campaign of moral reformation in the 1690s. Respectable people continued to castigate the poor, but it was their idleness rather than their immorality which tended to be emphasized.

Any discussion of the impact of Christianity on the English people must also take account of the fact that organized religion was only one of several different currents of belief and one that, with its emphasis on personal sin and punishment, was not particularly attractive for many of the people. Witchcraft, for instance, retained a powerful hold on the minds of the people. At the beginning of the Stuart period most educated persons, led by James I himself, believed in witchcraft and were prepared to enforce the laws which made its practice a capital offence. But from about the 1620s a growing scepticism and incredulity on the part of the educated classes resulted in the acquittal of most suspected witches. At the popular level, however, belief in both black witchcraft and in the more beneficent white witchcraft remained a strong one down to the nineteenth century and this division in belief provides a good example of a mental polarization which paralleled the increasing economic polarization of rural society.

Astrology provides another example of the same process. In the first half of the seventeenth century the astrologer was an influential figure in all levels of English society whose predictive skills could provide assistance in personal relationships or in business decisions and who could be called upon to give advice to those who had lost property or who were ill. However, in the second half of the century educated belief in

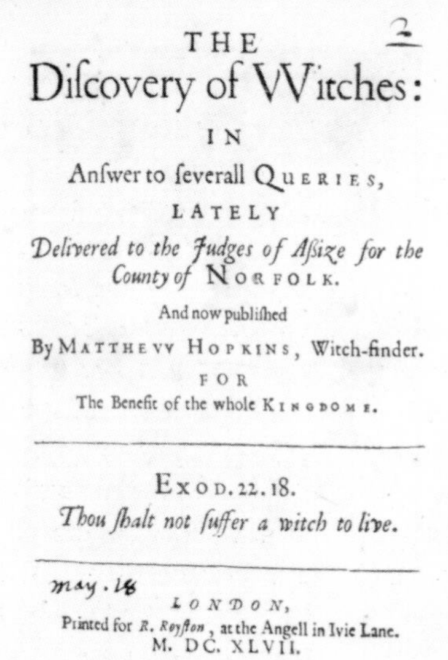
THE
Discovery of Witches:
IN
Answer to severall QUERIES,
LATELY
Delivered to the Judges of Assize for the County of NORFOLK.
And now published
By MATTHEVV HOPKINS, Witch-finder.
FOR
The Benefit of the whole KINGDOME.

EXOD. 22. 18.
Thou shalt not suffer a witch to live.

LONDON,
Printed for R. Royston, at the Angell in Ivie Lane.
M. DC. XLVII.

The bloody Almanack:
To which ENGLAND is directed, to fore-know what shall come to passe, by that famous Astrologer, M. JOHN BOOKER.
Being a perfect Abstract of the Prophecies proved out of Scripture, By the noble NAPIER, Lord of Marchistoun in Scotland.
The guide of Astrologers. The Joy of England.
The Crosse of Rome. The destruction of the World.
Rome London
LONDON,
Printed for Anthony Vincent, and are to be sold in the Old-Baily. 164

30. Matthew Hopkins, *The Discovery of Witches* (1647).
The son of a Suffolk clergyman, Matthew Hopkins began in 1644 a three-year career as a witch-finder, and contributed substantially to the East Anglian witch-craze of that time. With two assistants he rode round the counties and, for a fee, organized the detection and confession of witches. The Huntingdonshire vicar John Gaule remarked sceptically that 'every old woman, with a wrinkled face, a furrowed brow, a hairy lip, a gobber tooth, a squint eye, a squeaking voice, or a scolding tongue, having a rugged coat on her back, a skull-cap on her head, a spindle in her hand, and a dog or cat by her side, is not only suspected but pronounced for a witch.'

31. John Booker, *The Bloody Almanack* (1643).
John Booker, having earned his fame by reportedly predicting the death of the Protestant hero Gustavus Adolphus in 1632, devoted his prophetic powers to anti-royalist propaganda in the civil wars. Almanacs were published in massive numbers, and by the late seventeenth century they were selling at a rate of 400,000 copies a year. The 'noble Napier' is the inventor of logarithms, which were used for the species of astrological and millenarian prediction presented in Booker's pamphlet.

32. Winchester College School.
This school house (which has been attributed to Wren, but with no firm evidence) is a sumptuous example of the extensive building devoted to school education in the seventeenth century.

astrology quite suddenly collapsed and the astrologer became a joke rather than the respected man that he had been. There had, of course, always been some scepticism and many would have agreed with Edmund in *King Lear* (1606): 'This is the excellent foppery of the world, that, when we are sick in fortune, – often the surfeit of our own behaviour – we make guilty of our disasters the sun, the moon, and the stars.' Nevertheless this ability of both witchcraft and astrology to shift blame away from the individual was one of their main attractions; as well, astrology could claim to bring some order and predictability into an uncertain and insecure world. For these reasons astrology, like witchcraft, remained a firm belief in the minds of most people long after such systems had been rejected by their educated betters.

One reason for the growing disparity between popular and educated beliefs was the unequal access to education. The provision of schools grew considerably in the century before the civil war and was to continue to grow more slowly after 1660. An important part in this educational expansion was played by charitable foundations, particularly grammar schools, but the great majority of the 'petty', ABC or dame schools, which taught children the basic skills of literacy and numeracy, were set up on an *ad hoc* basis by parsons, lay teachers or 'dames' who perceived and met a growing local demand for education. Both Church and state placed considerable emphasis on the need for literacy in a godly commonwealth, for Protestantism was the religion of the word. Material motives stimulated literacy as well; commercial development provided an economic incentive and a great expansion of publishing in the vernacular offered scope for people to use their literate skills for enjoyment or instruction.

Several schools were technically free, but even 'free' schools charged for extras and most other schools charged fees, thus effectively restricting their clientele. Fees for elementary education were normally quite small, but even so could be too costly for the poor. There was also the problem of opportunity cost. The children of the poor might be expected to work from the age of six or seven and so provide their family with a small but often vital contribution to their income. This meant that even when the poor did go to school,

And Kings shall be thy nursing Fathers, and their Queens thy nursing Mothers. Isaiah 49.23.

THE
Childes first Tutor:
Or, The
Master & Mistris.
Teaching Children an easie and delightful way to learn the twenty four Letters, to spell, and read true English in a short time.
By FESTUS CORIN.
August 11. 1662.
Imprimatur Dan. Nicols, Reverendissimo in Christo Patri Archiepisc. Cantuar. Sacellan.
London, Printed for F. Coffinet, at the Anchor and Mariner in Tower-street. 1664.

The Childes Tutor.
Italica Letters.
A B C D E F G H I K L M N O
P Q R S T U V W X Y Z.
Small Italica Letters.
a b c d e f g h i k l m n o p q
r s t u v w x y z.
Vowels.
a e i o u y.
Consonants.
b c d f g h k l m n p q r s t v
w x y z.

a before b, is ab.
e before b, is eb.
i before b, is ib.
o before b, is ob.
u before b, is ub.

AB

The Childes Tutor
A B C D E F G H I K L M N O
P Q R S T U V W X Y Z.

Aa ap, ep, ip, op, up — The Ape will eat an Apple.
Bb ba, be, bi, bo, bu. — The Bear will bite.
Cc ca, ce, ci, co, cu. — The Cock will crow.
Dd da, de, di, do, du. — The Dog will kill the Duck.

Ab eb ib ob ub
ac ec ic oc uc
ad ed id od ud
af ef if of uf.

a e i o u are Vowels; all the rest are Consonants.

A4 4b

33. *The Childes First Tutor* (1664).
This manual, a basic guide to literacy, stresses the authority of the teacher, whose authority over his pupils is compared to that of monarchs over subjects. Crown and Church alike encouraged the growth of literacy in seventeenth-century England. Although the pamphlet teaches children 'to spell', the rigorous standardization of spelling came only in the eighteenth century.

which few did, they rarely stayed long enough to gain much benefit and soon forgot the little that they had learned. The situation was probably better in towns, where charitable schooling for the poor had a long tradition behind it and was to be considerably expanded at the very end of the Stuart period, particularly in London. However, the ethos of the charity school was that although the children should be taught, they should not be taught too much lest they get ideas above their station. The main emphasis was on the inculcation of the habits of deference and obedience. A charity-school child, it was said, should make a good servant.

One historian has estimated that the level of male literacy, defined as the ability to sign one's name, rose from 20 per cent in the mid-sixteenth century to 45 per cent in the early eighteenth century. Female literacy, although much lower, also rose from 5 to 25 per cent in the same period. This was certainly an improvement and represents a level unmatched elsewhere in Europe; but the figures make it clear that over half the population remained illiterate. That half, of course, was predominantly among the poor. Since a high proportion of gentlemen were already literate at the beginning of the period, it is clear that the main beneficiaries were those in the middling ranks of society. Such people were also in the forefront in demanding a new type of education as they sought a more practical schooling for

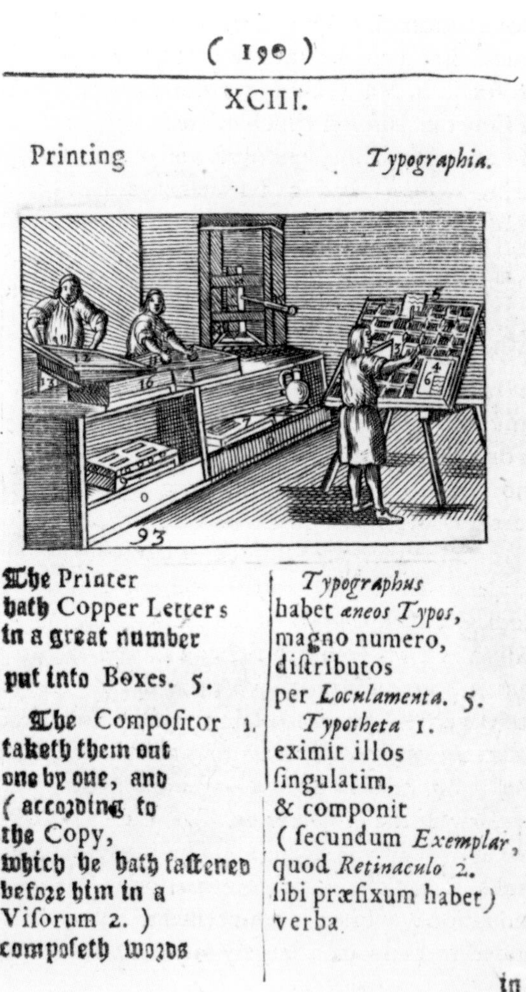

(190)
XCIII.
Printing — Typographia.

The Printer hath Copper Letters in a great number put into Boxes. 5.	Typographus habet æneos Typos, magno numero, distributos per Loculamenta. 5.
The Compositor 1. taketh them out one by one, and (according to the Copy, which he hath fastened before him in a Visorum 2.) composeth words	Typotheta 1. eximit illos singulatim, & componit (secundum Exemplar, quod Retinaculo 2. sibi præfixum habet) verba

in

34. An illustration from J. A. Comenius, *Orbis Sensualium Pictus* (1672 edition).
The volume of printing increased spectacularly in seventeenth-century England, and was the ally both of advancing Protestantism (the religion of the word) and of advancing literacy. Some writers, scorning publication as vulgar, circulated their works only in manuscript; but printers, publishers and booksellers were alive to the demands of a large readership eager for a plain, vigorous prose.

their children in subjects such as English, mathematics, accounting and foreign languages in place of the rigid classical curriculum of the grammar schools. Classical education remained important, however, both in preparing pupils for the two universities and in creating yet another cultural divide in society between those who could and could not read Latin.

The universities themselves underwent considerable expansion in their numbers of undergraduates in the period up to the civil war and also acquired a high reputation for learning and scholarship. Most of this increase came from the sons of the gentry who were attracted as much by the social advantages of contact with their peers as by the classical, humanist and religious education offered to them. Few took their degrees unless they were destined for the Church or the learned professions. Many went on from university to the Inns of Court in London which offered many of the facilities of a social finishing school as well as providing a smattering of legal learning. This generation of gentry, who grew up in the late sixteenth century and during the reigns of the early Stuarts, were therefore much better educated than their forefathers, a fact of some significance when one considers the religious and political debate of the period. However, a reaction set in after the civil war. Fewer sons of the gentry went to the universities or the Inns of Court unless it was necessary in order to prepare themselves for a professional career and the universities began a long period of decline in numbers and in the quality of their scholarship.

It can be seen that English society underwent some fundamental changes during the reigns of the Stuarts. Radical reorganization of the economy was to make the nation as a whole much richer and was to improve the material lot of nearly everyone. Such changes were accompanied by an increasing polarization in the social structure which widened the gulf between the few wealthy or reasonably well-off and the many poor, particularly in the countryside. This division was intensified by a cultural change as the upper and middling ranks of society became increasingly literate, secular and rational, while the poor remained illiterate and continued to cling to a largely superstitious view of the world. Cultural division bred contempt and encouraged the view that the only function of the poor was to work hard for low wages to support the comfort and the leisure of the increasingly respectable members of the middling and upper classes.

35. Statues on the façade of the Greycoat School, Westminster, early eighteenth century.
Whereas Winchester (see Pl. 32) catered for the rich, the Greycoat School was founded for poorer children. These sculptures on the school wall show two of the charity pupils in their Sunday best.

The unequal nature of English society was to generate some remarkable social criticism in the troubled years of the civil war and Interregnum, criticism which anticipated almost every radical idea of modern times. Such radicalism was, however, precocious. In normal times, there was little overt criticism of the social order and remarkably few attempts were made to subvert it by riot or rebellion. The English poor remained quiet and outwardly subservient, caught in a web of deference, patronage and economic dependence which their betters were careful to ensure was not broken.

47
The Queenes
and her
Children
Ambaßado
Trumpetts

CHAPTER TWO

Jacobean Politics 1603–1625

Monarchy and Institutions

Although the names of the main political institutions of England in 1603 are familiar to modern readers, their apparent identity with their modern equivalents can be misleading. Perhaps most obvious is the fact that the king's powers were enormously greater than those of modern constitutional monarchs. As James himself told his parliament in 1610, 'the state of Monarchy is the supremest thing upon earth; for kings are not only God's lieutenants upon earth and sit upon God's throne, but even by God himself they are called Gods'. Some of his contemporaries might have been shocked by James's analogy between kings and God, but most of them would probably have been no less shocked by the witticism of the eminent lawyer and savant, John Selden, who remarked that 'A King is a thing men have made for their own sakes, for quietness' sake'. Even Selden was at pains to stress the very great powers which *Rex Solus*, the king alone, exercised – the powers which constituted the royal prerogative.

The prerogative was the law as it concerned the king, and it concerned him differently from the way in which it concerned his subjects. In the first place his position was legally unique in that he could not be sued and subjects who sought redress for royal actions that had adversely affected their own legal rights had perforce to resort to petitioning rather than suing the king. Secondly, the king had the right (confirmed by a test case of 1627) to commit subjects to prison without having to cite the specific offences with which they were to be charged. Thirdly, control of foreign affairs, including the right to make war and peace, was vested entirely in the king; so was undisputed control of the armed forces of the realm, although in the absence of a standing army these were confined to the royal navy and the local militias. Fourthly, the king was technically the apex of a feudal pyramid. Feudalism as the prevailing form of social, political and military organization had passed away centuries before, but the king retained the feudal rights of wardship, which enabled him to sell the right to exploit the revenues of minors holding of him by feudal tenure; and of purveyance, which entitled him to requisition goods for the royal household below market prices. Fifthly, the king alone had power to summon, dissolve, adjourn and prorogue parliament, at least until 1641.

36. Drawing of the Entry Procession for the Investiture of Henry Prince of Wales in the Court of Requests, 1610. London, College of Arms, MS. WA, f. 47.
At the head of the procession Sir William Segar, Garter, bears the letters patent. Five peers bear the robe, the sword, the ring, the rod and the coronet. Behind them is the prince, escorted by two dukes. After his investiture Henry, the popular heir to the throne, held his court at St. James's, which was set apart for his residence. It attracted many more visitors than the court of his father. Henry's sudden death in 1612 caused widespread lamentation.

Parliaments met relatively infrequently when compared with their modern equivalents. Before the Long Parliament met in 1640 there were often periods of many years during which no parliament met. Even during the lifetime of a protracted parliament, such as James I's first parliament which lasted from 1604 to 1610, it sat intermittently for only a few weeks in each year. Further parliaments were called by James in 1614, 1621 and 1624. Whether parliament met or stayed in being was entirely a matter for the king's decision and in doing without parliaments between 1614 and 1621, and again between 1629 and 1640, the crown was acting entirely within its prerogative rights.

Parliaments normally met at Westminster, although the choice of venue was the crown's. The main reason for calling parliament was usually that the crown needed money. Parliament alone could grant the levies needed to finance extraordinary expenditure. It alone could grant the customs duties of tonnage and poundage, which it normally did for the life of each king at the beginning of his reign, though it neglected to do so for James's successor. But even here the king might resort to prerogative right to raise money. If, for instance, the realm was in imminent danger from foreign invasion, the king could raise emergency levies and thereby avoid the slow process through which parliaments were elected and grants voted and collected. Similarly, while parliament had the sole right to vote the customs duties of tonnage and poundage on exports and imports, the king claimed (and established by an important test case of 1606) the right to levy additional extra-parliamentary duties (impositions) on exports and imports in what he held to be the economic interests of the realm, even though the

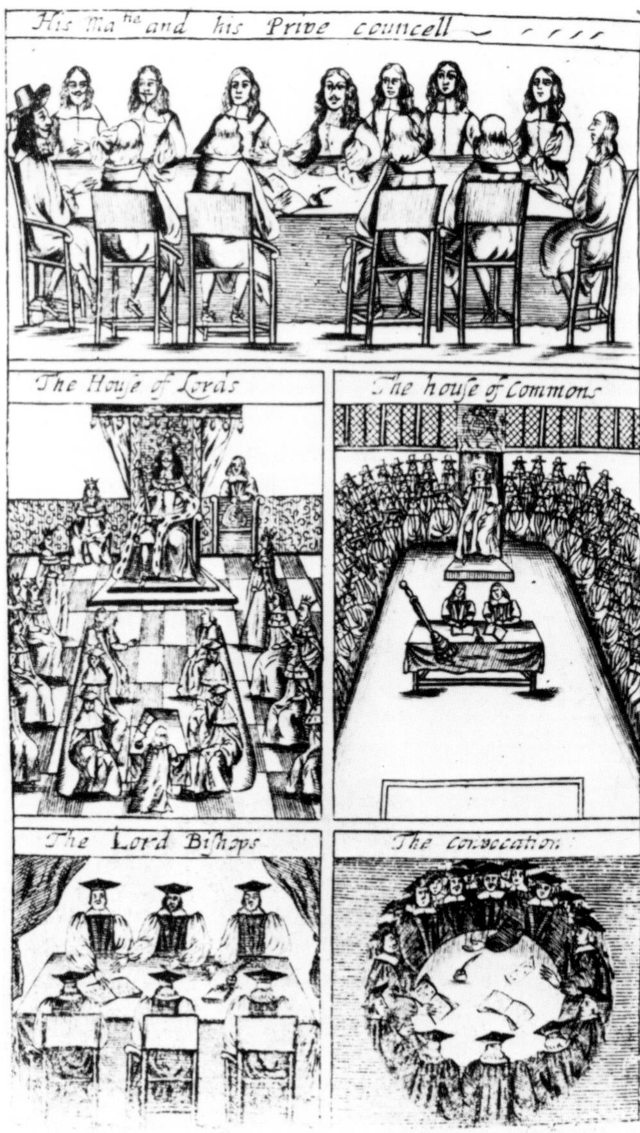

37. The Government of Charles I. Contemporary engraving. *The government of the nation, comprising king, Privy Council, House of Lords, House of Commons, the bishops and Convocation. Bishops were members of the House of Lords, although the dissolution of the monasteries by Henry VIII, by removing the monastic heads, had weakened clerical representation in the upper house. Convocation, the clergy's parliament, was normally summoned and dissolved at the same time as its secular counterpart, which viewed Convocation as a junior partner. Convocation fell into abeyance near the end of the Stuart period, when national political differences bitterly divided the clergy.*

usual purpose of such levies was to raise money for the crown.

Furthermore while only parliament – of which the king himself was an essential part – could perform the supreme legislative function of making statutes, the 'enlarging' power of his prerogative gave the king the right to dispense with the operation of statutes by the issue of licences to individuals to disregard those statutes. Similarly, his 'restraining' power allowed him to place restrictions (for example, by patents of monopoly) on what was otherwise free by common law. Most of such prerogative powers – such as the royal use of proclamations (a form of extra-parliamentary legislation) – were believed to serve the interest of both king and subject provided they were used with discretion. The danger was that the abuse of them might whittle away the power of statutes or parliament's control of taxation. Many of the constitutional disputes between the Stuarts and their parliaments derived from fears that prerogative government might become arbitrary government.

Besides the monarch, parliament consisted, then as now, of a House of Lords and a House of Commons. The latter was divided into county and borough members. There were two seats for each shire, whose MPs were elected on a property franchise which gave the vote to every adult male holding freehold land worth at least forty shillings per year. Inflation was continually reducing the real value of this property qualification and, in addition, there seems to have been an increasing tendency for the term 'freehold' to be loosely interpreted, with a resultant increase in the size of country electorates. Borough seats carried less prestige than county seats and here the size of the electorate varied bewilderingly from one borough to another, sometimes taking in a very high proportion of the adult male population of the borough and sometimes virtually restricting it to the mayor and corporation. Here also, however, was a trend towards a widening of the franchise, often because rival urban oligarchs were keen to expand their electoral following.

Today the government is drawn from the majority party in the House of Commons. In the early Stuart period there were no formal parties. Instead there were factional groupings whose members shifted perplexingly and often. The nearest thing to a modern cabinet was the Privy Council, today a largely honorific body, but then an organ that served to advise the monarch on the formulation of his policy as well as to execute and administer that policy through a stream of conciliar directives to such local authorities as Justices of the Peace and municipal governors. The early Stuart Privy Council was an unwieldy size, about twice as large as that of Elizabeth I under whom it rose never above twenty and, in the last decade of her reign, only to thirteen. By contrast the Jacobean council had risen to 35 by 1623 and under James's successor reached 42 in 1632. However, the attendance of many councillors was sporadic and an inner ring of councillors generally dominated business.

The personnel of the Council was heterogeneous in

terms both of social status and of political and religious outlook, ranging in the former case from the greatest noblemen in the land to commoners, who had played an important role under Elizabeth in steering government business through the House of Commons, but whose utility in this respect was lost on James who elevated all but a handful of them to the peerage. The main force behind the formation of the factional groups which divided the Council was sometimes religious or ideological. But no less, and probably more important was the fear of being overtaken by rivals for the royal favour. The leaders of court factions were, above all else, competitors for royal patronage: for offices, economic concessions such as export licences or monopolies, titles of honour, leases of royal land on favourable terms, and numerous other rewards from a monarch who, though short of cash, was rich in privileges which could be converted into money. In turn, courtiers could dispense this patronage to their own followers or clients and thus act as distributors of the royal bounty to less exalted individuals. The size of a courtier's following directly reflected the state of his influence with the monarch. If the monarch's favour was withdrawn, the patron's following tended to melt away; or at least to become reduced, as that of the Earl of Essex's had been by the end of the 1590s, to a frustrated group of men staking their all on a desperate coup. Such was the abortive revolt by the Earl of Essex in 1601, designed to break the stranglehold of his rivals for power at court; in the words of one of the conspirators, to 'seize the queen, and be our own carvers'.

The Character of King James

James I was 36 when he became King of England. The agreeable descriptions of his appearance in 1602 and 1607 by the English courtier-diplomat Sir Henry Wotton and by Nicolo Molin, the Venetian ambassador at the Court of St James, receive some support from the contemporary annalist and minor dramatist Arthur Wilson, who had no reason to love or flatter James. Wilson describes the king as 'of the middle size, rather tall than low, well set and somewhat plump, of a ruddy complexion, his hair of a light brown in his full perfection, had at last a tincture of white . . . His beard was scattering on his chin, and very thin: and though his clothes were seldom fashioned to the vulgar garb, yet in the whole man he was not uncomely'. Such a portrait is very different from the familiar image of the king by the nineteenth-century historian Macaulay, who based his description on those by biased and hostile contemporary memoir writers such as Francis Osborne and Sir Anthony Weldon. At Weldon's hands even James's apparent merits become defects: if his skin was 'as soft as taffeta sarsnet', this was because 'he never washed his hands, only rubbed his finger-ends slightly with the wet end of a napkin'. Weldon's account of the king's weak legs, clumsy gait, circular walk, large rolling eyes and 'his tongue too large for his mouth' complete a portrait which is as grotesque as it is unattractive. Such accounts of James's ungainly demeanour accord with Macaulay's portrayal of the king as a slobbering pedant whose lack of statesmanship undermined the monarchy that was to fall under his son. Yet James had been an undoubtedly successful King of Scotland before 1603 and historians have begun to ask whether he was an altogether ineffective King of England.

James's reputation, both during his life and after his death, has been largely influenced by comparisons between him and his predecessor. Elizabeth and James are unusual among English monarchs in their intellectual abilities and tastes. Both were able linguists. Elizabeth was probably the abler, as she was in the arts of oratory where her eloquence was the more effective for being sparingly employed. James spoke too often

38. Attrib. Adrian Vanson, *James VI*, 1595.
Oil on panel, $4\frac{5}{8}$ in. (11.9 cm.) diam.
Edinburgh, Scottish National Portrait Gallery.
James aged 29, eight years before his accession to the English throne. Son of Mary Queen of Scots, he became King of Scotland in infancy. In adulthood he imposed order on his native land, which had been bitterly divided by religious and noble feuds. In 1589 he married Anne of Denmark, who would become a patron of poets and artists in England.

39. James I portrayed in an English stained and painted glass panel, 1619. $16\frac{1}{2} \times 9\frac{1}{2}$ in. (50 × 24 cm.). Edinburgh, National Museums of Scotland.
The king is shown with crowned royal arms above, and crown, crossed sceptres and crossed swords on either side. As the French inscription would indicate, this panel was commissioned by the owner of an English private house, almost certainly Wroxton Abbey in Oxfordshire, to commemorate a visit by James I in August 1619.

and his speeches, though learned and sometimes not unimpressive, were frequently prolix and verbose and delivered in a hectoring, schoolmasterly tone unwelcome to his parliamentary audiences. Verbosity extended from his speech to his writings, for James was a prolific writer – the author of devotional treatises, some pleasing if undistinguished verse, political treatises (among them assertions of kingly authority and refutations of papal authority) and tracts on subjects ranging from demonology to the harmful effects of tobacco.

Elizabeth had been financially prudent to the point of tight-fistedness: James was open-handed to the point of financial recklessness. He encouraged a riot of extravagance that all but one of his Lord Treasurers despaired of curbing; the exception was Lionel Cranfield, Earl of Middlesex, whose efforts to impose economies from 1621 to 1624 aroused opposition which landed him in the Tower. As the courtier Dudley Carelton observed as early as 1604, 'we cannot say that the king hath been behind hand in liberality, for . . . he hath given away more plate than Queen Elizabeth did in her whole reign'. There was a similar contrast between them in the number of titles of honour they bestowed. Elizabeth made few knights and scarcely any peers.

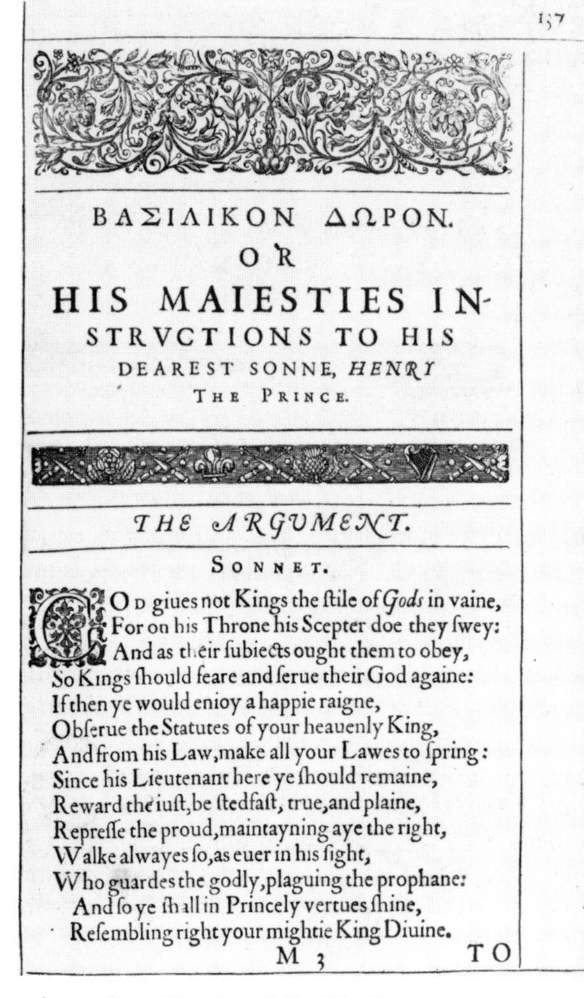

157

ΒΑΣΙΛΙΚΟΝ ΔΩΡΟΝ.
OR
HIS MAIESTIES INSTRVCTIONS TO HIS DEAREST SONNE, *HENRY* THE PRINCE.

THE ARGVMENT.

SONNET.

GOD giues not Kings the ſtile of *Gods* in vaine,
For on his Throne his Scepter doe they ſwey:
And as their ſubiects ought them to obey,
So Kings ſhould feare and ſerue their God againe:
If then ye would enioy a happie raigne,
Obſerue the Statutes of your heauenly King,
And from his Law, make all your Lawes to ſpring:
Since his Lieutenant here ye ſhould remaine,
Reward the iuſt, be ſtedfaſt, true, and plaine,
Repreſſe the proud, maintayning aye the right,
Walke alwayes ſo, as euer in his ſight,
Who guardes the godly, plaguing the prophane:
And ſo ye ſhall in Princely vertues ſhine,
Reſembling right your mightie King Diuine.

M 3 TO

40. A page from King James's *Basilikon Doron*, first published 1599.
This sonnet to his son and heir Prince Henry illustrates James's belief in the divine right of kings – a principle in which he instructed his subjects more often than was wise.

41. Satirical print by John Garrett.
Riotous courtiers weigh down the commonwealth while a plain countryman vainly begs his king to 'chase this rout away'. James's successor was to be less indulgent to debauchery. On acceding to the throne in 1625, Charles I refused to admit the brother of his favourite the Duke of Buckingham to the court, declaring that he would have no drunkards in his chamber.

James almost trebled the number of English knights by creating 906 in the first four years of his reign alone. In 1611 he created the title of baronet, which he sold in large numbers, and from 1615 peerages were also widely sold. Elizabeth's parsimony in the bestowal of honours had offered inadequate recognition of service to the realm and so had fostered dangerous discontent. James, instead of merely restoring the balance, debased the titles and thereby demeaned the monarchy which awarded them. The monarchs differed, too, in their public images and in their attitudes toward outward ceremony. Elizabeth's instinct for the dignity and pomp of monarchy was lost on James; as Arthur Wilson put it, 'those formalities of state were but so many burdens to him'. And whereas Elizabeth had made skilful use of informal and spontaneous contacts with her subjects, James, observed Wilson, 'did not love to be looked on . . . But in his public appearances the excesses of the people made him so impatient that he often dispersed them with frowns, that we may not say with curses'.

Two other of James's defects, much remarked upon by his contemporaries, were his cowardice and his homosexuality. Sir John Oglander of Hampshire called him 'the most cowardly man that ever I knew'. His fear of assassination was not surprising, for he was the intended victim of four plots between 1600 and 1605 alone: the Gowrie Plot in Scotland in 1600 and in England the Bye and Main Plots of 1603 and the Gunpowder Plot of 1605. He was said to pile furniture against the doors of his apartments and to wear quilted doublets and stuffed breeches as protection against murderous weapons. But his contemporary critics were unfair when they attributed to cowardice the pacific foreign policy which distinguished his reign. His decision to make peace with Spain in 1604 was a realistic one. The war had not gone well in Elizabeth's last years and the royal finances had become unable to meet its cost.

James's sexual tastes had a profound influence on the character and vicissitudes of Jacobean high politics. As Osborne all too graphically put it:

'A Great Living Laid Together'

ROBERT CECIL AND HATFIELD HOUSE

Francis Bacon (anticipating Le Corbusier) wrote that 'houses are built to live in, and not to look on'. Few of his great contemporaries practised that principle. The Home Counties sprouted a host of turreted fantasies, 'prodigy houses' like Kirby, Holdenby, Theobalds and Audley End. They were political 'power houses' as well. Robert Cecil's Hatfield was one of the greatest of these architectural symbols. He lavished nearly £40,000 on it before his death in 1612.

Cecil, Earl of Salisbury, tactfully exchanged his nearby family house of Theobalds with James I (who had stayed there) for Hatfield and lands in 12 counties.

1 Hatfield House, south front.
A nineteenth-century fire altered the aspect of the wings, but the centre preserves its original Italianate grandeur as the main entrance. Inigo Jones may have had a hand in this.

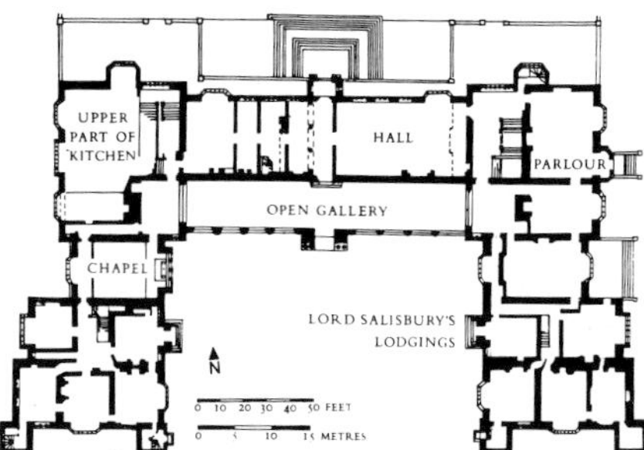

2 Plan of south front (former entrance front), 1611.
The rather sprawling and hotchpotch nature of the house on the wings is brought out on this plan.

3 Mosaic portrait of Robert Cecil, based on a portrait by Critz. Now in the Library, Hatfield House.
The heir of his father's political power, and like his father a builder, Cecil put up Salisbury House, 'Britain's Bourse' (a commercial centre), and Hatfield.

The earl still had houses in London, at Enfield, Quickswood and Cranborne. Francis Bacon quoted Pompey's remark to Lucullus about his fine summer villa: 'surely an excellent place for summer, but how do you do in winter?' Lucullus answered: 'Why, do you not think me as wise as some fowls are, that ever change their abode towards the winter!' A magnate demanded many functions of a house. It was the administrative centre of an estate or of a whole lordship. It was a focus for the training and education of distinguished youth, a pleasure-dome for indoor and outdoor pursuits, and a centre for local employment and social services. Its many functions have been summarized by Mark Girouard: 'It was an image-maker, which projected an aura of glamour, mystery or success around its owner. It was visible evidence of his wealth. It showed his credentials . . .' A single house could embrace all these roles for a country gentleman, but for a peer one would hardly suffice. At Cranborne, Cecil's villa of Lucullus, there was a rural life. At Salisbury House in Charing Cross there was his base for London political life – his main occupation – and the setting for his fine picture collection. Theobalds had been his 'progress palace' for entertaining his sovereign on those summer progresses and receptions through which the crown projected its image in cultural propaganda. Elizabeth I had stayed at Theobalds 13 times – and then her successor had claimed it as his own.

Cecil was a very rich man, but the Theobalds-Hatfield exchange was an expensive one. Like most office-holders he derived only a portion of his income from his official salary: perquisites helped to make up the rest. As Lord Treasurer, Master of the Wards, Secretary of State and beneficiary from the silk customs, Cecil was worth about £25,000 a year, about one-eighth of the income of the state. He set a hot and expensive political pace. His household alone cost £8,500 a year to run and his building schemes in the last five years of his life cost £63,000. It is a measure of the political value he set on these buildings that he owed £53,000 by 1611.

A new 'prodigy house' was needed to entertain his sovereign. It would be built from scratch to fulfil its purpose as a progress palace to house a visiting king and queen. Only one wing of the old building was preserved on one side, and £40,000 was borrowed at ten per cent to build and furnish a new one. Cecil supervised the building closely. Hatfield was a gigantic pavilion; yet it was not as large as Theobalds or Holdenby, and it abandoned the idea of courtyards and the inward-looking feeling which they generated. Instead it presented a compact T-shaped structure in which turreted wings balanced each other and were set off by gatehouses, turreted lodges, pavilions and statuary, all long since lost. The carefully prepared landscape was as important as the House itself, drawing the arriving visitor towards the stone-faced classical south front. Cecil apparently commissioned drawings for the north and south fronts to present two contrasting culminations of approach through lesser gateways and pavilions. The south wing was showy and the north austere.

The result resembled a hunting lodge built on a very large scale, a massive garden

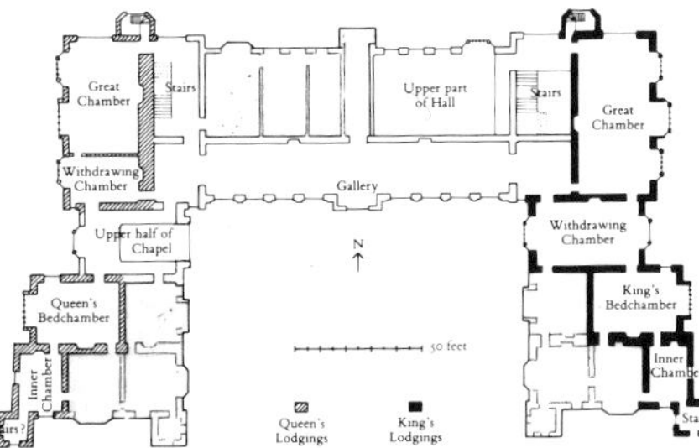

4 Plan of the King's and Queen's side, first floor.
Two households had to be accommodated, with formal separation in the wings, and a processional gallery joining them.

5 Hatfield House, north front.
This austere frontage looked on to the main garden.

pavilion. The house, though, has a hotchpotch quality about it, possibly reflecting the combined efforts of too many designers: Robert Lyminge the main designer and carpenter, Simon Basil the Surveyor of the King's Works, Thomas Wilson the earl's man of affairs and cost-watcher, and possibly, as the designer of the south porch, the young Inigo Jones. Yet the variety which makes the wings, especially, seem unplanned would have been admired by contemporaries. Contrast, diversity and fantasy were architectural virtues.

Indoors, Cecil's taste and patronage were seen in the ornate fireplaces of Maximilian Colt and the woodwork of John Buck, which still survive to dazzle the visitor as they were meant to impress royalty. The house was designed to express a political point. The royal party were given the whole first floor, with the king and his entourage in the east wing, and the queen in the west wing, their rooms connected by a grand gallery. A whole set of special furnishings had to be moved in for royal visits, but the chimney-piece in the king's bedchamber had a statue of James himself. A mosaic picture of Cecil decorates the queen's bedchamber, showing that Salisbury probably intended to live in it himself at other times. During royal visits the Cecils occupied the ground floor, while the second storey housed children and important servants. The house was a £40,000 stage set for the enactment of a drama of political etiquette. But Cecil died before his sovereign could visit the new residence, and his seventeenth-century descendants were not to match his political ability and influence. The house still stands in illustration of the place of conspicuous expenditure in Jacobean politics and of a great political career.

6 The Marble Hall by Robert Lyminge, 1607–11.
The hall and screen were rather old-fashioned, but the woodcarving is some of the finest surviving from the period.

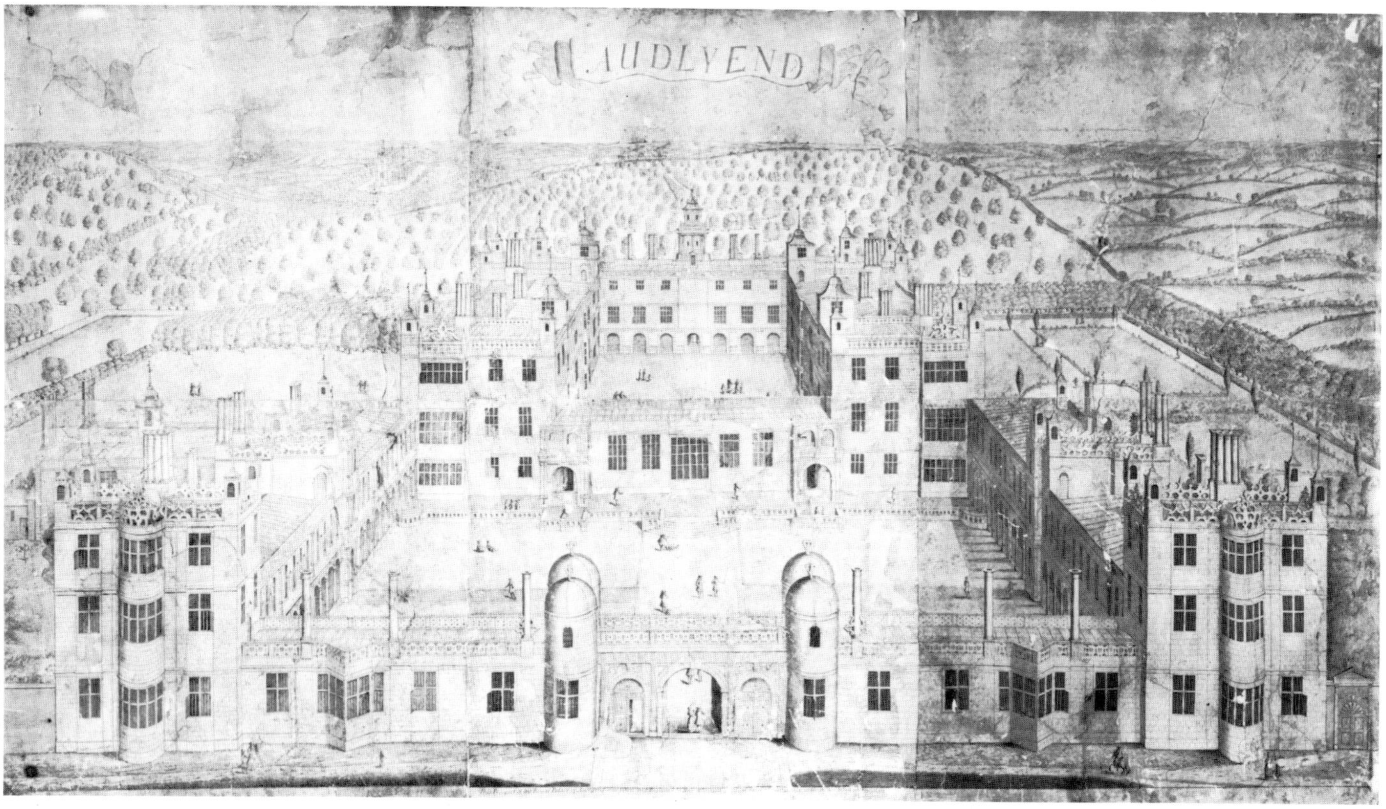

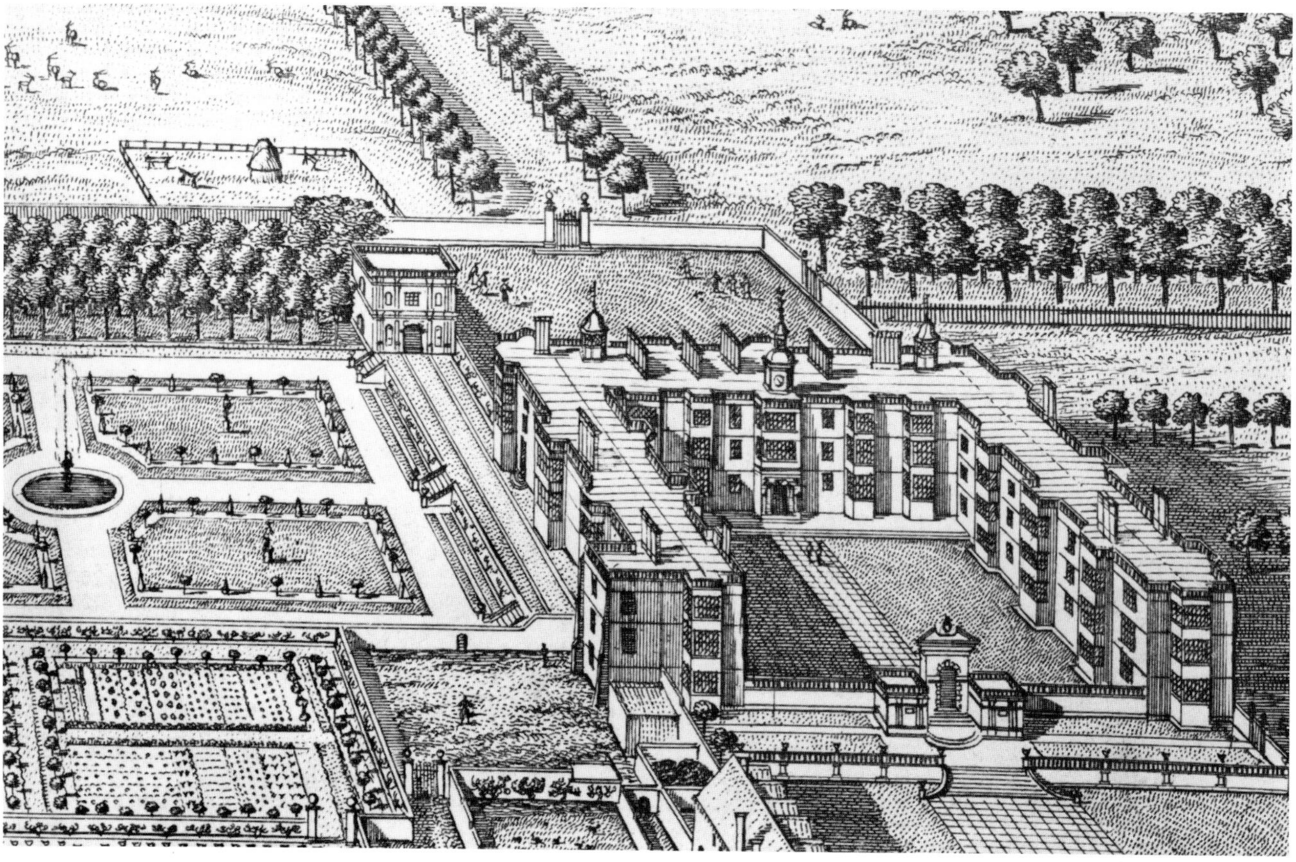

> his favourites or minions . . . like burning-glasses were daily interposed between him and the subject, multiplying the heat of oppressions in the general opinion . . . The love the king showed was as amorously conveyed as if he had mistaken their sex . . . Nor was . . . it carried on with . . . discretion . . . for the king's kissing them after so lascivious a model . . . upon the theatre as it were of the world prompted many to imagine some things done in the tyring-house that exceed my expressions no less than they do my experience.

Scandal – both homosexual and heterosexual – compounded the court's reputation as a centre of moral depravity, of ostentatious luxury and wild extravagance, of artificial sophistication and of grovelling sycophancy. Contemporaries fancifully compared those failings with the virtues of 'the Country', that part of the nation which the court had not corrupted, and which was portrayed as the centre of purity, simplicity, plain speaking and plain dealing. The contrast was a gross simplification, but its impact on the contemporary imagination was a forceful one. Even courtiers were dismayed by courtly practice. In 1611 Lord Thomas Howard wrote to Sir John Harington a letter, jocular in tone but serious in substance, lamenting the decline of those learned and virtuous accomplishments which a century earlier had been extolled by the Italian Castiglione in a treatise, *The Book of the Courtier*, a work that had become a classic in Tudor England. If Harington sought courtly advancement, warned Howard, he must learn to practise uninhibited dissimulation, to shower with praises the king's latest horse or favourite, and if need be to agree that 'the moon shineth all the summer'. Harington, Howard observed, had 'lived to see the trim of old times and what passed in the Queen's days'. Indeed he had; and in 1606 he noticed the contrast between the decorum of Elizabeth's court and the drunken riot that distinguished an entertainment for James and Christian IV of Denmark, the brother of Anne of Denmark whom James had married in 1589.

The court was the centre of economic racketeering. The favourably-placed courtiers who waxed fat on monopolies, customs farms, export licences and other perquisites often sublet them to syndicates of businessmen, a practice resented by other businessmen excluded from the profits and, at least in the case of monopolies, by consumers who bore the burden in the form of increased prices. Monopolies were violently attacked in parliament as well as by some of the foremost imaginative writers of the period, among them Ben Jonson, whose play *The Devil is an Ass* satirized the shady borderline between the court and the city of London.

42. Audley End, engraving by Henry Winstanley, 1676.
Like Hatfield (see Picture Essay, p. 54), Audley End was a prodigy house. It was built by the Howards on the Cambridgeshire–Essex border. James I slyly remarked that it might be appropriate for a Lord Treasurer but was too grand for a king. Only a portion of the house survives today.

43. Temple Newsam House, Leeds. Contemporary engraving.
Sir Arthur Ingram, a linen draper who rose to wealth and office under James I, built this Yorkshire house with his gains. Charles I stayed there in 1642 during the approach to civil war. Ingram's career illustrates the often unsavoury interaction of politics and high finance under James. But like other profiteers, Ingram was a philanthropist as well; he built a hospital at Bootham, York.

44. Satirical engraving of a patentee, 1624.
Monopolies were abolished by statute in 1624, the year of this cartoon, but the crown evaded the legislation by granting exemptions to it. One of the more grotesque episodes arising from the grant of monopolies occurred under Charles I, when complaints against the monopoly of a company of soap-boilers were brought before a tribunal headed by the Lord Mayor of London. Two washerwomen, one using the company's soap, the other an independent brand, scrubbed furiously in competition. The tribunal loyally ruled in favour of the monopoly, which was bringing £20,000 a year into the Treasury.

45. 'The Garden of Plenty', from Stephen Harrison, *Arches of Triumph* (1604).
One of at least seven arches designed by Harrison and erected for James's entry into London in 1604, the largest being 90 feet high and 50 feet wide. On this occasion of elaborate pageantry and complex allegory, the king was presented as a personification of divine providence and as a ruler whose peaceful and prosperous reign would resemble the Augustan era of classical Rome. The playwrights Ben Jonson and Thomas Dekker helped to devise the pageantry. Harrison's book preserves the ephemeral architecture of the event.

The Course of Jacobean Politics

A primary aim of Jacobean statecraft was to keep rival factions within the government under control and to avoid the domination of one group of courtiers and the consequent alienation of others. According to Secretary of State Sir Robert Naunton, James failed to maintain the Elizabethan balance between contending factions on the Council. But the balance had already broken down in Elizabeth's last years, when the bitter strife between Essex and Sir Robert Cecil had obliged the queen to choose between them. Cecil had enjoyed a scarcely-questioned ascendancy during the last two years of Elizabeth's reign, as he continued to do for the first four or five years of James's.

Created Earl of Salisbury in 1605, Cecil was the carefully trained and supremely able son of Elizabeth's great minister Lord Burghley, who had died in 1598. At the outset of James's reign Cecil was in alliance with members of that once-powerful interest the Howard family and especially with Lord Henry Howard, who became Earl of Northampton in 1604 and who revived the family's political fortunes. Howard was the son of the poet Earl of Surrey, whom Henry VIII had executed for treason in 1547, and the brother of the Duke of Norfolk, who had suffered the same fate under Elizabeth in 1572. Ambitious and malevolent, a man of great natural ability and an administrative reformer of unusual determination and capacity, Howard had spent long Elizabethan years in the political wilderness. But his sycophancy, which Elizabeth had distrusted, was more to James's taste, and before James's accession Howard and Cecil had contrived to poison his mind against their enemies, Sir Walter Ralegh and Lord Cobham. Consequently Ralegh and Cobham were removed from office on James's accession and, convicted of plotting against him, were placed in the Tower under suspended sentence of death. Ralegh was the victim of factional conflict again in 1618 when the sentence was put into effect.

In the early years of the reign the Howards and Cecil worked hand-in-hand, with Cecil emphatically the senior partner. In 1608, by then Earl of Salisbury, he was made Lord Treasurer. But his co-operation with Northampton suffered increasing strain and in 1610 Salisbury's hold on royal favour was gravely weakened by the failure of his 'Great Contract', an imaginative scheme to substitute a permanent property tax for purveyance, wardship and other antiquated feudal dues. The proposal would have involved major concessions by crown and parliament alike and the two sides could not agree terms. After Salisbury's death in 1612 James vested the Lord Treasurer's power in a commission containing a rough balance of councillors from different factions. Of these the two most powerful were the strongly anti-Catholic and anti-Howard group led by the Earl of Pembroke, Lord Chancellor Ellesmere and the new Archbishop of Canterbury, George Abbot, and the group dominated by the Howards themselves and led by Northampton and his nephew the Earl of Suffolk. Soon the Howards gained the upper hand and Northampton became the most important member of the government.

Yet as Northampton knew, the key to supremacy lay not in the Treasury but in the king's personal affections. Since 1607 these had been enjoyed by the handsome Scotsman Robert Carr. Carr had first come to England in 1603 as a page in James's Scottish train, but unlike

46. *The Death of the Gunpowder Conspirators,* engraving by N. de Visscher, 1606.
The Gunpowder Plot was a sensational piece of treason and further strengthened the anti-Catholic sentiment which had been nourished by Church and state under Elizabeth. The plot to blow up parliament at the opening of a new session in November 1605 was organized by Catholics apparently fearful of open persecution. When parliament reassembled in 1606 it passed fierce legislation against Catholics. Yet the laws do not seem to have been severely enforced. Most English Catholics were loyal to the crown and hoped that their loyalty would earn them toleration. This engraving captures the excitement aroused by the executions but is not to be trusted in its details.

many of his countrymen he had failed to find permanent employment at court. His luck changed four years later when he fell from his horse in the royal tilt-yard and broke a leg. The interest excited in James by this episode quickly became a passion. Carr was knighted, given lands and offices and became a centre of influence and patronage at court. In 1612 he was made Viscount Rochester. By that time it had become a principal objective of factional struggle to control the new favourite as well as his friend and adviser, Sir Thomas Overbury. Unhappily for the Howards, Overbury was as hostile to them as was the Pembroke faction. The Howards therefore set out to wrest Carr from Overbury's hold.

Their methods were at once ruthless and ingenious. For some time the versatile Rochester had been intimate with Suffolk's daughter Frances, and the Howards aimed to convert this liaison into a marriage. Frances, alas, was already married to the Earl of Essex, the son of Elizabeth's thwarted favourite. Divorce was an exceptional event in seventeenth-century England, attainable only through elaborate ecclesiastical proceedings. Even so, the Howards resolved upon it. Knowing that if they succeeded then his own influence over Rochester would be ended, Overbury urged Carr against the move. It therefore became necessary for the Howards to remove Overbury from the scene. First, in 1613, they arranged an offer of a diplomatic post abroad; when Overbury declined, his refusal was made a pretext for his imprisonment in the Tower, where he was subsequently poisoned, it transpired later, through the agency of Frances. But long before the disclosure that Overbury's death had been due to foul play the commission appointed to examine the flimsy case for the annulment – its deliberations protracted only by the moral scruples and political calculations of Pembroke's

'Every Virtue of a King, and of All in Him, We Sing'

PRINCE HENRY'S CHRISTMAS MASQUE, JANUARY 1611, *OBERON, THE FAIRY PRINCE*

We are in the old Banqueting House at Whitehall. The court is assembled and James I, Queen Anne and the Spanish and Venetian ambassadors have taken their seats. They are about to watch a masque by Ben Jonson, designed by Inigo Jones and with music and choreography by Alfonso Ferabosco and Robert Johnson. It is an entertainment devised for Henry, Prince of Wales and for his household, which consists of the most respected young aristocrats in England and which is a major centre of literary patronage. The prince is the object of general praise well beyond the conventional. Aged 16, he seems to contain precociously in his person all that his father is not. The king is slovenly, filthy-minded, undignified and flippant. The heir is handsome, accomplished in the arts, dignified, martial, earnestly Protestant and conscious of his regal mission ahead. Henry embodies a sharp contrast with the king. He is standing literally in the wings to act out an allusive masque which he has commissioned and in which he is about to star. The entertainment begins by revealing a set of rustic rockery by Inigo Jones.

2 The rocks from *Oberon*, Scene I. Pen and ink drawing by Inigo Jones. Chatsworth, Devonshire Collection.

1 A. Van Dyck, *Inigo Jones*, 1640. Lead drawing, $9\frac{1}{2} \times 7\frac{1}{2}$ in. (24.2 × 19.3 cm.). Chatsworth, Devonshire Collection.

The performance of *Oberon* has, unusually, 'a very large curtain painted with the Kingdoms of England, Scotland and Ireland'. Oberon represents King Arthur (whose legendary kingship of Great Britain was a common unifying idea in the masques of the period). Silenus, the 'Governor' of a chorus of satyrs, leads on his troupe, who are played by Shakespeare's Company, the King's Men. They convey a touch of the bibulous and the lecherous: 'Hath his tankard touched your brain?' and 'Are there any nymphs to woo?' The satyrs are the Anti-Masquers, the forces of disorder, whose presence in the masque counters the representation of courtly harmony and sometimes injects a note of criticism alongside the idealization of English rulers. 'They danced a ballet . . . with a thousand strange gestures, affording great pleasure'. Silenus announces the presence of Oberon and his 'fays' in a palace behind the rocks: 'Satyrs he doth fill with grace, every season, every place.' Jones's set, a mass of lights and transparent walls, is transformed. The rocks open. The satyrs taunt and threaten the sylvans who guard the door to Oberon's palace, but are asleep. More ribaldry follows and violence is threatened against the Fairy Prince's attendants.

The outside of Jones's palace is a superb classical construction which reflects the prince's taste. The set, the costumes and the music are a mixture of classical and medieval styles which bring together two fertile rivers of imagery: the world of Imperial Rome, of the Augustan age (which some poets compared with the rule of the new dynasty), and that of Edmund Spenser's Elizabethan epic poem, *The Faery Queen*. Oberon is given a genealogy linking him with the Welsh Henrys of the Tudor dynasty and with the Arthur who once ruled a united, peaceful Britain.

A cock-crow follows further singing and dancing and 'the whole palace opened, and the nation of fays discovered, and within, afar off in perspective, the knights masquers . . . at the further end of all, Oberon, in a chariot, which to a loud triumphant music begins to move forward, drawn by two white bears . . .' Prince Henry, two earls, three barons, five knights and two esquires enter and sing:

Melt earth to sea, sea flow to air
And air fly into fire,
Whilst we, in tunes, to Arthur's chair
[James on his throne in the Hall],
Bear Oberon's desire.

The forces of harmony have arrived and the satyrs' dancing is 'rude too late'. The Masquers, by their very presence, will subdue the grosser natures of the Anti-Masquers and harmony will be reasserted in the universe:

This is a night of greatness and of state,
Not to be mixed with light and skipping sport.
A night of homage to the British Court,
And ceremonies due to Arthur's chair
From our bright master, Oberon, the fair.

Two fays now sing Oberon's praise, stressing his majesty, wisdom, piety and knowledge, for 'every virtue of a king, and of all in him, we sing'. 'The Prince then took the Queen to dance', and 'then followed the measures, corantos, galliards, etc. till Phosphorus the day-star appeared, and called them away'. A final song ends the masque and 'the whole machine closed'.

Ben Jonson had for some years written masques for the households of the king, of the queen and of Prince Henry. A masque was a spectacle, an ordered series of dances with elaborate and colourful costumes. It was placed in a sumptuous court setting with architectural scenery and music. Such entertainments were regal and aristocratic. Usually they involved royal dancers and their aim was to illustrate unity, harmony and order, public virtues secured by monarchy and sanctioned by God. Dancing, itself an ordered ritual, was the centrepiece. The words, usually expressing a fable, pointed up the action and the colour. In this exotic entertainment, courtiers could not fail to appreciate the relationship between the king and God, which was developed in speeches in songs and in dances. For the well-read and initiated among the audience there were more subtle and complex messages. Jonson represented the alliance, common in his time, between the drama and the intellect, and his masques contained layers of allegorical allusions to myth and history.

When masques were commissioned by the king's household, the themes were much the same as those presented to Prince Henry, but the occasion was very different. James was liable to be drunk and the event might have an air of degeneracy and orgy that ill-suited the aesthetic and semi-religious pretensions of the masque. Prince Henry's entertainments reflected the correctness of his household and of his preoccupations. They spoke the truth. He really was a young prince devoted to learning, music and the arts. He led a virtuous life. His private tastes matched his public and political interests, just as his wholesomeness of living was reflected in his devotion to responsible Protestant kingship. His death on 6 November 1612 was therefore genuinely mourned. The poet Thomas Campion expressed that grief when he wrote,

And like a well tun'd chime his carriage was
Full of celestial witchcraft, winning all
To admiration and love personal.

4 *Two Satyrs*, pen and brown ink sketch by Inigo Jones. Chatsworth, Devonshire Collection.
These Anti-Masquers were played by the King's Men, Shakespeare's Company, and were probably the actors who took the roles in the masquing scene in *The Winter's Tale*, Act IV, Scene IV.

3 Oberon's Palace from Jones's designs. Pen and brown ink drawing. Chatsworth, Devonshire Collection.
The design (there are others surviving for the same scheme) combines a romantic medievalism with some classical motifs.

5 (right) Finished pen and brown ink sketch by Inigo Jones of Prince Henry as Oberon. Chatsworth, Devonshire Collection.
The Roman Imperial theme seems to be suggested openly here.

47. Hendrik Cornelisz Vroom, *The Arrival of the Elector Frederick of the Palatinate at Flushing, May 1613*. Oil on canvas, 43 × 80 in. (109 × 203 cm.). Haarlem, Frans Hals Museum.
The Prince Elector returns to the Continent with his bride, James's daughter Elizabeth. This was a powerfully symbolic moment in the history both of English and of continental Protestantism. England's more zealous Protestants, whose leaders were well represented in the party which escorted the couple of Flushing, hoped that the alliance would steer England into vigorous support of their co-religionists in Europe. James had other ideas.

ally Archbishop Abbot – granted the divorce and in December 1613 Rochester, now elevated to the Earldom of Somerset, was married to Frances Howard in great splendour.

Triumphant as the Howards' strategy had been, a cloud remained on their horizon: the need for a new parliament to grant the money necessary to arrest the alarming deterioration of the royal finances. Northampton had resolutely opposed the summoning of a parliament that he expected to favour his enemies, and it may be that when the assembly met he gave encouragement to the members whose virulent criticism of royal policy eventually provoked a dissolution. It certainly suited his purpose when one parliamentary attack followed another: on alleged electoral malpractice by the government; on the Scots (significantly by the MP John Hoskyns, a client of Northampton); on Bishop Neile of Lichfield, who had traduced members of the Commons for seditious utterances; and on royal favourites, 'spaniels to the king and wolves to the people'. The Addled Parliament, as it was called, lasted a mere nine weeks.

Its dissolution marked the zenith of the Howard hegemony, but Northampton died within a week of his triumph. Had he lived he would probably have been made Lord Treasurer. Instead the office went to his incompetent nephew Suffolk, who was to preside over the most disastrous episode in early Stuart financial history. Courtly expenditure and the royal debt bounded upwards under a regime whose tone was set by the morally-blind Suffolk, by his corrupt wife, by her creature Sir John Bingley, the Auditor of the Exchequer, and by business sharks such as Sir Arthur Ingram and Sir William Cockayne. Somehow this incompetent regime survived for three years. What destroyed it was not its ineptitude but a shift in the royal affections. By the end of 1615 Somerset, of whom the Howards had so skilfully made an ally, yielded in

James's favour to the youthful George Villiers. Villiers was a protégé of the anti-Howard faction, one of whose members, Archbishop Abbot, has left a vivid account of the stratagems which secured Villiers a place in the royal bedchamber. Successively the new favourite became a viscount, an earl, a marquis and in 1623, Duke of Buckingham. Somerset, whose petulant response to his rival's rise did not help his cause, was doomed to permanent disgrace when in 1615 his enemies succeeded in bringing to light the murder of Sir Thomas Overbury two years earlier. The Somersets were brought to a sensational trial and convicted of murder. Unlike their less exalted accomplices, they were spared execution. They were subsequently pardoned, but they never returned to court. The Howards' enemies followed these moves with criticisms of the financial corruption of the Howard regime and secured Suffolk's conviction and dismissal in 1618.

Suffolk's enemies had been eager for his power, but they were also concerned with the urgent need for financial reform. Between the fall of Lord Treasurer Suffolk in 1618 and that of Lord Treasurer Middlesex in 1624, reform was earnestly attempted. The departmental reorganization and the economies achieved by the Treasury Commission of 1618–20, and by Middlesex himself after 1621, produced for the first time in the reign a surplus of ordinary annual revenue over expenditure. Yet the vested interests of courtiers averted fundamental change. An overall deficit remained and the royal debt continued to rise.

The crown's financial position was worsened by England's growing involvement in the diplomacy of Europe, following the outbreak of the the Thirty Years War in 1618. The principal aim of James's foreign policy had been the creation for England of a pivotal place in an international system of balancing alliances. In 1613 he had secured the marriage of his daughter Elizabeth to the Protestant Elector of the Rhineland Palatinate; he hoped to balance that alliance by marrying his heir to the daughter of the King of Spain. Thus might James become the peacemaker of Christendom. His hopes were rudely shattered when in 1619 the Elector Palatine accepted the offer of the elective crown of Bohemia. The king of Bohemia was one of the seven electors to the Holy Roman Empire and Protestants throughout Europe welcomed Frederick's appointment as a significant shift of power in their favour. But the following year the indignant Habsburg Emperor drove Frederick not only from Bohemia, but from his hereditary dominion, the Palatinate. James I, who had thought his son-in-law's acceptance of the Bohemian crown needlessly provocative, could not silently acquiesce in his expulsion from his own territory. The English crown became involved in a series of alliances and initiatives designed to secure the Elector's restitution, all fruitless and expensive. It was increasingly clear that only a far more expensive measure, a resort to arms, could offer hope of Frederick's restoration.

These were the circumstances in 1621 in which James summoned the first parliament for seven years. It was gratifyingly zealous for the Elector and the Protestant cause, but its offer of two subsidies – a mere £160,000 – was hopelessly inadequate. MPs launched into criticisms of monopolies and of ministers, one of whom, Lord Chancellor Francis Bacon, Viscount St Albans, was impeached and dismissed. When parliament also debated matters of religion and foreign policy, which James believed to lie solely within his prerogative, he dissolved it. It had lasted from January to December.

1

Of Truth.

I.

WHAT *is Truth;* ſaid jeſting *Pilate;* And would not ſtay for an Anſwer. Certainly there be, that delight in Giddineſſe; And count it a Bondage, to fix a Beleefe; Affecting Free-will in Thinking, as well as in Acting. And though the Sects of Philoſophers of that Kinde be gone, yet there remaine certaine diſcourſing Wits, which are of the ſame veines, though there be not ſo much Bloud in them, as was in thoſe of the Ancients. But it is not

B onely

48. A page from Francis Bacon, *Essays* (1625 edition).
Made Lord Chancellor and Viscount St. Albans by James I, Bacon became a victim of factional rivalry at court and was impeached in 1621 on a charge of bribery – a harsh interpretation of the actions of a man who sought persistently to raise the standards of government. He produced a series of works, among them The Advancement of Learning, *that were designed to improve education and to set philosophical and scientific inquiry on a firmer footing. His other writings included a celebrated history of the reign of Henry VII. The intellectual influence of his works was enormous and persisted down the century.*

How could James, so short of money, now produce a credible foreign policy? The only alternative to a war seemed to be an alliance with the Emperor's natural ally, Spain, whose good offices would place the Elector back on his throne. It was a policy with grave risks, for in England the anti-Spanish sentiment of Elizabeth's reign still ran deep and Spain's terms were likely to be impossibly high: the conversion of Prince Charles to Catholicism and complete toleration for Catholics in England. In 1623, when Prince Charles and Buckingham left incognito for Spain in a bid to secure the prince's marriage to the Spanish Infanta, they were giving hostages to fortune. On the failure of their mission they abruptly reversed their policy. They returned to England determined to wage war on Spain, a policy which delighted many parliamentarians but horrified Lord Treasurer Middlesex who knew that war could not be financed. In the parliament of 1624 advocates of war combined with office-holders whose interests had been threatened by Middlesex's financial reforms to achieve the Lord Treasurer's impeachment, imprisonment and removal from power. Parliament did make a large (but inadequate) grant and military preparations began. Yet the war which parliament had been promised was not declared. All that happened was a calamitously mismanaged expedition of pressed Englishmen which crossed the channel under a German mercenary in January 1625 bound for the Palatinate, and which quickly melted away. James died two months later – the pacific foreign policy of his reign in ruins and with no alternative to it found.

49. *The Council of War.*
Engraving printed for Thomas Archer, 1624.
Besides his Privy Council, which became cumbersomely large in his reign, James formed temporary Councils of War in 1621 and 1624. That of 1624 was appointed to help recover the Palatinate for James's son-in-law. Although the Council proved ineffective, and was to be criticized in the parliament of 1626 for its role in the preparations for the disastrous military expedition of Count Mansfeld to Germany at the end of James's reign, it was ably manned, containing a wealth of military experience, much of it in Ireland. The picture was probably printed in an attempt to win confidence in and support for the military preparations. An accompanying poem lamely praises 'this heap of worthies': 'The soldier fights abroad, but these at home/Teach him to fight well: From these ten heads come/Those streams of counsel, by which war does stand/As safe as in the ocean does this land.'

The Jacobean Achievement

How successful was James I as king? Clearly his foreign policy, although it had long preserved peace, was ultimately unsuccessful. Yet it was not a less realistic one than that advocated by James's critics, who urged a Protestant crusade in Europe, but who never came to terms with its strategic and diplomatic complexities and who in parliament were not prepared to pay for it.

Religion caused James problems at home as well as abroad. In 1604 he called a conference at Hampton Court where he listened to Puritan complaints against Church ceremonies and against the poor quality of many clergy. Perhaps he did not take full advantage of the opportunity created by the conference for an understanding between the crown and the Puritans, and he did not implement all the reforms which were agreed upon there. But his reign did see an improvement, with his encouragement, in the quality of the ministry. He did not share the Puritans' enthusiasm for sermons and thought the profound and complex theological issues which Puritans sometimes raised in them unsuitable for simple listeners. He also disliked the persistent refusal of the less moderate Puritans to conform to Church ceremonies and services, and in 1604 he appointed the harsh disciplinarian Richard Bancroft, no friend to Puritanism, as Archbishop of Canterbury. Some men, unwilling to remain within an impure church, went into exile, first to Holland and later to America. But while James would not tolerate the extremists, his attitude to mainstream Puritanism was not an intolerant one.

In 1611 most Puritans could welcome the appointment of the old-fashioned Calvinist George Abbot as Bancroft's successor. Abbot lacked the energy to quicken the pace of reform himself, but at least his appointment was a defeat for the Arminian school of churchmanship, whose growth Puritans viewed with such dismay during James's reign. The English Arminians stood for elaborate Church ritual, which many contemporaries, accustomed to the bare and unadorned character of Elizabethan churches and worship, found hard to distinguish from Catholic practice. Arminians also reacted against the Calvinist doctrine of predestination contained in the Thirty-Nine Articles. The political problems that his successor courted by favouring the Arminians seem to emphasize James's good sense on this issue.

In studying the religious developments of the early seventeenth century, historians are too often conscious that civil war lay round the corner. Thus Jacobean Puritanism – in reality a largely conservative movement anxious to preserve the gains made by the Protestant Church of England during the previous reign – is sometimes discussed as if it were a revolutionary one. There is a comparable temptation concerning James's relations with his parliaments, many episodes of which become distorted when viewed as preludes to the parliamentary victory in the civil war. Certainly James's policies encountered opposition in parliament: opposition directed against monopolists and against the government-backed chartered companies that con-

50. Studio of Daniel Mytens, *George Villiers, first Duke of Buckingham.* Oil on canvas, 86 × 55½ in. (218 × 141 cm.). Private collection.

'A Mining and a Countermining Profession'

THE END OF SIR HENRY WOTTON'S FIRST EMBASSY TO VENICE, 1610

1 Odorado Fialetti, *Wotton received by the Doge of Venice*, *c.* 1606–10. Oil on canvas, $68\frac{1}{2} \times 104\frac{1}{2}$ in. (174×264.8 cm.). Royal Collection.
Wotton is seen standing before the Doge and Collegio of 25 principal senators of Venice.

Sir Henry Wotton, James I's ambassador to the Venetian Republic since 1604, took his leave on 7 December 1610 with the gifts and thanks of the Doge. He also received royal thanks on his return to England. James said 'he had known him in Scotland for a man of spirit and had loved him ever since'. 'Il volpone vecchio [the old wolf]', Italian diplomats called him.

James had first met him in 1601 when Wotton, travelling under the pseudonym Octavio Baldi, had warned the Scottish king of a plan to assassinate him. When James became King of England two years later, Wotton soon found favour. He exemplified a 'type' whose number grew in the Elizabethan and early Stuart period: the rich young Englishman who travelled abroad to learn and to prepare himself for a career in politics, in the academic world or in diplomacy. From a family of courtier-diplomats, he submitted himself to intensive travel and study. He had always sought foreign teachers, from Gentilis at Oxford, where he learned the civil law essential for diplomats, to Isaac Casaubon and Hugo Grotius abroad. He studied in Germany and travelled widely in Italy. After the fall of his patron the Earl of Essex in 1601, he travelled again in self-imposed exile. But such uncertainties were well behind him by 1610. He could be satisfied by his first embassy posting, which had re-established good relations with Venice and removed trade restrictions. It had also sustained the Protestant interest in the great conflict – the Interdict Crisis – between Venice and the Papacy in 1607–8.

In that conflict Venice scored a great political victory. Its long-running feud with the papacy about jurisdiction over the temporal concerns of the city had led to the last Interdict – an ecclesiastical ban by the papacy – in the history of the Church. Pope Paul V had challenged Venice's claims to buy and sell Church property and its right to try priests for secular offences. Spain, whom Englishmen saw as the Pope's intimate ally, supported him. The crisis attracted the attention of all the European powers. Many Catholic states shared Venice's anxiety about the Pope's temporal ambitions and admired her bid to establish sovereignty of jurisdiction within her territories. In Protestant countries enthusiasm for Venice's anti-Papal cause was sometimes enhanced by intellectual curiosity about Venice's elaborate and remarkably stable constitution and about its affinity with republican government of classical antiquity.

The events of 1606–7 belonged to a wider diplomatic context. Although the Dutch war of independence against Spain continued, hostilities between the major powers had been ended by the Treaty of Vervins between France and Spain in 1598 and by the Treaty of London between Spain and England in 1604. Now rulers longed for a period of peace and hoped for reconciliation among Christian princes. During the wars of religion of the later sixteenth century confessional rivalries had greatly weakened governments and brought chaos to international relations. At home, rulers strove to defuse religious conflicts and to balance the contending religious parties; abroad, they wanted the course of diplomacy to be determined by themselves and not by churchmen and religious enthusiasts.

Henry IV of France, who promoted Venice's challenge to Rome, subscribed to this position. So did James I of England, who had his own bitter memories of religious conflict in Scotland and who

2 Attrib. Alessandro Voratori, *Sir Henry Wotton*. Oil on canvas, $39 \times 32\frac{1}{2}$ in. (99×82.5 cm.). Oxford, Bodleian Library.
Wotton was from a Kentish family of courtiers. His life is lovingly told by Izaak Walton, author of lives of the Anglican divine Richard Hooker and of the clergyman-poet George Herbert, and of *The Compleat Angler*.

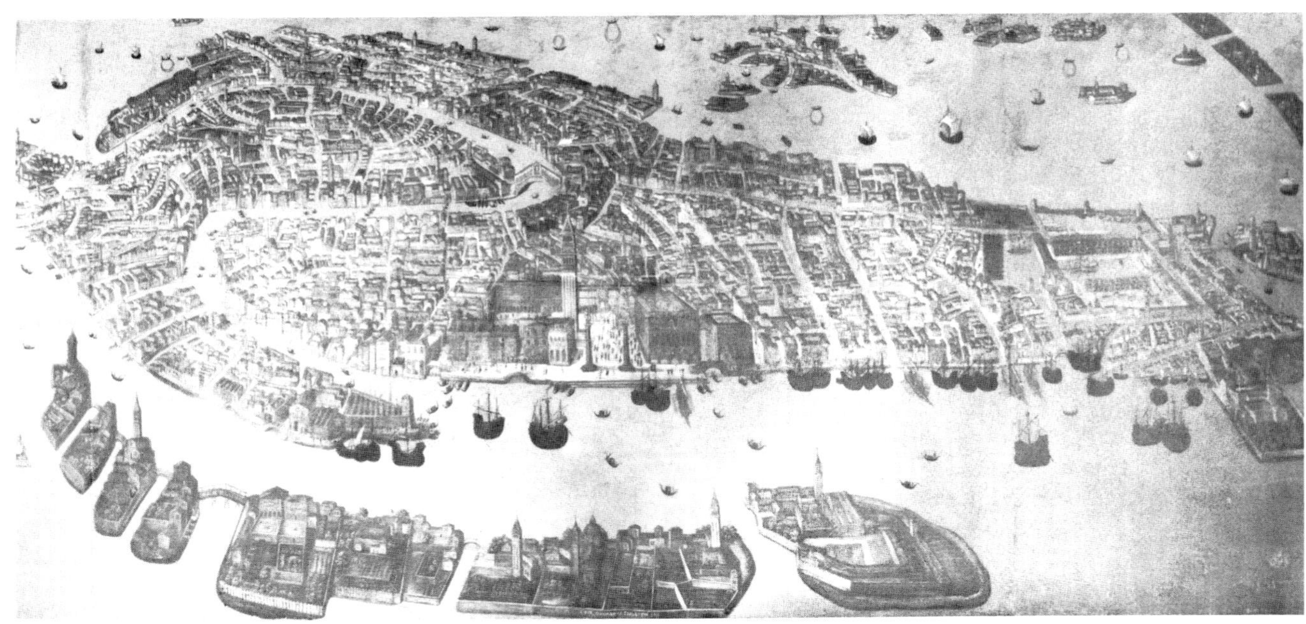

welcomed the Venetian triumph of 1607. James wanted a Europe peaceably united by co-operating princes. Within victorious Venice he saw natural allies for his programme. Some Venetian clergy and patricians were attracted by Protestant views of the papacy, perhaps even by Protestantism itself. The leader of this group was a Servite intellectual of European stature, Paolo Sarpi, theological advisor to the Republic during the Interdict. This was the setting for Wotton's first embassy to Venice from 1604 to 1610.

Wotton had close links with Sarpi and after the Interdict he nurtured a movement for religious reform in Venice, encouraging French, German and English Protestants there to collaborate in a secret church. Sarpi too seemed to encourage the idea of reformation for Venice, and he appeared to toy with Protestant ideas; but he must have known that Venice's devotion to the Virgin would prevent her from deserting the forms and doctrines of Catholicism. Cautiously he urged a 'Defensive League against the encroachers on the Jurisdiction of Princes'. Venice, he indicated, might join such a league, but Protestant princes must first settle the differences which had kept them divided during the Interdict. Wotton agreed, and understood Sarpi's reluctance to come out openly against the might of Rome and Spain. Yet his hopes remained high. As we watch him haunting Venice's churches and her art studios, buying books, pictures and glass, appreciating the chanting of nuns and admiring the flower girls in Chioggia, we see in him a genuine international cosmopolitan. His dream of a united Europe remained.

It was to be no more than a dream. During the Interdict James and Henry IV, both eager to make a mark on Italian politics, had been rivals in the struggle to resolve the crisis – and it was Henry who won. After the crisis the rivalries of princes persisted, but James continued to meddle in Italian affairs. In 1609 his book *A Premonition to all Most Mighty Monarchs, Kings, Free Princes and States of Christendom* provoked a scene which led to Wotton's departure from Venice. Dedicated to the Holy Roman Emperor, the Habsburg Rudolf II, the book was intended to advocate that princely unity against usurping powers on which James had set his heart. In it the king is at his best in defence of the rights of princes against Papal power, but at his worst in flippant remarks about the Virgin, puns about Bulls and horns, and jokes about popes as whores. No Catholic could have accepted James's book as a gift. Henry IV, who had outwardly converted to Catholicism to secure his throne, rejected the work, saying that writing was no business for a king. Others burnt their copies or tore them up. Wotton presented one to the Doge (the leading magistrate) and the 'collegio' (the ruling body). It was graciously received, locked away unread and banned in the Republic. Wotton protested and soon brought his embassy to an end. The Venetians placated James and maintained their friendly links with England (Wotton was still officially ambassador, even though he was back in England, until 1612), but the unreality of English policy stood revealed. Wotton embarked on many more embassies with the aim of effecting a union of princes, but the policy was a chimera. Wotton and men like him knew Europe well, but not well enough to produce a practicable foreign policy for England.

3 Attrib. O. Fialetti, *Venice*. Oil on canvas, approx, 7 × 16 ft. (2.13 × 4.9 m.). Eton College. This map-picture, acquired by Wotton during one of his three embassies to Venice, was presented in 1636 to Eton College, where he spent his old age as Provost.

4 Anon., *Paolo Sarpi*. Oil on canvas, 30 × 25 in. (76 × 63.5 cm.). Oxford, Bodleian Library.
Sarpi was an authority on mathematics and science as well as theology, and was an implacable enemy of papal claims to temporal power.

51. Title-page of the Authorized Version of the Bible (1611). *The Bible had first been printed in English under Henry VIII, at the time of the Reformation, but not until the Authorized Version was there a standard text. The Authorized Version was produced by a commission of divines set up with royal encouragement at the Hampton Court Conference of 1604. The frontispiece shows the saints of the ancient Church presiding over, and suggesting the historical credentials of, the Church of England. Some Puritans continued to prefer the 'Geneva Bible', which contained Calvinist glosses in its margins.*

trolled much overseas trade; against impositions; and against proclamations. Yet such opposition was not often successful. A statute of 1624 did restrict monopolies, but the exemption of corporate bodies enabled the chartered companies to retain their privileges. James continued to collect impositions and to issue proclamations (although not, it seems, with any intention of replacing statutes by them). The concessions that the king made on the occasions when he allowed the Commons to debate prerogative matters may indicate not the crown's weakness but, on the contrary, the strength of a king keen to involve parliament in the pursuit of reform. If a shift occurred in the balance of power between crown and parliament, it was in the crown's favour, not parliament's. Representative institutions seemed under threat in England as they were in Europe; and most MPs would have concurred with the statement of the select committee which lamented in the 'Apology and Satisfaction' of 1604 that 'the prerogatives of princes may easily and do daily grow; the privileges of the subject are for the most part at an everlasting stand'.

Yet to think in terms of conflict between crown and parliament is too simple. Thus the failure of the Great Contract in 1610 was the triumph not of parliament over the crown but of one court faction over another, both of them commanding a parliamentary following in their support. The same is true of the appointment in 1624 of parliamentary treasurers to supervise the spending of subsidies voted for war, and of the revival of the medieval procedure of impeachment in which the lower house accused and the upper house judged. Bacon fell in 1621 not because parliament asserted itself against a minister of the crown, but because Cranfield and Buckingham, for factional reasons, combined to be rid of him. The impeachment of Middlesex in 1624 was the achievement not of parliament but of Charles and Buckingham, who used their support in parliament to win a battle at court.

On one issue parliament did thwart the king: his plan for the union of England and Scotland, which the parliament of 1604–10 frustrated. Perhaps it is too easy to represent James's policy as a far-sighted anticipation of Oliver Cromwell's short-lived union of 1654 and the permanent one of 1707, and to treat the resistance of MPs to the novel concept of Great Britain as myopic. The Scottish adventurers drawn south to James's court were not the best advertisements for union and James was insufficiently sensitive to understandable English anxieties. But here, and perhaps elsewhere, it was the king who was innovative and his parliament conservative.

The Jacobean age has suffered more than it deserves from comparison with the Elizabethan. Even in cultural history many achievements often labelled 'Elizabethan' were produced under James I – among them some of the greatest works of Shakespeare, who died in 1616, the mature creations of Ben Jonson and John Donne in literature, and of William Byrd and John Dowland in music. The Elizabethan miniaturist Nicholas Hilliard found a worthy, perhaps even a greater successor in Isaac Oliver; and whereas

SEIANVS

HIS FALL.

Written
by
BEN: IONSON.

MART. Non hîc *Centauros*, non *Gorgonas, Harpyiasq;*
Inuenies: Hominem pagina nostra sapit.

AT LONDON
Printed by *G. Elld*, for *Thomas Thorpe.* 1605.

The Testimony of my Affection, & Observance to my noble Friend Sr Robert Townshend which I desire may remayne with him, & last beyond Marble.

52. A presentation copy of Ben Jonson, *Sejanus* (1605).
Sejanus, *performed in 1603, was much better thought of by Jonson than by its audience. His dramatic gifts are better seen in such comedies as* The Alchemist *and* Bartholomew Fair, *which brought whole cities to life. Yet the seriousness with which Jonson took this venture into historical and tragical writing is instructive. There was a growing interest in Roman history – and of the writings on it of Tacitus and Machiavelli, which Jonson closely followed in* Sejanus. *The emergence of the Roman history play answered that interest, Jonson apparently seeing* Sejanus *as his answer to Shakespeare's* Julius Caesar. *Jonson's play, like much early Stuart drama, had transparent contemporary implications. The story of the wicked favourite of the emperor Tiberius, it hints at a parallel often drawn in the seventeenth century, between the decline of republican liberty under the Roman empire and the decline of medieval liberty under Renaissance monarchy. Like other plays of Jonson,* Sejanus *aroused the suspicions of authority, which however was better pleased by the masques he wrote for James I and by some of his poems. With a high view of his literary calling, Jonson took more interest than most dramatists in the publication of his works.*

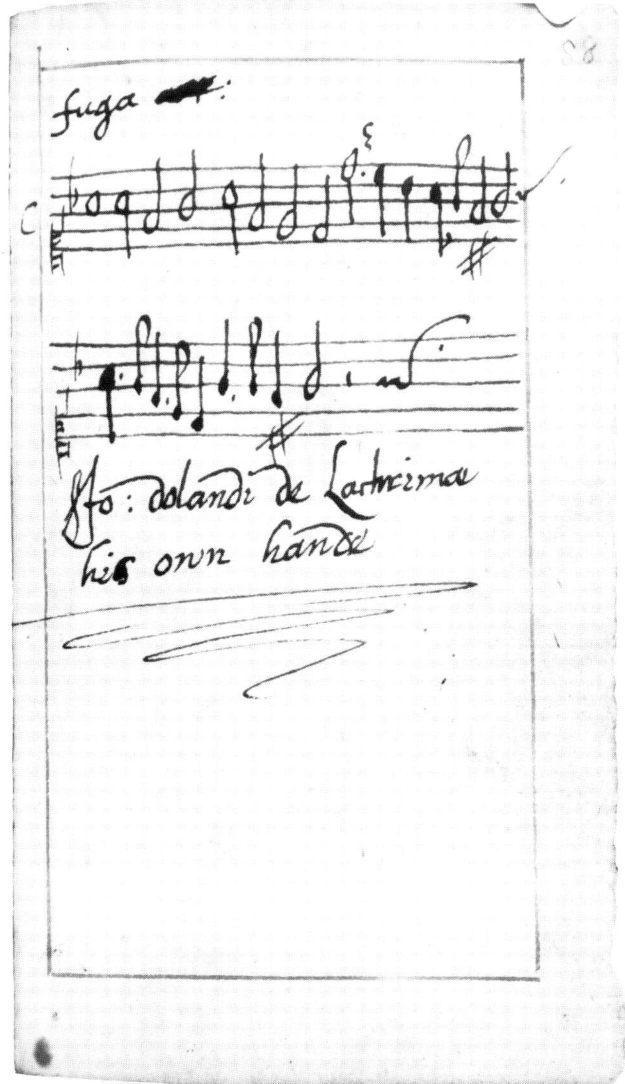

53. Fugue by John Dowland in the 'Album Amicorum' of Johann Cellarius of Nuremberg (1580–1619).
London, British Library, Additional MS. 27579, p. 88.
These bars, with Dowland's signature ('Doland'), belong to his Lachrymae, or Seven Tears, figured in seven passionate Pavans, *which was published in 1605 and dedicated to the queen, Anne of Denmark. Dowland spent much of his life abroad, where princely patrons were more appreciative of his work than in England.*

Elizabeth had been niggardly in her patronage of the arts and especially of architecture, the royal and courtly patronage of the Jacobean period produced in Inigo Jones the greatest architect that England – or rather Wales – had yet seen. Together with Ben Jonson, Jones brought a heightened and innovative sophistication to the court masque, the principal achievements of which belong to the reign of James rather than to that of his son with whom the masque is more usually associated. The great collaboration of Jones and Jonson, which flourished under James, collapsed in acrimony under Charles. And while Charles was a more spectacular and discerning patron and collector of painting than his father, the patronage bestowed by James and his queen on such foreign painters as van Somer, van Mierevelt, van Blyenberch and above all Mytens marked an artistic advance on the Elizabethan period. The Jacobean age was the precursor of what Sir Oliver Millar has described as 'the most spectacular moment in the history of English taste' in the next reign. That reign, however, was also to bring a crisis for the English monarchy and its temporary destruction.

CHAPTER THREE

Caroline Politics 1625–1640

The Character of King Charles

Charles I, like a number of other English monarchs, was not born the heir to his father's throne. Twelve years old on the death of Prince Henry, he found difficulty in escaping the shadow of that formidable elder brother, as from that of his elder sister Elizabeth, the Electress Palatine and popular heroine of the beleaguered Protestant cause in Europe. His father, disconcerted by Henry's independence of spirit, was careful to discourage any sign of it in his younger son, whom he dominated. Yet in adulthood Charles resembled his father as little as he did his elder brother. Cold, withdrawn, fastidious, even a little precious, he had none of James's grossness or uncouthness. Edward Hyde, who was to be his minister and the greatest historian of the reign, recalled of it that 'no man durst bring before him any thing that was profane or unclean; that kind of wit had never any countenance then'. Whereas James had despised ceremony, Charles 'kept state to the full, which made his court very orderly; no man presuming to be seen in a place where he had no pretence to be'. While the diminutive Charles fell literally short of the superb figure of regal majesty presented in Van Dyck's great baroque portrait of him, at least he embodied in his person something of that kingly *gravitas* that his father had lacked.

Charles swiftly raised the tone of the court. Within a fortnight of James's death it was reported that 'the court is kept more strict and private than in the former time'. Lucy Hutchinson, whose father held a courtly office under Charles (and whose husband was later to sign his death warrant), came to think of the king as 'a worse encroacher upon the civil and spiritual liberties of the people by far than his father'; yet she conceded that he was 'temperate, chaste and serious; so that the fools and bawds, mimics and catamites of the former court grew out of fashion; and the nobility and courtiers who did not quite abandon their debaucheries had yet that reverence to the king to retire into corners to practise them'. Admittedly, the most far-reaching reforms had to await the death of the greatest catamite of all, the Duke of Buckingham, in 1628. So did Charles's termination of the wanton grant of titles, from which Buckingham had been a principal beneficiary. Charles, like his father before him, was under the duke's spell. It was through the guidance and friendship of Buckingham, whom he had initially disliked, that Charles found himself and to some measure escaped his father's domination.

As the moral purpose of the court was elevated, so also was its aesthetic taste. Charles was the greatest connoisseur, patron and collector ever to reign in England. Even the great Rubens found at his court 'none of the crudeness that one might expect from a place so remote from Italian elegance'. Vast sums, by contemporary standards, went on works of art: £3000 to Rubens for the ceiling panels in the Banqueting House and more than £18,000 for the sumptuous collection of the Duke of Mantua – although Charles, not a bountiful man, was no soft touch.

Outside the court the king was ill at ease. Though a monarch could gain enormously from indulging his subjects' public expressions of loyalty, it was not until 1633 that Charles went to Edinburgh to be crowned King of Scotland. In the same year, as in 1626, he dropped plans for a royal procession of entry into the city of London, despite the cost and effort expended by the citizens in preparing pageants – an incident that exacerbated the already strained relations between crown and City. If expressions of loyalty were a problem to him, expressions of criticism were a greater one. He chose advisers who were content to echo his own views rather than those willing to make him face unwelcome truths. Like all authoritarian personalities, he found concession difficult and compromise distasteful. And he was

54. The Interior of the Banqueting House, Whitehall.
Designed by Inigo Jones in 1619, the Banqueting House was intended to announce a new age in English kingship. The formal geometry of the exterior would have stood out from the jumble of earlier buildings in neighbouring Whitehall, while in the huge hall, 110 by 55 feet, the grandeur and divinity of Stuart rule were emphasized. Foreign ambassadors were received here, and until 1635, when Rubens's ceiling was installed, the hall was the setting for court masques. Under James I the central focus was a large coffered niche where the king sat in state, like a living statue; but the niche was removed by his son. Rubens's paintings were apparently commissioned during his visit to England in 1629, and were finished by 1634; his fee was £3,000. The central oval contains the 'Apotheosis of James I', whose earthly labours are rewarded by his elevation to heaven. The central picture here visible at the far end celebrates the union of England and Scotland. James leans forward from his throne to accept the new-born and naked child of union, while cherubs above carry the arms of the united kingdom. But the plans of the early Stuarts to strengthen that union proved vain.

55. Daniel Mytens, *Charles I*, 1627.
Oil on canvas. Galleria Sabauda, Turin.
Painted for Charles's sister the Duchess of Savoy, the painting was approved by the king, who arranged a second sitting the following year for Mytens to bring it up to date. The background of the picture is an architectural fantasy constructed in 1626 by Hendrick van Steenwyck. Mytens, a Dutchman who came to England some time before 1618, was one of the many imported artists who made up the want of a strong native tradition. Given a house by James I, he was made 'king's painter' by Charles I, with a life pension; but he returned to Holland in 1630.

56. A Guard of James I, *c.* 1623–5.
British Library, Egerton MS. 1269, f. 11.
One of a series of impressions in the album of a foreign traveller to England.

57. A. Van Dyck, *The Madagascar Portrait* (Thomas Howard, second Earl of Arundel, with Aletheia, Countess of Arundel), *c.* 1639. Oil on canvas. $53\frac{1}{4} \times 83$ in. (135×211 cm.). Arundel Castle, Sussex, collection of the Duke of Norfolk.
To Madagascar on the globe point the countess, who bears an astrolabe and dividers, and the earl, who wears his peer's robes over his armour. The painting alludes to a bizarre and fanciful scheme, advanced by Prince Rupert in 1636 and revived by the earl in 1639, for colonizing the island; Arundel himself, the premier peer of England, intended to head the colony. Ships were commissioned, money raised, royal approval granted; but nothing came of a venture which, observed Rupert's mother Elizabeth of Bohemia, 'sounds like one of Don Quixote's projects'. Arundel was one of England's foremost patrons, connoisseurs and collectors of art, his enthusiasms including paintings, drawings, statues and marbles. The historian Clarendon, who disliked him, wrote: 'he was generally thought to be a proud man, who lived always within himself, and to himself, conversing little with any who were in common conversation'; but added, 'it cannot be denied that he had in his person, in his aspect and countenance, the appearance of a great man . . . He wore and affected a habit very different from that of the time, such as men had only beheld in the pictures of the most considerable men; all which drew the eyes of most, and the reverence of many towards him, as the image and representative of the primitive nobility, and native gravity of the nobles, when they had been most venerable.'

devious; Macaulay's picture of a monarch cursed by 'an incurable propensity to dark and crooked ways' has its truth. There was a vindictive streak too – the obverse of his strong sense of personal loyalty. In 1632 he refused permission for the body of Sir John Eliot, who had been the greatest enemy of his beloved Buckingham, to be taken from the Tower to be buried in his native Cornwall. So great was Buckingham's hold on Charles that his assassination in August 1628 – along with the dissolution of Charles's third parliament in 1629 – marks a fundamental dividing line in the reign.

The Last Years of Buckingham: Wars and Parliaments, 1625–1629

Charles married Henrietta Maria, the sister of King Louis XIII of France, in 1625 in fulfilment of a treaty of Anglo-French alliance in the previous year. Only 15 at the time of her marriage, the queen was described on her arrival in England as 'nimble and quick, black-eyed, brown-haired, and in a word a brave lady'. She came to England with firm instructions to convert her Protestant husband to the true Catholic faith and to improve the conditions of her co-religionists. The marriage, which was eventually so happy, had its initial difficulties. Sometimes the early storms are attributed to the malevolent influence of Buckingham, whose hold over her husband the queen is said to have resented and who is supposed to have seen in her presence a threat to his own ascendancy. The origins of this story, or at least of its exaggeration, lie in the reports of the queen's French entourage, notably her Grand Almoner the Bishop of Mende, her confessor Father Bérulle and her friend the Duchesse de Chevreuse. They, not Buckingham, were the principal source of marital discord, for they regarded Charles as a threat to their own

59. Gerrit Honthorst, *Apollo and Diana*, 1628. Oil on canvas, 140½ × 252 in. (357 × 640 cm.). Hampton Court, Royal Collection. *Mercury, personated by Buckingham, and with a Garter round his leg, heads a procession of the Liberal Arts as they pay homage to Apollo (Charles I, with Henrietta Maria beside him as Diana). Grammar, at the front of the procession on her knees and with an open book, is probably the Duchess of Buckingham. Then, with their symbols, come Logic, Rhetoric, Arithmetic and Music. At the bottom left Hatred (or Ignorance) and Envy are overthrown. The lady behind Diana's right shoulder is probably the queen's friend the Countess of Carlisle. It is not certain whether the picture was commissioned by the king or by Buckingham.*

58. *The Raising of the Siege of the Island of Rhé, 8 November 1627.* Oil on canvas, 127 × 100½ in. (322 × 255 cm.). Palace of Versailles. *In July 1627 an expedition led by Buckingham of some 6,000 men and some 100 ships effected a landing on the island of Rhé, close to the Protestant stronghold of La Rochelle. Buckingham saw in the island a base from which to assist the Protestants of southern France against a monarchy determined either to diminish the toleration they had enjoyed since the Revocation of the Edict of Nantes in 1598 or at least to reduce them to firm political obedience. Buckingham's army was weakened by sickness, by lack of discipline, and by the failure of reinforcements from England; the Huguenots of La Rochelle hesitated to incur royal wrath by supporting the expedition; and in November the English were driven from the island in a disastrously managed retreat. An Englishman, learning the news, called it 'the greatest and shamefullest overthrow since the loss of Normandy'. In the picture the relief expedition, exhorted by Louis XIII and Richelieu, sails from the mainland. Hopes of succouring the Protestants of Bordeaux were to be revived under Puritan rule in the 1650s.*

OVERLEAF

60 (left). A. Van Dyck, *Charles I on Horseback with Seigneur de St. Antoine*, 1633.
Oil on canvas, 145 × 106½ in. (368 × 270 cm.).
Buckingham Palace, Royal Collection.
Van Dyck, who had settled in England under James I, settled in London in 1632, when Charles knighted him and gave him an annual pension of £200 and a house in Blackfriars. Between that year and his death in 1641 the artist effected a revolution in English painting, and provided the images in which the Stuart court recognized its own ideals and by which posterity remembers it. The portrait of Charles I, modelled on an equestrian portrait by Rubens, was much admired by contemporaries. Van Dyck, it was observed, 'has so skilfully brought him to life with his brush, that if our eyes alone were to be believed they would boldly assert that the king himself is alive in the portrait, so vivid is its appearance.' Charles, an accomplished horseman, is attended by the Seigneur de St. Antoine, a riding-master and equerry of the crown.

61 (right). A. Van Dyck, *Henrietta Maria*, 1635.
Oil on canvas, 41½ × 33 in. (105.5 × 84.2 cm.).
New York, private collection.

domination of the queen and feared that he would convert her to Protestantism. Buckingham did see in the queen's household a new and vital sphere of political influence that he needed to penetrate, and his success in inserting his wife and mother as ladies of the Queen's Bedchamber antagonized the 'monsieurs', as Charles disdainfully called his wife's French attendants. In 1626 the monsieurs were expelled and the marriage began to improve. After Buckingham's death two years later, the queen – despite her failure to understand some of Charles's dearest principles and especially his religion – was supremely able to give him the love and support he so needed.

The marriage alliance that had brought Henrietta Maria to England was a keystone of the anti-Habsburg and anti-Spanish foreign policy pursued by Buckingham from the time of his return from Madrid in 1623. In the autumn of 1625, when war with Spain had become open, a naval expedition to Cadiz failed ignominiously. This was but one of the disasters of foreign policy that marked the early years of Charles's reign. Soon Buckingham had contrived to draw England into war not only with Spain but with France. For the latter conflict the expulsion of the monsieurs was partly responsible, but the main explanation lies with the duke's diplomatic miscalculations.

Possibly Buckingham was the victim of bad luck and less incompetent than has traditionally been supposed, but the elaborate plans with which he aimed to secure the restoration of the Palatinate – plans far beyond the resources of English means or influence – smack of *folie de grandeur*. Eager for French support against Spain, he set out to topple the great minister of Louis XIII of France, Cardinal Richelieu, whom he mistakenly supposed to be an implacable enemy of Anglo-French cooperation. It was Buckingham's aim to orchestrate a series of insurrections within France and of invasions by her neighbours, until a desperate Louis was obliged to replace Richelieu with councillors more amicably disposed to English aims. The duke's own contribution to this grand design was to lead a naval expedition in 1627 to the island of Rhé in order to relieve the Protestant Huguenots of nearby La Rochelle, whose disobedience Richelieu was determined to crush. The expedition, like that to Cadiz two years earlier, was a fiasco and Buckingham's grand design failed on all fronts. In 1627–8 the duke had created not the network of anti-Habsburg and anti-Spanish alliances at which he had aimed, but the threat of encirclement by a Franco-Spanish alliance. As Lord Admiral he bore a particular responsibility for the futile attempts to revive Elizabethan glories at sea. In 1628 Buckingham was preparing a second expedition to La Rochelle when he was assassinated at Portsmouth by a junior naval officer John Felton who, though his motives had been more spiteful than patriotic, became something of a popular hero in the weeks before his execution. The financial and military burdens of the duke's humiliating wars had produced an alarming growth of popular unrest.

That unrest was compounded by the government's religious policy. Charles was not the crypto-Catholic that Puritan zealots supposed him to be and in 1625 he accepted parliamentary demands for a stiffer enforcement of the recusancy laws against Catholics, even though secret clauses of the French marriage treaty obliged him to show them favour. Yet he aroused acute

50 AN APPEALE

for ever. To bring this his Decree and unchangeable purpoſe to paſſe, it was neceſſary he ſhould, and ſo hee did, purpoſe, and ſo effect the creation of man and all mankinde, neceſſarily alſo, unto life or death. So that the *major* part of mankinde by farre, periſhing everlaſtingly from GOD, did ſo periſh, becauſe GOD had decreed irreverſibly and irreſpectively, that they ſhould ſo periſh, and indeed made them that they might ſo periſh inevitably. For the will of GOD is the neceſſity of things, ſay YOUR *Maſters* out of S. AUGUSTINE miſ-underſtood. This is no malicious relating of the doctrine of YOUR Side, that delight to be ſtiled *Calviniſts*. The firſt counſell, purpoſe, and decree of GOD was thus: Before the works of his hands of old, meerly and irreſpectively to declare his power (I cannot ſay his juſtice) and what hee might and would doe upon his creatures, *for his glorie ſake, hee made the wicked* AGAINST, *nay* FOR *the day of vengeance*. The meanes to bring this his purpoſe to paſſe, was Creation; and the cauſe of his creating man, was to effect it.

CALVIN, *Inſtit*. 3. 21. 5. *Prædeſtinationem vocamus æternum* DEI *decretum, quo apud ſe conſtitutum habuit, quid de unoquoque homine fieri vellet. Non enim* PARI *conditione* CREANTUR *homines: ſed alijs vita æterna, alijs* DAMNATIO *æterna* PRÆORDINATUR. *Itaque prout in alterutrum finem quiſque* CONDITUS EST, *ita vel ad vitam, vel ad* MORTEM

62. A page from Richard Mountagu, *Appello Caesarem* (1625). *The clergyman Mountagu wrote provocative works in support of the High Church position favoured by the king and Laud. His writings aroused angry responses in parliament in 1626 and again in 1628. Here Mountagu is attacking the Calvinist doctrine of predestination. The areas of disagreement between Calvinists and Arminians on the question of predestination and free will were often narrow but were none the less bitter, Calvinists seeing in the Arminian position, as in the Laudian emphasis on ceremony and ritual, a return towards popery. The king made his suppport for Mountagu clear by awarding him the see of Chichester in 1628.*

suspicions by the enthusiasm with which he espoused High-Church ceremonialism and sacramentalism and the separation of altars in the east end of churches. Promotion was given to High-Churchmen who stressed the divine right both of kings and of bishops. Among them was William Laud, who was made Bishop of London in 1628.

Charles, who left the formulation of foreign policy largely to Buckingham, was his own master in religious matters. Here Buckingham's own position had kept men guessing. Would he adopt the High-Church, Arminian position of his king, or the Puritan or Calvinist posture of such leading politicians as the Earl of Pembroke and Lord Saye and Sele? Buckingham came off the fence in 1626 when he held a conference to discuss doctrinal issues at York House, his house in the Strand. His declaration of support for Arminianism was a grave blow to Saye and Sele and other Puritans, whose pressure had obliged Buckingham to call the conference and who had hoped to secure from it a forthright condemnation of Arminianism and in particular of the Arminian royal chaplain Richard Mountagu. Mountagu had published a tract which ostensibly attacked Catholicism but which seemed to Puritans to condone more Catholic practices than it condemned. The king, who had already protected Mountagu from impeachment in parliament, ratified his support by raising him to the see of Chichester in 1628.

Religious controversy and the disasters of war and diplomacy provided the unsettling background to the three parliaments which met in the opening years of the reign in 1625, 1626 and 1628. Buckingham came under fierce attack in all of them. In 1625, when he was suspected of arranging secret pro-Catholic clauses in the French marriage treaty, his failings as Lord Admiral were pointedly criticized by the Commons' refusal to make the customary grant of tonnage and poundage for life, a tax earmarked for defence of the seas. Until 1626 Buckingham could at least expect some support from Puritan politicians who, though dismayed by his diplomatic ineptitude, at least welcomed the anti-Spanish bias of his policy. But the failure of the Cadiz expedition and the outcome of the York House Conference left him virtually isolated and exposed him to the proceedings of impeachment brought against him in the parliament of 1626. Pembroke, who had supported the duke in the parliament of 1624, now led the moves against him. In the Commons Buckingham was confronted by his former clients Sir John Eliot and Sir Dudley Digges and by members who belonged to Pembroke's great empire of electoral and court patronage: Sir Benjamin Rudyerd, William Coryton and Dr Samuel Turner, the man who first introduced the articles of impeachment into the lower house.

Pembroke used impeachment as a political weapon much as the duke had done against Lord Treasurer Middlesex in 1624, though the risks were now much greater in view of the favourite's uniquely privileged position. The charges ranged from Buckingham's misuse of office and his self-enrichment and self-aggrandizement to his foreign policy and the religious affiliations of his relations, and concluded with what seemed like an insinuation that the duke had poisoned James on his deathbed. It may be that Pembroke aimed not to secure Buckingham's conviction but merely to

63. Engraving of Sir Edward Coke.
Coke, lawyer and politician, vigorously defended the claims of the common law against the pretensions both of the crown and of other branches of the law. A privy councillor and member of parliament, he was a powerful obstructive force against attempts to enlarge the royal prerogative; this was one of the issues that brought him into conflict with Francis Bacon. Coke's Institutes, *published under Charles I, became the bible of the common law and had an enduring influence in both England and America.*

64. *The Sovereign of the Seas.* Contemporary engraving. Greenwich, National Maritime Museum.
The engraving was published as propaganda for the tax of ship money. The Sovereign of the Seas, *built in 1637, was a prestige ship. There was widespread agreement about the need to improve the navy and also to clear the coasts of pirates; and Charles could reasonably claim that the cost of these activities should be more widely spread. But the extension of the tax had disturbing legal and constitutional implications, and at the trial in 1637 of John Hampden, who refused to pay the tax, five of the twelve judges showed surprising independence by voting against the crown. Even so, Charles had won his case.*

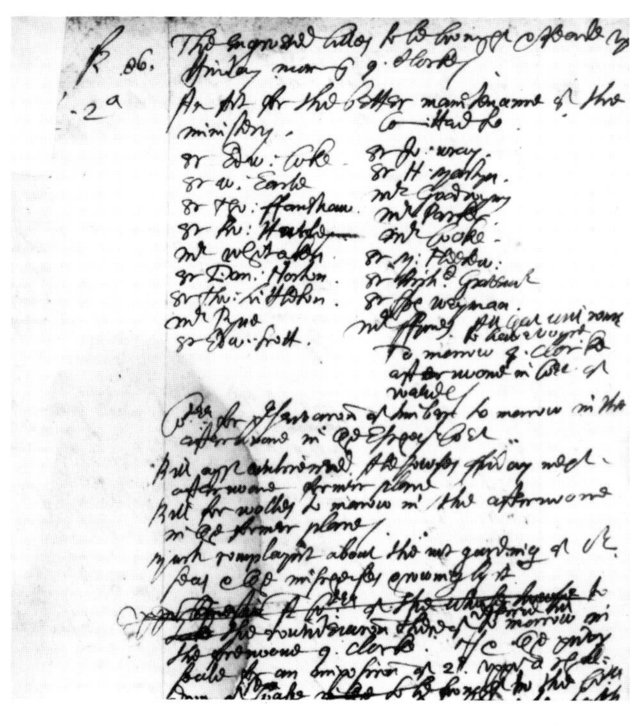

65. Journal of the House of Commons, 7 May 1628. House of Lords Record Office.
A page from the Journal of the House of Commons, kept by the Clerk of the House. In the earlier seventeenth century the Commons' record of its proceedings became fuller, although its journal was not printed until the eighteenth century. The page begins: 'The engrossed bills to be brought and read upon Friday morning 9 clock./An Act for the better maintenance of the ministry.' The act (or bill) is entrusted to a committee, headed by Sir Edward Coke, which is to meet 'tomorrow 4 clock afternoon in the Court of Wards'. Puritan moves to supplement the incomes of ministers were opposed and eventually suppressed by the king and Archbishop Laud.

use the charges against him as a bargaining counter. Thus if Buckingham would yield some of his powers and offices – and in particular if he would resign as Lord Admiral – then parliament might vote a generous grant and quietly drop the impeachment. But the impeachment process, once set in motion, was hard to stop. In the Commons, Eliot and Digges displayed an appetite for ducal blood that hints of compromise could not assuage; and in the Lords, the Earl of Bristol (fighting his own defence against a charge of treason) brought newly-damaging charges against the favourite. Buckingham's conviction was forestalled only by the King's decision to dissolve the parliament.

Parliament had voted no money. Charles resolved to raise funds without it through a forced loan. Five knights who refused to contribute to it were arbitrarily imprisoned and brought to a trial in the King's Bench in 1627 which had wide implications. The judges aroused grave dismay by their ruling that the king's command could legally imprison his subjects without specifying the offence. Here was an issue which came to the forefront of Charles's third parliament in 1628 – an issue that parliament's Petition of Right was an attempt to resolve. Modern liberal democracies accept the abrogation of some basic liberties of the subject in wartime in the confidence that peace will restore them. The MPs of 1628 lacked that confidence. In the Petition and in the debates which surrounded it, they sought a strict definition of the law on four critical issues raised by Charles's domestic and foreign policies: arbitrary taxation, arbitrary imprisonment, the billeting of soldiers in households and the scope of martial law. The king's first reply to the Petition succeeded only in provoking a fresh drive against Buckingham and the Arminians. Even his second more conciliatory response was followed by two formal Remonstrances from the Commons, one against Buckingham and the Arminians, the other against unparliamentary collection of tonnage and poundage. MPs such as Eliot and John Pym were not seeking to extend the power of parliament or to alter the balance of the constitution; they were seeking to defend ancient liberties which they believed to be in fundamental danger.

Adjourned in the summer of 1628, the parliament met again early in 1629. By then Buckingham had been dispatched by the assassin's knife. Yet his death failed to appease MPs and the parliament ended in pure theatre when, with the Speaker forcibly held in his chair, the Commons voted a Protestation against Arminianism, popery and unparliamentary taxation. The king drew the conclusion from the persistence of opposition after Buckingham's death that 'the duke was not alone the mark these men shot at, but only as a near minister of ours taken up on the by in their passage to their more secret designs . . . to abate the powers of our Crown, and to bring our government into obloquy'. Henceforth he resolved to rule without parliaments, at least until MPs had acquired the habits of loyalty and obedience. The diplomatic consequences of this decision were as conspicuous as its domestic ones, for Charles was now in no position to finance wars. Peace was made with France in 1629 and with Spain in 1630.

The Years of Personal Rule

No parliament met in England between 1629 and 1640. Looking back to these years of 'personal rule' across the intervening horrors of civil war, royalists such as Clarendon were to recall a period when the country enjoyed a peace and prosperity denied continental countries who simultaneously endured the miseries of the Thirty Years War. Yet Clarendon admitted that 'all these blessings could but enable, not compel us to be happy'. Charles, eager for a period of beneficent and unchallenged royal rule, had given leading offices to some able men who had criticized his policies in the 1620s – notably William Noy, who as Attorney General introduced the regular levying of Ship Money, and above all Thomas Wentworth, the later Earl of Strafford, who served Charles first as President of the Council of the North and then from 1633 as Lord Deputy of Ireland. Yet the court, despite the picture of harmony carefully projected by masques and paintings, was riven by conflict.

In the first half of the 1630s three main contending factions could be discerned. A pro-Spanish group was led by two men who were later to convert to Catholicism: Lord Treasurer Weston, created Earl of Portland in 1633, and his Chancellor of the Exchequer Sir Francis Cottington, the principal negotiator of the peace with Spain in 1630. Bitterly opposed to this group and to the corruption and dilatoriness of Portland's administration was William Laud, who became Archbishop of Canterbury in 1633. In due course Laud was to find a firm ally in Wentworth, but in the earlier years of the decade Wentworth was connected with Portland and Cottington. By contrast, Secretary of State Sir Francis Windebank, who owed his office to Laud's influence, defected to the Portland faction.

The third group centred on the queen. Henrietta Maria's reasons for disliking Portland were quite different from Laud's. She resented the Treasurer's efficient controls on her household expenditure and disliked his leanings toward Spain. Goaded by the French ambassador in London, she sought to steer her

'. . . Beloved of Two Kings' . . . and 'The Most Excellent Painter that England hath yet Bred'

ENDYMION PORTER AND WILLIAM DOBSON

In 1623 the young Charles, Prince of Wales, disguised as 'John Smith' and wooing the Spanish Infanta in eccentric fashion, scaled the walls of her garden; one of his companions on that occasion was that cosmopolitan courtier Endymion Porter. A Gloucestershire gentleman, Porter was partly Spanish and Spain was the key to his career. He spoke the language and had the contacts. Employed by the early Stuarts as both diplomatic envoy and art collector, he was a courtier of the age of European Baroque. As the seventeenth-century antiquarian and gossip Anthony Wood said, 'he was a great man beloved of two kings, James I for his admirable wit and Charles I . . . for his general learning, brave style, sweet temper, great experience, travels and modern languages'.

As Groom of the Bedchamber, Porter was close both to Buckingham, his patron and his relative by marriage, and to Charles as both Prince and King. In the early years of Charles's reign Porter lost ground when the abortive Spanish match, which he had promoted, gave way to the marriage with Henrietta Maria, who disliked him. He came into his own only in the 1630s, the heyday of the Caroline court. By the outbreak of civil war in 1642, when he was 55, the best part of his career was behind him. He went into exile in 1645. In 1647, when parliament discussed peace terms with the king, Porter was one of the few men whom it insisted on excluding from pardon. He died of natural causes on his return to England in 1649.

2 A. Van Dyck. *Self-Portrait with Edymion Porter*. Oil on canvas, 47 × 56¾ in. (119 × 144 cm.). Madrid, Prado. A tribute by the painter to their friendship.

1 William Dobson, *Endymion Porter*, c. 1643–45. Oil on canvas, 59 × 50 in. (150 × 127 cm.). London, Tate Gallery.

Porter shared the king's aesthetic tastes and helped to give his court that image of refined aestheticism which a nostalgic posterity has heightened. He filled several useful artistic functions for Charles. He acted as intermediary between him and art dealers such as Nicholas Lanier and Balthazar Gerbier; he arranged for the Dutch painter, Daniel Mytens, to become King's Drawer in 1625; he disposed of royal patronage to Orazio Gentilischi in 1626 and, in the late 1630s, to Peter Paul Rubens to whom were entrusted the Banqueting House decorations; in 1627 he negotiated the sale of the century, in which the Duke of Mantua sold his picture collection to Charles I; he helped secure Van Dyck's services for the king and became his friend. Porter was himself a collector and connoisseur of paintings, alongside wealthier enthusiasts like Buckingham and Arundel. He was also a poet. His poems were published and he was both a patron of and part of the circle of Donne, Herrick, Dekker and William Davenant. 'Let there be patrons; patrons like to thee/Brave Porter! Poets ne'er will wanting be' (Herrick).

Endymion's role as patron is superbly exemplified by what has been described as 'one of the rare masterpieces of English painting from the seventeenth century' – the famous portrait by William Dobson. Admired by contemporaries, the painting was engraved for quantity production some time before 1646. Dobson was a product of the artistic milieu which Porter had done so much to foster. Born in 1611 he was much younger than Porter. Early in life, with his family left destitute, he was forced to seek his fortune as a painter. He was never properly trained, and his work shows it. He learned the rudiments of his trade from Sir Robert Peake, the engraver and picture-dealer, and from the German Francis Cleyn, who painted allegories and supervised the tapestry works at Mortlake. Perhaps more important for both his career and his development as a painter was his decision to live in St Martin's Lane, the artists' quarter near to the court. There he picked up both knowledge and commissions. He soon knew about Caravaggio and painted at least one canvas in his manner. His portrait compositions were based on Van Dyck's; and from Cleyn he acquired a liking for allegorical devices in his portraits. But the greatest influence on him was Charles I's own picture collection, which had been so assiduously put together with Porter's help. From these pictures Dobson assimilated the colour and brushwork of Venice and the baroque bravura of Flanders. 'Had his education been answerable to his genius', writes Richard Graham, 'England might have been justly proud of her Dobson, as Venice of her Titian, or Flanders of her Van Dyck.'

Wiliam Dobson painted royalists in civil war Oxford. His style, depicting lavish

3 William Dobson, *Self-Portrait,* c. 1642–6. Oil on canvas, 23 × 27 in. (58.3 × 68.4 cm.). Collection of the Earl of Jersey.

fabrics and luscious flesh tints, well served the dashing cavaliers at Charles's wartime court. His painting of Porter may have been made in Oxford, or alternatively just before the war while they were both in London. Porter looks careworn, but his clothing and the theme of the painting seem to be pre-war. The composition was modelled on a painting, now destroyed, of the Emperor Vespasian by Titian in Charles's collection. Porter is seen as a country gentleman and a courtly patron, characterized as the first by the hunting pose, the wheel lock rifle, retriever, page and dead hare, and as the second by the bust of Apollo and the allusions on the classical frieze to sculpture, painting and poetry. This painting asserted that it was possible to be a true Englishman and to like contemporary European taste. But for many Englishmen the life-style of a man like Porter was unacceptable. It represented something profoundly un-English, and seemed to symbolize Catholicism and tyranny. It was a style about to go down in defeat, but Dobson's brush captured it forever.

4 A. van Stalbemt and J. van Belcamp, *A View of Greenwich, c.* 1632. Oil on canvas, $34\frac{1}{4} \times 42\frac{1}{2}$ in. (87 × 107 cm.). Windsor Castle, Royal Collection.
Porter attends on Charles I and his Queen above Greenwich. He is the florid figure on the left with his left hand on a stick.

5 A. Correggio, *Mercury instructing Cupid before Venus.* Oil on canvas, 61 × 36 in. (155 × 91.5 cm.). London, National Gallery.
This picture was bought for Charles I by Porter as part of the great Gonzaga sale at Mantua in 1627.

husband in a pro-French and anti-Habsburg direction. This was a policy that Puritans – whatever their feelings about Henrietta Maria's and France's Catholicism – were bound to favour, for it was increasingly clear that only in alliance with France might England hope to thwart the Habsburgs in Europe and restore the Palatinate.

Thus there emerged a curious alliance between a fervently Catholic queen and militantly Protestant noblemen, among them the Earls of Pembroke and Northumberland, Viscount Dorchester (the former diplomat Sir Dudley Carelton) and above all two brothers, the Earls of Warwick and Holland. These men, Holland especially, possessed the courtly graces and *savoir-faire* which their enemies and rivals, Portland and Laud, altogether lacked. They opposed Portland for his foreign policy and Laud for his High-Churchmanship and his persecution of Puritans. Only in 1637, with the departure of the French ambassador and the arrival in England of the exiled French queen mother and of Henrietta's childhood friend the Duchesse de Chevreuse – both of whom were bitter opponents of their country's anti-Habsburg policies – was Henrietta's alliance with the anti-Spanish party sapped.

Meanwhile the balance of power at court had been altered in favour of Archbishop Laud by the death of Portland in 1635 and by his replacement as Lord Treasurer in the following year by Laud's protégé William Juxon, the Bishop of London. Yet the more powerful Laud became, the harder those men excluded from the court found it to distinguish between his High-Churchmanship and the promotion of Catholic conversions by the queen, especially from 1637. Opponents they might be, but the queen and the archbishop were viewed as fellow agents in a court plot to restore England to Rome.

Charles saw Laud's insistence on uniform and ordered worship as a prime means to national unity. In reality it had the opposite effect. Devout men, instinctively loyal to the institutions of Church and state, were shocked and alienated by measures which seemed to undermine the Calvinist doctrinal foundations of the Church of England. Puritans eager to improve the quality of the ministry from within the

66. A. Van Dyck, *Archbishop Laud, c.* 1638.
Oil on canvas, 48 × 38 in. (121.6 × 97 cm.).
Cambridge, Fitzwilliam Museum.
Laud was Bishop of London from 1628, and thanks to the king's support became the dominant influence in the Church well before his succession to the see of Canterbury in 1633. His predecessor, James's appointment George Abbot, had been more sympathetic to the Puritans. Yet there was a Puritan streak to Laud's temperament, as the unadorned background to this portrait suggests.

67. After A. Van Dyck, *Thomas Wentworth, Earl of Strafford, c.* 1633. Oil on canvas, 50½ × 40 in. (128 × 102 cm.).
London, National Portrait Gallery.
Wentworth, a Yorkshire gentleman, was imprisoned for opposing the forced loan of 1627. Next year his abilities were recognised at court. Able, ruthless and self-serving, he became President of the Council of the North and then, from 1633, Lord Deputy of Ireland. In both positions he enforced the government's will with energy and determination, and to Ireland he brought overdue financial and administrative reform. But his methods antagonized landowners and officials both in the north of England and in Ireland, who played leading roles in his destruction by the Long Parliament in 1641.

Church found themselves under attack. 'Lecturers', whose sermons supplemented parochial services, were silenced and the devout benefactors who financed them came under attack. The activities of the Church courts – which often punished sins that were as offensive to Puritans as to Laud, but which could be aimed at Puritans themselves – were extended, and the prerogative courts of High Commission and Star Chamber were used to punish Laud's critics. The economic and political control of the Church established by the laity during the Reformation seemed to be threatened when Laud fought to recover lands for the Church and to increase its income, and when churchmen were appointed as JPs or even given high secular office, as Bishop

68. The nave of Old St. Paul's Cathedral.
Engraving by Wenceslaus Hollar.
Like so many English churches St. Paul's cathedral suffered neglect from the time of the Reformation. The cathedral and the yard around it were treated as places of business and recreation; there was perpetual noise; and a man who was called before the Court of High Commission on a charge of making water against the building replied that he did not know it was a church. As Bishop of London, Laud decided to restore dignity and sanctity to the cathedral. In the work of restoration, Inigo Jones acted as Surveyor. Some of the money came from the king, some from collections organized by Laud's friends among the bishops. The restored church was destroyed by the Great Fire of 1666, after which Wren's cathedral was built in its place. Wenceslaus Hollar, a native of Prague, has left us with many of the most familiar visual images of seventeenth-century England.

Juxon was in 1636. Most divisive of all were Laud's innovations in Church ceremony and his elevation of the priest's authority and sacramental role. To a modern ecumenical churchman, Laud's belief that the Roman Church was not a false church, only an erroneous one, looks like open-minded tolerance. To the seventeenth-century Protestant zealot such views were anathema. Rome was the Antichrist, the Whore of Babylon.

Charles, like his archbishop, was subjected to the unjust but fatal smear of popery. For had he tried seriously to convert his queen to Protestantism or to curb her recruitment of Catholic converts? Why was he so affable to the papal envoy George Con, whose very presence at court was offensive to firm Protestants? It was true that, like Laud, Charles rigorously exacted recusancy fines on Catholics, but was this not merely to raise money; and did not Catholic priests get off suspiciously lightly? Even the king's aesthetic tastes exposed him to suspicion, for the art of Italy and the southern Netherlands which he loved had a decidedly Catholic flavour and iconography. William Prynne, that vigilant detector of popery, saw the royal collection as evidence of a plot to 'seduce the king . . . with pictures, antiquities, images and other vanities brought from Rome'.

Charles's commitment to Laud was perhaps his greatest political mistake. How successful was his personal rule in other respects? The urgent need for administrative reform persisted, but so did the financial and political constraints which had thwarted it in the previous decades. The wars of the 1620s left a heavy legacy of debt, which ate into the crown's ordinary revenue of the 1630s when the government was obliged to borrow in order to repay. In 1637 the anticipations of the revenue for repayment of debt were around £315,000, a sum even higher than that at the end of the war seven years earlier. The burden had mounted

69. John Lilburne 'whipped after the cart's tail' in 1637.
Contemporary engraving.
In 1637 the London apprentice John Lilburne was accused before the Court of Star Chamber of printing radical Puritan books. Lilburne's ability to dramatize his grievances – a trait which was to be turned against Puritan governments in the 1640s and 1650s – made the trial a cause célèbre, *and placed Lilburne's name alongside those of William Prynne, Henry Burton and John Bastwick among the martyrs of Caroline and Laudian absolutism. He was whipped from the Fleet to Palace Yard, and put in the pillory. In the 1640s Lilburne led the Levellers; in the 1650s he became a Quaker.*

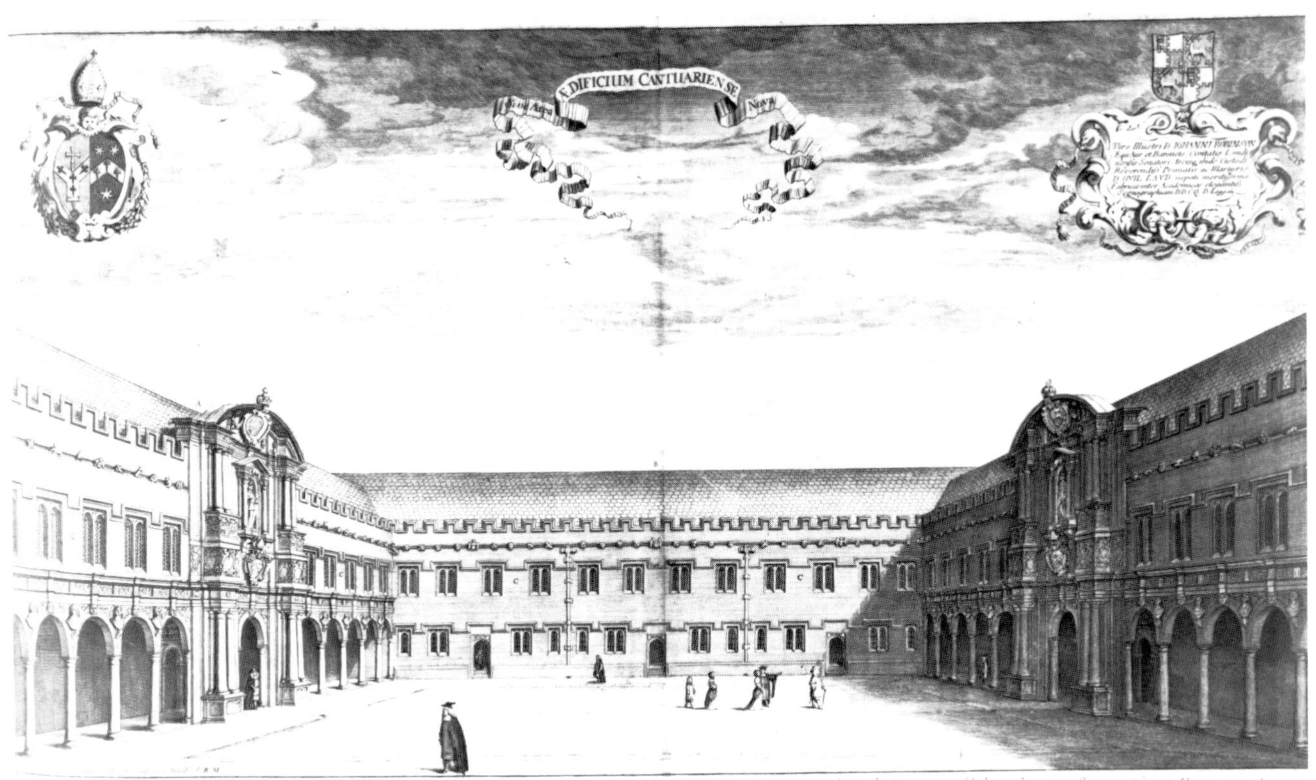

70. The Laudian Quadrangle at St. John's College, Oxford. Engraving by D. Loggan.
In 1630 Laud resolved 'to build at St. John's in Oxford, where I was bred up, for the good and safety of that college'. Canterbury Quadrangle was completed by 1636, when during a ceremonious royal visit to Oxford it was shown to the king and queen, who were represented by impressive bronze statues by Hubert le Sueur above the colonnades. The quadrangle is Gothic in design, classical in decoration. Control of the universities was essential to control of the Church. In Oxford and Cambridge alike, Arminians were promoted to high office by Laud and Charles. Laud, who had been President of St. John's under James I, reformed the statutes of the university in the 1630s. The nineteenth-century historian Carlyle wrote of him that in public life he remained confined by the mentality of 'a college tutor'.

in spite of increases in the ordinary revenue achieved during the decade. The most remunerative innovation was the conversion of Ship Money from an emergency tax on coastal regions to a regular levy on the whole country. The tax yielded £730,000 between 1634 and 1640 and the money was devoted to necessary improvements of the navy. Other financial expedients devised by the government during these years were the enhancement of income from wardship and monopolies; the levying of fines for the encroachment on what had once been (in some cases centuries earlier) royal forests; and the equally archaic levy of fines on gentlemen worth £40 a year who had failed to present themselves for knighthood at Charles's coronation.

The government's money-raising techniques were as unpopular as they were ingenious; and the regime's financial difficulties vitiated all its attempts at reform. Commissions were set up to examine excessive fees paid to officials (who could reasonably reply that they needed them, for their stipends had not kept pace with inflation), to investigate the erection of new buildings in London contrary to royal proclamation and to enquire into depopulation caused by the enclosure of common land. But the usual outcome of at least the first two of these initiatives was not a cure of the abuses, but the licensing of offenders who thus bought their way out of trouble. In other spheres reform was often stillborn or else lost its impetus. The crown knew that if it were to acquire effective control over its officials it would need to convert the occupancy of many office-holders from life-tenure to tenure during the royal pleasure. Yet only the most tentative steps were taken towards so major a challenge to vested interests. Campaigns of economy in the royal Household, Wardrobe, Armoury and Ordinance were energetic in the early years of personal rule, less so thereafter. In local government the Privy Council instituted in 1631 a more rigorous supervision of JPs and more thorough-going instructions for poor relief and for the control of vagrancy and food supplies, but these measures derived less from long-term thinking than from the govern-

'A Precedent Fit for Posterity to Imitate'

JOHN HARRISON AND ST JOHN'S CHURCH, LEEDS

John Harrison was a prominent wool merchant in early seventeenth-century Leeds. The Harrisons and families such as the Skeltons, Hilarys, Cookes and Marshalls were part of a merchant and manufacturing oligarchy in a town whose main business was the making, dyeing and finishing of cloth made from Dales wool. It was a place of thriving business and a growing population of 6,000.

The ruling families were central to the town's spiritual and institutional life as well as to its business prosperity. In the early Stuart period Leeds, once a royal manor, was still establishing its municipal independence. Under James I and Charles I there were three landmarks in that development. In 1619 a Pious Uses Committee was established to administer the town charities, which were allegedly being embezzled by the crown bailiff. Then in 1625 Leeds obtained a charter of incorporation from the crown. Thirdly, in 1629 a syndicate bought up the crown's manorial rights and freed the town from its subjection to the royal bailiff. The men dominating these steps towards municipal freedom were from the merchant oligarchy. John Harrison was distinguished among them for the extent of his Christian charity.

Harrison had invested his wool profits in property, giving surpluses from his rents to charity and maintaining storerooms with food and clothing for the poor. His appealing generosity generated stories around him like the one which related that as a child he had given his cloak to a beggar. In 1647 it was reported that he had presented a tankard of gold to the imprisoned Charles I. His communal grants were prodigious and from the 1620s he developed a whole new street north of the Headrow (see map). There he built new accommodation for the Grammar School at a cost of £300, and extensive almshouses opposite it. Alongside the almshouses Harrison proposed to build St John's Church, which would create a large religious-educational complex for the newly incorporated Leeds.

The need for a new church in the town centre was real. There were 5,000 potential communicants numbered in the opening years of the century, for whom the parish church of St Peter and its subordinate chapels could hardly have been sufficient. Harrison's proposed foundation was in the tradition of the lay endowment of chapels and preaching ministers as an expression of piety and an instrument of social discipline designed to reduce the threat of social unrest. His initiative came at a time of reli-

1 Exterior of St John's, Leeds before nineteenth-century remodelling. From Thoresby, *Ducatus Leodiensis*, (1715).
The strapwork on the porch is now lost. Note Harrison's almshouses behind the Church.

2 Portrait of Archbishop Neile of York. St John's College, Cambridge.
Neile had great difficulty in dealing with large northern parishes where reform was needed, but where it tended to be provided by Puritans.

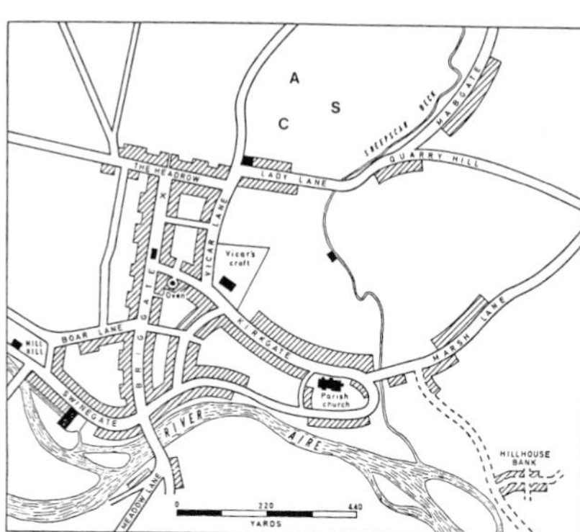

3 Early seventeenth-century Leeds, from *Leeds and Its Region*, British Association for the Advancement of Science (1967), based on a reconstruction of Leeds in 1612 by Prof. D. Ward.
The letters A, C and S show the approximate location of Harrison's almshouses, church and school.
Leeds had ten out-townships, but in the centre there was only one church, St Peter's, until Harrison developed the area north of the Headrow from the 1620s.

gious tension in Leeds. The Laudian Archbishop of York, Richard Neile, was unhappy about the large parish with its outchapelries and about the increasingly Puritan outlook of both its priests and its people. The attitude of the Church to an endowment like Harrison's was mixed. On the one hand, such pious public spirit in the provision of facilities for worship could hardly be opposed, for Leeds needed those facilities and only laymen were able to pay for them; yet at the same time, lay philanthropy weakened the clergy's control. And what if the provision were Puritan? This was Archbishop Neile's dilemma when faced by Harrison's generosity.

The dilemma was compounded by the proximity of St John's to St Peter's. Neile saw the danger of rivalry between the two churches in an area where religious passions were easily aroused. He also feared that the Puritans might take over both churches. Harrison's nephew Henry Robinson, recently Vicar of Leeds, was a Puritan, and Harrison proposed to appoint as minister to the new church the Vicar of Ledsham, Robert Todd, reader at St Peter's and a notorious leader of the 'godly' there. For the future it was decided that the Vicar, the Alderman (mayor) and three members of the Corporation should act as patrons to St John's. It looked as if Leeds would be dominated by two Puritan churches, both supported by the town's leading philanthropist.

The consecration of St John's took place on 31 September 1634. Neile took the precaution of sending his chaplain, the Laudian John Cosin, to deliver the consecration sermon on the text, 'Let all things be done decently and in order'. That was in the morning. In the afternoon, Todd preached, flatly contradicting what Cosin had said. It looked as if Neile's fears were fully justified.

But is the label 'Puritan' pinned too easily? Sometimes it obscures complexities and shifts of loyalty. By the 1650s, when Church and king had been destroyed, Harrison was writing to Todd regretting his patronage: 'Time was when you called me patron and remembered me in your prayers, but now patrons are out of date and so many churches be tithe barns. To pray for any in public is (called) popish and prelatic: the time was when I suffered for you under the royal party, more than you will suffer for me under the parliament but oh! the times.' Harrison's moderate Puritanism, which wished to reform the Church from within rather than overthrow it, had been overtaken by national events.

St John's itself throws uncertain light on Harrison's religious views. In one sense it is a very 'Protestant' church, open and double-naved, built in an old-fashioned, Yorkshire, late Gothic style with nave and south aisle of equal width within a parallelogram and with a western tower attached. In exterior appearance it is like the parish churches of Wakefield and Halifax; but

4 Interior of St John's today.

inside, the church is unusual – and un-Protestant – with its column carvings of acanthus and ball ornament, and its oak roof with carved corbels and plastered ceiling of roses, oak-leaves, acorns and vines. The screen separates the chancel from the nave in an entirely 'Laudian' manner and is accompanied by sumptuous pews. Carvings of scrolls, diamonds, circles and obelisks and balusters with Ionic capitals may be of provincial workmanship, but their designs come from Serlio and from German and Flemish pattern books. This is not at all the accepted idea of Puritan decor. The church's plan was 'open' for the active lay participation in worship that Puritans liked, but the chancel was separated from the congregation, a feature which suggests a sacramental view of the services and is reminiscent of a church like St Katherine Cree in London, which was consecrated by Laud himself. It may be that the designs at St John's were by Francis Gunby, who was hired to work at nearby Templenewsam by Harrison's courtier friend, Sir Arthur Ingram. If so, that might explain the metropolitan decor in the church. Gunby had also carved the screen at Wakefield and Leeds would not have wished to be outdone. Its screen furnishings were to be the best that money could buy and fashion achieve.

The church survives, sadly redundant, as a puzzling tribute to its patron. Harrison died aged 77 in 1656, and the entry in the parish register for 1 November of that year lists his benefactions, 'a precedent fit for posterity to imitate'.

5 Detail of screen in the chancel, St John's. An aura of Flemish Baroque is conveyed by the sophisticated wood carving.

6 Watercolour by Norman Shaw of the interior of St John's, Leeds in 1865. Reproduced from D. Linstrum, *West Yorkshire, Architects and Architecture*, Lund Humphries, 1978.
Shaw was responsible for restoring the Church in the last century and for saving much of the woodwork.

ment's alarm at the economic distress prevalent at the start of the decade and at the outbreak of food riots in the west country; once the hardship had passed, so did the government's reforming energy.

Without a parliament, critics of government policy had no national forum for the expression of opposition. But outlets for discontent remained. Grand Juries could present the grievances of their counties in petitions; Puritan leaders could meet in the town and country houses of such peers as the Earls of Bedford and Warwick; the great London chartered companies could discuss the sour fruits of their cooperation with the crown; and the Corporation of London could organize itself for the acrimonious legal and financial battles it fought with the crown in the 1630s. Three new companies for transatlantic trade and colonization – the Massachusetts Bay Company founded in 1628 and the Providence Island and Saybrooke Companies founded in 1630 – were at least as significant as centres where militant Puritans and leading parliamentarians of 1628–9 could gather as they were as contributions to commerce and colonization, spheres in which the Massachusetts Bay Company alone had significant success.

Grievances persisting from the 1620s were joined by fresh ones. Although the exigencies of war, which had brought unpopular pressure by central on local government in the 1620s, had passed, tension was created in the localities by the crown's determination to make the county militias more efficient. Lords Lieutenants and their deputies harried magistrates and employed muster-masters whose operations had to be financed by the communities affected by them and who roused constitutional anxieties by removing control of the militia from the local gentlemen who had traditionally run it. Its interference in the traditional ways of the counties was a significant source of the government's unpopularity. Thus Ship Money was disliked not only because it was a non-parliamentary tax, but because its assessment tampered with customary systems of local ratings. Yet in spite of John Hampden's stand against Ship Money in the famous case in the Court of Exchequer in 1637, the yield of the tax did not fall spectacularly until 1639. Then the levy was widely resisted not only by the people who paid it, but by under-officers of sheriffs responsible for its collection. The breakdown of Ship Money owed less to events in England than to developments outside it. For England was at war again and Ship Money was one of a number of rapidly accumulating burdens on the localities.

War with the Scots and the End of Personal Rule, 1638–1640

This time England's enemy was not France or Spain, but the Scots who had rebelled against the ecclesiastical innovations introduced by Charles into his northern kingdom. For the king's High-Church policies were still more hated in Scotland, where Presbyterianism had been established in the previous century, than in England. Charles's father had succeeded in reviving episcopacy in Scotland, but only in a weaker form than its English counterpart. Deprived of a resident dynasty since the Stuart acquisition of England, Scots viewed Charles's attempt of 1637 to impose a prayer book modelled on the English one as an assault upon their national as well as their religious identity. There were riots in Edinburgh and in 1638 Scottish Presbyterians flocked in their thousands to sign a National Covenant defending their religion against what they regarded as neo-papist subversion – a view shared by English Puritans, some of whom saw in the Scottish troubles a means by which Laudianism might be brought down in England. The General Assembly of the Scottish Church in 1638, filled with men who had taken the Covenant, not only annulled Charles's recent innovations but declared the abolition of episcopacy.

Only by military force could Charles now hope to impose his policies on Scotland. His decision to use it was a critical moment in the history both of Scotland and of England. His attempted invasion of the northern kingdom in the 'First Bishops' War' proved a fiasco, and when the Scots threatened a counter-invasion Charles was obliged to accept a cessation of hostilities at the Treaty of Berwick in June 1639. At least the treaty gave the king a breathing space in which to husband resources for a fresh offensive, but the truth was that his mobilization of an army, which had roused great discontent in England, had also stretched his financial resources to breaking point.

It is not inconceivable that there would have been a civil war in England even without Charles's calamitous blunders in Scotland: that (say) rebellion might eventually have been provoked had Buckingham not been removed by assassination in 1628, or had Laudianism had time to provoke still deeper hostility in England. Even so, when the personal rule collapsed in 1640 no one in England yet thought in terms of civil war. The king's policies and advisers were widely hated, but the institution of monarchy was still revered. In April 1640, when Charles at last summoned a parliament, he approached it in a sanguine mood hoping to secure from it the financial support that would enable him to dictate terms to the Scots. His optimism was probably encouraged by Wentworth, whom Charles had brought back from Ireland as a strong man to resolve the crisis and whom he was shortly to elevate to the earldom of Strafford.

In any event the parliament – the Short Parliament as it came to be called – proved far more interested in redressing long-term grievances than in aiding the king's Scottish policy. It was quickly dissolved. In August Scottish invaders put the English to rout at Newburn on the Tyne and occupied Newcastle. Charles secured peace only by the Treaty of Ripon, which left the Scottish army in possession of most of England north of the Tees and obliged the crown to pay £850 per day for its upkeep until a permanent peace had been concluded. Next, he summoned a council of peers for advice and in September resolved to summon the parliament – the Long Parliament as it was to be – that met in November. In calling it, Charles was still aiming principally to raise the money with which to reduce the Scots to obedience. But the men who met in that parliament, and probably even some of the king's own councillors, had other ideas. The Long Parliament presented a challenge to Charles's policies far more profound than that which its predecessor had offered six months earlier; and on Charles's response to that challenge the fate of two nations depended.

71. A. Van Dyck, *Charles I in Three Positions*, 1635.
Oil on canvas, $33\frac{1}{4} \times 39\frac{1}{4}$ in. (84.5 × 99.7 cm.).
Windsor Castle, Royal Collection.
This work, probably begun in 1635, was sent to Rome the following year as the model for a bust commissioned by Charles. When the bust arrived in England in 1637 it was admired 'not only for the exquisiteness of the work but the likeness and near resemblance it had to the king's countenance'; it was destroyed by the fire at Whitehall Palace in 1698.

Englands Miraculous Preſervation Emblematically Deſcribed, Erected for a perpetuall *MONVMENT* to Poſterity.

THis Ark cal'd Union hath not her Peer
On Earth, & 's laden with a fraught ſo dear
To her Almighty Pilot, that no waves
Of might or malice rais'd b' infernal ſlaves
Of human ſhape and lofty high eſtate,
Nor yet their father that inveterate
Old Serpent raging 'gainſt this bleſſed Bark
The *Antitype* of righteous *Noahs* Ark
Can make to ſink or ſplit upon the rocks
Of ruine, maugre all their furious knocks
Of powdered bals, and force of armed ſteel
By violence to make this *Ark* to feel
Their wrathful open rage, when neither plots
Nor treacheries faſt tyed with the knots
Of vows, and Sacraments of miracles,
Impoſtures, fachinations, and ſpels,
Eſpouſed intereſts of Potentates
Forraign and home-bred Soldiers, and Prelates;
Threats, Promiſes, and Proteſtations,
Aulick Libels, Lyes, and Defamations,
Nor all the cunning, ſtudy, pains, and ſweat
Of all Malignant Foxes ſmal, and great;
In Court, and Campe, City, and Countrie,
Nor in this *Ark* (if any lurking lie)
Can break this Churches Trinity of State
Deſcribed here, nor make them violate
That pious Covenant, which holds them faſt,
And is indeed that Veſſels maineſt Maſt,
By which ſhe ſaileth through the troubled ſeas
Of her affairs; and now hath found ſome eaſe,
Thanks be unto that heavenly Cynoſure
Above the Stars, which gives a light t' allure
Her Mariners, and yet wil give light more
T' unfold the ſecrets of the *Romiſh* Whore,
The helliſh darkneſs of thoſe miſts and foggs
Of blaſphemies, and errors, which thoſe froggs
Or unclean Spirits from the Beaſt proceeding
(whoſe thoughts upon Reformers blood are feeding)
Have now unbowelled, and ſpread about
To put the light of *Reformation* out,
And with new *Hydra*-headed hereſies
(Like to that ſmoke) t' obſcure the cleareſt skies
Of ſacred Truth (a devilliſh deſigne
More dangerous, then was the Powder-Myne)
And raiſe tempeſtuous ſtorms about this *Ark*,
And now they cannot beat by force, they *bark*
Belch, and diſgorge their *Stygian* deſpight
'Gainſt the Protector of this *Ark* outright;
And ſtil their horrid rage doth more abound
Becauſe this *Ark* of Union is not drown'd;
But wait a while, and ſee this curſed crew
Pertake of that reward, that's here in view:
For fix your eyes upon theſe Seas of ire
Involving thoſe, that did 'gainſt th' *Ark* conſpire:
See here ſome headleſſe floating in the waves
Of direful death, ſome dead, and wanting graves:
See all their warlike Engines, and their Forces,
Now as feeble as their liveleſs Corſes;
See theſe bloody men and their Commiſſion
To kil Innocents brought to perdition;
And they that living yet thought it no ſin
To leave this *Ark*, now wiſh they had kept in;
But now they are the ſcorn of time, and fate,
Who did this toſſed Bark deſpiſe, and hate,
Augmented more in that they did remove
The Royal Steers-man, whom our *Ark* doth love.
But ſee theſe noble Champions (lately ſix)
Guarding th' aſſaulted Union, and fix
Themſelves to courage, valor, care, and love
To bring to reſt this toſſed *Turtle*-dove.
Their brave atchievements *Chronicles* ſhal ſpeak,
And learned Volumes; but my pen's too weak
To tel their worth, or their due praiſes ſpread,
Whom great *JEHOVAH* hath ſo honored.
Draw neer, kind Reader, do but view this peece,
'Tis not of *Jaſon*, nor of his Golden fleece
That here is *Emblem'd*, nor the high renown
Of *Hectors* Acts ere *Troy* was battered down,
That here we ſhew you, but it doth preſage
A watry Landskip of a weeping Age.
The *Ark* that rideth here whoſe tender *Wals*
Contains in her our *Engliſh Admirals*,
For *Reformation* ſwimming on the Main,
'Gainſt Superſtition which ſo much did raign:
Charge on, charge on, the guard of *Pluto* al,
The *Pope*, the *Biſhop*, and the *Cardinal*:
But you had beſt retire, 'tis all but vain,
For *truth* hath gotten higher, and ſhe wil raign.
Here Reader pauſe, and judge our Land is free,
A Chronicle for our poſteritie;
For *God* hath brought them, lo their pride doth ſwage
And we made happy in a peaceful Age.
Had not the *LORD* bin for us, they had won,
And cloth'd this Land with red confuſion;
But now ſail on you worthies through the Ocean
Of ſad diſtempers, let your winged Motion
Out pace the flight of Egles, that aſpire
Go take your Senſers fil'd with zealous fire:
Let *truth* cōmand the way, by her the *Ark* is guided,
And let the *Goſpel* ſway, and *Errors* be avoyded:
Great *God* of wind & ſea, who ſearcheſt thro' the dark
Who didſt command old *Noah* to enter in the Ark,
Direct this *ARK* unto the Key of peace,
Command deliverance that our Wars may ceaſe.

An Apoſtrophe to the Church.

THen woman thou whoſe clothing is the Sun,
Ceaſe to complain, nor ſay thou art undone;
For thou haſt ſuffered harder things of yore,
Than now; weigh with the preſent times before.
Seeſt thou not how thy ſad and heavy night
Of fears and ſorrows now are vaniſht quite:
Triumphing days thy late griefs do beguile,
And *Halcyon* times begin again to ſmile.
Behold how rugged *Mars* is poſting hence,
Seeing thee armed ſo with heav'ns defence:
Outward enmity ſhal not hurt a jot,
If thine inteſtine Errors hurt thee not.
Then wipe thy blubbered face, and lay aſide
Thy mourning weeds, and like a loving Bride
With ſpirit mounted on a heav'nly flame
Spread abroad thy Bridegrooms glorious fame;
What tongue of mortal, men or *Seraphim*
Can tel ſufficiently the praiſe of *him*.

By *John Leceſter*.

LONDON, Printed for *John Hancock*, and are to be ſold at his ſhop, at the entrance into *Popes-head* Ally. 1646.

CHAPTER FOUR

The Civil Wars 1640–1649

The Challenge from Parliament, 1640–1641

When the Long Parliament met in November 1640, the political situation had changed dramatically even in the six months since Charles had dissolved the Short Parliament. The humiliating Scottish victory on the Tyne should have shown him how little most Englishmen supported his quarrel with the Scots. The collapse of Ship Money and other non-parliamentary sources of finance in the face of a national tax strike left his revenue in ruins. The Scottish army remained in occupation of northern England and the English Parliament had both to find the £850 per day that Charles had agreed to pay it and to finance the English forces that stood facing it.

The calling of the parliament was very popular and more of the people were involved in the elections than ever before. To an unprecedented extent candidates appealed to their constituents on major national issues. The Commons themselves encouraged this politicization of the electorate. In town constituencies, which accounted for over four-fifths of the House, members elected on a traditional narrow franchise were frequently challenged by others elected by a more popular vote. By 1640–41 the Commons regularly settled the dispute in favour of the latter, assuming that every adult male inhabitant had a vote unless there was a statute to the contrary. The outcome was a severe defeat for the court. Less than half as many royal servants were returned as in James I's first parliament and even the king's candidate for the Speaker's chair lost his election. Out of just over 500 original members, 80 was about the maximum whose connections aligned them with the court and the House expelled 16 of those as monopolists or for other unacceptable activities.

Charles so completely misjudged the nation's temper that he counted on this parliament to support him in prosecuting his war against the Scots. The fact that it took him a month to realize his error shows how feeble a grasp he had of political realities. The great majority in both Houses could agree that they had four main tasks besides finding money: to remove and punish the 'evil counsellors' who had sustained the personal rule; to reverse the Laudian innovations in religion; to pass legislation that would make non-parliamentary government henceforth impossible; and to persuade the king to appoint ministers and councillors whom parliament could trust. The prevailing temper was conservative. Members thought that England was uniquely fortunate in her ancient constitution and that they had only to prune away some relatively recent abuses and excrescences to make her happy again. They were more divided over religion, for the Laudian regime had provoked an unhappy polarization in the Church; but the majority would probably have settled for retaining its episcopal government and its much-loved liturgy without drastic change. The idea that they might embark on a civil war within two years would have shocked them immeasurably. Royalists and parliamentarians did not yet exist as parties; the very words as we know them had not yet entered the language. If anyone had been asked in 1640 whether he was a royalist or a parliamentarian, his puzzled answer might have been that he was both.

There was the nucleus of a leadership in both Houses in a group of Puritan peers and MPs who had been associated in colonizing ventures of the 1630s, especially the Providence Island Company. They included the Earl of Warwick, the Earl of Holland, Viscount Saye and Sele, and Lord Brooke in the Lords, John Pym, John Hampden, Oliver St John, Sir Benjamin Rudyerd and a dozen others in the Commons. Pym had increasingly made his mark in the parliaments of the 1620s as a champion of constitutional rights and an implacable opponent of Arminianism, and he was now advancing to a position of leadership among the more responsible opponents of the court. He gained it largely through his eloquence, his burning conviction and his command of parliamentary tactics, but also through the special patronage of the influential Earl of Bedford and his circle, whose spokesman he was in the Commons.

72. *England's Miraculous Preservation Emblematically Described,* a Puritan pamphlet of 1646.
The king, the queen, Laud and Strafford are among the royalists who struggle in the water while the parliamentary ark is guided to safety by its leaders. Encircled at the top and bottom are the leaders of the parliamentary armies of the civil war. Puritans repeatedly saw a divinely intended significance in parallels between contemporary political developments and the events of the Old Testament, and were attracted by the idea of an ark of the covenant between God and his chosen in England.

The role of the peers in the politics of the Long Parliament has generally been underestimated.

It was Pym who led the Commons in impeaching Strafford, and Laud followed his friend to the Tower on 1 March 1641. Other pillars of the personal rule such as the Lord Keeper Sir John Finch and Secretary of State Sir Francis Windebank escaped impeachment by flight. In February Charles gave his reluctant assent to the Triennial Act, which breached his prerogative right to summon parliaments only when he pleased. The act provided that no more than three years should ever elapse without a parliament meeting and that after three years a parliament should assemble even if the crown had failed to summon one. Yet the measure illustrates the conservative instincts of a parliament which cited medieval precedents in support of the act, and which (here as elsewhere) aimed not to innovate but rather to secure the constitutional balance that it believed the personal rule to have undermined. There were few omens yet of the radical changes to come. In March and April 1642, when Strafford was subjected to a great show-trial in Westminster Hall, it steadily became clear that the Commons' charges of treason were not going to convince the Lords, his judges. That was just, because whatever Strafford had committed, it was not treason. A more extreme faction than Pym's, led by Sir Arthur Hesilrige, dropped the impeachment in favour of an act of attainder, which did not require Strafford's conviction by due process of law but simply pronounced him guilty and sentenced him to death.

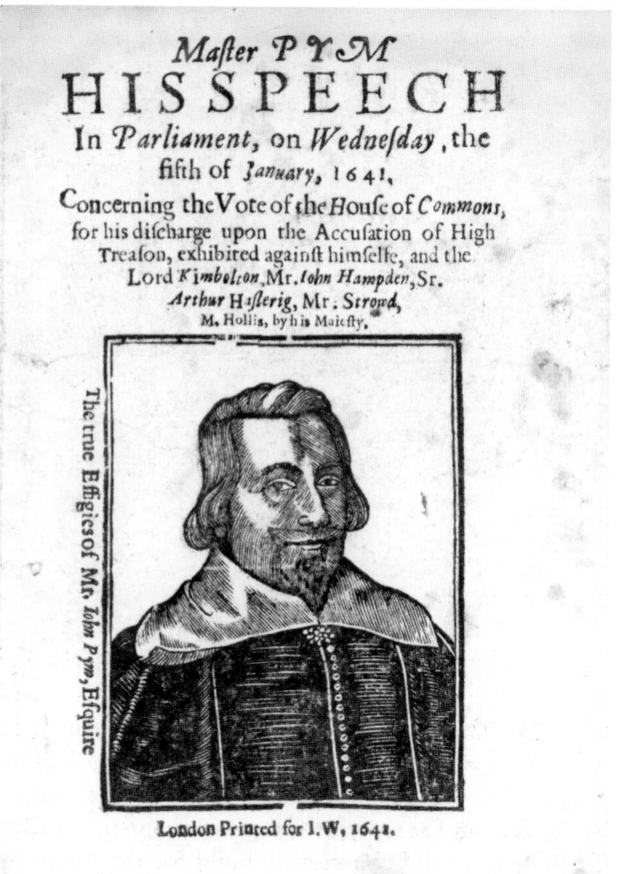

Master PYM
HIS SPEECH
In *Parliament*, on *Wednesday*, the
fifth of *January*, 1641,
Concerning the Vote of the *House* of *Commons*,
for his discharge upon the Accusation of High
Treason, exhibited against himselfe, and the
Lord *Kimbolton*, Mr. *Iohn Hampden*, Sr.
Arthur H*asterig*, Mr. *Strowd*,
M. Hollis, by his Maiesty.

The true Effigies of Mr. *Iohn Pym*, Esquire

London Printed for I. W, 1642.

73. A printed speech by John Pym (1642; 1641 old style).
Pym was one of the foremost politicians of the parliamentary party, which he helped to hold together as its divisions emerged. His death in 1643, at a black time for the parliamentary war effort, was a grave blow to it. Like other members of the Long Parliament he published his speeches in order to appeal to a wider audience. Here he remonstrates against the king's attempt to arrest the five members in January 1642. In the seventeenth century the year was normally taken to begin on 25th March rather than 1 January; we would date the pamphlet 1642.

This was countering tyranny with tyranny and it produced the first serious split in both Houses. The Commons passed the attainder by 204 votes to 59, the Lords by only 26 to 19 – and only after Pym had made out, with careful timing and on flimsy evidence, that Charles was prepared to use his northern forces and the Tower garrison against the parliament. Many MPs and peers absented themselves rather than be parties to the attainder, but few were brave enough to oppose it. Indeed the 59 'Straffordians' were put in fear for their lives by the great crowds that, orchestrated by the parliamentary leadership, now filled the streets baying for Strafford's blood. This was a new element in politics, and it was fear of what the mob might do to the queen that made Charles, in utter misery, assent to the act. As at every crisis of confidence in these years there was intense suspicion of a popish plot close to the throne, and Pym exploited rumours of Henrietta Maria's involvement in plans for a military coup against parliament and for the calling in of French troops.

Strafford's execution was a tragedy on more than a personal level, since it made it much harder for the king and the parliamentary leaders to come to terms. Bedford and his allies had an ambitious plan for putting the king's revenues on a sound and regular footing in return for Bedford's own appointment as Lord Treasurer, Pym's as Chancellor of the Exchequer, St John's as Solicitor-General and other places for their friends. Bedford was willing to see Strafford's life spared, but he contracted smallpox at a critical moment and the Earl of Essex's hard line against the earl – 'Stone dead hath no fellow', he said – carried the Lords. Bedford died on the very day that Charles gave way. Whether he could have saved Strafford is uncertain; still more, whether his scheme would have worked. It might have foundered upon Charles's reluctance to accept any limitations and upon the Commons' reluctance to face up to the basic cost of government. Nevertheless the only hope of a return to normality rested on Charles's willingness to appoint ministers and

74. The Trial of Strafford, 1641. Contemporary engraving.
Strafford, in the dock, faces his judges. The king and queen watch at the far end in the boxes to Strafford's left.

councillors whom parliament could trust and with whom he could work. He had shown some readiness to do this in February when he added six reformist peers including Essex and Saye and Sele to the Privy Council, but after May he almost gave up trying. Feeling guilt over Strafford's death himself, he could not do business with those who had the man's blood on their hands.

On the same day that he bowed to the attainder, Charles also assented to a brief act whereby the present parliament could not be dissolved without its own consent. The object was merely to strengthen parliament's credit for the huge loans that it was raising, and no one foresaw that the assembly would sit for twelve more years and even return to power in 1659–60. But the parliament did consciously build for the future in the series of constitutional measures that it enacted between June and August. These abolished the prerogative courts of Star Chamber and High Commission, brought all customs duties, new and old, firmly under parliamentary control, and outlawed Ship Money and all the other financial expedients of the thirties. All these acts claimed a basis in ancient law and all were to survive the restoration of the monarch in 1660. Collectively they restricted the royal prerogative very considerably and Charles assented to them only because he had to do so.

Those statutes raised little controversy, but religion was already arousing much more. All MPs could agree in denouncing popish plots and Arminian innovations; the rift lay between those who wanted simply to restore the latitudinarian Anglicanism which they remembered from the later years of James I, and those who thought that the time had come at last for a thorough reformation. The latter welcomed the Root and Branch Petition which was presented in December 1640 over the names of 15,000 London citizens and was followed by similar mass petitions from nineteen counties. It called for the abolition of bishops and of the whole Church hierarchy 'root and branch', and condemned the Book of Common Prayer as 'framed out of the Romish Breviary, Rituals [and] Mass-book'.

Several currents besides these mass petitions raised the religious temperature during 1641. One gushed from the pulpits, and especially from the marathon sermons that well-known Puritan divines preached to parliament on the days that it set aside for fasting and humiliation. Another flowed from the Scottish ministers who came to London with the commissioners sent by their country to treat with Charles and who proselytized for Presbyterianism. But the most potent current was that of millenarianism. For over twenty years there had been growing interest in the biblical prophecies about the 'last times', particularly those promising the overthrow of Antichrist and the thousand-year rule of Christ's saints that would ensue before Christ himself returned in majesty to pronounce the Last Judgement and bring the world's history to an end. For nearly eighty years Englishmen had been taught by John Foxe's *Book of Martyrs* to identify Antichrist with the Pope, and one complaint of the London Root and Branch Petition was that the Arminians had dared to doubt that tenet of Protestant orthodoxy. The rapid overthrow of ecclesiastical tyranny, lately in Scotland and now in England, coupled with the heavy blows to the Catholic cause in the Thirty Years War, especially since the revolts of Catalonia and Portugal in 1640, suggested that the downfall of Antichrist had begun and that England was to play a glorious part in it, as Foxe had promised. In this hope, the poet Milton laid aside his deeply felt vocation to write a great Christian epic so that he could advance the anti-episcopal cause with his pen.

But would parliament take a radical line? In May 1641 the Commons was pursuing the limited objective of excluding the bishops from the Lords, but when the upper House refused to consider such a measure the Commons, in anger, gave two readings to a Root and Branch bill for abolishing bishops altogether. They were deeply divided over it, however. They debated it weekly all through the summer, but it was still not ready when the first session ended on 9 September, so it lapsed. It may have failed more through lack of time than lack of support, but it would not have passed a full House of Lords.

Most peers and MPs ended this longest session in parliament's history in sober hope. A treaty had been concluded with the Scots, whose army had at last left English soil. The English army was being paid off as fast as money could be found. The Irish army, which Strafford had threatened to bring over, was at least partly disbanded, too, though ominously Charles had sent orders to halt the process. Arminianism was dead – even Charles had abandoned it – and a great series of statutes had remedied all the immediate constitutional grievances. *Détente* was in the air and with it a widespread hope of a fresh start.

Lurching into War, 1641–1642

Why did such a hope prove illusory? The answers lay in both Ireland and Scotland, but above all in the king. Instead of staying at Westminster, cultivating a certain reaction of feeling in his favour and concentrating on building a government of constitutional royalists as he might still have done, he set off for Scotland in August and stayed until mid-November. He could not bear to accept the new curbs on his prerogative as final. Since parliament had enacted them, however, only parliament could repeal them unless he could bring force to bear on it. From this time onward force was never far from his mind. He travelled north to explore the potential of a nascent royalist party among the Scottish nobility, but he won little but distrust for himself, despite conceding the abolition of episcopacy in Scotland and the Scottish Parliament's right of advice and consent in all appointments of councillors, judges and officers of state. He was to fight a civil war rather than make similar concessions in England.

While he was away a dreadful rebellion erupted in Ulster, the province so heavily subjected since 1609 to English and Scottish settlement. The native Irish whom the settlers had dispossessed, desperate at the English parliament's venom towards all things Catholic, rose *en masse* to recover their right to their lands and their faith. They slaughtered some thousands of Protestant settlers and reports soon exaggerated the 'massacre' fifty-fold. The rebel leaders proclaimed themselves the king's loyal subjects and exhibited a commission from him, purporting to authorize them to recover their lands. It was a forgery, but Charles's intrigues in Scotland and his suspicious contacts with Irish leaders made his complicity all too believable. The rebellion spread through Ireland like wildfire and in England it heated the fear of popery into a fever. No single event did more to set the stage for civil war.

Pym's leadership had lately been insecure, but the terrible news restored it. He carried the Commons in requesting the king to 'employ such counsellors and ministers as shall be approved by his Parliament', or they would take their own measures to recover Ireland. Soon after, they made their first moves towards asserting parliamentary control over the militia. These were to be two of the main issues of the civil war. On 22 November they passed the Grand Remonstrance, ostensibly an account of the state of the nation, but really a bitterly partisan indictment of fifteen years' alleged misgovernment which was all blamed upon a conspiracy of 'Jesuited Papists', corrupt bishops and

(7)

and preſumptuous Injuſtice of ſuch Miniſters as durſt break the Laws, and ſuppreſſe the Liberties of the Kingdom, after they had been ſo ſolemnly and evidently declared.

Another Parliament diſſolved, 4 *Car.* the priviledge of Parliament broken, by Impriſoning divers Members of the Houſe, detaining them cloſe priſoners for many moneths together, without the liberty of uſing Books, Pen, Inke, or Paper, denying them all the comforts of life, all means of preſervation of health, not permitting their wives to come unto them, even in time of their ſickneſſe. And for the compleating of that cruelty, after yeers ſpent in ſuch miſerable durance, depriving them of the neceſſary means of Spirituall conſolation, not ſuffering them to go abroad to enjoy Gods Ordinances, in Gods Houſe, or Gods Miniſters to come to them, to adminiſter comfort unto them in their private Chambers: and to keep them ſtill in this oppreſſed condition, not admitting them to be bayled according to Law, yet vexing them with Informations in inferiour Courts, ſentencing and fining ſome of them for matters done in Parliament, and extorting the payments of thoſe Fines from them, enforcing others to put in ſecurity of good behaviour, before they could be releaſed.

The impriſonment of the reſt which refuſed to be bound, ſtill continued; which might have been perpetuall, if neceſſity had not, the laſt yeer, brought another Parliament to relieve them; of whom, one died, by the cruelty and harſhneſſe of his impriſonment, which would admit of no relaxation, notwithſtanding the imminent danger of his life, did ſufficiently appear by the declaration of his Phyſitian: And his releaſe, or at leaſt, his refreſhment, was ſought by many humble Petitions. And his bloud ſtill cries either for vengeance, or repentance of thoſe Miniſters of State, who are at once obſtructed the courſe, both of his Majeſties Juſtice and Mercy.

Upon the diſſolution of both theſe Parliaments, untrue and ſcandalous declarations publiſhed, to aſperſe their proceedings, and ſome of their Members, unjuſtly to make them odious, and colour the violence which was uſed againſt them. Proclamations ſet out to the ſame purpoſe; and to the great dejecting of the harts of the people, forbidding them, even to ſpeak of Parliaments.

B 2 After

75. A page from *The Grand Remonstrance* (1641).
This was the document in which the leaders of the parliamentary opposition to Charles recounted the evils of his reign. Here it relates the events of 1629. The MPs who were then imprisoned included Sir John Eliot, who died in the Tower. A propaganda document, heavily biased, the Remonstrance passed the Commons only narrowly, but the image of Caroline rule which it created was to endure across the centuries.

clergy, and councillors and courtiers working for foreign powers. Yet the Grand Remonstrance passed the Commons only after fierce argument and by a bare eleven votes, and the Lords never passed it at all. A moderate royalist party was beginning to emerge that was anxious to preserve a balance between king, Lords and Commons, opposed to novel departures from the 'fundamental laws', deeply attached to the liturgy and government of the Church of England, and outraged by the parliamentary leadership's increasing use of the mob as an engine of political pressure. Ranged against this party were those who believed, with Pym, that the gains they had made so far would never be secure unless further constitutional constraints were imposed on the king.

Charles was deceived by the warmth of Edinburgh's farewell to him and of London's welcome on his return late in November. He gave several rash provocations in December, the worst being his appointment of a murderous bravo as Lieutenant of the Tower of London, whom he was forced to remove after three days for fear of a popular uprising. But his crowning folly was on 4 January 1642 when he led several hundred armed followers, or 'cavaliers', to the parliament-house and attempted to arrest five leading members. Persuaded that only a few malevolent spirits were perverting the parliament and that they were planning to impeach the queen, he had attempted to impeach them first, but the Lords had demurred at the unconstitutional procedure. The five escaped just in time. The Commons took refuge in the City, set up a committee of safety and prepared for armed resistance. The citizenry seemed on the brink of revolution and even the staid corporation had swung round to Pym's support. Finding his capital too hot for him, Charles left Whitehall on the 10th and the Commons returned to Westminster in triumph.

Charles's violent affront to parliament brought the two Houses closer together, for he had impeached a peer, the future Earl of Manchester, as well as the five MPs. In February the Lords passed a Commons' bill which excluded the bishops from the upper House and the clergy from all secular office. They also passed the Militia Bill to place all the trained bands in the counties, the only land forces then afoot in England, under parliamentary control. The king assented to the former but rejected the latter, whereupon the two Houses passed it as the Militia Ordinance and commanded all subjects to obey it, notwithstanding his refusal. If there was a single point at which civil war became inevitable it was on 15 March 1642 when parliament thus challenged both the king's share in the legislative process and his power over the ultimate sanction of the state, its armed forces. Who, he could ask, was breaching the fundamental laws now?

Charles's response was to withdraw to York and the polarization of the nation accelerated. His public declarations made an appealing case for him. They were largely drafted by men who had previously been his critics: chief among them Sir Edward Hyde (the future Earl of Clarendon), Hyde's friend Lord Falkland and Sir John Culpepper. In those declarations Charles stood forth as the defender of the Church of England against Puritan iconoclasts, as the guarantor of the ancient government by king, Lords and Commons against radical innovators, and as the upholder of the time-honoured ranks and orders of society against levelling mobs. Many country gentlemen, believing in all these things,were dismayed by the zeal with which Pym, Hampden, St John and their party in the Commons, and Saye and Sele, Warwick, Essex and others in the Lords advanced during the summer from claiming the militia to raising an army. The parliamentarians' reply was that they had been driven to extreme measures by a king who had become irresponsible, untrustworthy and incapable of the exercise of his office; for while his public utterances spoke the language of Hyde and Falkland, his actions spoke that of the queen, Lord Digby (a recent convert to ultra-royalism) and other high-flying cavaliers. On top of the affair of the five members, he encouraged a gathering of armed followers at Kingston-upon-Thames, planned to secure Portsmouth, sent the queen abroad to pawn the crown jewels and purchase arms, and attempted in person to seize the large magazine of arms in Hull. His continued contacts with Catholic powers kept alive the notion that behind his acts lay a popish plot.

In public argument the main points of contention concerned parliamentary control of the armed forces and of appointments to the king's government. But when men took sides, religion played a powerful part in determining their choices. The religious issue was not clearly defined; for the Grand Remonstrance had not directly threatened either episcopacy or the Prayer Book – it had merely called for a synod of divines to advise on reforms. As late as April 1642 parliament declared that it would abolish nothing in the government or liturgy of the Church but what was evil, unnecessary or burdensome. Yet when Charles summoned his supporters to join him at York, the effect was to leave the Root and Branch party in the majority at Westminster; and though many a moderate Anglican sided with parliament, a deep attachment to the faith and worship of *Ecclesia Anglicana* became one of the strongest motives for rallying to the king. Conversely, those now emerging as the most committed and militant parliamentarians were men such as Oliver Cromwell, Sir Henry Vane the younger and the Cheshire gentleman Sir William Brereton, who believed that a thorough reformation was needed to fit England for her promised role as an elect nation. Vane had recently returned from Massachusetts, where his championship of radical Puritanism had provoked a constitutional crisis in the infant colony. He was to be one of Cromwell's most intimate political allies.

Among less militant members there was often little difference of principle between moderate parliamentarians and constitutional royalists, especially as king and parliament professed to be standing for much the same things. Being alike mostly conservative, such moderates differed mainly as to whether they saw King Charles or 'King' Pym as the greater menace to the order that they wished to preserve. In more than half the English counties the gentry attempted, finally without success, to conclude local treaties of neutrality. Most towns and townsmen viewed the prospect of war with equal dismay and would have kept out of it if they could. Exceptions were found where the governing corporation was strongly Puritan, but there were also more royalist towns than used to be realized. Local circumstances and interests often coloured people's perceptions of the national issues: as in Wiltshire and Leicestershire, two counties in which many of the gentry chose sides according to which rival magnate they regarded as their patron; or as in Newcastle and Chester, where the king won support by granting commercial privileges to the ruling oligarchies. Recent detailed studies of particular counties and towns have shown how complex the pattern of allegiance could be and how unsafe it is to generalize about social or economic distinctions between royalists and parliamentarians. Such distinctions can quite often be found locally, but the social line of division could differ markedly between adjacent counties: between Northamptonshire and Leicestershire, for instance, and between Kent and Sussex. It still seems broadly true, however, though with large local exceptions, that rather more of the biggest landowners were royalist and that rather more of the middling sort of yeomen, lesser merchants and independent craftsmen were parliamentarian, especially in areas like the West Riding and south Lancashire and Somerset where cloth manufacture and Puritanism went together.

The First Civil War, 1642–1646

The summer of 1642 saw many contests for the control of territory between parliamentarian deputy lieutenants executing the Militia Ordinance and royalist commissioners executing the king's more archaic 'Commissions of Array'. When it came to raising effective forces, however, the armies were initially composed on both sides mainly of regiments and companies raised personally by colonels and captains who risked their fortunes for causes in which they deeply believed. Early on, a high proportion of the rank and file were volunteers. The king gave the signal for war by raising his standard at Nottingham on 22 August. At first it seemed touch and go whether he would raise an adequate army at all, but he emerged from the confused, indecisive battle of Edgehill on 23 October with one clear advantage: the road to London lay open to him. He was halted only by a massive turn-out of trained bands, apprentices and other volunteers at Turnham Green.

Parliament was badly shaken and an emerging peace party drove it into negotiating with the king on much easier terms than it had demanded in June. But Charles – now at Oxford, which was to be the royalist capital in the civil war – had sniffed the scent of victory and indeed the campaigns of 1643 almost won him the war. His nominal commander-in-chief the Earl of Forth (later Earl of Brentford) was a gouty, boozy old professional and a limited asset, and his initial appointment of six royalist magnates as lieutenant-generals of limited regions was not a success. But reorganization between July 1643 and April 1644 placed all Wales and the Marches under his German nephew Price Rupert and all the west and south-west under Rupert's brother Prince Maurice, leaving the Earl of Newcastle commanding the north-east down to Lincolnshire.

Parliament's Lord General, the Earl of Essex, was like Forth a somewhat slow and heavy man and he had far less military experience, but he was dogged in adversity and carried great weight in the Lords. He operated, not very effectively, against the king's army around Oxford; a smaller army under Sir William Waller, which opposed Maurice in the west and south, was initially more successful. An Eastern Association army was formed in East Anglia under the Earl of Manchester with Cromwell as lieutenant-general commanding the cavalry. In Yorkshire Lord Fairfax and his son Sir Thomas headed another small army, which gained control of the West Riding towns and joined hands with the parliamentarians in Hull. Of other local forces the most notable was Sir William Brereton's in Cheshire.

It was Sir Ralph Hopton – who had voted for Strafford's attainder and personally presented the Grand Remonstrance to the king – who launched the first great tide of royalist victories from Cornwall. The Militia Ordinance had turned this strongly Protestant, even Puritan country gentleman from a sharp critic of the court into a heroically active royalist. He triumphed at Bradock Down in January and at Stratton in May, then overran Devon and joined forces with Maurice. He mauled Waller's army at Lansdown on 5 July, and though badly wounded helped to destroy it at Roundway Down eight days later. The victors then joined Rupert in storming Bristol, and parliament reeled under the loss of England's second port. Gloucester soon lay under siege and a royalist rising in Kent briefly threatened London itself. Meanwhile Newcastle had routed the Fairfaxes at Adwalton Moor and was advancing to besiege them in Hull.

Parliament was thoroughly demoralized and Pym temporarily lost control of it. Two events in September, however, hushed the clamour for peace. Essex performed his finest military feat by leading a scratch army to the relief of Gloucester and saving it on its return march from the royalists' fierce onslaught at Newbury. Simultaneously, parliament's commissioners to the northern kingdom, Sir Henry Vane among them, concluded a treaty with the Scots, who realized that if the king was victorious their own turn would come next. But there was a price to pay for their promised army of 21,000 men besides its financial cost: the Church of England was to be brought into the closest possible conformity with the Presbyterian Kirk of Scotland. The terms were embodied in the Solemn League and Covenant, to which every adult male in both kingdoms was supposed to swear. The trouble was that most of the English people remained attached to Anglican worship and Church order and that, among critics of the Church, radical Puritanism had been taking other forms than Presbyterianism for over a generation.

At the same time the king, through his lieutenant the Marquis of Ormonde, concluded a truce known as the Cessation with the Catholic Confederation, which now controlled most of Ireland. The Cessation released a few thousand of the king's forces – Protestant and mainly English troops who had been resisting the Irish confederates – for service in England, but the military gain hardly compensated for the odium that Charles incurred through treating with Irish papists.

On 8 December Pym died of an internal abscess, perhaps as much a casualty of the war as Hampden and Falkland, who had both fallen in action. His patient management had laid the administrative foundations of future victory: the monthly assessments, the excise and the equally unpopular county committees which brought the money in and met the other local demands of war. The royalist war effort, though more systematically organized than used to be realized, was rarely as effective and in the long run it was more hated because it allowed less local partcipation. Pym's other great con-

'Here is Nothing but Providing of Arms'

THE OUTBREAK OF THE FIRST CIVIL WAR IN WARWICKSHIRE

1 Henry Paert after Cornelius Johnson and Van Dyck, *Spencer Compton, 2nd Earl of Northampton.* Oil on canvas, 49 × 40¼ in. (124.5 × 102.2 cm.). London, National Portrait Gallery.

2 Robert Greville, 2nd Lord Brooke. Engraving by R.S. London, National Portrait Gallery.

Three weeks before Charles I raised his standard at Nottingham in August 1642, the Warwickshire county community was, in effect, already at war. Leaders on both sides grasped the county's key geographical position in the centre of England. Robert Greville, second Baron Brooke, Speaker in the Lords and a vigorous opponent of the court and all its policies, was transferring the Banbury artillery to his castle at Warwick. Barring his path was Spencer Compton, second Earl of Northampton. Compton was as hot for the king as Brooke was cold. He was the king's Master of the Robes and had been Charles's friend since accompanying him on the Madrid wooing expedition of 1623. Brooke and Compton could not have been less alike. The earl, a courtier who knew where his duty and loyalty lay, was not a political animal. Brooke was.

Brooke was also a Puritan. In his youth he had undergone one of those conversion experiences that made Puritans of many seventeenth-century Englishmen. He had written spiritual treatises which pleaded for liberty of conscience and which influenced the development of Milton's ideas In the 1630s he promoted that centre of Puritan political opposition to the personal rule of Charles I, the Providence Island Company. In 1640 he helped negotiate the Treaty of Ripon which kept the Scottish army in England with English money. Northampton had opposed the Treaty and supported the king at York. The enmity of Northampton and Brooke guaranteed a bitter time for Warwickshire, for 'the county is like a cockpit spurring against each other'.

In every county in the summer of 1642 the decision men had to make was whether to obey parliament's Militia Ordinance and prepare to fight the king, or to respond to Charles's Commissions of Array and prepare to fight the parliament. Some counties tried to organize neutrality pacts that would keep the war outside their boundaries. In the villages of Warwickshire men found themselves approached both by Deputy Lieutenants brandishing the Militia Ordinance and by the Commissioners of Array. The inhabitants of Nether Whiteacre near Sutton Coldfield resolved their dilemma by reporting for training to both sides and hoping to fight for neither. Yet feelings in the county ran too high for neutralism to prevail. In any case, a county which was not secured for one side or the other risked invasion by 'foreigners' eager to annexe it to their cause. In 1642 Warwickshire determined its allegiance for itself.

As early as June, rival groups were wearing ribbons (made in Coventry) as distinguishing marks. Northampton, commissioned to organize the Array in the county, knew he must act fast. He knew that Brooke might well be joined by his fellow Puritan leader Lord Saye and Sele, whose estates were across the border in Oxfordshire. He knew that owners of manor houses were securing their homes against him, and he knew that the towns of Coventry and Birmingham were controlled by a zealous Puritan magistracy. In Coventry, whose city fathers he tried to win over, he was obliged to make a quick getaway 'out of the back door of the Black Bull' on 25 June. In Birmingham 15,000 swords were being made for the parliament's Lord General, the Earl of Essex. Brooke secured the county's trained bands and their weapons, and the king's cause seemed to be lost.

But was it? Among the gentry, the Warwickshire antiquarian William Dugdale believed that 92 accepted the king's Array and only 26 the Ordinance, while 50 'stood neuter'. Probably the county could have swung either way and a decisive act of war by either side would have determined the issue. Yet neither of them wished to risk failure, or the alienation of potential supporters, by striking the first blow. Instead, the county drifted into violence as acts of plunder were perpetrated in attempts to intimidate opponents and neutrals.

The nearest that Warwickshire came to an open battle before Charles had raised his standard was on 30 July at Kineton, the village below Edgehill, which was to figure in the famous battle of 23 October. The July confrontation had its chivalrous aspect, probably because neither side wished to incur the odium of starting hostilities. From 10 a.m. until 5 p.m. the two sides parleyed. Northampton proposed a combat either between the two leaders themselves or between the 20 best men from each side. Brooke compromised. He made an offer, which Northampton accepted, to return the guns to Banbury while he consulted parliament and to give three days' notice if he intended to move them again. This agreement, which resolved the confrontation at Kineton, worked to Brooke's advantage; for soon afterwards, having driven the royalists out of his way, he was able to move the guns from Banbury and get them into Warwick Castle, his home.

Once the king had raised his standard, Warwickshire was bound to be drawn into the wider conflict. In August the king

3 Photograph of the Warwickshire countryside looking down on to Kineton from Edgehill.
Banbury, in Oxfordshire, was a regional centre, and had guns and a magazine in 1642. Brooke carried the ordnance from there to Warwick via Kineton.

4 Woodcut from *The Bloody Prince, or a Declaration of the most cruel practices of Prince Rupert and the rest of the Cavaliers* (1643). On 3 April 1643 Rupert sacked Birmingham and was said to have burned down 80 houses. The event was typical of Rupert and added to the sufferings of centrally placed Warwickshire.

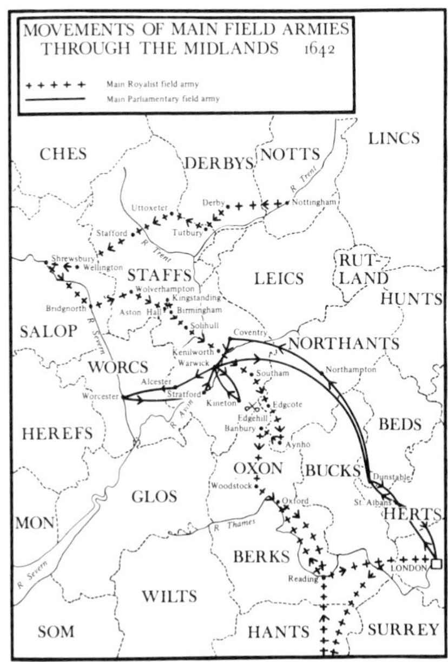

5 Map of the movements of the main field armies through the Midlands, 1642 from Roy Sherwood, *Civil Strife in the Midlands 1642–51*, Phillimore Press, 1974.

approached the county from the north. Northampton tried to secure strongholds for him by seizing the magazine at Banbury in Oxfordshire and by laying siege to Warwick Castle. Edward Peyto, its governor, hung out emblems of the struggle ahead, a red flag of defiance, his Bible and a winding sheet. Northampton's cannon kept blowing up bits of Warwick Church. The king, who was by now in the county, was also in difficulties. He stormed Coventry on 19 August, a move which permanently alienated it and other towns. Coventry was swiftly relieved by Brooke, and Northampton raised his siege of Warwick by 23 August. The king moved north again to regroup and Warwickshire was won for parliament.

By now the parliamentary field army under Essex had arrived in the county at Southam with the soldiers crying out for a 'dish of cavaliers for supper'. Northampton challenged them with his remaining forces, and a skirmish, largely an artillery duel, ensued there. Few were killed or injured. But the lines of conflict in the county were now firmly drawn. Both Brooke and Northampton were to pay the price of their commitment. In 1643 Brooke was killed by a bullet in the eye during the attack on Lichfield, and Northampton died at Hopton Heath. The county for which they had fought was to endure much suffering in the civil war, and was to be subjected to the grasping rule of a parliamentary county committee made up largely of militants drawn from outside the county's traditional landed rulers.

76. Medal struck to commemorate the siege of Bristol in 1643. London, British Museum.
The surrender of Bristol to the royalists on 26 July 1643 was a grave blow to the morale of parliament, whose governor of the city, Nathaniel Fiennes, a son of Lord Saye and Sele, was court-martialled; he survived to become a councillor of Oliver Cromwell during the Protectorate. The two sides in the civil war fought hard for control of the large ports, parliament being the more successful.

tribution was to mobilize a solid 'middle group' in parliament, which steered a steady course between the defeatism of the peace party and the divisive radicalism of some of the war party.

The Scottish army entered England as parliament's allies in January 1644 under Alexander Leslie, Earl of Leven, who had risen in the Swedish service under the great Gustavus Adolphus but now, in his sixties, had grown paunchy and cautious. He failed in an attempt on royalist-held Newastle and his progress during that long hard winter was painfully slow. Better news for parliament came from Cheshire, where Sir Thomas Fairfax joined Brereton, and together they roundly beat Lord Byron at Nantwich on 25 January; but when Sir John Meldrum besieged Newark, Rupert made a lightning march to its relief and reconquered most of Lincolnshire before returning to the Marches. The balance of the first quarter's campaigning lay decidedly with the king until Waller raised the parliament's shaken morale with a timely victory over Forth at Cheriton in Hampshire on 29 March.

The fortunes of war turned dramatically in April and May when the Scots, the Fairfaxes and the Eastern Association army converged on York and besieged the Earl of Newcastle there. That brought Rupert north again to the rescue, though he took a wide sweep through Lancashire, storming and plundering Stockport, Bolton and Liverpool on his way. His arrival before York triggered the biggest and bloodiest battle of the war, a clash of five armies on Marston Moor on 2 July. The allies outnumbered the royalists by nearly three to two, but many of them broke and fled – including Leven and Lord Fairfax themselves – before Cromwell's and the Scottish cavalry followed up their victory on the left flank by retrieving a near disaster on the right. The royalists lost about 4,000 dead, including most of Newcastle's brave whitecoated infantry; the allies only about 300.

With York and a vast territory lost to the king and his northern army shattered, the allies might have won the war quite quickly if Essex and Waller had joined up and brought the king's main army to battle while Rupert was unable to reinforce it. But Essex had decided in June to take his army to the relief of Lyme Regis and (he hoped) the reconquest of the south-west. He sent Waller on his own against the king, but at

77. Frontispiece to Francis Quarles, *The Shepherd's Oracle* (1646).
Charles defends the tree of religion from the attacks of Puritans who hack at its root, as in the Root and Branch Petition. Charles also defends the tree against papists, for royalist propagandists were as anxious as Puritans to associate their opponents with the forces of subversion and of popery. Charles, who was to be so effectively portrayed after his death as a martyr to the Church of England, had in reality played fast and loose with it during the negotiations with parliament concerning the religious settlement. Yet popular Anglicanism preserved a strong base of royalist support throughout the civil wars and Interregnum.

Cropredy Bridge near Banbury Waller came off the worse, and thereafter mutiny and desertion incapacitated him for weeks to come. Essex met a far worse disaster. He got himself trapped in Cornwall and had to escape with his cavalry by sea, leaving nearly 6,000 infantry to surrender. In the north the Scots took a long rest before besieging Newcastle, which fell in October. They contributed little thereafter; Charles's champion, Montrose, and his Highlanders were wreaking such havoc back at home that Leven's army was constantly depleted by demands from Edinburgh for relief. Parliament finally roused a lethargic Manchester and the remains of Essex's and Waller's forces into engaging Charles's main army again, but thanks mainly to Manchester they bungled a fair chance of destroying it at the second battle of Newbury.

It was not merely incompetence that made parliament's aristocratic generals squander their chances of victory, but an onset of doubt as to what they were fighting for. Before Marston Moor they could see the struggle as essentially defensive: to prevent the royalists from reversing by force what the parliaments of both kingdoms had achieved by statute. But Marston Moor opened up a prospect of total victory, and Essex and Manchester and their kind did not like it. Total victory might give the radical men in the war party and the firebrands in Cromwell's cavalry what they were suspected of wanting: drastic change in the constitution, perhaps threatening monarchy itself; a flood of sectarian heresy in religion; even a subversion of the social hierarchy, destroying the privileges and deference due to noblemen, knights and gentlemen. A negotiated peace and a return (with adjustments) to traditional order were what they desired.

To Cromwell such an attitude was a betrayal, and he denounced Manchester, his own general, before the House of Commons for his 'backwardness to all action'. The victories of his cavalry, the famous Ironsides, had enhanced Cromwell's growing parliamentary stature. This was no personal vendetta, however, for his purpose was to prepare parliament for the remedies with which he and his allies hoped to end the military stalemate. One was a Self-Denying Ordinance, requiring members of both Houses to resign their military commands and civil offices. This would remove the aristocratic generals, whose commitment to outright victory was so doubtful. The other was to forge a 'New Model' army out of the battered remains of the old ones: an army that would go wherever it was sent and pursue victory single-mindedly, undeflected by local ties or political interest. Much of the winter was spent in a struggle over these measures, which split both Houses and often set them against each other. The Lords rightly sensed that Essex and Manchester were primary targets, and there was talk at Essex's town house of impeaching Cromwell. But a combination of the middle group and the war party got both measures through – the Self-Denying Ordinance being redrafted so as not to preclude reappointment – and the Lords finally gave way on both early in April 1645.

The New Model was not in origin or intention a political army and it did not become one until 1647. Its general, the 32-year-old Sir Thomas Fairfax, was as non-political and unfanatical as could be wished. Its regiments were as far as possible taken intact from the

78. From *A Pious and Seasonable Perswasive to the Sonnes of Zion*, a pamphlet of 1647.
A plea for unity between Presbyterians and Independents, the leading religious factions on the parliamentary side, against their common enemies. Royalist writers were able to make much of their enemies' divisions over religion, which principally concerned the correct form of church government and the proper degree of liberty of conscience.

79 (overleaf). The Battle of Naseby, from Joshua Sprigge, *Anglia Rediviva* (1647).
The decisive battle of the civil war. The parliamentary army, with the village of Naseby behind it, has Cromwell commanding the right wing of the horse, and Ireton facing Rupert on the left. The king, shown in front of his forces before the battle, was to fight from behind the front line; even so, the more cautious parliamentarians had scruples about firing on their sovereign. Cromwell seems to have had no such doubts. He was to recall of the morning of the battle how, lining up his forces, 'I could not, riding about my business, but smile out to God in praises, in assurance of victory, because God would, by things that are not, bring to naught things that are.'

THE DESCRIPTION OF THE ARMIES OF
Sr Thomas Fairefax his Excellency, as they were
the Fower
Dust Hill
Prince Rupert
Prince Maurice
Sr Barnard Astley
The Left Wing Commanded by Comissary Generall Ireton
Maior Generall Skippon
Comissary Generall Ireton
Coll Riches Regiment
Coll Fleetwood Regiment
Hardres Waller
Farny Hill
The Mill Hill
The traine guarded with firelockes
NASBYE
Printed for John Partridge

AND FOOT OF HIS MAJESTIES, AND
rall bodyes, at the Battayle at NASBYE;
of June 1645
The Generall
The right wing of horse commanded
By Lieutenant generall Cromwell

best of Manchester's, Essex's and Waller's armies, which now ceased to exist, but their infantry was so depleted that over half the foot soldiers had to be newly recruited or pressed. The Ironsides that Cromwell had commanded in the Eastern Association army furnished the bulk of the New Model horse, and they already had such a reputation for religious enthusiasm and unorthodoxy that the Scots were deeply distrustful of them. The Lords tried to reject 51 of Fairfax's nominees for commissions, many if not most of them radical men, but the Commons ensured that nearly all his recommendations were approved. The New Model's original officers covered a wide religious and political spectrum and they kept their politics to themselves while the war lasted. Most were drawn from the gentry, especially in the senior ranks.

The year 1645 brought striking evidence to confirm Cromwell's warning to parliament that the people were growing sick of the war. Spontaneous associations of countrymen calling themselves Clubmen appeared, first in Shropshire, then in Worcestershire and Herefordshire and later in half a dozen other counties in western and southern England and south Wales. They were neither royalist nor parliamentarian but neutralist, and their general purpose was to see off the troops of either side that plundered or oppressed them.

The year's fighting began with mixed fortunes and confused purposes. Parliament's strategy was distorted by a natural desire to rescue Taunton from Lord Goring's long siege, and the king's by a similar concern to save Chester from Brereton's. But a more purposeful campaign developed after parliament had ordered the New Model to besiege Oxford. To draw it off, Rupert, who had been made commander-in-chief in November, launched a swift and ruthless assault on Leicester. The ensuing sack was terrible, but the move succeeded because parliament promptly ordered Fairfax to lift the siege of Oxford and seek out the king's army. Rupert had already concentrated his own and Byron's forces and he sent repeated orders to Goring to bring his, too. His decision to tackle the New Model while its infantry were still raw would have been a sound one if Goring had obeyed. But Goring did not; nor did Rupert wait for the considerable army that Lord Gerard was bringing from Wales. Consequently Rupert had 9,000 men at most and Fairfax nearly 14,000 when he risked battle at Naseby near Market Harborough on 14 June. Even so, his brave infantry came near to victory before Cromwell brought his cavalry against them. Cromwell had just been appointed lieutenant-general with the overall command of the cavalry, at Fairfax's urgent request; he had joined the army only the day before. Commanding the right wing, he halted his regiments after they had beaten the king's northern horse and brought them back in time to save the foot from rout and win the battle, whereas Rupert dissipated his own successful charge on the other flank in a quest for plunder.

Naseby proved to be the decisive action of the war. Goring, whose 5,000 horse might have saved it, lost half his army when the New Model fell upon it at Langport. Rupert advised the king to treat for peace, but Charles replied that 'God will not suffer rebels to prosper, or his cause to be overthrown'. Yet one blow followed another, the hardest being Rupert's surrender of Bristol in September. For this Charles stripped him of his command, but it was unjust; victory had made the New Model irresistible. The remaining royal forces were defeated in detail and the war ended with the siege of Oxford and its surrender in June 1646. Charles was no longer there; he had slipped out incognito and given himself up to the Scots in Newark.

The Search for Settlement, 1646–1648

The civilian population had suffered far more heavily from the war than used to be appreciated. They had been taxed to an unprecedented degree, with the monthly assessments levied much further down the social scale than the old parliamentary subsidies, and with the excise falling on many articles of common consumption. They were lucky if they had not had horses, fodder or household goods commandeered, or soldiers billeted on them with or without payment. Plunder and the destruction of property were not rare experiences, especially in towns, where lengthy sieges inflicted untold misery. Peace brought a respite from death and devastation, but the burdens of war taxation, 'free quarter' and turbulent soldiers persisted. Roughly twice as many troops remained afoot as were in the New Model, without counting the Scots, and the various provincial forces were generally less disciplined than Fairfax's, being even more irregularly paid. Soldiers mutinied in at least 20 English counties in 1646 and 17 in 1647. Nearly £3 million was owed to all these forces in back pay and to find the money to pay them off was an appalling problem.

Their pay and their future became a major political issue. Since 1645 parliament had tended to polarize between two parties, known as the Presbyterians and the Independents. The usage of these terms was complex, for they had both a religious and a political meaning. They were used initially to describe the conflicting positions taken up in the debates on the settlement of the Church. The Presbyterians were those who wanted the Presbyterian church settlement that parliament, aided by a synod of divines known as the Westminster

Assembly, was drawing up in accordance with the Solemn League and Covenant. (For more on Presbyterianism see p. 136.) The Independents saw in this scheme merely the replacement of intolerant Anglicanism by intolerant Presbyterianism. They wanted protection for 'independent', voluntarily-formed congregations; and they had some sympathy for the radical religious sects who pleaded for the liberty of conscience of which Presbyterians were keen to deprive them.

But soon men were labelled Presbyterian or Independent because of their political as well as their religious convictions: often the MPs who were most alarmed by religious radicalism were those who most disliked the political pretensions of the army, where the feeling in favour of liberty of conscience was strong. These 'political Presbyterians', as heirs to the peace party of the civil war, were keen to see the king restored to his throne. Even though some of them had doubts about the Presbyterian religious settlement, they were obliged to support it because they depended on the city of London, where religious Presbyterianism had taken strong root, and on the Scots, who had fought the war for it. 'Political Independents' covered a wider spectrum, from sincere monarchists to a few barely concealed republicans such as the Berkshire MP Henry Marten. They were distinguished until 1646 by their pursuit of total victory and after that by their unwillingness to disband the New Model until the king had

A new Sect of Religon Descryed, called
ADAMITES:
Deriving their Religion from our Father *Adam*.
Wherein they hold themselves to be blamelesse at the last day, though they sinne never so egregiously, for they challenge Salvation, as their due, from the innocencie of their second ADAM.
This was first disclosed by a Brother of the same Sect, to the Author, who went along with this Brother, and saw all these Passages following.
By Samoth Yarb, Batchelor in Arts.

Downe Proud Flesh Downe

80. *A New Sect of Religion Descryed,* an anonymous tract of 1641. *A rare and unusually explicit pamphlet deriding the libertinism which magistrates, ministers and Puritans saw everywhere in seventeenth-century England, and to which – if we can believe hostile voices – the breakdown of authority in the 1640s gave an enormous boost. The belief mocked here, and subsequently attributed to the Ranters, was the 'antinomian' one that the elect had no reason to wear clothes, having regained the innocence which Adam's fall had lost. A related antinomian principle, that the elect were free from the bounds of moral law, was thought to occasion much orgiastic pleasure.*

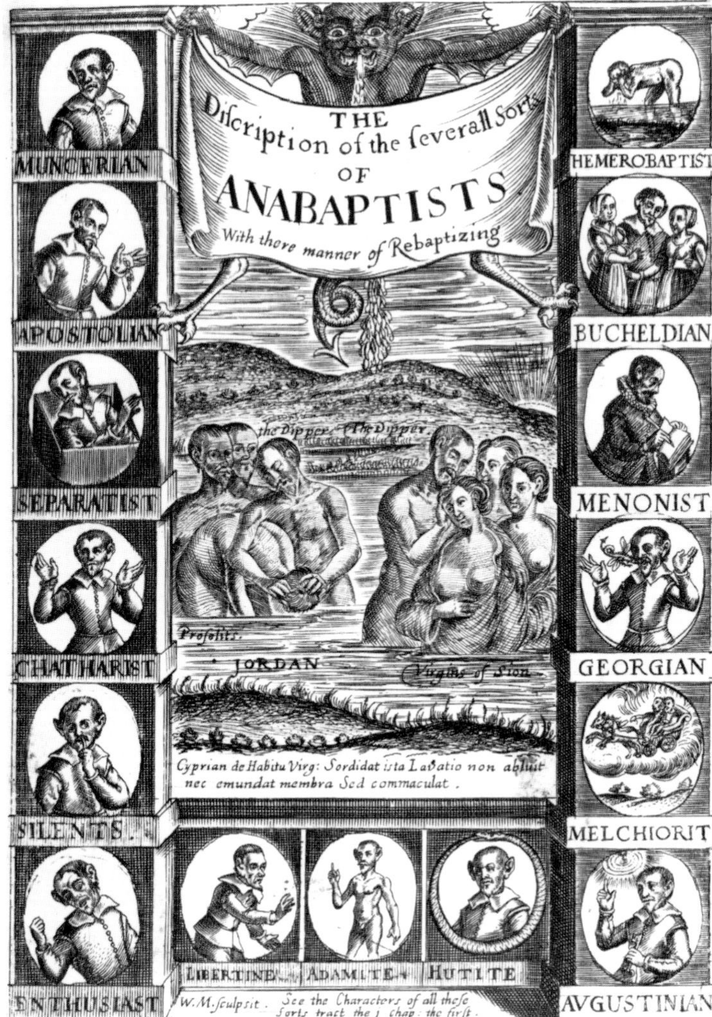

81. Daniel Featley, *The Dippers Dipt* (1645), title-page.
This satirical woodcut mocks the Baptists, a small but determined sect which had grown up in the early seventeenth century and which achieved a much wider appeal during the civil wars. Its members believed in adult baptism, although they were divided about predestination. Of the radical groups of the Puritan Revolution, the Baptists – or 'anabaptists' or 'dippers' as their enemies called them – were those to whom Oliver Cromwell was closest and whom he was most anxious to protect from persecution. Most parliamentarians were hostile to them, and shared the views about them of Featley, a chaplain to Charles I.

'Hot Service at Cropredy Bridge'

THE OXFORD CAMPAIGN AND THE BATTLE OF CROPREDY BRIDGE, 1644

1 Anon., *Sir William Waller*. Oil on canvas, $27\frac{1}{2} \times 23\frac{1}{4}$ in. (69.9 × 59.1 cm.). London, National Portrait Gallery.
Sir William Waller (1597–1668) was dubbed 'William the Conqueror' by some, but his military achievements scarcely seem to justify the name.

On 29 June 1644 the parliamentary general Sir William Waller faced his sovereign across the River Cherwell near Banbury in Oxfordshire. Charles I commanded an army of about 5,000 horse and 3,500 foot. The parliamentary army had about the same number of cavalry as the king's, and more than 1,000 additional infantry.

Both armies must have been weary. Charles had lost an important battle to Waller at Cheriton in Hampshire on 28 March. After his victory Waller had been dubbed 'William the Conqueror', and as a result of it the royalists were forced, as the king's secretary put it, 'in place of an offensive to make a defensive war'. Charles then withdrew to his temporary capital at Oxford. Yet Waller, after securing Hampshire, was unable to follow up his victory. Many of his troops were from the West Country, many from London. They disliked fighting so far from home. The reluctance of regionally-recruited armies to fight national campaigns was a problem for both sides. In response to it they had fought a series of regional campaigns, hoping that regional successes would eventually add up to national success. Overall, this strategy had served the king well. By the end of 1643 the Marquis of Newcastle controlled most of the north for him, Hopton and Prince Maurice secured most of the west country and Charles himself dominated the Thames Valley from Oxford.

On the parliamentary side, Waller had become aware by the summer of 1644 of the disadvantages of the regional strategy, and had to come to rue the divisions in aim and command which it had caused. He urged a full rendezvous of all parliamentary field armies for a decisive battle; and he had his way.

Where should the battle be fought? Possibly in the north, if only the Scottish army and the parliamentary forces could unite; possibly in the west, where several strongholds were still preserved by brave local troops; or possibly in the midlands, in an attack on the king himself. Some parliamentarians were reluctant to fight their sovereign in person, dreading the thought of killing him and uncertain what they would do if they captured him. Even so, it was against the king's army that Waller and parliament's Lord General, the Earl of Essex, led a united army of 28,000 men to Oxford in a move designed to force the 'grand battle'. At first it was successful. The king had sent a considerable force under Prince Rupert to the north to secure Lancashire and to prepare to face parliament and the Scots. He had also pulled in much of his West Country field army around Oxford, and by securing strong garrisons in towns such as Banbury, Reading, Abingdon and Wallingford he hoped to hold his Thames Valley position. Occasional cavalry sorties on the model of the Battle of Chalgrove in 1643 would help. But Charles pursued an indecisive strategy. Faced by the advance of Essex and Waller he had foolishly pulled in his outer garrisons, and the parliamentarians were poised to take Oxford. 'I confess', admitted Charles to Rupert, who had urged a bolder course, 'the best had been to have followed your advice'.

But Essex and Waller made mistakes too. They failed to coordinate their pincer movement on Oxford, and on the night of 3 June Charles slipped out of the city and moved with his army towards Witney. Waller pursued him with day and night marches, but the king escaped. Had the chance of the decisive battle faded? Waller thought not. Essex thought it had, and went off with his army to relieve Lyme in Dorset. Piecemeal regional strategy had returned. Waller was very angry with Essex who had 'undertaken my task in the West'.

Both Charles and Waller then began a fortnight's marching and counter-marching across the Cotswolds between Oxfordshire and Worcestershire. Both were undecided about the next move. Charles marched as far as Bewdley, pursued by Waller who expected the king to cut loose and make for the north to join Rupert. In June hot days alternated with rainy ones in the Cotswolds, and both armies were tired by the weather and by the long marches. At last the king decided on a strategy. He would threaten Buckingham and give the impression of advancing on the Eastern Association army of the parliament. This was sensible, for it might force that army to stay in East Anglia and prevent it from joining the Scots in the north. But Waller kept to Charles's heels. On 29 June, looking over the village of Cropredy from the south side of the Cherwell, he faced the king.

THE
SOULDIERS
Pocket Bible:
Containing the most (if not all) those places contained in holy Scripture, which doe shew the qualifications of his inner man, that is a fit Souldier to fight the Lords Battels, both before he fight, in the fight, and after the fight;
Which Scriptures are reduced to severall heads, and fitly applyed to the Souldiers severall occasions, and so may supply the want of the whole Bible; which a Souldier cannot conveniently carry about him:
And may bee also usefull for any Christian to meditate upon, now in this miserable time of Warre.

Imprimatur, *Edm. Calamy:*

*Jos.*1.8. This Book of the Law shall not depart out of thy mouth, but thou shalt meditate therein day and night, that thou maist observe to doe according to all that is written therein, for then thou shalt make thy way prosperous, and have good successe.

Printed at *London* by *G.B.* and *R.W.* for *G.C.* 1643.
Aug: 3d

2 Title-page of *The Soldier's Catechism* by Robert Ram (1644).
This pamphlet presented the parliamentary cause as God's cause.

Waller had shown at Cheriton that he could beat the royalist cavalry, which had seemed invincible. Now he had the additional advantage of a good position on Bourton Hill (see map). Happily he had caught the king's army on the march and stretched out for miles along the Banbury–Daventry road, its vanguard so far ahead that it could scarcely turn round to give battle. That seemed to leave the rest of Charles's army exposed across the Cherwell opposite the two crossings of Cropredy Bridge and the ford at Slat Mill. Emboldened by his earlier success, Waller sent troops under John Middleton over the bridge while he himself seized the ford to tackle the royalist commanders opposite, the Earls of Cleveland and Northampton. This was a tactical error, for it allowed Waller to deploy only a part of his army across two narrow river crossings to face likely cross fire from the main and rear columns of the royalists. Middleton attacked across Cropredy Bridge, but Cleveland fought well and some of Middleton's men wastefully pursued some royalists towards Hays Bridge and lost the momentum of the attack. Northampton turned back Waller at Slat Mill. The parliamentarians were caught with insufficient troops across the river to sustain their advance, and with their backs to the river, were exposed to the threat of a royalist counter-attack.

Cleveland broke a second charge by Middleton across the bridge and that proved to be decisive. The parliamentarian troops retreated towards the bridge crying 'the field is lost, the field is lost . . .' The London regiments subsequently claimed to have prevented a worse disaster: 'by the courage of the Kentish regiments and that of the Hamlets we got down two drakes [guns] on to the bridge and staved them off bravely . . . that ere night they could not brag of their winning'. But the royalists could and did. The morale of Waller's army collapsed, especially in the City brigades where there were mutinies. Waller complained about these Londoners. Like all men fighting away from home they were 'come of their old song, "Home, home" . . . an army compounded of these men will never go through with their service . . .'. This may have been a fair criticism but it was not an excuse for the reverse, the true blame for which lies in Waller's decision to loose his cavalry across the Cherwell. As Clarendon remarked of Waller, Cropredy Bridge had 'even broke the heart of his army'.

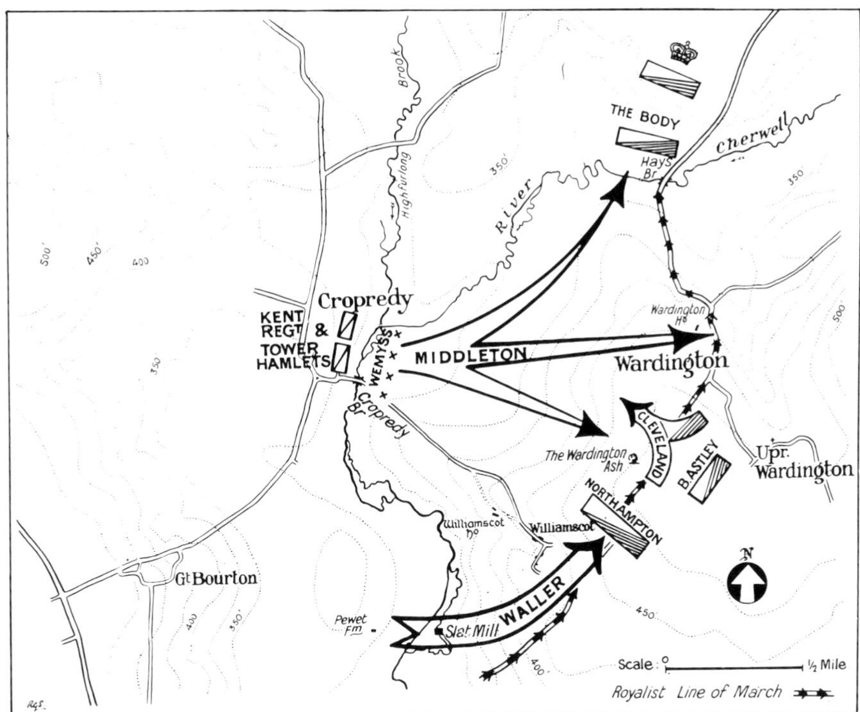

3 Map of the Battle of Cropredy Bridge. From M. Toynbee and P. Young, *Cropredy Bridge, 1644*, Roundwood Press, 1970.

4 Slat Mill near Cropredy today. Waller led his detachment across the Cherwell here to face the Earl of Northampton.

bound himself to terms that would keep him from further mischief. But keeping up the army after the war was unpopular and steadily robbed them of their wartime majority in the Commons, so they and the army made common cause in mutual defence. A measure of religious toleration was an important plank in the Independent platform.

The peace terms that parliament sent to the king in July 1646, the Propositions of Newcastle, were impossibly stiff, for they combined the religious demands of the Presbyterians and the Scots with the stringent political restraints favoured by hardline Independents. But the leading Presbyterians were prepared to treat on easier conditions, which they communicated to him through diplomatic channels; he then put them forward (in part) as counter-offers. They greatly strengthened their position when they successfully steered parliament and the City into negotiating the withdrawal of the Scottish army in February 1647, upon which Charles was handed over to parliament's custody. With little apparent danger that the Scots might try to restore him now, the Presbyterians felt free to proceed with a large-scale disbandment of forces as a prelude (they hoped) to a deal with the king. Justice and national interest might have suggested that they should start by disbanding the unruly provincial forces and draw on the New Model for whatever standing army needed to be kept up, since it contained the finest fighting regiments and the most volunteers and veterans. But (apart from one brigade in the west) the Presbyterian-dominated parliament *began* with the New Model, offering its men a straight choice between disbandment with six weeks' pay in cash (the cavalrymen were 43 weeks in arrears) or enlistment in a relief force for Ireland. The only exceptions were five cavalry regiments – 3,000 officers and men at most out of an army of over 22,000 – which were to form part of a standing force of 6,400 horse and dragoons; the only permanent home army that parliament envisaged apart from small local garrisons.

Although the New Model had kept out of politics so far, it contained Cromwell, his son-in-law Henry Ireton and several other officer-MPs who were strong political Independents; there can be no doubt that the political Presbyterians saw it as a potential threat to their plans for settling the kingdom. They wanted to break it up. But in the spring of 1647, when the army was quartered at Saffron Walden in Essex, they provoked it too far and not only over its pay. The soldiers spontaneously got up a petition to Fairfax late in March, protesting at their unjust treatment. The Commons got wind of it and voted that any soldiers who persisted with it were 'enemies of the state and disturbers of the public peace'. They stirred up a hornets' nest.

The soldiery, again spontaneously, elected representatives from each troop and regiment and by May these 'agitators' had a close-knit organization of their own. Many officers supported them and most of the army now presented a concerted refusal to enlist for Ireland until its grievances were remedied and its affronted honour satisfied. Early in June, Fairfax yielded to the pressure of the agitators and the advice of the officers and called all the regiments to a general rendezvous near Newmarket in defiance of parliament's orders for piecemeal disbandment. The agitators organized their own coup: they abducted the king from Holmby House in Northamptonshire, where parliament was holding him, and brought him to army headquarters. At the rendezvous the whole army entered into a mutual covenant not to disband until its traducers were removed from power and its grievances redressed to the satisfaction of a General Council of the Army, which was to include two officers and two soldiers elected by each regiment. This gave the agitators formal status, but it brought them under a degree of control.

The New Model, claiming that it was 'not a mere mercenary' army but the dedicated defender of the people's liberties, next affirmed its own broad principles for the settlement of the kingdom and brought charges for the impeachment of eleven leading Presbyterian MPs. It showed no feeling against the king as yet. Indeed Ireton, acting in close liaison with Lord Saye and Sele and other influential Independent peers, put before the General Council that met at Reading on 17 July some 'Heads of the Proposals' for restoring him on conditions less unacceptable to him than parliament's Propositions of Newcastle. Their limitations on his prerogative were less humiliating and their religious provisions far more liberal, extending to the tolerance of Anglican worship.

But before these terms could be properly debated and negotiated, the Presbyterians in London, encouraged by some MPs, launched a desperate attempt at counter-revolution. A violent mob invaded both Houses on the 26th and terrorized their members into inviting the king to Westminster forthwith. The formidable City militia was mobilized and thousands of additional horse and foot were raised from the ex-soldiers who swarmed around London. The Speakers of both Houses and many members fled to the army, but others sat on at Westminster and defied it. Clearly the army had to move into the capital, but before it did so Cromwell and Ireton strove hard to persuade Charles to accept the Heads of the Proposals. Had he pledged himself to them, the army would have escorted him as well as the fugitive Speakers and members back to Westminster when it marched in on 6 August. But he waited to see whether the London counter-revolutionaries would do his business, and even when they collapsed without striking a blow he would not commit himself. He missed his best chance of regaining his throne with honour; but he was counting on playing off the parliament and the army against each other and he still had one eye on Scotland.

The next two months were an anticlimax. The Independent peers and the army commanders still wanted to treat with the king, but the Commons remained an uncertain quantity and in the army at large there were growing doubts about him. From 9 September the General Council of the Army met weekly in Putney Church, close to headquarters, and this helped to preserve a broad consensus across the ranks. But the soldiery were increasingly subjected to propaganda by the Levellers, whose London-based movement had been developing a full political programme at much the same time as the army's own entry into politics. The Levellers had very little to do with the army's initial revolt, but they did bid for the agitators' allegiance during the summer and autumn. Their ideas about equal natural rights for all men, including the right to consent to the government they lived under, had a wide appeal, especially to the literate and sophisticated cavalry troopers. But the full Leveller programme – including the supreme authority of annual or biennial popular assemblies, disestablishment of the Church, radical reform of the law and annually elected magistrates in place of gentry JPs and municipal oligarchies – could only be achieved by defying parliament as it was and launching into revolutionary action. That would have meant breaking the army's public pledges; besides, it was against the soliders' interests. Parliament had been granting much under pressure that the army sought, including more regular pay, better provision for arrears, indemnity for acts committed in war and a mili-

82. From *Knavery of the Rump*, a set of satirical playing cards of 1679.
The card mocks the flight of the army's supporters from Westminster in July 1647, with William Lenthall, the pliable Speaker of the House of Commons, at their head carrying the mace. The memory of such events was assiduously kept alive by the political successors to the royalists in Charles II's reign, to whose propaganda these cards belong.

83. Attrib. Robert Walker, *Henry Ireton*.
Oil on canvas, 49 × 39½ in. (124.5 × 100.3 cm.).
London, National Portrait Gallery.
From a Nottinghamshire gentry family, Ireton became Cromwell's right-hand man in the New Model army, and also his son-in-law. He owed his rise less to military prowess than to the clarity of his mind and to his skill in drafting documents setting out the army's position. It was Ireton who, late in 1648, steered the army officers into the decision to bring the king to trial.

tary establishment of 26,400 officers and men.

The Levellers, disappointed by the response of all but a handful of the agitators, late in September engineered the emergence of some new agents or agitators to proselytize for them in the army. Their famous leader John Lilburne initiated this move from the Tower, where he had been imprisoned by parliament for writing vociferous pamphlets that accused it of establishing its own tyranny in place of the king's; but the main organizers were John Wildman and the agitator Edward Sexby. The new agents appeared in only five out of two dozen regiments and it is doubtful whether even the five ever elected them, but they and their Leveller mentors formed a little caucus quite separate from the General Council. They published a manifesto in October that accused the high officers, especially Cromwell and Ireton, of reneging on the undertakings that they and the army had made in June.

Foundations of *Freedom;*

OR AN

AGREEMENT

OF THE

PEOPLE:

Propoſed as a Rule for future Government in the Eſtabliſhment of a firm and laſting PEACE.

Drawn up by ſeverall wel-affected Perſons, and tendered to the conſideration of the

Generall Councell of the ARMY.

And now offered to the Conſideration of all Perſons who are at liberty by Printing or otherwiſe, to give their Reaſons, for, or againſt it.

Unto which is annexed ſeverall Grievances by ſome Perſons, offered to be inſerted in the ſaid Agreement, but adjudged only neceſſary to be inſiſted on, as fit to be removed by the next

REPRESENTATIVES.

Publiſh'd for ſatisfaction of all honest Intereſts.

London, Printed for *R. Smithurſt,* 1648.

84. *Foundations of Freedom; or an Agreement of the People* (1648), title-page.
Late in 1648 a tactical struggle developed between the Levellers, who proposed a revised version – its title-page seen here – of their Agreement of the People *of 1647 as a basis for a political settlement, and the army leaders, who were worried by the radicalism of the document and reluctant to commit themselves to a programme which involved the speedy dissolution of the Long Parliament as a prelude to sweeping constitutional and social changes. In the weeks before the execution of Charles I the officers were able first to modify the* Agreement *and then to ensure that parliament would lay it aside. There were no general elections for a further five years; few of the Leveller reforms were implemented; and in the first half of 1649 the Levellers were broken by Cromwell and Ireton as a significant political force.*

This led to a lengthy confrontation between their caucus and the General Council, and three days of it are recorded and preserved in the famous Putney debates. Discussion centred on a new Leveller document, *An Agreement of the People*, which would have settled the country's government on the basis, not of acts of parliament, but of all the 'free-born' people's signatures to the *Agreement* itself. The clash of ideas between the Levellers' fundamental democracy and Ireton's and Cromwell's reasoned conservatism is memorably vivid, but behind the play of theory the real question was whether the army was free to impose a solution by force (for only by doing so could the *Agreement* have been launched), or whether it should hold to its constitutional course. Even while the debate went on, the Levellers and the new agents were inciting the soldiery to disobey their commanders. The proposition that free men had a right to vote for their legislators unless somehow they had forfeited it attracted wide support at Putney; but its implementation by force did not, and many were growing worried that the divisions in the army were threatening to incapacitate it.

Then on 11 November Charles fled from the army's custody to the Isle of Wight. At Carisbrooke he found himself still a prisoner, but his object was to negotiate with commissioners recently arrived from Scotland without having the generals breathing down his neck. A shift in Scottish politics had opened a possibility of military aid without his having to take the Covenant.

During the next week Fairfax addressed all his regiments at a series of three rendezvous. Two regiments staged a brief mutiny at Ware in Hertfordshire in the name of the *Agreement*; the rest proved firmly loyal and indeed glad to recover their old solidarity and discipline and sense of common purpose. It was timely; for on 26 December Charles signed a secret Engagement with the Scots whereby they were to send him an army and he was to call the cavaliers to arms again. He had deliberately abandoned the path of negotiation and gambled on the renewal of war.

85. The Farndon Civil War Window.
Church of St. Chad, Farndon, Cheshire.
The stained glass, which may date from the Restoration, commemorates royalist soldiers of Cheshire.

'He Loveth our Nation and Hath Built Us a Synagogue'

PURITANISM IN ACTION – ROBERT DYNELEY AND HIS CHAPEL

In the West Riding village of Bramhope, eight miles from Leeds, stands 'one of the most valuable of *incunabula* of Protestant or Puritan ecclesiastical planning in England' (Sir Niklaus Pevsner). It is a chapel, a plain oblong structure with mullioned windows and a belfry, and is one of the few churches built during the Interregnum. It owes its existence to the zeal of one man, the local gentleman of Bramhope, Robert Dyneley.

Bramhope was part of the very old parish of Otley. It was also, like many other old parishes in the north of England, very large. Protestant reformers thought it too large. With their emphasis on sermons, on communal participation in the liturgy and on hearing and reading the Bible, they were offended by the underprovision of church-building and clergy, particularly in these 'dark corners of the land'. Many northern townships had no church of their own, or at best a chapel-at-ease. How were more buildings and ministers to be provided? Church and state offered only piecemeal help. By the time of the civil wars of the 1640s, when the state disintegrated, it was clear that effective change could only come from local action. In Bramhope Robert Dyneley took the initiative on behalf of his community.

1 External view of the chapel today. The chapel is more or less unchanged externally, and was well restored in the 1960s.

Dyneley may have been responding to a wider movement in the area. In 1648, West Riding incumbents and 'lecturers' (that is, preaching ministers without benefices) signed a *Unanimous Attestation* and *Serious Protestation against Church-desolating and Soul-damning Errors.* They called for regional cooperation by West Riding gentry and clergy to give the county godly discipline, more preaching and proper clerical maintenance. Puritan ministers had hated Laud, but in the 1640s they were no less distressed by the spread of heresy which followed the collapse of church discipline and press censorship in the civil war. Among them were William Clarkson, Vicar of Adel, the parish next door to Bramhope township, and Thomas Chapman, parson of Denton, which lay the other side of Otley parish. Both men were clients of the Fairfax family, who belonged to a network of Yorkshire gentry families which had been formed by marriages, by Puritan feeling and by political cooperation on the parliamentary side: the Stapletons, the Wentworths, the Arthingtons, the Stanhopes, the Hawksworths – and the Dyneleys. The initiatives of these men may have been connected with parliament's attempts in the same year to introduce a Presbyterian Church government and to suppress vice and blasphemy. But local ecclesiastical schemes were usually closer to the heart of Puritanism than national ones were. So it was in the West Riding.

Robert Dyneley built his chapel in 1649 on a small plot of land adjoining his manor house in keeping with the proprietory link between hall and church which was traditional. The creation of this private-enterprise church was not easy. 130 acres of waste ground and common land had to be prised, by agreement, out of the villagers. Eventually enough ground, valued at 6s. 8d. an acre, was yielded to a group of five trustees drawn from Dyneley's Puritan friends and neighbours: Sir George Wentworth, Sir Charles Fairfax, the MP Henry Arthington, Walter Hawksworth and John Stanhope. These men were to pay a minister and had the power to deprive him. His appointment was in the hands of the same men together with Dyneley himself and Robert Todd, curate of St John's, Leeds, probably the most active reforming clergyman of the region. One George Crossley was 'found to be duly qualified and gifted for the holy office' of minister. The arrangement seems to have operated unhindered throughout the Interregnum. It was the gentry who had taken the initiative and it was they who retained control.

After the restoration of Charles II in 1660, when the Anglican Church was restored and when the government cracked down on Puritanism and Dissent, Dyneley seems to have successfully defended his rights against the Anglican Church. Elsewhere in the region, the restored Church was more successful in annexing Puritan church enterprises. Oliver Heywood, among the most famous Puritan preachers of his day, was expelled from his church at Coley, near Halifax, another privately owned church in a large parish. In his diary Heywood tells of the survival of the Bramhope experiment: 'Because I could not personally go to my own chapel . . . I went to hear Mr. Crossley at Bramhope, who by good providence of God yet holds up the work of public preaching without conforming. After dinner, Mr Dyneley, the gentleman of the place, moved me to preach in the afternoon.'

In 1666 Dyneley was indicted at Pontefract sessions for running a 'conventicle', the term used to describe a meeting of Puritans. The Conventicle Act of 1664 was used against him, but the case was dismissed. Maybe the Yorkshire gentlemen who heard the case sympathized with Dyneley's claim that the Church could not touch private property standing on private land, and were loath to interfere with property rights vested in Dyneley's control of the chapel. Heywood makes it clear that the

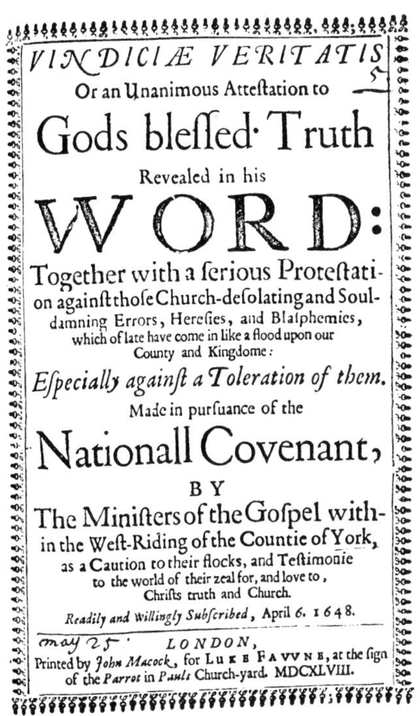

VINDICIÆ VERITATIS

Or an Unanimous Atteſtation to

Gods bleſſed Truth

Revealed in his

WORD:

Together with a ſerious Proteſtation againſt thoſe Church-deſolating and Soul-damning Errors, Hereſies, and Blaſphemies, which of late have come in like a flood upon our County and Kingdome:

Eſpecially againſt a Toleration of them.

Made in purſuance of the

Nationall Covenant,

BY

The Miniſters of the Goſpel within the Weſt-Riding of the Countie of York,

as a Caution to their flocks, and Teſtimonie to the world of their zeal for, and love to, Chriſts truth and Church.

Readily and willingly Subſcribed, April 6. 1648.

may 25

LONDON,

Printed by *John Macock*, for LUKE FAVVNE, at the ſign of the *Parrot* in *Pauls* Church-yard. MDCXLVIII.

2 Title-page of the *Unanimous Attestation* and *Serious Protestation against Church-desolating and Soul-damning Errors* (April 1648).

the day after (being saturday feb 8 1667) according to a call and promise, my wife and I rode to Idle in Calverley parish, where (the place being vacant) I preacht the day after, being Lords day, and had a very numerous congregation, the Lord graciously assisted, and preserved me in safety, on munday I went to Rawdon and preacht there that night, on the thursday to Bradford, visited Mr Brooksbank lodged with Mr Watkinsons, the day after called at Mr Sharps where was appointed a meeting that day, but it was put off by businesse, and so we came home that night, and found all well blessed be god, on friday I went again to little Horton, and Mr Waterhouse, Mr Dawson Mr Sharp and I kept the day upon a solemne occasion and oh how my heart was inlarged in the duty.

3 (below) Otley and surrounding parishes, based on the map published by the Institute of Heraldic and Genealogical Studies, Canterbury.
Otley parish contained about 14 out-townships. The parishes get larger as we move further west. Those in the lower valleys of the Wharfe, Aire and Nidd contain rich farmland and are small. Those in the middle and upper dales become progressively poorer and larger.

4 A page from Oliver Heywood's *Diary*, from the edition by J. Horsfall Turner (Brighouse, 1882).
Heywood's preaching and pastoral visits to dissenting communities were extensive and continuous. Here is part of a busy week which included visits to Idle and Rawden, only a few miles from Bramhope.

Bramhope practices were not unique in their post-1660 survival. At Menston, Arthington and Rawdon, conventicles were thriving. Certainly, ejected ministers continued to find a pulpit well into the 1680s. On 14 November 1689 Robert Dyneley was buried, aged 83. John Hepworth, in a letter to Ralph Thoresby the antiquarian, described how he preached the funeral sermon: 'and you all know what he hath done as to the setting up of worship amongst us. He loveth our nation and hath built us a synagogue. . . . By the care and diligence of this worthy person we have a chapel erected and endowed with a competent maintenance for a preaching minister. I wish that the gentry and those who have good estates would follow the example and give something to pious uses: that they would augment ministers' maintenance when it is poor and inconsiderable.'

It was an unavailing plea, for the Puritan gentry were no more. The chapel continued to function under its original trust deeds in spite of their doubtful legality and of some feeling that the church was not properly consecrated. It must be supposed that the services became closer to legal Anglican practice. Certainly the eighteenth-century fittings and the Dyneley memorials of that period of orthodox Anglicanism adorn the church today. The building is a reminder of the religious ideals held by many seventeenth-century English gentry who desired to bring God to the out-townships of a sprawling northern parish and into the hearts of men.

86. A. Van Dyck, *George and Francis Villiers*, 1635.
Oil on canvas, 54 × $50\frac{1}{4}$ in. (137.2 × 127.7 cm.).
Windsor Castle, Royal Collection.
After the assassination of their father these children of the first Duke of Buckingham, here painted in boyhood, were 'bred up by the king's charge, with his own children, the same tutors and governors'. They fought for the king in the civil wars. In 1648 the elder, George, escaped abroad, but Francis was killed in action at Kingston aged 19. George would return to England to become a leading politician of the Restoration period.

87 (opposite). A. Van Dyck, *Philip, Fourth Lord Wharton*, 1632.
Oil on canvas, $52\frac{1}{2}$ × $41\frac{3}{4}$ in. (133 × 106 cm.).
Washington D.C., National Gallery of Art.
Seen here aged about nineteen – when he is reported to have been the greatest beau in England, proud of exhibiting his fine legs in dancing – Wharton was firmly Puritan in the civil wars. But he broke with his friend Cromwell in 1648–9, the time of Pride's Purge, of regicide, and of the abolition of the House of Lords. Subsequently he resisted all Cromwell's attempts to win his support for the Interregnum regimes.

Philip Lord Wharton
1632 about yͤ age
of 19.
Sʳ Ant: Vandike

The Second Civil War and Regicide, 1648–1649

The second civil war began with insurrections in south Wales (in April 1648), Kent (in May) and Essex (in June) that were initially directed more against the county committees and other unpopular agencies of parliament than in favour of the king. Cromwell suppressed the first and Fairfax moved against those in Kent and Essex, but not before committed royalists had taken them over and much of the fleet had declared for the king. They erupted far too early, however, to be assisted by the Scots, whose army was slow in reaching the border and even slower thereafter. The Duke of Hamilton, who had promoted the Engagement, had difficulty in raising an army at all and he had to command it in person because the best Scottish officers would not fight for an uncovenanted king. Only about 3,600 men could be raised in northern England to support it. Cromwell fell on the combined Anglo-Scottish army at Preston on 17 August with a force less than half its size and in two days of battle and pursuit he annihilated it. The southern royalists, who had long been besieged by Fairfax in Colchester, surrendered on receiving the news and the second civil war was virtually over.

Long before these victories, parliament had decided to treat again with the king. They did not want him restored by Scottish arms, but neither would the majority risk allowing the triumphant army to dictate the peace. So they opened a long negotiation with him at Newport on the Isle of Wight, and he kept it going by making concessions which he privately admitted were insincere. The army sensed a betrayal of all it had fought for; most of it now regarded him as 'a man of blood' with the guilt of all the dead in this second war on his hands. Fairfax was hopelessly irresolute; Cromwell was evading a decision by lingering over the siege of Pontefract, where a die-hard royalist garrison still held out. But Ireton had no qualms. At a second attempt he united the Council of Officers in demanding that the king be tried for his life. Late in November the army seized him again and marched on London. Ireton's plan was that it should dissolve the parliament and recognize the 'faithful' members as caretakers until a new one was elected, but those members would not permit a dissolution by the army. They preferred a purge. On 6 December and the days that followed, soldiers under the command of Colonel Thomas Pride stood outside the Commons and prevented MPs who had striven to conclude the 'Treaty of Newport' from entering the chamber.

'Pride's Purge' at first left an active core of only 70 or so members who set up what they called a High Court of Justice, consisting nominally of 135 commissioners – MPs, army officers and others who were thought to be their supporters – to try the king for making war on his people. Milton saw the king's trial as an act of exemplary justice and wrote *The Tenure of*

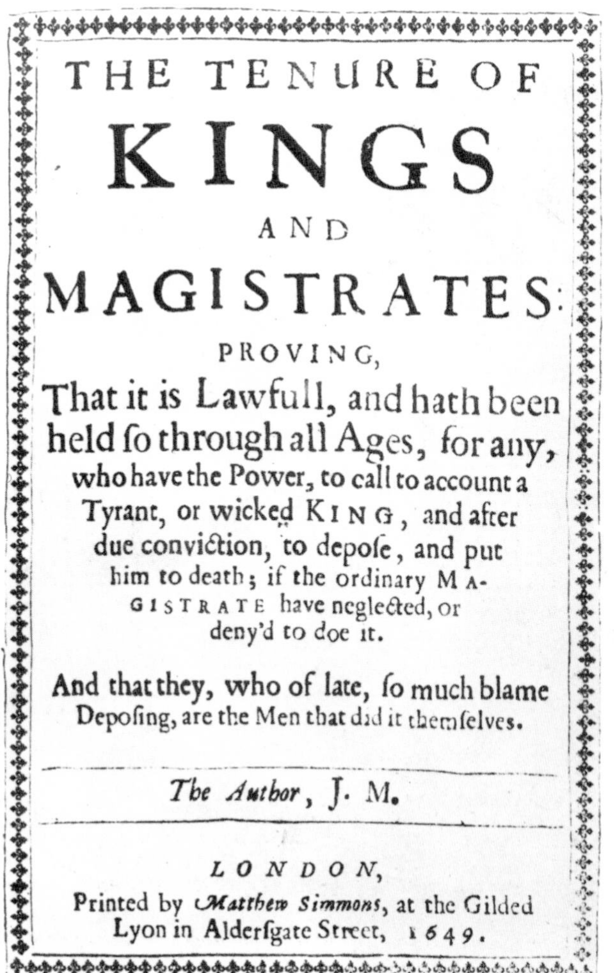

THE TENURE OF

KINGS

AND

MAGISTRATES:

PROVING,

That it is Lawfull, and hath been held ſo through all Ages, for any, who have the Power, to call to account a Tyrant, or wicked KING, and after due conviction, to depoſe, and put him to death; if the ordinary MAGISTRATE have neglected, or deny'd to doe it.

And that they, who of late, ſo much blame Depoſing, are the Men that did it themſelves.

The Author, J. M.

LONDON,

Printed by *Matthew Simmons*, at the Gilded Lyon in Alderſgate Street, 1649.

88. John Milton, *The Tenure of Kings and Magistrates* (1649). *The title-page of Milton's pamphlet of February 1649 summarizes the thesis that kings are accountable to the people. Milton wrote to justify the moves which led to Charles I's execution and to counter the vigorous Presbyterian criticism of Pride's Purge and of the regicide. The 'ordinary magistrate' who had 'neglected or denied to do it' was the parliament which the army, 'who have the power', purged in December 1648. Like the purged parliament on whose behalf he wrote, Milton at this stage hesitated to condemn the institution of monarchy. Charles I, rather than kingship, was the principal target, and Milton concerns himself only with the evils of 'a tyrant, or wicked king'. The act abolishing kingship in March 1649 was ambiguously worded, and it was not until May that the new regime declared itself a 'commonwealth or free state'. Later in 1649 Milton wrote an unsuccessful reply to that immensely successful piece of royalist propaganda,* Eikon Basilike, *'the king's book'. He was employed by the republic's Council of State, and published apologias both for it and for the subsequent Cromwellian protectorate.*

Kings and Magistrates to justify it. Cromwell was at first less sure. He had returned from the north on the evening after Pride's Purge and given it his blessing, but had striven behind the scenes until late in December to find some way of avoiding the ultimate penalty. But Charles now refused all compromise and Cromwell, finally convinced that providence had pronounced against the king and his cause, became the most unyielding of the regicides. Seventy members of the High Court, just over half, sentenced him to death; 59 signed his death warrant. From his trial to the final scene on the scaffold outside Inigo Jones's Banqueting Hall in Whitehall on 30 January, Charles played out with faultless dignity and courage the tragic role that his proven unwillingness to accept the political or religious consequences of his defeat, and his equally proven untrustworthiness as a negotiator, had cast upon him.

The execution of the king sent out a wave of shock and revulsion not only through England and Scotland, but through the whole continent of Europe. When Charles had been called upon at his trial to answer the parliament's charge in the name of 'the good people of England', Lady Fairfax had cried from the public gallery, 'It is a lie!' She was quite right. The army and the remnant of the Commons now had power, but the events which had given it to them earned them a depth of unpopularity that they were never to overcome.

89. *Andrew Marvell,* by an unknown artist, *c.* 1655–60.
Oil on canvas, $23\frac{1}{2} \times 18\frac{1}{2}$ in. (59.7 × 47 cm.).
London, National Portrait Gallery.
The son of a Yorkshire clergyman, Marvell was abroad during the civil war years. Having returned to England he addressed poems to royalists in the late 1640s. His 'Horatian Ode' of 1650 expresses the ambivalence of his feelings about the rise of a new Cromwellian order, and contains the only lines to have done justice to the execution of the king in January 1649, when Charles 'nothing common did or mean/ Upon that memorable scene'. Soon afterwards the poet became tutor to Fairfax's daughter Mary at Appleton House in Yorkshire. Under Cromwell he found employment first as an agent in France and then as a colleague of his friend Milton in Cromwell's secretariat. He wrote poems in praise of Cromwell on the first anniversary of his rule as Protector in 1654 and on his death in 1658. After the Restoration, as MP for his native Hull, he became a Whig pamphleteer.

90 (overleaf). Weesop, *The Execution of Charles I in 1649.*
Oil on canvas, $64\frac{1}{2} \times 117$ in. (163.2 × 296.8 cm.).
By permission of the Earl of Rosebery.
In the cold weather Charles wore an extra shirt so that he would not shiver and give the impression of fear. On the scaffold he made an effective speech against his 'arbitrary' judges and 'the power of the sword', and reminded his hearers that 'A subject and sovereign are clear distinct things . . . I have a good cause and I have a gracious God; I will say no more.' To his chaplain William Juxon he observed, 'I go from a corruptible to an incorruptible crown, where no disturbance can be, no disturbance in the world.' The block beneath which he had to place his head was unusually low. Among the spectators was the schoolboy Samuel Pepys. So was another boy who would never forget the sound that broke from the crowd when the axe fell, 'such a groan as I never heard before, and desire I may never hear again.'

THE GREAT SEALE OF ENGLAND 1651
THE IRISH SEA
THE BRITISH SEA

IN·THE·THIRD·YEARE·OF·FREEDOME·BY·GODS·BLESSING·RESTORED·1651

CHAPTER FIVE

Cromwellian England 1649–1660

The Rule of the Rump, 1649–1653

Between the execution of Charles I in January 1649 and the restoration of his son in May 1660, England was governed without a king. It was governed too without the House of Lords, most members of which had supported Charles in the civil wars and which was abolished in 1649 as 'useless and dangerous'. The new rulers declared that 'the commons of England, in parliament assembled, have the supreme power in this nation', and that the country would 'henceforth be governed as a Commonwealth and Free State by the representatives of the people in parliament'. But England neither was nor wished to be represented by a House of Commons from which royalists had long been excluded, which had been deprived by Pride's Purge of more than half the members who had opposed the king in the wars, and which had supervised the judicial murder of the king. During the Interregnum 'supreme power' lay not with parliaments, but with the Cromwellian army, the creator and destroyer of a series of unsuccessful regimes. The army did not covet military rule. It wanted a republican government answerable not to the traditional 'kingly' or 'lordly interest', but to the people, 'the original of all just power'; and even if it rarely explained who 'the people' were, it respected and often observed many principles of civilian and constitutional rule. But it also had a programme which it was determined to implement, and which held little appeal to a nation exhausted by the wars, demoralized by a postwar trading depression and desperate for settlement and stability.

The army believed that the victories it had won and the blood it had spilled entitled it to a share in the resolution of the conflict. It also saw itself as the patron of civilian groups – religious sectaries and radicals in the wartime administration in the counties – whom its presence alone sheltered from the wrath of postwar reaction. With those groups the soldiers, or at least some of the most influential of them, shared a compelling vision. The army's triumphs, they believed, had marked it as the instrument of providence, raised by God to purify the land of its social and institutional corruptions. England was a chosen nation as Israel had been; and in the 1640s God's elect, his 'saints', had been miraculously delivered from the Egyptian bondage of Laudian persecution, had crossed the red sea of civil war blood, and were now entering a promised land. The regicide was to be the prelude to more revolutionary changes. The purge of God's enemies in parliament would be followed by a purge of local government and by the elevation there of 'honest' radicals generally less well-born than the leading gentry who traditionally administered the counties. The archaic language and the complex proceedings of the common law would be reformed, so that all clients could understand them and would be spared the exorbitant fees exacted and the immoderate delays practised by those 'verminous caterpillars', the lawyers. Then there would be electoral reform: for if the authority of parliaments derived from their representative function, it followed that the unrepresentative and haphazard distribution of constituencies should be overhauled and the many rotten boroughs swept away. There might be an extension of voting rights, perhaps even a universal male franchise, although radicals were sufficiently alert to the shortage of popular support for their programme to moderate and then forget that demand. The restrictive privileges of trading companies would be removed, as would inequitable terms of land tenure.

Above all there would be religious reform. Virulent anticlericalism was directed by radicals at ministers ('dumb dogs') too slothful and ignorant, or too preoccupied with the outward formalities of worship, to satisfy lay hunger for spiritual experience and for animating sermons. It was aimed, too, at tithes, the compulsory levy by which the clergy was financed. Instead of the uniform and intolerant state Church which had been sought in an Anglican form by Laud in the 1630s and in a Puritan form by Presbyterians in the 1640s, the army demanded liberty of conscience,

91. The Great Seal of England, 1651.
The seal, made in 'the third year of freedom by God's blessing restored' – the first being 1649, the year when monarchy was abolished – shows England ruled by its sovereign representatives, the members of the Rump of the Long Parliament that held power after Pride's Purge. The new-found sea power of the republic is lauded by the seal, which also suggests England's aspiration towards a union of the British isles, an aim achieved in 1652–4. During the rule of the Rump there were rarely as many members in attendance as are shown here. The word 'restored' appeals to the idea of an ancient free constitution suppressed by the rise of monarchy.

S.C.

at least for those sects in whom it could recognize godliness of spirit. During the wars the collapse of the Church of England and of press censorship had made room for an unprecedented degree of religious variety and experiment. Troops had found that differences of belief among them had impaired neither their comradeship nor their sense that they were fighting the Lord's battles. God, they believed, allowed his followers to worship Him in different forms, as the light He had given them would direct. In a host of voluntarily gathered congregations, individual experience rather than conformity to man-made systems of belief and practice was seen as the key to religious authenticity.

Some thinkers, John Milton among them, wanted a total separation of Church from state. Most radicals, however, were eager to put the resources of the state behind the purification of the Church. In that, at least, they resembled the orthodox Puritans represented in the Long Parliament both before and after Pride's Purge. The demand for reform was not a radical preserve. The Puritan gentry, whose political outlook in the opening stages of the Long Parliament had been so conservative, viewed the nation's religious problems in a more zealous spirit. They had long striven to improve the quality of the ministry and to spread or 'propagate' the gospel in those 'backward parts of the land' – especially Wales and the north – where popery and superstition had proved most resilient. They were susceptible, as their excitement during the popish scares of 1640–2 had shown, to moods of apocalyptic despair and messianic hope; and they were as keen as the army to suppress the vice, the drunkenness and the blasphemy which they believed to be rife in England and which were certain to provoke divine punishment on the nation were they not eliminated. In more secular matters they often favoured at least a moderate degree of legal and electoral reform; for they resented both the endless litigation which disputes about the possession and inheritance of land involved and the massive electoral patronage which the rotten boroughs had given to the crown and to a handful of wealthy noblemen. But reforming enthusiasm had been discredited by the democratic agitation led by Levellers and sectaries in the 1640s and by the New Model's hated interventions in politics. The Puritan gentry discerned in the army's programme a threat not merely to institutional vested interests – in which some of them had stakes – but to the entire social order. And many MPs, sharing the Presbyterian belief that religious variety was in itself offensive to God, were bewildered and appalled by the rise of the sects. 'We shall have as many religions as there be men of different judgements', prophesied the Presbyterians after the regicide; 'so farewell Protestant religion.' Of all the army's demands, liberty of conscience was that which it pressed most consistently during the Interregnum and which its enemies most firmly resisted.

No one was more anxious for liberty of conscience than Oliver Cromwell, the dominant figure in the army

92. Samuel Cooper, *Oliver Cromwell*, 1649.
Miniature. London, National Portrait Gallery.
The earliest known portrait of Cromwell, painted in the year of Charles I's execution. It was until recently supposed to be of the Cromwellian colonel Robert Lilburne.

(1349) **Numb. 85.**

Mercurius Politicus.

Compriſing the ſumme of all Intelligence, with the Affairs and Deſigns now on foot in the three Nations of *England*, *Ireland*, and *Scotland*.

In defence of the Common-wealth, and for Information of the People.

——*Ita vertere Seria.* {Hor. de Ar. Poet.

From *Thurſday*, January 15. to *Thurſday*, January 22. 1652.

O go on upon our old Subject of a *free-State* or *Government by the People*, as it is conſtituted in a *due and orderly ſucceſſion of their ſupreme Aſſemblies*; and to prove its excellency above all other Forms, wee ſhall make matters yet more evident by *Reaſon*.

A *Tenth Reaſon* is, becauſe under this Government, the People are ever endued with a more Magnanimous, active, & noble Temper of ſpirit, then under the grandeur of any *ſtanding Power* whatſoever: And this ariſeth from that apprehenſion which every particular man hath of his owne immediate ſhare in the *publick Intereſt*, as well as of that ſecurity which he poſſeſſeth in the enjoyment of his *private Fortune*, free from the reach of any *arbitrary Power*. Hence it is, that whenſoever any good ſucceſs or happineſs betides the Publick, every one counts it his own; If the Commonwealth conquer, thrive in Dominion, wealth, or honour, he reckons all don for himſelf; If he ſee diſtributions of honour, high Hhhhhhhh Offices,

93. *Mercurius Politicus*, 15–22 January 1652 (new style).
One of a series of editorials in a weekly government newspaper urging the superiority of republican to monarchical government. A new confidence is evident in such assertions after the defeat of the royalists at Worcester in 1651. The editor, Marchamont Nedham, was a friend of Milton and of Marvell. The Rump, having secured a tight control of the press by a censorship act of September 1649, allowed only reporting and comment favourable to the regime. In general its newspapers concentrated more on events abroad than at home – where, as one of them put it, 'to have no news is good news'. Even so, the newspapers seem to have been quite widely read. The government relied upon them for the communication of information and of attitudes to its representatives in the localities and overseas.

– a Huntingdonshire squire of limited means whose military exploits had raised him from provincial obscurity and from the backbenches of the Commons, and whom soldiers and sectaries, seeing him as the agent of their plans, urged to think of himself as England's Moses. The sects were his political constituency. The intimacy of the bonds he had formed with his troops had left an indelible impression on him; and amidst the perplexities of politics in the 1650s, when God's wishes were so much harder to discern than in the outcome of civil war battles, he would yearn for the companionship and the certainties of those earlier years. The combination – which to his enemies betokened fathomless hypocrisy – of his unshakeable commitment to God's cause and his intuitive capacity for effective political manipulation was of critical importance in the aftermath of the regicide. While others wavered amidst the problems which beset the new republic, he had the decisiveness to act and the courage and authority to lead his followers into the uncharted political waters of kingless rule. Yet those problems impelled him not towards revolutionary courses, but towards cautious and conciliatory ones. They impelled others in the army in the same direction.

94. 'The Scots Holding their young Kinges Nose to the Grinstone'. Contemporary print.
The cartoon illustrates Charles II's humiliating dilemma of 1650. After the defeat of his supporters in Ireland the previous year, he could turn only to Scotland. There he had to woo the Presbyterians, who had fought against his father in the 1640s, but whose dislike of the Stuarts was exceeded by their hatred of the sectarian republic in England. They agreed to fight for Charles II only on conditions which gravely impaired his sovereignty. But the Scottish defeat at Dunbar at least had for Charles the consolation of weakening the Presbyterians' hold over him.

Even the junior officers, generally the most eager advocates of reformation, accepted in 1649 that their reform programme must be postponed.

The infant Commonwealth needed urgently to widen the basis of its acceptance. Above all it needed the support, or at least the forbearance, of political Presbyterianism: that is, of that broad section of opinion which had opposed Charles I in the war but which had wanted to see him restored honourably to his throne, and which had been shocked by Pride's Purge and the execution – the events which had driven Presbyterians from power. The danger now was that further manifestations of army radicalism, either in politics or in religion, would provoke Presbyterians into supporting the Stuart cause. The government faced the threat of royalist insurrection at home and of royalist invasion from abroad. Charles II, who dated his accession from his father's execution, learned of the regicide in Holland, one of the countries where his wandering exile would find him during the coming eleven years. The new king was gratified by the unanimous condemnations of the regicide by his fellow European monarchs. Their protests were not accompanied by practical offers of arms or money; for the English republic had a mighty army and navy behind it, and the great powers of France and Spain, at war with each other, both saw in the Commonwealth a powerful potential ally. Yet the new republic could not predict the reluctance of European monarchs to espouse the royalists' hopes of restoration. Both the domestic and the foreign policies of all the Interregnum regimes were to be profoundly influenced by the Stuart danger. In 1649 the gravest royalist peril came from Ireland and Scotland. From a British perspective the English civil wars had been merely a part of a war in three kingdoms; and only in England had the royalists been defeated and disarmed.

In these circumstances, the army dropped the demand for fresh elections that it had persistently made until its accession to power. Instead it permitted the survival until 1653 of that remnant of the Long Parliament, the 'Rump', which had survived Pride's Purge. The wars had transformed the character of parliament. Before 1640 parliaments had sat only for short periods at long intervals and had had no place in the executive. The Long Parliament, by contrast, became first a war machine and then the government. The Rump entrusted executive power to a Council of State which consisted largely of MPs and which was firmly subordinated to the Commons. Yet while the Rump gave itself revolutionary powers, few of its members had revolutionary aims. Some of them had taken part in the king's trial, like the republican Henry Marten

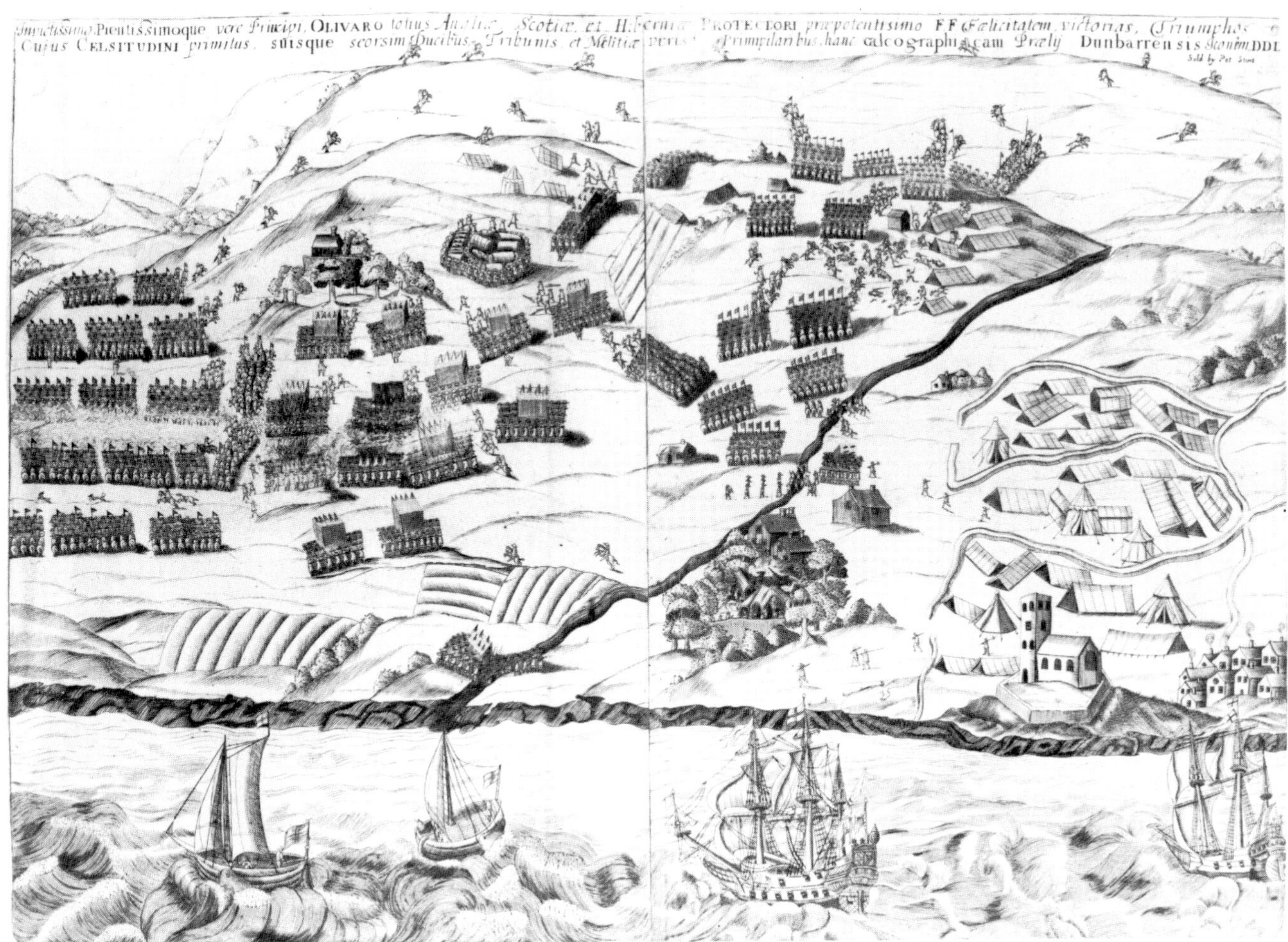

95. The Battle of Dunbar, 1650. Contemporary engraving. Oxford, Ashmolean Museum.
This print was made for Payne Fisher, the panegyrist poet of the Cromwellian period. Cromwell's forces are in the bottom right-hand corner, close to the town of Dunbar, and supplied from the sea. Cromwell won no more important or more surprising a victory than at Dunbar. Trapped on the coast, apparently at the mercy of the Scots, he succeeded in tempting them down from the hills into battle. On the night before the fight, knowing the odds were heavily against him and that the godly cause for which he fought seemed on the verge of extinction, he reportedly bit his lip until the blood came from it. After the victory he 'did laugh so excessively as if he had been drunk, and his eyes sparkled with spirits'. In his triumph he wrote to parliament urging it to 'relieve the oppressed', 'hear the groans of poor prisoners', 'reform the abuses of all professions; and if there be anyone that makes many poor to make a few rich, that suits not a commonwealth.' He was often to be uncomfortably reminded of those sentiments during his later periods of relative conservatism.

who had befriended the Levellers. But many if not most of Marten's parliamentary colleagues were conventional Puritan country gentlemen whose purpose in agreeing to sit in the purged parliament was not to further the army's programme, but on the contrary to moderate the revolution's course. A number of such men joined the Rump only after the regicide, with which they had had nothing to do.

From the summer of 1649 to that of 1651, domestic politics were overshadowed by Cromwell's campaigns in Ireland and Scotland. In 1649, determined to break the Irish resistance quickly, he rescued the English republic by his massacres, which have left so dreadful a memory, at Drogheda and Wexford – although Ireland was not to be wholly subdued for a further three years. In 1650, having returned to England a conquering hero, he invaded Scotland and against all the odds defeated the Scots at Dunbar. After a further year's campaign he pursued the enemy army into England and eliminated it at the battle of Worcester in September 1651. These campaigns, and the suppression of royalism in England, had to be supported by massive taxation at home – taxation inflicted by a government which was also driven, by its lack of support in the provinces, to impose on them a degree of centralized authority greater than that which had earned Charles I so much unpopularity in the 1630s. In 1649–50 the Rump sought to drive a wedge between royalists and Presbyterians by requiring all citizens to make a promise – an 'engagement' – of loyalty to the republic. To the government's dismay the Presbyterians, instead of being won over by the mild wording of the test, protested vigorously

96. The gatehouse, Llanhydrock House, Cornwall, 1651.
One of the few elegant buildings to have been raised in England during the Interregnum, the gatehouse was put up in 1651 on Lord Robartes's estate at Llanhydrock in Cornwall. The Robartes family had acquired great wealth through trade in tin and wool in the sixteenth century, and was raised to the peerage in 1625. In the 1630s Robartes built a fine gallery and library, the plaster barrel ceiling showing richly decorated biblical motifs. In the civil wars he fought prominently for the parliamentary cause in the West Country, but like his fellow peer Lord Wharton (see Pl. 87), he withdrew from politics after the events of 1648–9; the gatehouse was a product of his retirement. After the Restoration he was made Lord Deputy of Ireland. Clarendon called him 'a man of more than ordinary parts, well versed in the knowledge of the law, and esteemed of integrity not to be corrupted by money. But he was a sullen, morose man, intolerably proud, and had some humours as inconvenient as small vices, which made him hard to live with.' His wife, who seems to have met that challenge, was a daughter of the parliamentary leader the Earl of Warwick.

against its interrogation of their consciences. Cromwell's campaigns did win for the Commonwealth a measure of support in England, for some Englishmen's hatred of Irishmen and Scotsmen seems to have gone still deeper than their dislike of regicide. When Charles led the Scottish army towards Worcester in 1651, few Englishmen rose to join him. Even so, much of the king's support in Scotland came from religious Presbyterians, and Presbyterians in England were dismayed to find their country at war with their co-religionists. Their scruples were shared by Lord General Fairfax, who in 1650 embarrassed the government by resigning his command rather than lead the

THE
Declaration and Standard

Of the *Levellers* of *England*;
Delivered in a Speech to his Excellency the Lord Gen. *Fairfax*, on *Friday* laſt at White-Hall, by Mr. *Everard*, a late Member of the Army, and his Propheſie in reference thereunto; ſhewing what will befall the Nobility and Gentry of this Nation, by their ſubmitting to community; With their invitation and promiſe unto the people, and their proceedings in *Windſor* Park, *Oatlands* park, and ſeverall other places; alſo, the Examination and confeſſion of the ſaid Mr. *Everard* before his Excellency, the manner of his deportment with his Hat on, and his ſeverall ſpeeches and expreſſions, when he was commanded to put it off. Together with a Liſt of the ſeverall Regiments of Horſe and Foot that have caſt Lots to go for *Ireland*.

Imprinted at *London*, for *G. Laurenſon*, *April* 23. 1649.

The Ranters Declaration,

WITH

Their new Oath and Proteſtation; their ſtrange Votes, and a new way to get money; their Proclamation and Summons; their new way of Ranting, *never before heard of*; their dancing of the *Hey* naked, at the white *Lyon* in Peticoat-lane; their mad Dream, and Dr. *Pockridge* his Speech, with their Trial, Examination, and Anſwers: the coming in of 3000. their Prayer and Recantation, *to be in all Cities and Market-towns read and publiſhed*; the mad-Ranters further Reſolution; their Chriſtmas Carol, and blaſpheming Song; their two pretended-abominable Keyes to enter Heaven, and the worſhiping of his little majeſty, the late Biſhop of *Canterbury*: A new and further Diſcovery of their black Art, with the Names of thoſe that are poſſeſt by the Devil, having ſtrange and hideous cries heard within them, *to the great admiration of all thoſe that ſhall read and peruſe this enſuing ſubject.*

Licenſed according to order, and publiſhed by M. *Stubs*, a late fellow-Ranter

Increaſe multiply
VVe have over com the Devil

Imprinted at London, by J. C. MDCL.

97. *The Declaration and Standard of the Levellers of England* (1649).
In April 1649, a time of grave economic hardship, a band of poor people occupied and planted land on St George's Hill near Walton-on-Thames in Surrey, and invited others to join them in a colony where all goods would be held in common. The settlement was dispersed by an angry crowd, Cromwellian soldiers among them. The leaders of the 'Diggers' were William Everard, a former radical trooper of the New Model, and the eloquent pamphleteer Gerrard Winstanley. Whereas Lilburne and his friends, who were nicknamed Levellers, repudiated the term and declared their belief in property, the Diggers called themselves Levellers (as here) or 'True Levellers'. Everard's refusal to take off his hat before his superiors, referred to here, anticipated a principle of the Quakers in the 1650s. The vigorous and radical programme advanced by the Diggers in 1649 indicates the high but vain hopes of social transformation raised by the execution of the king.

98. *The Ranters Declaration* (1650).
One of the pamphlets hostile to the Ranters produced in 1650, a year when the sect was reported to be spreading widely and when the Rump passed severe legislation against adultery and blasphemy. The celebration of Christmas, mocked here, was a target of persistent and unavailing Puritan criticism. The date written on the title page, 'Dec[ember] 17', is inscribed by the contemporary London bookseller George Thomason, a Presbyterian who greatly helped subsequent historians by making a collection of more than 20,000 pamphlets during the Puritan Revolution and noting the dates of their appearance. The collection is now in the British Library.

August. 1. 1653

The true manner of the fitting of the Parliament of the Commonwealth of England, &c. Together with a perfect Catalogue of their Names, and for what Places they Serve.

Alfo the Names of the Members of the feverall Committees, and the Places where they fit, for People to make their Addreffes to them, to regulate the Abufes of the Commonwealth.&c.

A Lift of the Parliament men.

Berks.
SAmuel Dunch
Vincent Goddard
Thomas Wood.

Bedford.
Nathanael Taylor
Edward Cater.

Buckingham.
George Fleetwood
George Baldwin.

Cambridge.
John Sadler
Thomas French
Robert Caftle
Samuel Warner

Chefter.
Robert Duckenfield
Henry Birkinhead.

Four Northern Counties.
Charls Howard
Robert Fenwick
Henry Dawfon
Henry Ogle,

Cornewal.
Robert Bennet
Francis Langdon
Anthony Rous
John Bawden.

Derby.
Jervas Bennet
Nathanael Barton.

Devon.
George Monk, *one of the Generals at Sea.*
John Carew
Thomas Sanders,
Chriftopher Martin
James Erifey
Francis Rous
Richard Sweet

Dorfet.
William Sydenham
John Bingham

Effex.
Joachim Matthews
Henry Barington
John Brewfter
Chriftopher Earle
Dudley Templer.

Glocefter.
John Crofts
William Neaft
Robert Holmes

Southampton.
Richard Norton
Richard Major
John Hildefley

Hertford.
Henry Lawrence
William Reeve.

Hereford.
Wroth Rogers
John Herring.

Huntington.
Edward Montague
Stephen Phefaunt.

Kent.
Lord Vifcount Lifle
Thomas Blount
William Kenrick,
William Cullen
Andrew Broughton

Lancafter.
William Weft
John Sawrey
Robert Cunliff

Leicefter.
Henry Danvers
Edward Smith
John Prat.

Lincoln.
Sir Will. Brownlow
Richard Cuft
Barnaby Bowtel
Humphrey Walcot
William Thompfon.

Middlefex.
Sir William Roberts
Auguftine Wingfield
Arthur Squib.

Monmouth
Phillip Jones.

Northampton.
Sir Gilbert Pickering
Thomas Brook

Norfolk.
Robert Jermy
Tobias Freere
Ralph Wolmer
Henry King
William Burton

Nottingham.
John Oddingfels
Edward Clud.

Oxon.
Sir Charles Wolfley
William Draper
Dr. Jonathan Goddard

Rutland.
Edward Horfeman

Salop.
William Botterel
Thomas Baker.

Stafford.
George Bellit
John Chetwood.

Suffolk.
Jacob Caley
Francis Brewfter
Robert Dunkon
John Clark,
Edward Plumftead

Somerfet.
Robert Blake *one of the Generals at fea.*
Iohn Pine
Dennis Hollifter
Henry Henly.

Surrey.
Samuel Highland
Lawrence March

Suffex.
Anthony Stapeley
William Spence.
Nathanael Studeley

Warwick,
Iohn St. Nicholas
Richard Lucy

Wilts.
Sir Ant. Afhley Cooper
Nicholas Green
Thomas Eyre.

Worcefter.
Richard Salway
Iohn Iames.

Yorke.
George *Lord* Evre
Walter Strickland.
Francis Laffels
John Anlaby
Thomas Dickenfon
Thomas St. Nicholas
Roger Coats
Edward Gill.

London.
Robert Titchborn
John Ireton
Samuel Moyer
John Langley
John Stone
Henry Barton
Praife-God Barbone.

Wales.
Bufhy Manfel
James Philips
John Williams
Hugh Courtney
Richard Price
John Brown.

Scotland.
Sir James Hope
Alexander Bredy
John Swinton
William Lockart
Alexander Jefferies.

Ireland.
Sir Robert King
Col. John Hewfon
Col. Henry Cromwel
Col. John Clark
Daniel Hutchinfon
Vincent Gookyn.

Called in by the Parliament, fince they fate.
Lord Gen. Cromwel
Major Gen. Lambert
Major Gen. Harifon
Maj. Gen. Desborough
Col. Matth. Tomlinfon

The *Councel* of *State.*

Lord General *Cromwel*
Major Gen. *Lambert*
Major Gen. *Harrifon*
Maj. Gen. *Desborough.*
Sir *Gilbert Pickering*
Col. Tomlinfon
Col. Bennet
Col. Stapeley
Col. Sidnam
Col. Jones
Mr. Jo. Carew
Mr. Walt. Strickland
Mr. Moyer
Major Salloway
Sir Anth Afhley Cooper
Sir Charls Wolfley
Sir James Hope
Lieu. Gen. Fleetwood
Mr. Broughton
Col. Hewfon
Alderman Tichborne
Col. Norton
Mr. Lawrence
Mr. Courtney
Mr. Major
Mr. Howard
Col. Montague
Mr. St. Nicholas
Mr. Williams
Mr. Holften

A Committee for the affairs of Scotland.
LOrd Gen. Cromwel
Maj. Gen. Lambert
Major General Harrifon
Alderman Titchborn
Captain Charls Howard
Mr. Alexander Jefferies
Mr. Henry Henly
Mr. Danvers
Major Thomas Sanders
Mr. Nathaniel Tailor
Mr. John Sawrey
Mr. Robert Fenwick
Mr. John Odenfels
Mr. John St. Nicholas
Mr. Nathanael Studley.

The Quorum feven, and to fit in the Houfe commonly called The Lords Houfe.

A Committee for the affaires of Ireland.
Lord Gen. Cromwell
Maj. Gen. Lambert.
Sir Robert King
Mr. Spence
Col. Cromwel
Mr. Frere
Col. Hewfon
Col. Hutchinfon
Col. Clark
Mr. Manfel
Mr. Gookin
Mr. Clark
Col. Weft
Col. Phillip Jones
Mr. Francis Brewfter.
The Quorum or any five to meet in the Lords houfe.

A Committee for difcovery of Bribery, fraud, breach of publick Truft, and publique Debts.
Sir Gilbert Pickering
Mr. Strickland
Col. Bingham
Mr. Sadler
Col. Duckenfield
Col. Kenrick
Col. Montague
George Lo. Evre
Mr. Wil. Reeve
Mr. Bowtell
Mr. Hildefley
Mr. Cafell
Mr. Laffells. Or any five of them, to fit in the Dutchy Court.

A Committee for the Army.
Col. Sidenham
Mr. William Lockart
Col. Norton
Col. Clark,
Mr. Wil. Lockart
Mr. Wolmer
Col. Pine
Mr. Lucy
Col. Weft
Mr. Cuft
Mr. Horfeman
Mr. Clud
Mr. Fleetwood
Mr. Neaft
Col. Bennet
Mr. Anlaby.
Quorum five.

A Committee for the Law
Sir Antho. Afhley Cooper
Sir Wil. Roberts
Sir Wil. Brownlow
Maj. Gen. Desborough
Col. Matth. Tomlinfon
Mr. Sadler
Col. Blount
M. Jo. Brewfter
M. Taylor
M. Jervas Bennet
Mr. Gill
M. King
Mr. Swinton.
Mr. Nath. Barton
Mr. Coates
Mr. Wingfield
Mr. Spence
Mr. Moyer.
Col. Weft.
Quorum 5. *To fit in the* Chequer Chamber.

A Committee to confider of the Treafury.
Maj. Gen. Harrifon
Mr. Squib
Col. Bennet
Col. James.
Col. Blount
Mr. Wolmer
Mr. Jacob Caley
Mr. Cunliffe
Mr. Birkinhead
Mr. Stone
Mr. Botterel
Major Bawden
Mr. Barington
Alderm. Ireton
Mr. Moyer
Mr. Hildefley
Sir Wil. Roberts
Mr. Anlaby
Mr. Thomfon
Col. Weft
Or any five of them, to fit in the Court of Wards.

A Committee for advancement of Learning.
Mr. Strickland
Mr. Sadler
Mr. Lawrence
Mr. Wingfield
Dr. Goddard
Col. Barton
Mr. Spence
Sir Anth. Afhley-Cooper
Col. Sidenham
Alderm. Tichburn
Col. Montague
Mr. Lockart
Sir. Robert King
Col. Blount
Sir Wil. Roberts
Mr. John St. Nicholas
Col. Matthewes
Mr. Cuft.
The Quorum to be five and to meete in the Dutchy Chamber.

A Committee for Tythes.
Major Gen. Harrifon
Mr. Sadler
Sir Antho. Afhley Cooper
Col. Barton
Praifegod Barbone
Col. Blount
Mr. Highland
Alder. Titchburn
Maj. Generall Desborough
Col. Clark
Mr. Strickland
Col. Sidenham
Col. Danvers
Sir Wil. Roberts
Mr. Jefferies
Mr. Spence
Mr. Squib
Mr. Wolmer
Mr. Weft
Col. Kenrick
Mr. Freer
Capt. Stone
Mr. Taylor
Mr. Wingfield
Col. Rous
Mr. Moyer
Major Horfeman
Mr. Plumftead
Mr. Herring
Mr. Courtney
Mr. Gill
Mr Swinton
And the care hereof is committed to M. Sadler, M. Taylor, and Col. Weft to fit in the Chequer Chamber.

A Committee for the poor, and regulating Commiffions of Peace; for Alms-houfes, and for Printing.
Mr. Baldwyn
Mr. Ogle
Mr. Chetwood
Maj. Sanders
Mr. Wood
Mr. Draper
Mr. Langdon
Mr. Thomas St. Nicholas.
Mr. Brook
Mr. Cater
Mr. Green
Mr. Bennet
Mr. Barton
Mr. Barrington
Mr. Tompfon
And all that come, to have voices to fit in the Queens Court.

A Committee for receiving Petitions.
Col. Rous
Mr. Dunch
Alderman Ireton
Mr. Barbone
Dr. Goddard
Mr. Crofts
Mr. Henry Barton
Mr. Freer
Mr. Earle
Mr. Jermy
Mr. Matthews
Mr. Hildefley
Mr. Erifley
Or any five of them, to fit in the Painted Chamber.

A Committee for Prifons and prifoners.
Mr. Anlaby
Mr. March
Col. James
Mr. Price
Mr. Highland
Mr. Herring
Mr. Bellit
Mr. Brown
Mr. Williams
Mr. Wingfield
Mr. Rogers
Mr. Cullen
Mr. Prat
Mr. Vin. Goddard
And any five of them, to fit in the Chequer Chamber

A Committee for the bufinefs of Trade, Corporations, and for receiving Propofitions for advance of the Commonwealth,
M. Sam. Warner
M. Sweet
M. Ald. Ireton
Mr. Hutchinfon
Mr. Dickenfon
Mr. Dawfon
Mr. Stone
Mr. Wood
Mr. Jefferies
Mr. French
Mr. Templer
Mr. Plumfteade
Mr Dunkon
Mr. Clarke
Mr. Moyer
Col. Bennet
Mr. Holmes
Mr. Coates
Mr. Barton.
Or any feven of them, to fit at Whitehall, in the old Councel Chamber.

FINIS.

London Printed by R. I. for Peter Stent 1653.

expedition to Scotland. Cromwell, long the effective leader of the army, at last became its titular head.

So long as the threat from Ireland and Scotland continued, the army took pains to distance itself from the radical fringe: from the Levellers, whose mutiny of May 1649 Cromwell crushed at Burford in the Cotswolds; from the Diggers or 'True Levellers', who went beyond Lilburne in seeking the abolition of private property and who to that purpose established a commune on St George's Hill in Surrey; and from the Ranters, whose colourful challenges to conventional morality and theology provoked the Rump into passing severe Puritanical legislation. But the army had merely suspended its reforming aspirations. In the weeks of radical excitement after Dunbar in 1650 the Rump was obliged to legislate for greater religious freedom and for the conversion of legal proceedings into intelligible English. Next year the victory at Worcester freed many officers, Cromwell at their head, to return to civilian politics and concentrate on the achievement of godly reformation. Yet once more Cromwell proved a restraining as much as a galvanizing influence. His instincts were always to preserve as broad a base for the revolution as possible and to work for reform in cooperation with existing institutions. As so often in the Interregnum he found himself a broker between the parliamentary and the military classes, urging reform on his fellow MPs and counselling patience to his officers. In pursuit of that strategy he was a stabilizing force. Yet there was always an unpredictable, not to say volcanic side to the character of a man who would suddenly turn on those moderate allies whom he had carefully cultivated and vilify them, in language close to that of his most radical followers, as agents of Antichrist.

So it was with the Rump Parliament. All Cromwell's efforts to secure constructive reform from it in 1651–3 were thwarted by a dilatoriness and an obstructiveness that can be explained largely by the House's hatred of the army. In the eyes even of republican MPs, who owed their share of power to the military coup of 1648–9, the army was the mere servant of parliament, not its master. Time and again during the Interregnum mistrust and anger would divide civilian from military politicians when the sole hope of both groups of implementing their unpopular (and frequently overlapping) programmes lay in cooperation between them. It was to be their inability to work together that finally destroyed the Puritan cause in 1659–60. In April 1653 the Rump disgusted Cromwell and the officers first by refusing to renew the Commission for the Propagation of the Gospel in Wales that had been set up three years earlier, and then by resolving to hold parliamentary elections that were likely to return an assembly even less sympathetic to the army's programme than the Rump was. On 20 April Cromwell led his musketeers into the chamber and, having vituperatively castigated former intimate friends as 'drunkards' and 'whoremasters', forcibly cleared the chamber. 'Thus', recorded the MP Bulstrode Whitelocke, 'was this great parliament which had done so great things, famous through the world for its successes, wholly at this time routed.'

Cromwell wanted parliamentary elections – in time. Parliaments were the principal means through which he might hope to reconcile the nation's natural leaders to Puritan rule. But first he needed to educate those rulers: to persuade them to understand the army's perspective and to accept the principle of liberty of conscience. An interim government of hand-picked Puritan notables would set the godly reformation in progress and, by practical legislation and moral example, would begin to Puritanize, and so to stabilize, the land. Such a body was the assembly of about 140 men, chosen by army officers, which gathered in July 1653 and which is known to history as Barebone's Parliament after the colourfully named London leatherseller Praisegod Barebone, who was elected to it. It was characteristic of Cromwell, and a surprise to those who suspected him of vaulting ambition, that having found himself with naked and absolute power after the coup of April he had hastened to divest himself of that burden. Barebone's, like the Rump before it, was given executive as well as legislative power; and Cromwell did not make himself a member of it.

The year 1653 was a heady one. Radical agitation during the Rump's last months had aroused messianic expectations among the sects and the army. The belief held by orthodox Puritans that they were living in the latter ages of the world was converted by 'Fifth Monarchy men' into a conviction that God had appointed them to inaugurate, if need be by force, the imminent thousand-year rule of the saints. The Fifth Monarchists had a powerful patron among the leading officers in Thomas Harrison, who in 1653 was rivalling Cromwell's role as patron of the sects; and Cromwell, although no Fifth Monarchist, was affected by the

99. *The true Manner of the Siting of the Parliament of the Commonwealth of England,* a broadsheet of 1653.
Although chosen by the army rather than by the electorate, Barebone's called itself a parliament and followed parliamentary procedures. Among the members listed in this broadsheet, which appeared on 1 August 1653, are George Monck (Devon), who was to command the army in Scotland under the protectorate and to engineer the restoration of monarchy in 1660, and Anthony Ashley Cooper (Wiltshire), a leader of the moderate Cromwellians in the assembly, who was to become Earl of Shaftesbury and the leader of the Whigs under Charles II. The allocation of seats to Ireland and Scotland was a novel feature of Barebone's, although the principle had already been accepted by the Rump.

apocalyptic public mood. In consequence Barebone's contained the most radical (as well as some of the socially least weighty) men to participate in the governments of the 1650s. When it met, the assembly solemnly assured the nation of its 'more than usual expectation of some great and strange changes coming on the world, which we believe can hardly be paralleled with any times, but those for a while before the birth of our Lord and Saviour Jesus Christ'. Barebone's was not the assembly of hare-brained fanatics that subsequent Cromwellian propaganda was to portray. But Cromwell believed that its extensive and well-intentioned plans for reform of law and Church would alienate groups that he was anxious to conciliate and might even lead to anarchy. In December another swift military coup handed power back to his hands. Barebone's, he came to think, had been 'a tale of my own weakness and folly'.

The Politics of the Protectorate, 1653–1658

In 1649–53 sovereign parliaments had replaced sovereign kings. In exercising that unchecked sovereignty, the Rump had been too conservative for Cromwell's liking, Barebone's too radical. Henceforth he accepted the need for a constitutional balance in which a single ruler would restrain and be restrained by parliaments. He had contemplated such a solution in 1647 when he had offered, in the 'Heads of the Proposals', to restore Charles I on generous terms in return for guarantees of reform and toleration; and in 1651 he had floated the suggestion of 'a government with somewhat of monarchical in it'. Cromwell was never a committed republican. He was never 'wedded and glued to forms of government', which were 'but dross and dung in comparison of Christ'. He was impatient with advocates of rigid formulas in state and Church alike. Men must follow where God's providence led, not prescribe to Him with constitutions of their own invention. Cromwell left constitution-building to others. Previously his architect had been his son-in-law and fellow officer Henry Ireton, who died in 1651. In December 1653 the role was taken by the young and ambitious officer John Lambert, who came forward with the Instrument of Government. By the provisions of this constitution Cromwell would rule as Lord Protector, assisted by an executive council and by parliaments of fixed frequency and duration. The first parliament would meet in September 1654 after Cromwell and his councillors had initiated moderate reforms.

How would this constitution be welcomed by the bulk of the nation committed neither to the Stuarts nor to Cromwell? Would it reconcile the political Presbyterians? The new regime did have its attractions to them. Cromwell had put an end to parliamentary tyranny and could present himself as the saviour of society after Barebone's; and the idea of a balanced constitution to which he had turned had been favoured by Presbyterians in their own negotiations with the king in the previous decade. In the opening months of the Protectorate Cromwell made overtures of national reconciliation. The Rump's 'engagement' of loyalty was at last withdrawn; Presbyterians were encouraged to return to local government and in the elections of 1654 had their first opportunity since Pride's Purge to take part in national political life; and although royalists were to remain disenfranchised throughout the 1650s, some who had abandoned their past loyalties were drawn into the Cromwellian administration, while others were allowed privately to persist with the Anglican worship that the Long Parliament had outlawed. Gradually, too, Cromwell reduced the size of his army. In this he dared not act rapidly, partly because he needed a defence against the Stuarts, partly because without an army he would have no bargaining power when he pressed parliaments for reform. He moved more quickly in reducing the taxation by which the army was supported: perhaps too quickly, because by sacrificing financial need to political conciliation he set the regime on a path of mounting indebtedness.

If only Cromwell's overtures to moderates could win him parliamentary endorsement of the Instrument, then his authority would lie not merely in armed coups but in the consent of a broad section of the gentry. To his anger, the parliament that met in 1654 declined his request for statutory ratification of the constitution. He moved quickly to exclude the most determined of his critics. On 12 September, eight days after the parliament had assembled, MPs once more found soldiers outside the chamber. Only members who would sign a declaration of basic loyalty to the Protectorate were permitted to resume their seats: a test which the outraged republicans, who believed that the sole legal authority still lay with the Rump which Cromwell had expelled in April 1653, refused to subscribe. Yet even without them, parliament attempted a major revision of the Instrument. It reasserted the principle of the army's subordination to parliament, demanded a much speedier reduction of the forces than Cromwell would allow and assailed the Instrument's provision for liberty of conscience. When Cromwell dissolved it in January 1655 the assembly had passed not a single piece of legislation. Once more Cromwell ruled solely by virtue of the sword. Soon his taxes were challenged in the courts in cases which ominously and ironically echoed the Ship Money case of the 1630s.

In Cromwell's usurpation, as they termed his elevation to the Protectorate, his various enemies – republicans, Presbyterians and royalists – discovered a common hatred. Republicans, unalterably opposed to the rule of a single person, were irreconcilable; Presbyterians in the parliament of 1654–5 had rejected his hand of friendship; and soon there came a perilous reminder of the persistence of discontent among royalists. Their plan for a national rising in March 1655 was thwarted, as were all royalist conspiracies of the Protectorate, by bad organization, by divided leadership and by the penetration of often indiscreet cavalier deliberations by the intelligence service of Cromwell's Secretary of State John Thurloe. Only in Wiltshire, under John Penruddock, did the rebellion get off the ground; and it was crushed easily enough. Yet Cromwell was startled by the extent of the plotting and by the obduracy of royalists who, he believed, should have recognized the hand of divine punishment in the outcome of the civil wars. His sense of isolation now strengthened, he turned from conciliation to repression. Anglican services were forbidden and restrictions placed on Cavaliers' movements. By the end of 1655 the country had been subjected to systematic military rule. England and Wales were divided into eleven districts, each presided over by its Major-General. The initial responsibility of the Major-Generals was to crush conspiracy, and this they achieved. But they were given

100. A page from Izaak Walton, *The Compleat Angler* (1653). *The attraction of Walton's work, which went into several editions, was enhanced by its appeal to royalists driven by Cromwellian rule out of political life and into the cultivation of rural pursuits. For Wotton see the Picture Essay, p. 66.*

The Epiſtle

know I ſpeak the truth.

Sir, this pleaſant curioſity of Fiſh & Fiſhing (of which you are ſo great a Maſter) has been thought worthy the pens *and* practices *of divers in other Nations, which have been reputed men of great* Learning *and* Wiſdom; *and amongſt thoſe of this Nation, I remember Sir* Henry Wotton *(a dear lover of this Art) has told me, that his intentions were to write a Diſcourſe of the* Art, *and in the praiſe of* Angling; *and doubtleſ*

101. Major-General Charles Worsley to John Thurloe, 17 December 1656. Bodleian Library, MS. Rawlinson A.33, f. 429. *The Major-Generals wrote regularly to John Thurloe, Cromwell's Secretary of State, describing their attempts to raise reliable militia forces in their regions and to identify royalists for punishment and taxation. This letter of Charles Worsley, Major-General for Lancashire, Cheshire and Staffordshire, begins: 'Sir, by my last I gave you an account of what trial we had made at Stafford and Middlewich and also that tomorrow we meet at Preston for this county of Lancaster of which I hope likewise to give you a good account shortly.' The optimism of the earlier letters of the Major-Generals was to fade in 1656, partly because the limits of regional support for their efforts had become clear, but partly too because the government gave them too little guidance and too little money. Worsley, driven by a sense of providential mission, was perhaps the most vigorous of the Major-Generals. None of them suppressed more alehouses or listed more royalist estates for confiscation. He died exhausted in 1656 aged 34. The chance survival of Thurloe's massive correspondence, which was discovered in an attic well after the Restoration, provides an indispensable source for the Protectorate.*

moral responsibilities as well. If parliament would not help Cromwell to Puritanize the nation, then the army would do it itself. The Major-Generals, Cromwell was to claim when the experiment had been abandoned, had been 'more effectual towards the discountenancing of vice and the settling of religion than anything done these fifty years'.

Around the rule of the Major-Generals there has grown a legend of military oppression which obscures the limits both of their impact and of their unpopularity. There was no novelty in the presence of soldiers in the localities. From the time of the civil wars the provinces had grown used to the movement and quartering of troops and to soldiers acting frequently if unofficially as tax-collectors or policemen. The protection given by Major-Generals to the law-abiding was not unwelcome; nor, to many, was the orthodox Puritan morality which they promoted when they suppressed alehouses or enforced observance of the sabbath. In any case their administrative duties, energetically as they pursued them, were well beyond their resources. They strove to cooperate with, rather than to replace, the gentry-dominated commissions of the peace and the other organs of local government; but they were cold-shouldered, and those of them who lacked local connections were unable to penetrate the intricacies and the secrets of provincial life. The most unpopular aspect of the Major-Generals' rule seems to have been the decision to finance them by an income tax on all civil war royalists, even on those who had determined to live peaceably. The county communities, which had been divided by national events in 1642, had been gradually reuniting in their opposition to national events since 1648. Presbyterians and royalists who had fought each other in the wars began to resume the dinner-parties and the bowling matches and the marital negotiations which had traditionally helped bind them together. Now they were appalled by a policy which might have been designed to reopen the wounds of war.

Yet when, in September 1656, financial exigency drove Cromwell to summon another parliament, he encountered a much more cooperative assembly than its predecessor. Its friendliness owed something to the efficiency with which the government had disqualified its most severe critics of the regime from sitting, but more to the coordination of a group of MPs led by the Anglo-Irish Protestant Lord Broghil, a brother of the scientist Robert Boyle. Broghil tentatively supported Charles I in the 1640s, Cromwell in the 1650s and Charles II in the 1660s. He led a younger generation of politicians who saw that the inflexible allegiances and the high ideals of their elders had produced only bloodshed and chaos and bitterness. In the spring of 1657 Broghil's party persuaded parliament to offer Cromwell the title of king. Their purpose was not to endorse military rule, but on the contrary to tie Cromwell to traditional constitutional constraints and, by making a civilian ruler of him, to isolate him from army radicalism. With the title, parliament offered a new constitution which, although retaining the essential features of the Instrument, would return to normality in other ways. Not least, it would restore a second chamber: not the House of Lords (although some Puritan peers would be invited to sit in it), but a nominated assembly representing the various interests which might accept Cromwellian rule.

Recent events had made the prospect of a second chamber attractive to Cromwell. In December 1656 the Commons, emulating the Rump by assuming judicial powers, tried the Quaker James Nayler within its walls. The Quakers of the 1650s were not always the respectable pacifists of later times. Indeed they were probably the most frightening as well as the largest of the sects produced by the Puritan revolution. Roaming through the country, they broke up church services, divided communities, challenged the authority of magistrates and published intemperate demands for radical social change. In 1656 Nayler, a charismatic figure followed by adoring women, rode into Bristol on a donkey in the manner of Christ's entry into Jerusalem. Outraged MPs warned each other of the divine punishment that would visit the nation should they fail to avenge God's honour. Cromwell was as shocked as MPs by Nayler's blasphemy. But if the Commons could act unchecked against Nayler, what was to prevent it from persecuting those more sober sectaries whom Cromwell loved and whom the army was determined to protect? A second chamber would set a hedge to the tyrannical intolerance of the Commons.

Cromwell warmed to the Humble Petition and Advice, which at last offered him parliamentary sanction for his rule, and he wooed the House by jettisoning the rule of the Major-Generals. Yet he balked at the title of king. Nothing could do more than his acceptance of the crown to restore the sense of legality on which a lasting settlement must depend. But Cromwell's officers, self-appointed guardians of his conscience, interpreted the proposal as a bait to apostacy; and although their mutterings were unlikely to produce serious mutiny, the Protector feared their reproaches. On the path to his elevation Cromwell had already lost many intimate friends. Pride's Purge had divided him from his godly allies among the constitutionalist parliamentarians such as Lord Wharton and William Pierrepoint. The dissolution of the Rump had earned him bitter accusations of betrayal from such MPs as

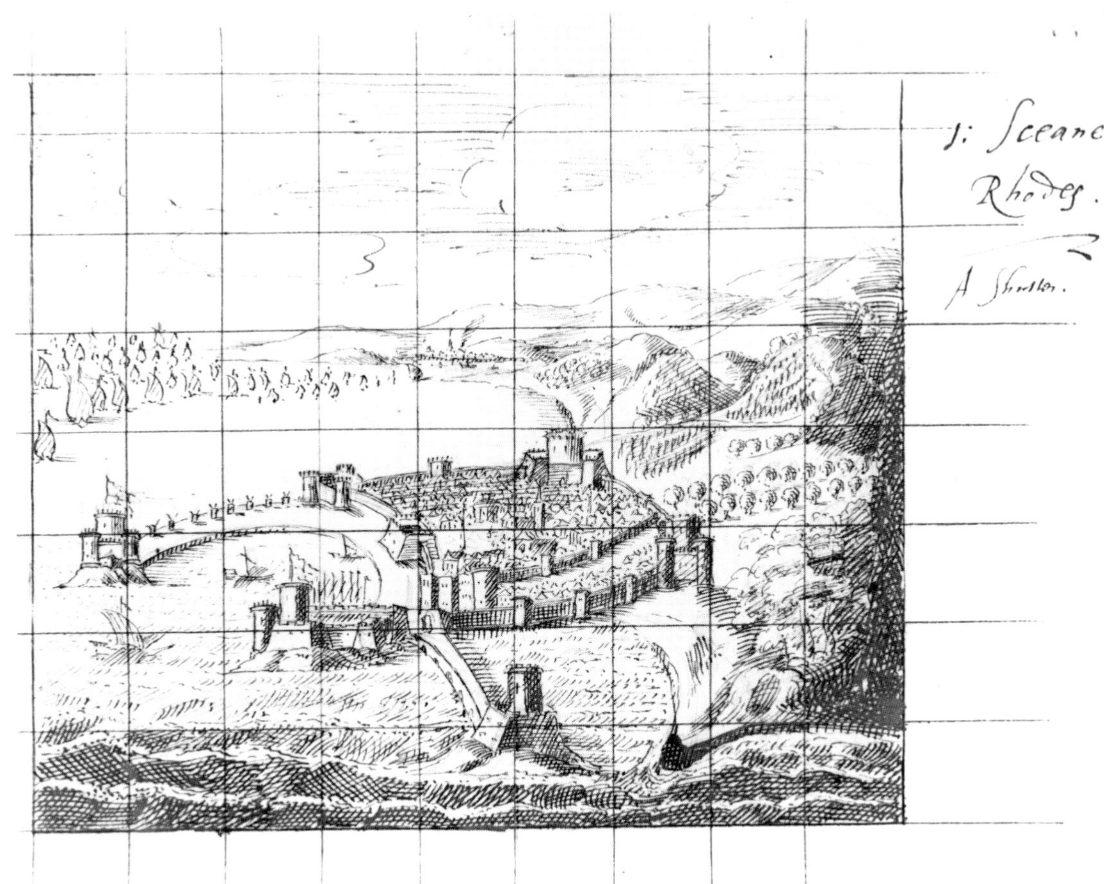

102. Stage design for *The Siege of Rhodes* (1656). Chatsworth House. *The play* The Siege of Rhodes *was produced at Rutland House in 1656, the text being sung* 'stilo recitativo'*; this was perhaps the first English opera. Although the closeness of Davenant to the Cromwellian regime can be exaggerated, music did flourish at the Protector's court. Among the actors in* The Siege of Rhodes *were the musicians Matthew Locke and the father of Henry Purcell (for whom see the Picture Essay, p. 226). John Webb, a pupil of Inigo Jones, produced the designs. The work was performed again with extensive revisions in 1663.*

Sir Henry Vane and Sir Arthur Hesilrige, his allies in the darkest days of civil war. At the dissolution of Barebone's he had broken with Thomas Harrison and other radical sectaries. From all sides he was reviled as a traitor whose ambition had destroyed the godly cause. To replace a Stuart monarchy with a Cromwellian one would be the loneliest of choices.

In May 1657, after weeks of solitary prayer and tortured indecision, Cromwell refused the crown. He was an ill and ageing man. Yet his political skills had not deserted him. Cleverly he persuaded parliament to enact the Humble Petition with the title of Protector, not of king. In the short term this was a wise enough decision, which once more displayed his ability to arbitrate between parliament and army. Even without the crown he was able to return to more traditional ways during 1657. His court became more stately and 'monarchical'; in provincial government tamed ex-royalists were once more welcomed back; and Anglican worship was almost openly permitted. In 1658, during the last months of Cromwell's life, there were fresh if unavailing moves to make him king. Yet in May 1657 he had missed his greatest opportunity to secure the nation's confidence and to give permanence to Puritan rule. His refusal of the crown gave fresh heart to his generals, above all to his relations John Desborough and Charles Fleetwood, men whose inflated stature derived from his favour and whose fondness for military solutions to his political problems seemed to have become discredited by his abandonment of the Major-Generals. Broghil's party in parliament, on the other hand, was demoralized by the failure of its initiative; and when the Commons, having adjourned in June, reassembled in January 1658, Cromwell found it a much less amicable body. The republicans, whom Cromwell had decided to readmit, led the attack on the powers and composition of the new second chamber and worked with discontented officers to raise trouble in the army. Cromwell stifled discontent in February by abruptly dissolving parliament and by purging the soldiery, but the episode was a foretaste of the problems that would arise once his restraining hand had been removed. The dissolution left the government without a policy, and on the Council a deadlock between the civilian and military factions persisted until Cromwell's death in September 1658 at the age of 59.

Cromwellian Policies

To outward appearances the Interregnum is a period of political sterility, in which frequent and fruitless changes of regime reflect the uncertainties and contradictions of Cromwell's purpose. It is certainly a period of frustrated hopes. Yet beneath the broken surface of the politics of the 1650s lay positive and consistent goals – even if Cromwell, as any politician must, changed his emphases and priorities under the pressure of events. His constitutional expedients were successive attempts to find a framework within which a reform programme could be executed and accepted, and a commonwealth fit for God's eyes created. That programme did not have the cutting social edge of reforms demanded by radicals: he was ever eager to preserve 'the ranks and orders of men, whereby England hath been known for hundreds of years'. It was a constructive and practical programme none the less.

First, he pressed consistently for law reform. In 1652 he persuaded the Rump to set up a commission chaired by the prominent lawyer Matthew Hale which devised a detailed scheme for extensive procedural changes. The Rump rejected the report as too radical, Barebone's as too conservative. In the Protectorate, seeking a middle path, he effected piecemeal improvements. Yet the law was probably the area where his reforming ambitions achieved least; for lawyers were no less skilful in the seventeenth century than they have always been in deflecting lay demands for simplified and cheaper procedure, and Cromwell's concern to give his rule an air of legitimacy made him reluctant to introduce measures which might provoke judges into resigning. His reform of the electoral system was more extensive. An elaborate scheme for geographical reapportionment and for the removal of rotten boroughs, based on proposals devised by the army in 1647–9 and the Rump in 1650–3, was incorporated into the Instrument of Government. In consequence the parliaments of 1654 and 1656 were elected in accordance with a reform quite as far-reaching as that of 1832. But whereas the Great Reform Act was to aim at pleasing the industrialized middle classes, Cromwell's pre-industrial reforms appealed to provincial country gentlemen, who wanted the regions to be represented not by the clients of courtiers and great noblemen who had long represented rotten boroughs but by their own kind. The change Cromwell effected was not a populist one. As Protector he favoured the redistribution of seats, but not a numerical extension of the electorate.

Government policy was not the sole source of reforming energy in the 1650s. In some areas, JPs and town officials devised novel schemes of poor relief. In religion, local initiatives led to the appointment of 'godly' ministers and to improvements in their stipends. In the 1640s the Long Parliament had replaced the Anglican Book of Common Prayer with Puritan forms of worship and had sought to impose a Puritan morality and a Puritan theology on the nation. It had also set up a Presbyterian form of Church government. Instead of the episcopal hierarchy imposed from above, a new chain of command was to work upwards from the parishes where Puritan laymen and Puritan clergy would run the churches and send representatives to regional assemblies and, through them, to national ones. The system was modelled on New Testament precept and on the example of Calvinist Geneva and Scotland, although it differed from foreign models in giving more control to Puritan laymen than to Puritan clergy, whose powers even the most zealous of English reformers viewed with suspicion; English anticlericalism ran even deeper than English Puritanism, and the new Presbyterian Church was firmly subordinated to the laity's representatives in parliament. In any event Presbyterian organization made headway only in a few areas – partly because Pride's Purge deprived Presbyterianism of its political base. Instead of the disciplined uniformity envisaged by orthodox Puritans, there was a variety of improvised local solutions that dismayed them by permitting both the survival of many inadequate or 'scandalous' ministers and the proliferation of sectarian heresies, some of them voiced by radicals who declined to go to church and worshipped privately among themselves. By 1649 there was in effect no national Church. The Puritan divine Richard Baxter of Worcestershire was eager to create one. He wanted to instil confidence into godly ministers and to help them rescue their parishioners from soul-destroying errors and from the despair about their own salvation which the theological wrangles of the 1640s had made widespread. Baxter's initiative lay behind the Association Movement of the 1650s, in which in a number of county ministers, who were conventionally Puritan in fundamental matters of faith and worship, learned to sink their differences in lesser ones and to cooperate in the propagation of the gospel.

In Baxter's eyes, Cromwell's ecclesiastical policy was too indulgent to the sects. To men who vainly urged the abolition of tithes, however, it seemed not radical enough. Cromwell rejected the intolerance of Presbyterians, but he shared their belief in the need for a national Church. His scheme of reconstruction was drawn up in 1652 by the minister John Owen, Cromwell's Vice-Chancellor of Oxford University. Like the Hale report on law reform of the same year, Owen's plan was thwarted by reactionary resistance in the

Rump and by radical resistance in Barebone's. Unlike the Hale report it was fully implemented – with some constructive amendments – under the Protectorate. Two bodies of commissioners were established. The first, the Triers (a term taken over from the Presbyterians), met in London and examined candidates for ordination. Representing a variety of Puritan beliefs, the Triers were permitted to test only the moral and doctrinal soundness of candidates, not their ecclesiastical preferences. The other commissioners were the Ejectors, who collaborated with Puritan gentry in the shires to weed out scandalous ministers.

Both bodies were bitterly attacked by Anglicans, although it is remarkable how many clergymen who had served under Laud accepted the changes brought by the Puritan Revolution and were able to retain their livings under successive Puritan regimes. Newly ordained Presbyterians, Congregationalists and Baptists learned to live alongside them and each other – sometimes even sharing the use of church buildings – in an ecclesiastical system that was at once stable and comprehensive – even if Cromwell never succeeded in establishing the Confession of Faith which would have given it a basis of doctrinal agreement. Slow to boast in other matters, Cromwell declared of his religious settlement that 'there hath not been such a service to England since the Christian religion was perfect in England'. Baxter conceded that the quality of the ministry had been greatly improved by Cromwell's policies, which accorded with the traditional Puritan concern for the propagation of the gospel. An alliance of godly ministers and godly magistrates would, Cromwell hoped, create a sober, virtuous, Puritanized ruling class whose example the nation would follow. Instead of sending their children abroad to be corrupted by grand tours in popish lands, the nobility and gentry would educate their children either at the Puritanized universities of Oxford and Cambridge, which the Long Parliament and then Cromwell reformed to that end, or at the college he founded at Durham for the sons of northern gentry.

Outside his Church, Cromwell created conditions in which diversity of religious practice became a habit. His tolerance is not to be mistaken for modern religious toleration, which derives from religious indifference. Cromwell's concern was to prevent persecution from breaking that lifeline of salvation through which God's grace reached the soul. Unlike the rigid Presbyterians, he believed that on the godly man's path to salvation truth might temporarily be mingled with error, which if left alone would pass with time. But Cromwell was a Calvinist who knew that most men were predestined from eternity to eternal torment, and despite the private magnanimity of his character he shared the Puritan indifference to the unredeemable. If he allowed some toleration to Anglicans, it was largely in the hope of winning their political support. If he was gentle with Catholics, it was to strengthen his bargaining hand with his Catholic ally France. When he readmitted the Jews, a group which had been expelled in the Middle Ages, to England in 1655–6, it was not because he sympathized with Jews or because he wanted trading benefits, but because he knew as a Puritan that the barrier between Jew and Gentile must be broken down before Christ came again.

If in the domestic field Cromwell had little success in persuading the Rump Parliament to introduce reforms, he was still less able to influence its foreign policy, which as Protector he rapidly reversed. He did concur with the Rump, however, in wanting to make effective use in Europe of the huge army and the improved navy which the civil wars had left behind. The early Stuarts, lacking those assets, had in Puritan eyes cut humiliating figures in Continental diplomacy, where they had appeased Catholic monarchies while the very survival of Protestantism was at stake in the Thirty Years War (1618–48). Yet when in 1652 the Commonwealth went to war, it was not against a Catholic power or a monarchy, but against the Dutch, a fellow Protestant republic which in a protracted war of independence had recently freed itself from the rule of Catholic Spain. Members of the Rump, led by Sir Arthur Hesilrige and Thomas Scot who drew England into the war, believed that she could become mighty abroad only when her international economic disadvantages had been overcome. The tiny Dutch nation, through superior techniques of capital and shipbuilding, had performed the economic miracle of seventeenth-century Europe. It had captured the maritime carrying trade; its fishing flourished; and it had captured markets, inside and outside Europe, from which England must dislodge it were its own economic potential to be realized.

The Rump did make gestures of friendship to the Dutch, and schemes were floated in the early 1650s for a division of the world's trade between the two nations and for an intimate alliance against Catholic powers; but the Dutch were not interested. Having founded in 1650 a Council of Trade devoted to commercial improvement and enterprise, the Rump in 1651 passed a Navigation Act which, with the aim of strengthening English shipping and her balance of trade, required that goods be imported into England only in English ships or in ships belonging to the country of their origin – a measure which in essence the restored monarchy, so scornful of republican innovation in other spheres, was to preserve in 1660. Dutch anger was intensified by the Rump's insistence that Dutch ships strike sail to English ones in acknowledgement of the maritime sovereignty claimed by the Commonwealth around the British Isles. The issue sparked off the Anglo-Dutch war of 1652–4, the first of three such conflicts over two decades. Initially the war went badly for England, but a reorganization of naval administration late in 1652 was followed by a 'huge crack of a sea victory' off Portland in February 1653. When Cromwell forcibly expelled the Rump two months later its members thought the Dutch to be on the brink of defeat; his usurpation, they came to believe, had squandered England's opportunity to become Europe's leading commercial and maritime power. Nostalgically they compared the military and naval exploits of their rule with the achievements of republics of classical antiquity. Milton, an apologist for the Rump as later for Cromwell, thought that England might have become 'another Rome'.

While Barebone's concentrated on domestic reforms in the summer and autumn of 1653, Cromwell encouraged peace talks with the Dutch. As Protector he swiftly ended the war and set out to form a series of Protestant alliances. There was an anachronistic element in this policy, for after the Thirty Years War common religious sympathies were no longer a firm basis for international cooperation. Under Caroline rule Cromwell and his fellow beleaguered Protestants had thrilled to the exploits of King Gustavus Adolphus of Sweden, whose crack army had turned the tide of war against the Catholic Habsburgs. But the new and bellicose Swedish king Charles X, with whom Cromwell allied in the hope that he would emulate Gustavus's example, proved more interested in outwitting the Protestant Dutch and Danes in the struggle for mastery of the Baltic. Yet Cromwell's diplomacy was less naïve than it may look. Beside his religious enthusiasms lay a shrewd eye for England's interests in the Baltic, a vital source of her naval stores, and in the North Sea. He stood up to the Dutch in commercial arguments and made them help him isolate the Stuarts in European diplomacy. Even when he espoused the cause of persecuted Protestant groups, like the 'slaughtered saints' of Piedmont whose sufferings Milton lamented and on whose behalf the Protector organized a national relief fund, his tactics served to strengthen his diplomatic hand. God's servants, Cromwell knew, must be wise as serpents in His cause.

By making peace with the Dutch in 1654, Cromwell freed himself to pursue a bellicose policy elsewhere in Europe. The most pressing question before him was which side to take in the Franco-Spanish war. Both were Catholic countries, but it was Spain rather than France which England habitually identified with the cause of international popery, and Spain – 'Antichristian' Spain – whose enmity Cromwell chose. Whereas the Rump's war with the Dutch, although favoured by many mercantile interests, had been disliked in the provinces of England, Cromwell's war with Spain, which roused memories of Elizabethan greatness, was more acceptable to the gentry and so broadened the domestic base of support for the Protectorate. MPs were evidently impressed when Cromwell, demanding money for the war, reminded them that popish Spain was the 'natural enemy' of England. The cause of the Stuarts, driven by Cromwell's diplomacy into Spanish hands, was tarnished by that association. Yet Cromwell's war with Spain was slow to bear fruit. At first he may have hoped that it could be confined, as for a time Queen Elizabeth's had been, to the Americas, where the Protector revived the piratical ambitions which had flourished in her reign, but which (to Puritan disgust) had been discouraged by the early Stuarts. In 1654, seeking a base in the Caribbean from which to destroy Spain's inter-continental economy, perhaps even to launch the conquest of Spanish America, the government dispatched a disastrously ill-organized expedition to the island of Hispaniola (now Haiti), where it was humiliatingly routed by a handful of Spaniards. Cromwell interpreted this failure as a divine punishment for the nation's sins: his enemies interpreted it as a divine punishment for his usurpation. The expedition did, however, proceed to take Jamaica, which with time was to prove so important an acquisition. Its short-term value was impaired by the Protector's failure to persuade God-fearing New Englanders to leave their homes to populate it. Even though Massachusetts and the northern colonies had generally favoured the Roundhead cause in the 1640s, they had taken advantage of England's immersion in civil wars to achieve a greater independence of the home country. Further south, where Virginia and Barbados had supported the royalists and had been reduced to obedience by the Rump's navy in 1651–2, Cromwell was content with the outward obedience of those colonies, and interfered little in their internal affairs. Even so, the Navigation Act strengthened the colonies' commercial dependence on England.

Cromwell's war with Spain soon extended to European waters, and for a while the conflict seemed a mistake. Merchants grumbled at the damage to their trade in the Mediterranean and in Spanish Flanders; the enemy resisted the inducements offered by Robert Blake, the English general at sea, to engage; and the belief that the capture of Spanish silver fleets would

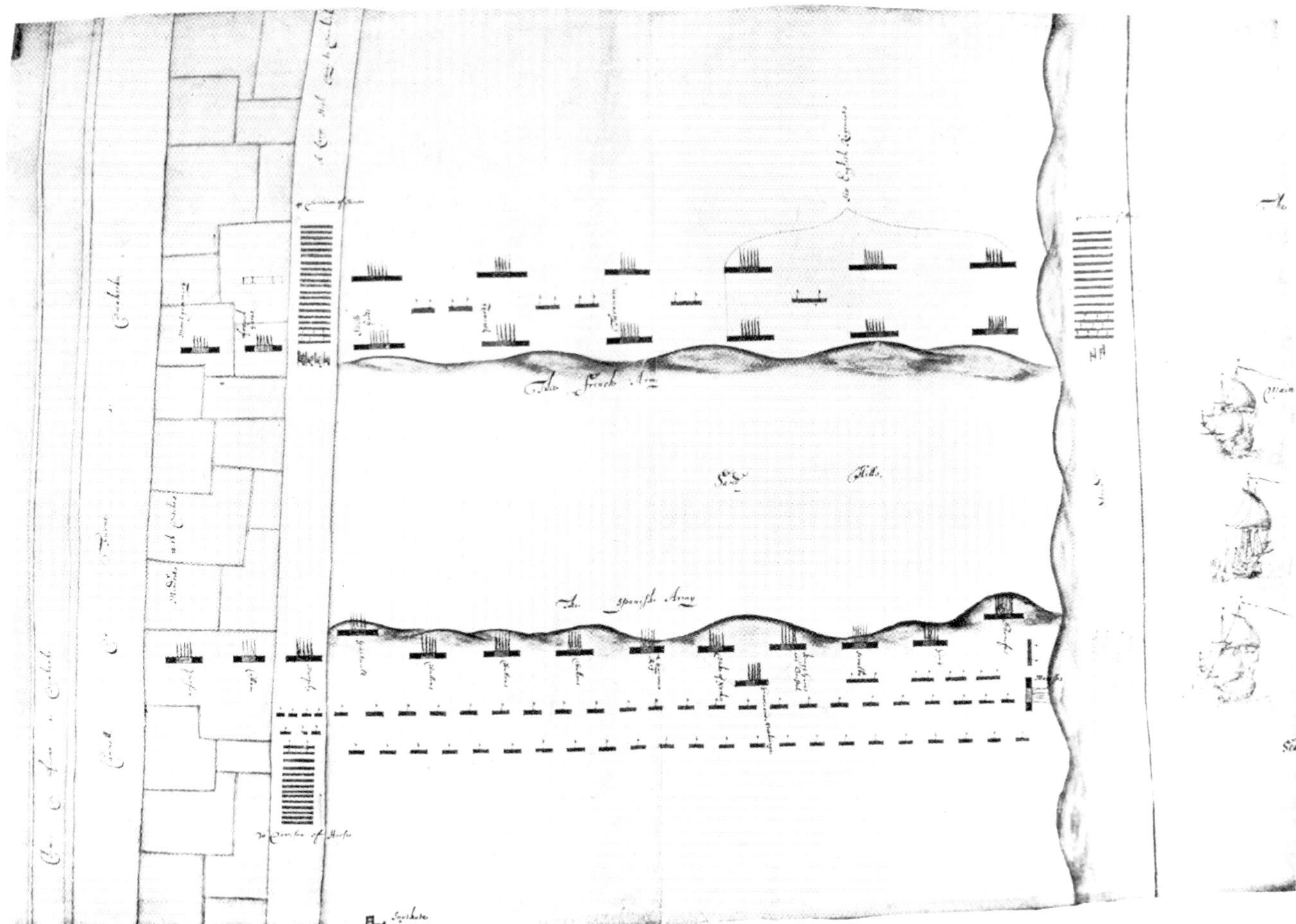

103. Sir Bernard de Gomme, plan of *The Battle of the Dunes*. British Library, Add. MS. 16370, f. 67.
On 4 June 1658 the joint Anglo-French army drove the Spanish army off a ridge of sand dunes between the sea and the high road to Dunkirk, a triumph which made the surrender of Dunkirk only a matter of time. The English forces, with their ships on the sea to their left, are on the left side of the allied forces. After the battle the English forces were 'generally cried up for their unparalleled courage' at the French court, and the Spaniards acknowledged that 'they came on like beasts'. The triumph belonged largely to the commander of the English forces, Sir William Lockhart, a Scotsman and former royalist who had married into Cromwell's family and who as Cromwell's ambassador at Paris had smoothed the path of the Anglo-French negotiations that produced the joint campaign in Flanders. Dunkirk proved an expensive acquisition and was sold to the French in 1662 – a decision that earned the restored monarchy some unpopularity.

meet the cost of war proved a mirage. But in April 1657, four months before his death, Blake brought off a spectacular victory at Santa Cruz in Tenerife which damaged the Spanish supply lines; and in 1658 a joint Anglo-French expedition in Flanders won Dunkirk for England and so gave her the base on the Channel seaboard she had lacked since Mary's loss of Calais a century earlier. The regimes of the Interregnum had made Europe tremble; and when in 1667 the Dutch fleet humiliated England by sailing into the Medway, Pepys noticed how men recalled of Cromwell's rule 'what brave things he did, and made the neighbour princes fear him'.

The motives of national security and religious zeal which were combined in Cromwell's foreign policy were blended, too, in his treatment of Ireland and Scotland, countries both subjected to military occupation during the 1650s after the defeat of the royalists there. Englishmen thought of Catholic Irishmen as barbarians who had massacred hundreds of thousands of Protestant settlers in 1641, an episode in the memory of which legend counted for more than fact. Massive transplantation of Catholics cleared the way for fresh English settlers, many of them Cromwellian soldiers. Punishment exceeded common sense, for the English removed to remote corners of the island not only landlords but tenants who could have worked the land for the new owners. Cromwell and his friends, grasping little of the country's social complexities, talked of Ireland as a 'white paper' on which they could experiment with reform of law and religion. From 1655 more realistic policies began to prevail, thanks largely to the presence in Ireland of Oliver's younger son Henry, whom his father, having for long balanced his power

'To Thy Victorious Pencil All, That Eyes and Minds Can Reach, Do Bow'

PETER LELY AND HIS PATRONS DURING THE INTERREGNUM

When Samuel Pepys called on Peter Lely in October 1662 and again in July 1666, he found the artist busy and with a full order book. In Post-Restoration London, Sir Peter Lely's skills were sought by patrons from the king downwards (see p. 197). Yet it can be argued that with commercial success there came some diminution of the originality and spontaneity of his earlier years, which are less familiar but no less important for English art.

Lely (pronounced lily) become a painter under contemporary Dutch and Flemish influence. His was always to be a derivative art. Born in Westphalia as Pieter van der Faes, his roots in both blood and taste were Dutch. He was painting professionally in Haarlem by 1637 and probably arrived in England in 1643 – not a propitious time for painting commissions, and Dutch and Flemish painters seeking work in England were common enough. Indeed Lely's earliest work on landscapes followed the style of van Poelenbergh, a successful Dutchman also working in England. To Dutch pastoral landscapes Lely added a mellow colouring picked up from Flemish artists, especially Van Dyck. Lely was accomplished at using the artistic innovations of others, and his pastoral concert scenes and genre portraits of individual musicians are very similar to those of Terbrugghen. His works of the late 1640s pictured Lely's circle of friends, who included the graver of the king's mint, Thomas Rawlins, and the Cavalier poet, Richard Lovelace. Lely became free of the Painter-Stationers Company in October 1647.

1 Peter Lely, *Self Portrait*. Oil on canvas, 42½ × 34½ in. (108 × 87.6 cm.). London, National Portrait Gallery.
Probably painted about 1660, the portrait displays Lely's assurance and success, and his mastery of the Baroque portrait conventions.

2 Peter Lely, *The Concert*. Oil on canvas, 48½ × 92½ in. (123 × 234.5 cm.). Courtauld Institute of Art, Lee Collection.
A fine example of Lely's early 'Concert Champêtres', an allegory with music in the service of love and beauty. The bass violinist may be Lely himself and the painting evokes his circle in the late 1640s.

Lovelace's poems were set to music in these years by Henry Lawes and John Lanier, and this precious atmosphere of poetry and music, characteristic of much of royalism in the wake of civil war defeat, was depicted by Lely in informal portraits of the musical friends in their circle. But Lovelace regretted Lely's need to turn for a living towards more formal portraits, 'dull counterfeits' as he called them. Lely suffered from the 'transalpine barbarous neglect' of an 'un-understanding land' which demanded portraits rather than pastorals.

In concentrating on formal portraiture Lely was angling for Van Dyck's place and reputation. Cornelius Johnson, who might have been a rival, had returned to Holland, and Dobson was dead. Lely's new patrons were the owners of great houses: houses that were already hung with pictures commissioned from Van Dyck, and owners who were men brought together by marriage and political sympathies – the Earls of Northumberland, Leicester, Pembroke and Salisbury among them. Having remained in London during the civil war, they were simultaneously royalist in instinct and loyalty but parliamentarian in their dislike of the Laudians and of the way in which Charles I had conducted politics. Most of Lely's work of 1648–50 was done for these families. Some of the best are portraits of Charles I and his children painted during their house arrest when the victorious parliament had sent them to the home of the Earl of Northumberland. These portraits acquired some of Van Dyck's modelling and colour and often contain atmospheric

3 Peter Lely, *Charles I with James, Duke of York*. Oil on canvas, 50 × 57¾ in. (126.4 × 146.7 cm.). Syon House, Collection of the Duke of Northumberland.
The Earl of Northumberland paid Lely £20 for this work, which was painted when the imprisoned king was allowed to visit his children in 1647 at Syon House, the earl's London house.

4 Peter Lely, *Sir William Compton*, Oil on canvas, 48½ × 40¼ in. (123.5 × 102 cm.). London, Ham House.
One of Lely's pictures of members of the Sealed Knot, a painting executed under Elizabeth Murray's patronage. The post-Restoration frame is a fitting setting for this portrait.

landscapes and Arcadian conceits. In 1654 Lely had reached the top of his profession by creating an image of Oliver Cromwell and was described by James Waynwright as 'the best artist in England'.

Before the dissolution of the Long Parliament in April 1653, Lely tried to sell to the Commonwealth government the idea of commissioning large pictures for the Banqueting House, Whitehall, which would celebrate civil war victories and show the Council of State and the parliament in session. His aristocratic patrons like Northumberland were behind the scheme. They thought that such art might help to stabilize the regime by glorifying its past in the same room as Rubens's *Apotheosis of James I*. Lely, unsullied by an association with the pre-war court, was well placed to be the artist of the new government. But his most intriguing patron during the Protectorate years was Elizabeth Murray, Countess of Dysart (1626–98), a woman whose association with Lely before and after 1660 helped to link the culture of the Protectorate with that of the Restoration. The daughter of Charles I's 'whipping boy', the Scotsman William Murray (himself an art patron), Elizabeth inherited her father's political skills and artistic tastes. She married Sir Lyonel Tollemache in 1647 and her children succeeded her in the earldom.

The Interregnum years were not easy for the countess. She supported both sides, belonging to the royalist secret society, the Sealed Knot, and exercising influence as a friend of Oliver Cromwell (gossip said – groundlessly – that she was his mistress). She was a useful but a dangerous woman to know. Lely knew her well and his first portrait of her is one of his best. It seems to capture Bishop Burnet's description of her as a woman 'of great beauty but of far greater parts: has a wonderful quickness of apprehension, and amazing vivacity in conversation: had studied not only divinity and history, but mathematics and philosophy: but what ruined these accomplishments, she was restless in her ambition, profuse in her expense, and of a most ravenous covetousness: nor was there anything she stuck at to compass her end, for she was violent in everything – a violent friend and a much more violent enemy'. For her house at Ham, Lely painted portraits of young men involved in the Sealed Knot. His links with these royalist families brought him the friendship of Hugh May, a fellow artist, an architect and a royalist agent. Lely's association with May brought him favour at the Restoration and helped to make him king's Principal Painter in 1661. Like his patrons, Lely had survived the Interregnum. He and the Countess of Dysart (see pp. 162–3) would both go on to greater fame.

5 Peter Lely, *Elizabeth Murray, Countess of Dysart*. Oil on canvas, 48½ × 46⅝ in. (123.5 × 118.4 cm.). London, Ham House.
The picture shows Lely's spectacular mastery of fluid brushwork, to create sumptuous costume effects and atmospheric landscapes.

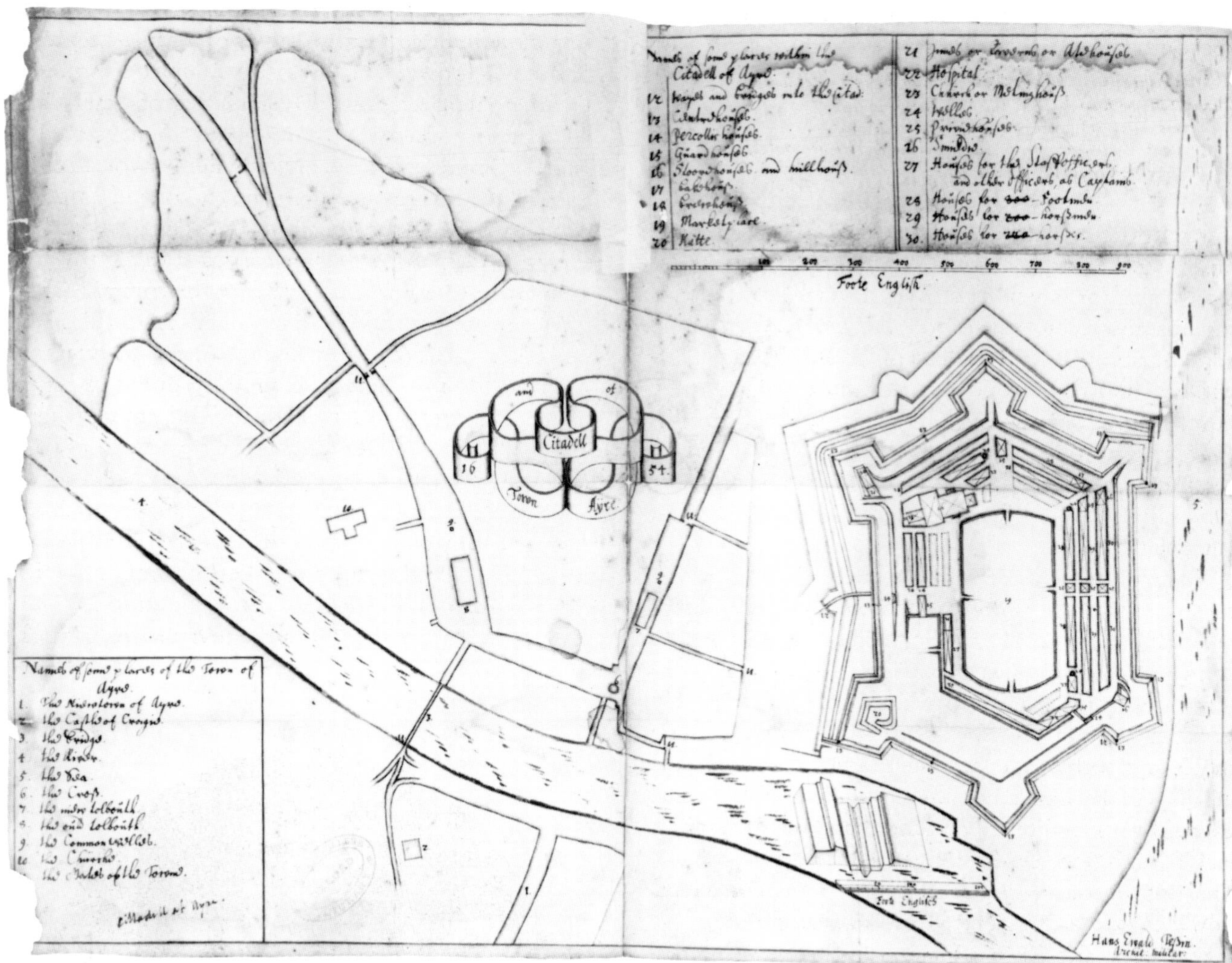

104. The citadel of Ayr under Cromwellian rule, from a contemporary engraving in Worcester College, Oxford.
The occupying Cromwellian army of the 1650s built impressive fortresses in Scotland at Inverlochy, Inverness, Ayr, Perth and Leith. That at Ayr was begun in 1652. In 1653 Robert Lilburne, Monck's predecessor as commander of the forces in Scotland, wrote that it was 'in very great forwardness and the outworks completely built: it is a most stately thing and will be very strong, only I conceive it is a great deal too large, and will put the state to much charge in maintaining it.' In 1657 there were about 500 soldiers quartered there.

against that of army radicals, at last made Lord Deputy in 1657. A friend of Broghil (the leader of the 'kingship party' in that year), Henry saw in him and his like – the Protestant landowning families which had settled in Ireland under Elizabeth and the early Stuarts – the key to settlement and security. These men, while glad of a Cromwellian presence to protect them against Catholics, wanted none of the army's social experiments. Henry ensured that they were spared them.

In Scotland – where the focus of nationalism was provided not by Catholics but by Presbyterians who, if they seemed to Cromwellians misguided, were at least fellow Protestants – military occupation took more conciliatory forms, especially after the suppression of Glencairn's royalist rising in 1653–4. In 1654 the Protectorate, following a plan drawn up by the Rump two years earlier, replaced the Stuart union of the crowns with a more far-reaching union of republics which was intended to bring real benefits to Scotland. The oppressive social privileges and legal jurisdictions of the great Scottish landowners were removed; the English system of commissions of the peace was introduced alongside revivified Scottish courts; and the achievement of law and order was welcomed by many, especially in the towns. The Scots were given representation at Westminster, as were the Irish; but in both countries many of those elected to Cromwell's parliament were Englishmen or English nominees. In Scotland as in Ireland the Cromwellians failed to establish a firm social base for their rule. The programme to win the Presbyterian Church, the Kirk, to the principle of toleration was a daunting and largely barren one; and the benefits derived by Scotland from union were probably outweighed by the huge taxation which supported the occupying army and which impeded the economic reconstruction needed after the ravages of war.

The Fall of the Republic, 1658–1660

If Cromwell was unable either to hold the Puritan movement together, or to create the godly commonwealth for which he strove, nevertheless his personal authority in the army and the realization by parliaments that no settlement could be achieved without him did enable him to secure the domestic peace which was essential if Puritanism and reform were to take root. After his death no one was able to rival that achievement. Within two years the Puritan Revolution had collapsed and Charles II was on the English throne.

The Humble Petition and Advice required Cromwell to nominate his successor. There is some doubt whether he did so, but in September 1658 his eldest son Richard, aged 31, whom Oliver's advisers deemed the Protector to have named, succeeded smoothly enough. He had played no part in the wars, had no radical sympathies and lacked his father's hold over the army. Yet he had advantages, not least the respect earned by his civility of demeanour and by his manifest lack of ambition. Unlike Oliver, Richard was unlikely to sabotage constitutional settlement by armed coups. Some constitutionalist parliamentarians, thinking that single rulers should be amiable rubber stamps, hoped more from Richard than from Oliver. He showed more grit than was expected of him. He summoned a parliament in February 1659 and, although the republicans made trouble in it, most of its members were amenable enough. What the parliament would not do was to treat the army with the deference that the army demanded. Richard, obliged to choose between parliament and army, first vainly ordered the army to obey parliament's provocative demands and then yielded to the army by sanctioning the dissolution of parliament. His power broken by the officers, he resigned in May. The Protectorate was over.

In its place the army restored the Rump, which it had expelled six years earlier. In this unholy alliance, radical euphoria and a common hatred of Cromwellian rule temporarily enabled many soldiers and civilians to forget the differences between them. It could not last. The Rump fatally attenuated its already narrow base of power by purging Cromwellians from the army and from local government. Now the 'godly' cause fell apart; and in the months ahead politicians who had devoted their lives to a profoundly earnest cause were caught in labyrinthine and fruitless manoeuvres which to a modern mind seem worthier of a banana republic or a comic opera. The army turned out the Rump in October, replaced it by a Committee of Safety and restored it once more in December. A new trading depression increased the nation's hunger for a settlement which, it was by now plain, no one in England could provide. In the opening months of 1660 republicans were helpless as the tide moved strongly towards a Stuart restoration. On 1 January the commander of the army in Scotland George Monck, resentful of the political pretensions of his fellow officers in England, resolved to move his forces south to impose a settlement. The forces in England, divided among themselves, could not prevent him. In February he persuaded the Rump to readmit those MPs whom Colonel Pride had purged in 1648. Thus restored, the Long Parliament dissolved itself in March to make way for a freely elected assembly, the Convention, which met in April and welcomed back the king in May. Essentially it was the political Presbyterians who, in

105. Richard Cromwell, by an unknown artist.
Miniature on vellum, $2\frac{1}{8} \times 1\frac{3}{4}$ in. (5.4 × 4.4 cm.).
London, National Portrait Gallery.
Richard Cromwell, Oliver's eldest son and his successor as Protector in 1658–9, was allowed to live peaceably after his fall from power and again after the restoration of monarchy in 1660. Oliver, nervous of appearing to endorse the hereditary principle to which many in his army were opposed, had taken only tentative steps to prepare Richard for high office.

alliance with Monck, brought Charles II back. In 1648 they had planned to restore his father on strict conditions; but in 1660 the current of pro-monarchical feeling proved strong enough for Charles to avoid Presbyterian restraints and to preserve his father's sovereignty intact.

When Puritans observed the profane popular rejoicing which greeted their downfall – the roasting of rumps, the erection of maypoles – they reflected that Charles owed his restoration not to any initiative of his own, but solely to the Puritans' divisions, for which God had deservedly punished them. Puritanism had achieved more as a destructive than as a constructive force. The zeal of Puritans had given them revolutionary hopes and a revolutionary vocabulary, but not a basis for preserving political unity or for meeting practical challenges of constitution-building. The only profound political thinkers of the Puritan Revolution – Thomas Hobbes, whose *Leviathan* (1651) examined the basis of political obligation and indeed the psychological basis of all political activity; and James Harrington, whose *Oceana* (1656) advanced a sophisticated socio-economic explanation of the civil wars and urged his countrymen to model their government on classical and foreign republics – were rejected by Puritans, whose political muddle-headedness they scorned. The nation did not want to be Puritanized – certainly not if the costs were to be constitutional chaos, military rule and fiscal and economic hardship. In 1660 most of Cromwell's constructive achievements, discredited by their association with his rule, were swept away as the reaction against reform gathered strength. In that reaction lay a determination, which was profoundly to influence the politics of the coming generation, that civil war should not come again. The most conspicuous legacy of the revolution was a bitter one: the entrenchment of that politics of polarization and vilification which the hatreds of civil war had created and which was to persist through the remainder of the Stuart age.

GOOD
Counſel and Advice,
REJECTED;
By Diſobedient men.
And the dayes of
OLIVER CROMWELLS
Viſitation paſſed over;
AND ALSO OF
RICHARD CROMWEL
his Son, late Protectors of theſe Nations.

And the many precious Warnings neglected by them, and ſet at naught, which from time to time the Servants of the Lord gave unto them, as declared in theſe following Letters; Whereby all may ſee the kindneſs of the Lord towards them, by his faithful Invitations to them, and their own Apoſtacy and careleſneſs, who rejected Warning till the time and day of their viſitation is ſhut up with the vail of darkneſs and reproach, which lies over them, and their precious day of love is ſpent, and cannot be re-called.

Put to publick view, by one that wiſhed well to them in their day, and is a Friend unto all that love Righteouſneſs, and hates Oppreſſion.

LONDON,
Printed for *Thomas Simmons*, at the Bull and Mouth near Alderſgate, 1659.

110. f. 119. (1)

107. *Good Counsel and Advice Rejected*, a Quaker tract of 1659.
This pamphlet by the Quaker Edward Burrough celebrated the fall of the Cromwellian Protectorate, which Quakers, in common with many other political and religious radicals, hailed as a moment of divine deliverance and as the long-postponed dawn of true reformation.

106. J. M. Wright, *Thomas Hobbes*, *c.* 1669–70.
Oil on canvas, 26 × 21½ in. (66 × 54.6 cm.)
London, National Portrait Gallery.
Hobbes was one of the great European thinkers of the seventeenth century. Born in the year of the Armada, he called himself a 'child of fear', and in a number of works, of which Leviathan *was the most sophisticated, he produced a system of ideas that answered to the political insecurity of the Puritan Revolution. In tracing men's beliefs and behaviour not to their conventional moral assumptions but to their needs and passions, and in arguing that men owed obedience to any government which held power over them and offered them protection, he aroused charges of atheism that echoed down the remainder of the century. Hobbes's political ideas were closely related to his studies in mathematics and in physics. He knew Galileo and disputed with Descartes. His friends included William Harvey, who discovered the circulation of the blood, and Ben Jonson.*

CHAPTER SIX

The Restoration 1660–1688

Themes of Restoration Politics

The year 1660 appeared to mark the triumph of conservatism. The reaction against the disturbing anarchy and radicalism since the death of Cromwell produced a wave of nostalgic sentiment for royalty and the ancient constitution and of hope for the reunification of a deeply divided nation. In the rejoicing of the Restoration, it seemed that all the political experiments of the civil war and Interregnum had been forgotten and that the new regime was supported by a divine blessing, which alone could explain so miraculous a change in political fortune. To an audience that had learned by experience that revolution could raise worse horrors than those it overcame, the clergy of the restored Church of England preached submission and obedience to the Lord's anointed. England needed and wanted a strong, legitimate authority.

The political mood of the country was reflected in the conservative nature of the constitutional settlement. Although a Presbyterian group in the House of Lords briefly tried to impose conditions on Charles's return in 1660, they were defeated by the very speed of the Restoration, and Charles and his most trusted minister, the Earl of Clarendon, avoided making any of the concessions that had been demanded of Charles I. The king remained free, as he had always been, to appoint and dismiss his ministers as he pleased; his complete control over the kingdom's militia was admitted in an Act passed in 1661; and the repeal of the 1641 Triennial Act in 1664 replaced the requirement to meet parliament every three years with a more vague (and less easily enforceable) undertaking. Parliament reverted to its traditional role as a representative body which approved taxes to supplement the king's own income for his extraordinary needs, which alerted the king to the grievances of his subjects and which legislated for the good of the nation.

But the stability of the restored regime depended on its financial health as much as on the conservatism and goodwill of its subjects. In 1660 the Convention Parliament's enthusiasm was so high that it willingly voted an increase in the crown's annual income to £1.2 million – a sum greater than that which had allowed Charles I to avoid meeting parliament during the 1630s. But overvaluation of the existing revenue and appalling errors in calculation meant that the extra permanent taxes voted to bring it up to that amount fell short by over £300,000; although this was to some extent amended by the following parliament, until the late 1670s receipts from the revenue never matched the rosy expectations of the early 1660s. On his accession Charles found himself encumbered with a debt of at least £925,000; and the money given by the Convention Parliament for the disbandment of most of the army and units of the navy could not match the growing arrears of pay and debt and the need to replenish military magazines.

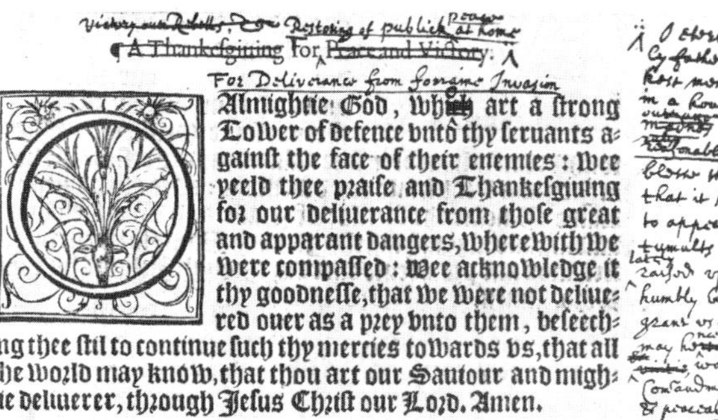

¶ A Thankesgiuing For Peace and Victory.

Almightie God, which art a strong Tower of defence vnto thy seruants against the face of their enemies: wee yeeld thee praise and Thankesgiuing for our deliuerance from those great and apparant dangers, wherewith wee were compassed: wee acknowledge it thy goodnesse, that wee were not deliuered ouer as a prey vnto them, beseeching thee still to continue such thy mercies towards vs, that all the world may know, that thou art our Sauiour and mighty deliuerer, through Iesus Christ our Lord. Amen.

¶ A Thankesgiuing For deliuerance from the Plague.

Lord God, which hast wounded vs for our sinnes, and consumed vs for our transgressi-

108. Charles II touching for the King's Evil.
Contemporary engraving by R. White.
Cambridge, Magdalene College, Pepys Library.
Charles II, understanding the strength which monarchy derived from its sacred character, revived the ritual of touching for the 'king's evil', scrofula. After a reading from the Gospel, a surgeon (on Charles's left) would bring forward the sick, 'who kneeling, the king strokes their face or cheeks with both his hands at once: at which instance a chaplain in his formalities says, "He put his hands upon them, and he healed them".' The severely Protestant William III declined to use the ceremony.

109. Proposed changes by Bishop John Cosin in the Book of Common Prayer. Durham University Library.
During the 1660s, when the Church emphatically supported the Crown's claim to the obedience of its subjects, Bishop Cosin of Durham, one of the 'highest' churchmen of his time, proposed changes in the Prayer Book, among them this giving of thanks for 'restoring of public peace at home'. It begins: 'O eternal God our heavenly father, who alone makest men to be of one mind in a house, and stillest the madness (or outrage) of a raging (or violent) and unreasonable people, we bless thy holy name that it hath pleased thee to appease the seditious tumults which have been lately raised among us . . .'

110 (right). Dirk Stoop, *The Coronation Procession of Charles II.* Oil on canvas. Private collection.
On 23 April 1661, St. George's day, the king proceeds from the Tower to Westminster for his coronation ceremony. The pageantry and rituals of power, with which Puritans had never felt at ease, returned with conviction at the Restoration. The festivities of the coronation were accompanied by a thunderstorm, which the king's friends interpreted as an expression of heavenly joy, and his Puritan enemies as a sign of divine condemnation.

111 (below). Jan Wyck, *Banqueting Hall and Whitehall Palace from Horseguards Parade.* Oil on canvas. Private collection.
Whitehall remained the centre of the court until a fire of 1698 destroyed most of its principal buildings – although by that time William III, a sufferer from asthma, already preferred the healthier air of his new palace at Kensington.

112 (opposite below). Dutch School, *The Great Fire of London, 1666.* Oil on canvas, $35\frac{1}{4} \times 59\frac{3}{4}$ in. (89.7×151.6 cm.). Museum of London.
Beginning in a baker's house in Pudding Lane on the Sunday morning of 2 September 1666, in an area where the water-engine happened to be out of order, the fire was swiftly carried by wind into the heart of the city, and lasted for five days. On the Sunday night the burning of St. Paul's afforded light enough to read by, and on the Thursday the pavements were still hot enough to scorch the shoes. The fire consumed 373 of the 450 acres within the city wall, and is believed to have destroyed 80 parish churches and more than 13,000 houses. Although the spectacular scale of the combustion was beyond comparison, fire was a source of frequent hazard and destruction in the largely wooden English towns. Since Guy Fawkes, the danger of fire and the danger of popery had been associated in the public mind, and the Great Fire helped to foster the suspicion of popish arson that was to surface at the time of the Popish Plot in 1678.

Partly as a result, the Restoration government was constantly short of money, subject to occasionally severe cash crises and perpetually at the mercy of its allies abroad, of parliament or of the City. In this fact lay the root of the problems of the monarchy in the 1660s and 1670s and of many of the developments of the reign. For by depending so much for its financial survival on the taxes granted by the House of Commons, the government itself helped to enhance parliament's prestige and influence. Charles's foreign wars made the problem worse, increasing his dependence on parliamentary supply in order to wage them and making him more vulnerable to popular discontent: all the great crises of the reign, in 1667, 1673 and 1678, were associated with the failure of government appeals for money to continue, or to pay for, unsuccessful wars.

In December 1660 the king dissolved the Convention, which had restored him to the throne, and in April 1661 a new parliament, the 'Cavalier Parliament', was elected. At first it seemed that this parliament, called amidst rapturous royalist sentiment, was the most amenable that could be had. Later, when by-elections and disillusionment had altered its character, it still seemed too risky to exchange this well-known devil for the unknown one of a general election. Consequently, the same parliament was not dissolved until 1679: because of the government's frequent appeals for money over the seventeen years of its existence, there were only two years in which it failed to meet. As a result, the structure of parliamentary politics began to change over the course of the reign: factions had more time in which to form and develop as MPs spent more time at Westminster; opposition to the government became more efficiently co-ordinated; politicians seeking power became adept at forming their own groups in either House, which could be used to support or oppose government policy; ministers became more blatant in the techniques they used to manage the House of Commons.

113. Samuel Cooper, *Charles II*, 1665.
Miniature. The Hague, Mauritshuis.
Charles II five years after the Restoration, aged 35. Samuel Cooper, a Londoner, was called by Pepys 'the great little limner in little'. A musician and a linguist, he wrote verses and was the uncle of Alexander Pope.

The structures of local politics were changing as well, under the impact of events at Westminster. With no general election between 1661 and 1678, local interest in the struggles at Westminster might have atrophied. But in the divisive politics of the late 1670s and early 1680s, the parties that had developed within parliament, known as 'Whigs' and 'Tories', began to appeal to the country at large in a way reminiscent of 1641. The electoral inactivity of 1661–78 was followed by three general elections in quick succession in which the parties did all they could to generate a high level of excitement and awareness of the issues involved, pulling the counties into a closer relationship with the politics of London.

The reunification of a divided nation was as important as the reassertion of royal power. In their eagerness to reconcile past enemies, Charles and Clarendon worked hard to get the Act of Indemnity and Oblivion through parliament in 1660, pardoning all those involved in the revolutionary regimes save only those who had signed the death warrant of Charles I. Presbyterians and ex-Cromwellians who had collaborated in the re-establishment of the monarchy were rewarded and their affections retained with grants of office and favour. Presbyterians and Anglicans could agree on the need for unity. Both had been shocked by the proliferation and increasing stridency of the radical religious sects which had thrived with the relaxation of ecclesiastical authority in the 1640s and 1650s: their sometimes violent millenarianism and contempt for traditional values disposed gentry of varying religious persuasions to favour a power capable of checking their growth and guaranteeing stability.

There, however, agreement ended. Presbyterians hoped that their objections to the ritual and hierarchy of the Anglican Church would be taken into account and a religious settlement devised to allow their 'comprehension' within it. The more extreme Anglicans bitterly contested any such concessions, expecting the uncompromising reconstruction of the Church for which they had fought and for which the martyr King Charles I had died. They regarded Presbyterians as almost as dangerous as the sects, their principles incon-

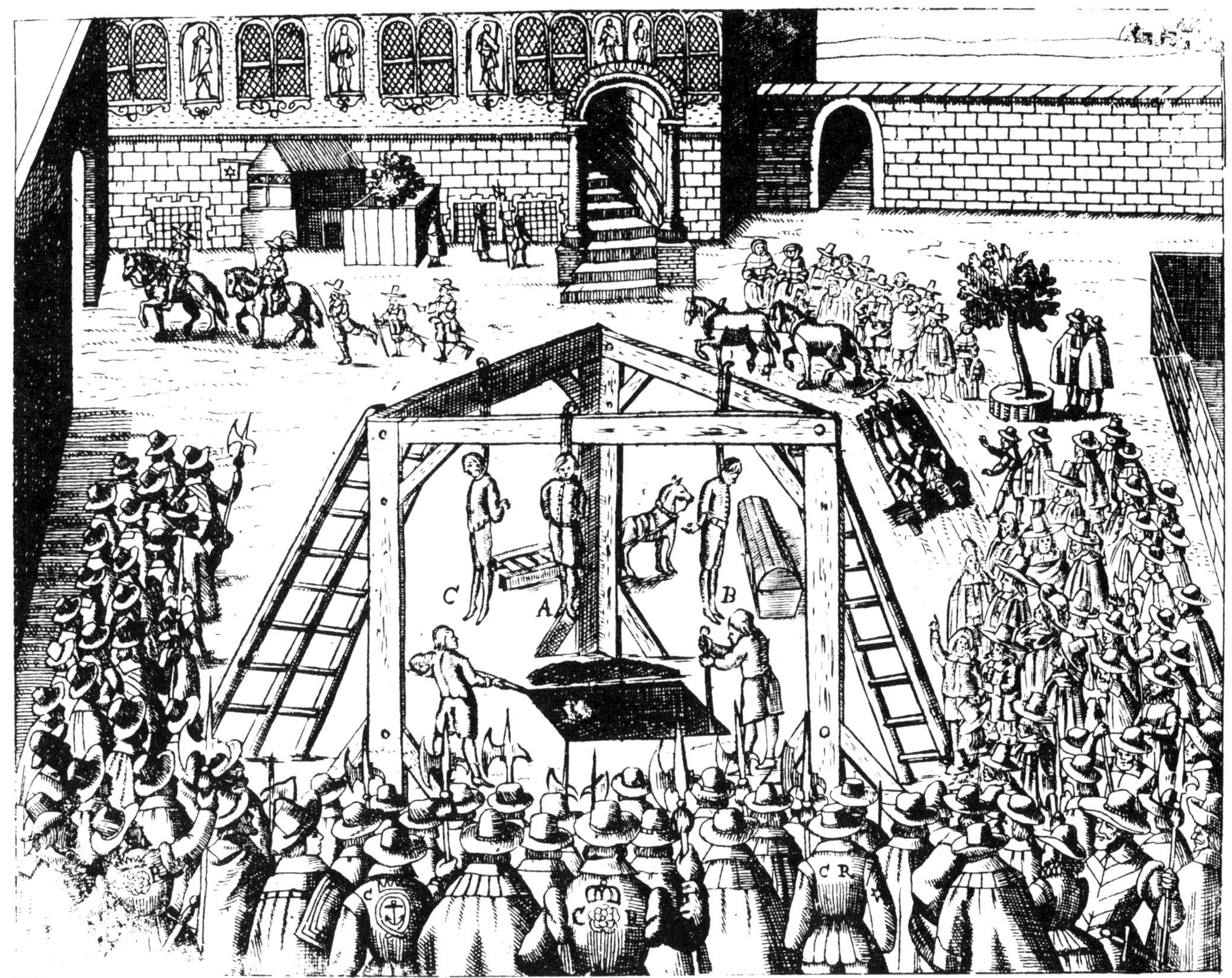

114. The Execution of the Regicides, October 1660. Contemporary engraving.
Only a handful of those who had signed the death warrant of Charles I in 1649 were executed at the Restoration, but their deaths in 1660, when they were hanged, drawn and quartered, acquired a vivid martyrological status. Oliver Cromwell's body was disinterred from Westminster Abbey and publicly mutilated. Some regicides had managed to escape to Switzerland or Holland or the new world, but three of them were brought back from Holland to be executed in 1662.

sistent with monarchical power. The sects themselves simply hoped for the toleration of their own styles of worship outside the established Church. The small Catholic population, too, hoped that the loyalty shown by many of them during the civil war might incline the king to reward them with religious freedom, an aspiration that Charles seemed willing to grant.

If the unity of 1660 was illusory, the apparent reaction towards royal authority was also very far from complete. For the moment, the terror of anarchy and radicalism demanded the reconstruction of a powerful monarchy; but Englishmen dreaded the example of other European states in which representative assemblies had decayed and in which, it seemed to them, tyrannous 'absolutist' monarchs enforced their will by vast standing forces. The experience during the Interregnum of a government supported by military power alone had reinforced their hatred of such regimes and their permanent armies. For the moment, too, the fear of popery, which had poisoned men's minds against Charles I and his government, was transcended by the fear of the radical Protestant sects; but it was too strong to be permanently eclipsed. The propaganda of the Interregnum powers had already had some effect in arousing suspicion of the genuineness of Charles's devotion to the Protestant religion. Charles and his ministers would have to tread extraordinarily carefully to avoid awakening such anxieties.

115 (overleaf). P.C. Van Soest, *The Dutch Attack on the Medway, June 1667*. Oil on canvas, 26 × 43 in. (66 × 109 cm.). Greenwich, National Maritime Museum.
A Dutch painter celebrates the English humiliation. Planned in late May, the coup was carried out on 12 June. The English fleet, in dock at Chatham, was hopelessly under-prepared and under-defended, and only narrowly escaped total destruction. The subsequent inquiry revealed incompetence and corruption on a grand scale. Clarendon was made the scapegoat.

The government's policies further from home helped to revive these fears. In Scotland, the nursery of Presbyterianism and of the civil war, the Episcopal Church was harshly reimposed and the ensuing nonconformist rebellion in 1666 bloodily crushed. A subservient Scottish Parliament was dissolved in 1663 after it had granted the king a sizeable permanent revenue and powers to raise a large army. Subsequently Charles ruled the country through the Duke of Lauderdale, his brilliant but brutal Secretary of State. Scotland appeared to demonstrate the style of absolutism of which Charles II was capable; Ireland seemed to show his religious preferences. In attempting to sort out the chaos created by the Irish Catholic rebellion of 1641 – by the activities of royalist and parliamentarian armies and by the consequent confiscations and resettlement of the land – the government showed more favour to loyal Catholics than was politically tactful, offending the by now entrenched Protestant interest. Royal policy in Ireland could be seen as pro-Catholic and anti-Protestant, a fact which seemed highly ominous to those who looked for ominous signs.

English popular prejudices and preferences in foreign policy were beginning to shift with the changes in the balance of European power. The Treaty of the Pyrenees in 1659, which ended the long Franco-Spanish wars, also marked the end of Spanish hegemony in Europe; while in 1658–61 France emerged from a period of civil war and instability stronger than before with a young king, Louis XIV, who was determined to ensure the absolute security of its borders, and to succeed to that position of European pre-eminence which the Habsburgs, ruling in Spain and in the Empire based on Austria, had held for so long. English popular opinion was quick to replace Spain with France as the ogre of the European scene. Charles II, however, cherished ambitions of an association with the power and the glory of the renascent French monarchy from the beginning of his reign. In 1662 his marriage to Catherine of Braganza, the Infanta of Portugal – a country allied to the French in their continuing attempts further to undermine Spanish power – formed the basis of a close understanding with France. English opponents of the government soon drew their own conclusions: that Charles took his inspiration from Louis's absolutism, which he hoped to imitate in England. Towards the Dutch, English feelings were more ambivalent. On the one hand, commercial competition between the two nations was intense and had already produced the war of 1652–4; on the other, English opinion had usually been sympathetic to the small Protestant state constantly subject to attack by its Catholic neighbours. There was a dynastic link as well. The hereditary 'stadthoulder', or highest dignitary of the Dutch republic, was William, Prince of Orange, a brilliant young general and politician, and the son of Charles II's eldest sister, now dead. After the king and his brother James, Duke of York, and their progeny, William was next in line to the English throne. When Louis XIV, in alliance with Charles, began to threaten Dutch independence, it was easy to play on pro-Dutch, anti-French, anti-absolutist and anti-Catholic sentiment to arouse opposition to Charles's policies at home.

Popularity could as easily be squandered by the personality of the monarch as by his policies. 'There was in no conjuncture more need', Clarendon observed, 'that the virtue and wisdom and industry of a prince should be evident, and made manifest in the preservation of his dignity, and the application of his mind to the government of his affairs.' Charles was charming, affable, witty and clever, but hardly virtuous, wise or

116. Notes passed between Charles II and Clarendon, 1660. Oxford, Bodleian Library.
A chance documentary survival preserves a series of notes passed between Charles II and Clarendon to relieve the tedium of Privy Council meetings. In this example Charles begins: 'I would willingly make a visit to my sister at Tunbridge for a night or two at farthest, when do you think I can best spare that time?' Clarendon: 'I know no reason why you may not for such a time (2 nights) go the next week, about Wednesday, or Thursday, and return time enough for the adjournment of parliament: which yet ought to be the week following. I suppose you will go with a light train.' Charles: 'I intend to take nothing but my night bag.' Clarendon: 'Yes, you will not go without 40 or 50 horse!' Charles: 'I count that part of my night bag.'

117. The Church of St. Charles the Martyr, Tunbridge Wells, built 1676–82.
Tunbridge Wells was a small place in the seventeenth century, centering on the wells which made it a watering resort. Henrietta Maria spent six weeks there in a tent in 1630, taking the waters.

industrious. His political adroitness was marred by a cynicism which eroded trust in himself and in his government; his religion was not deep (although many suspected Catholicism), his capacity for hard work small. He found it difficult to withstand the importunity of courtiers, a fault which could cloud his political judgement and deplete royal finances. His mistresses were notorious: the two most lasting, Barbara Palmer, Duchess of Cleveland ('the Lady', as Clarendon euphemistically referred to her), and Louise de la Kéroualle, Duchess of Portsmouth, were politically powerful and deeply unpopular. His favour to Catholics and an admiration for all things French, which he acquired during his years in exile, aroused the suspicion of a xenophobic nation.

The profane, irreverent and hedonistic court over which Charles presided bred intense factional intrigues. Despite his indolence, he was wary of dependence, never entirely trusting the men who conducted his affairs; consequently they could never entirely trust him. Rising politicians encouraged this distrust in the hope of replacing his ministers, or else played on his well-known inability to resist pressure by arousing so much discontent against them in parliament and at large that he would be all too willing to part with them.

Clarendon and the Second Dutch War, 1660–1667

For the first few years of the Restoration, Charles relied mainly on three men who were products of the war, known for their devotion and long service to the royalist cause. Clarendon, the Lord Chancellor, and the Duke of Ormonde (soon appointed Lord Lieutenant

118 (left). P. Lely, *Edward Hyde, Earl of Clarendon.*
Oil on canvas. London, Middle Temple Library.
As a young man Hyde opposed the policies of Charles I's personal rule, but rallied to him in the face of what seemed to him the parliamentary extremism of 1641–2. After the regicide, as one of Charles II's leading ministers in exile, he resisted the moves of other royalists to seek agreement and compromise with Puritans disaffected by the Cromwellian regimes, and argued – rightly as it proved – that in time the divisions within the Puritan cause would enable Charles to return to his throne without strict conditions. Clarendon had deep intellectual interests. He wrote a variety of essays, a long work on Church history, a reply to Hobbes, a celebrated autobiography, and an account of the Puritan Revolution, his History of the Rebellion, *which was begun in the wake of royalist defeat in 1646 and completed during his second exile after 1667. Published in 1702, it towers above most other writing of history, and all other writing of contemporary history, of the Stuart age.*

119 (above). Studio of John Greenhill, *Anthony Ashley Cooper, First Earl of Shaftesbury.*
Oil on canvas, 82 × 55 in. (207 × 140 cm.). Private collection.
From a gentry family on the Wiltshire-Dorset border, Anthony Ashley Cooper was raised to national influence as a young man by Oliver Cromwell, but broke with him over Cromwell's armed interventions in politics.

of Ireland), had been companions of the king's exile; the Earl of Southampton, the Lord Treasurer, was one of the most respected of royalist peers. Clarendon, in particular, saw his task as the reconstruction of the legitimate power of the monarchy and of the unity and harmony of the nation. The new parliament called in 1661 was intended to achieve this ambition. By 1664 it had done much to reassert royal authority. The Triennial Act of 1641 was repealed; extra revenues were settled on the crown in an (unsuccessful) attempt to make up the deficiency in the finance granted in 1660; extraordinary grants to assuage immediate financial problems were voted; a new Treason Act and a Corporation Act, which allowed the government to carry out a comprehensive purge of the members of borough councils, were passed.

One issue, however, disturbed the concurrence of parliament with royal policy. The Church of England had been restored along with the monarchy: in 1660 bishops were appointed to the many sees that had for a long time lain vacant; cathedral chapters were reassembled; ministers ejected from their parishes under the Puritan regimes flooded back. Charles and Clarendon originally hoped to obtain Presbyterian conformity to a moderated Anglican Church, leaving the other sects, whose loyalty to the regime was doubtful, outside, to be persecuted into compliance and extinction. Presbyterians were promised major concessions in Church worship and organization and a revision of the Prayer Book was ordered to take account of their objections. But partly because of the Presbyterians' own political incompetence and partly because the new parliament was dominated by extreme Anglican royalists, these promises were not fulfilled. The new Prayer Book contained only minor alterations; nearly 1,000 ministers appointed during the Interregnum who refused to accept it were removed from their livings by virtue of the new Act of Uniformity, passed by parliament in 1662. In 1663 the government's attempt to honour its promises by obtaining powers from parliament to grant individuals dispensation from the statutes enforcing religious uniformity was rejected: strong Anglican sentiment allied to disquiet about the constitutional implications of acknowledging a royal

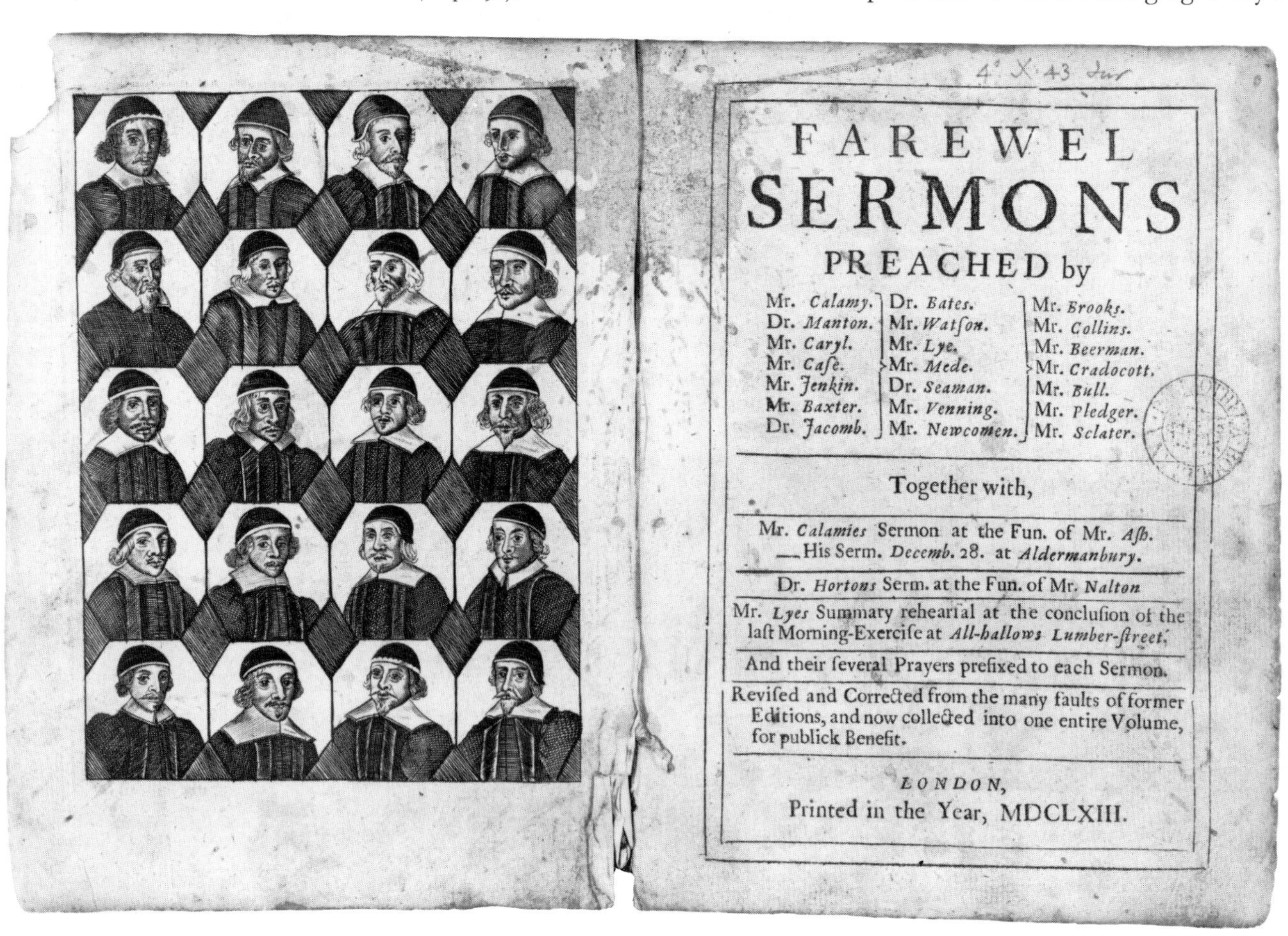

FAREWEL
SERMONS
PREACHED by

Mr. *Calamy.* Dr. *Manton.* Mr. *Caryl.* Mr. *Caſe.* Mr. *Jenkin.* Mr. *Baxter.* Dr. *Jacomb.*
Dr. *Bates.* Mr. *Watſon.* Mr. *Lye.* Mr. *Mede.* Dr. *Seaman.* Mr. *Venning.* Mr. *Newcomen.*
Mr. *Brooks.* Mr. *Collins.* Mr. *Beerman.* Mr. *Cradocott.* Mr. *Bull.* Mr. *Pledger.* Mr. *Sclater.*

Together with,

Mr. *Calamies* Sermon at the Fun. of Mr. *Aſh.*
—His Serm. *Decemb.* 28. at *Aldermanbury.*

Dr. *Hortons* Serm. at the Fun. of Mr. *Nalton*

Mr. *Lyes* Summary rehearſal at the concluſion of the laſt Morning-Exerciſe at *All-hallows Lumber-ſtreet.*

And their ſeveral Prayers prefixed to each Sermon.

Reviſed and Corrected from the many faults of former Editions, and now collected into one entire Volume, for publick Benefit.

LONDON,
Printed in the Year, MDCLXIII.

120. *Farewell Sermons preached by Mr. Calamy*, etc., 1663.
The clergymen who could not accept the Act of Uniformity in 1662 included many who, had the Restoration Church settlement been only a little broader, might well have been prepared to remain within the Church. Among those whose withdrawal was noted here is Richard Baxter (see p. 136).

121. The Royal Hospital, Chelsea, designed by Sir Christopher Wren, 1682–91.
The funding by the crown of naval hospitals at both Chelsea and Greenwich indicates the impact of the naval wars on English minds in the later seventeenth century.

right to override parliamentary statutes had aroused angry opposition.

After 1663 the government abandoned its attempts to make it possible for Presbyterians to conform to the Church, partly because of the discovery of Presbyterian involvement in a plot against the regime in Yorkshire late that year. When new acts against nonconformist meetings and ministers were passed in 1664 and 1665 in an attempt to crush the growing problem of religious dissent, Charles and Clarendon did nothing to prevent them. Rather than inducing their conformity to the Established Church, however, the Act of Uniformity pushed the Presbyterians into holding alternative religious services and into developing closer links with the other nonconformist sects.

But it was war, rather than religion, that finally destroyed the post-Restoration consensus. Anglo-Dutch commercial rivalry could not be effaced by a mere change of government: friction between the traders of the two nations often flared into open violence at sea or in the colonies. In 1664 moves by both sides to bring the other to see sense over their claims produced tension and confrontation and finally slipped into a war which neither wanted. A powerful navy had been among the more useful legacies Charles had received from the Interregnum governments, and the hard work and zest for efficiency that his brother James, Duke of York, the Lord Admiral, encouraged in Samuel Pepys and his colleagues in the Navy Board were already beginning to pay dividends. But to bring the fleet up to a fit condition for fighting required not only enormous energy, which they were willing enough to supply, but also money. In 1664 the government's debt stood at £1.25 million and war ruined the prospects of recovery, obstructing the trade on which taxation fed. Although parliament voted a total of £5 million for the war, the money came in too slowly to avoid near bankruptcy by 1667.

The war was indeed a disaster. It began well enough with a victory over the Dutch fleet off Lowestoft. But at the beginning of 1666 France and Denmark, reluctantly honouring their treaty obligations, entered the war in support of the Dutch. English naval reverses followed at Bergen and then in the Four Days' Fight in June. The fleet did manage to end the year's campaigning with two successes – the battle on St James's Day in July and Sir Robert Holmes's destruction of the Dutch East Indies fleet in August – but war had been shattering for the economy. Both England and Holland had been visited by the plague which raged through London in the summer of 1665. In the capital it probably killed over 100,000 people during the year, perhaps a quarter of the total population. The court hastily packed its bags and left for the country. Parliament and the law terms were held at Oxford. Just when the plague had virtually died out, London was struck again by the Great Fire, which in four days in September 1666 destroyed much of the City and the East End. The Dutch interpreted it as divine retribution for Holmes's raid; many Englishmen saw a popish plot.

As so often during the reign of Charles II, war pre-

122. J. M. Wright, *Astraea returns to Earth*, the Whitehall Ceiling, *c.* 1660.
Oil on canvas, 90 × 56 in. (228.6 × 142.2 cm.). Nottingham Castle Museum.
John Michael Wright, a Scotsman noted principally for his portrait, was a rival to Lely in Restoration England. Virgil's prophecy of a golden age, to be ruled by the virgin Astraea, or justice, was extensively employed in the propaganda of European monarchs of the sixteenth century, not least by Elizabeth I of England. By the reign of Charles II, the time of the scientific revolution, such mythological parallels perhaps carried less conviction.

cipitated a political crisis. The austere, devout and rather pompous Clarendon had never lacked enemies at court, but so far these had failed to persuade Charles to dismiss one of his most able and loyal servants. By 1666, however, the dutiful parliament of 1661 had become an angry one, furious at what it saw as the incompetence and corruption of the royal ministers who had mishandled the war, and whipped up by ambitious and influential courtiers like the Duke of Buckingham, anxious to seize the opportunity to increase the odium against the present ministers and to force their way into office. In response to a threatened Dutch invasion, Charles had enlarged the small army he had retained as a royal guard, providing parliamentary critics of the court with the opportunity to reawaken the old anxieties about a standing army. At the beginning of 1667 the government was at its wits' end for money. Peace negotiations had already begun and to save unnecessary expense the fleet was not fitted out for the new season's campaigning. Here was an excellent opportunity for the Dutch admiral, De Ruyter, to avenge Holmes's attack by sailing up the Medway as far as Chatham, burning and capturing some of the greatest ships of the English navy – a suitable end for a war that was almost catastrophic in its effect on English politics. Peace was concluded in July 1667, by which time royal debts had increased to about £2.5 million and bankers were refusing the government credit. The disasters of the war were blamed on a negligent administration and Clarendon received the full impact of popular bitterness. It was a dangerous moment for a precarious regime.

Charles's solution was to surrender to the popular clamour. He needed little persuading to demand Clarendon's resignation and to take Buckingham into the government. Fearing trial and execution on trumped up charges, Clarendon fled to France in December 1667, where he remained until his death in 1674. During the early 1660s he had set himself to recreate the power and authority of the monarchy along traditional lines, independent of parliament, but conscious that it rested still on the goodwill and affection of its subjects and that parliament remained the best expression of that relationship. But the war wrecked all that, ruining the consensus of 1661 and for the moment killing off the beginnings of a recovery in royal finances that would have freed the government from the necessity of constantly having to ask parliament for money.

The 'Cabal', 1667–1673

Buckingham's rise added new problems. There was little cohesion among those now in power, who regarded each other with suspicion as competitors in the struggle for the succession to Clarendon's position of pre-eminence. Buckingham's great strength was the king's friendship: despite his troublesome behaviour Charles had difficulty in withholding his favour from so witty a drinking companion. But profligate as he was, he was also an astute politician, balancing royal favour with a faction in the House of Commons, with the assiduous cultivation of popularity and with an extensive territorial power base in Yorkshire. The Secretary of State, the Earl of Arlington, was less ready to share the king's dissolute habits, but his ability and his possession of a group in the Commons likewise made him useful to the king. Sir Thomas Clifford and Lord Ashley, the most prominent members of the commission which had taken over the management of the Treasury from Southampton on his death in 1667, were both men of sound financial and political sense. If Lauderdale, the King's Scottish Secretary, was added, the initial letters of the ministers' names could be arranged to spell 'cabal', and the name stuck despite the fact that the ministers themselves were almost as disunited as it was possible for a group of men to be.

The new generation of politicians hounded Clarendon's supporters from office; Ormonde was dismissed in 1669 from his post as Lord Lieutenant of Ireland. With the new ministry came a reversal of the religious policy of Clarendon's later years. Buckingham (a royalist during the civil war, but renowned for his friendships with Presbyterians and religious radicals) and Ashley (who had been close to Cromwell) encouraged an attempt in early 1668 to secure the loyalty of nonconformists by passing through parliament bills both for comprehension of Presbyterians inside the Church of England and for toleration of others outside it. They were, as before, bitterly opposed by the Archbishop of Canterbury, Gilbert Sheldon, and thwarted by the Anglicans in the House of Commons; the only result was to provoke a new act against nonconformist meetings in early 1670.

The new ministry also tried to court popularity by tapping the general antipathy to France, which had been strengthened by her participation in the Dutch war. Louis XIV had mounted a full-scale invasion of the Spanish Netherlands in the summer of 1667, and in January 1668 Arlington joined Dutch and Spanish ministers in an alliance aimed at forcing him to end his war and return his gains. But if Charles had been for a time irritated by the French action during the Anglo-Dutch war, he soon reverted to his old belief in the advantages of their friendship, and in August 1668 reopened negotiations with France for a closer *rapprochement*. Ultimately these led to the conclusion of the

'Inferior to Few of the Best Villas in Italy'

HAM HOUSE AND THE LAUDERDALES

1 Attr. Henry Danckerts, *The South Front of Ham House*, c. 1675. Oil on canvas, $18\frac{3}{4} \times 32\frac{1}{2}$ in. (47.8 × 82.2 cm.).
This painting in the South Closet at Ham House shows the E-shaped Jacobean house 'filled in' by the new south front, and the formal layout of the gardens.

John Evelyn enjoyed visiting other people's houses, and was especially fond of those villas built for the Restoration aristocracy which lined the Thames near Richmond. Of these the finest was Ham House, 'furnish'd like a great prince's'. Built in 1610, it was remodelled during the century to make it a larger and more formal house for successful politicians. The transformation was effected principally by William Murray, first Earl of Dysart.

Architecturally, Ham was not remarkable and its new cross-wing (see plan) was unspectacular. What are remarkable are the decor and furnishings of the house, and their extraordinary survival to the present. The remodellers themselves were a notable husband and wife, John Maitland and Elizabeth Murray, first Duke and Duchess of Lauderdale.

John Maitland, even allowing for the contemporary capacity for uncharitable observation, was not a nice man to know. 'He was the coldest friend and the most violent enemy that ever was known,' said Bishop Burnet. Even a close friend, no less than Charles II, had his snuff box altered to prevent Maitland dipping into it, and at royal suppers 'this lord though not invited, ever intruded himself'. But Charles was loyal to his friends and fellow debauchees, and Maitland was both of these. A promoter

2 Peter Lely, *The First Duke and Duchess of Lauderdale*. Oil on canvas, $53\frac{3}{4} \times 64\frac{1}{4}$ in. (136.8 × 163 cm.). Ham House.
'Both $\mathrm{y^e}$ Graces in one Picture'. It is in a fine contemporary frame.

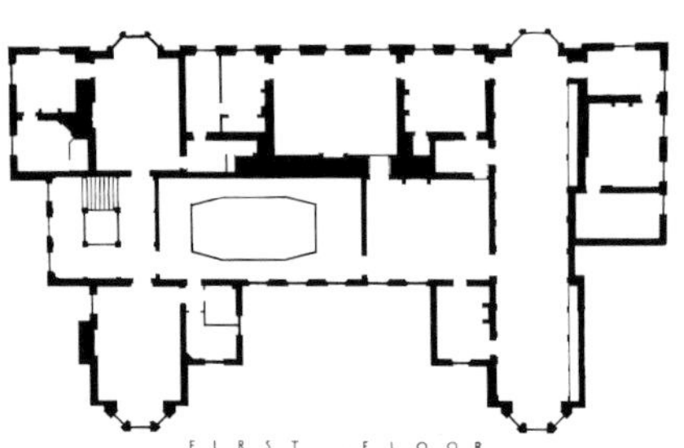

3 Plan of the first floor.
The queen's suite dominates the centre of the house and all the rest, including the gardens outside, is planned around it.

of Charles's cause in Scotland in 1651, he had been with him at Worcester, and after the battle was imprisoned until 1660. The length of the imprisonment, unusual among Cromwell's political prisoners, was a measure of the dislike he aroused. His life may have been spared only because of the influence of his future mistress and wife, Elizabeth Murray. Maitland was a turncoat.

Politics was Maitland's main preoccupation. To enter Scottish political life, he had taken the Solemn League and Covenant and been a Covenanting leader. If he had a principle it was that peers should rule and Scottish peers should rule Scotland. He had deserted the clerical world of the Covenant to support a kingship which would secure power for the big Scottish landowners, including himself. Appreciating that political power in Scotland had to be secured in London, he was able after 1660 to exert more or less sole control in Scotland, a domination he exercised with a reputation for harshness and corruption. Lauderdale was the only member of the 'cabal' (see p. 161) whose political career survived its fall. In 1672 he was raised to a dukedom. His first wife died and he was free to marry Elizabeth.

Both partners were strong-willed, unscrupulous and greedy, but Elizabeth even more so than John. 'All applications were made to her, she sold places and disposed of offices, and took upon her . . . to direct his private conduct likewise,' wrote Bishop Burnet. The pair had common cultural and artistic interests. Lauderdale, who read Latin, Greek and Hebrew, was interested in history and divinity, and he was a builder. In Scotland he rebuilt Thirlestone House and introduced the Baroque with the new wing at Holyrood.

4 William Van de Velde the Younger, *Sea-piece*.
This is one of four paintings by the Dutch marine master, and there are many others like this, inset within the plaster and woodwork décor.

Ham, with its furnishings and gardens, was his greatest achievement. It has an air of Holland about it with its inset paintings, four of them sea-pieces by William Van de Velde the Younger. There were Dutch joiners at work, too, alongside English craftsmen, and much of the furniture is Dutch. Portraits by Lely and his contemporaries offer a cross-section of Restoration portrait painting. But in the inventory of 1677 it is the furniture which conveys the greatest sense of luxury. The rooms housing it are often little exquisite closets off the main reception rooms. Marquetry and plasterwork set off lacquered cabinets and silk covered chairs. All these indicate wealth and taste, but they also signify that Ham was a product and expression of political status as well.

Its political character is best seen in the queen's suite in the centre of the first floor. The centrality is emphasized by the gardens, which are disposed around the principal bedroom with a studied symmetry. The layout and furnishings embody a political protocol where persons below the royal family are housed progressively further away from the queen herself. A model of the bedroom as it was when Queen Catherine of Braganza stayed there in 1680 shows the high Portuguese bedstead raised on a dais which is separated from the rest of the room by a small balustrade. In the adjoining closet, a tiny room of imitation marble with gilded plaster reliefs, the initials J. E. L. remind the queen of her hosts. A planned hierarchy dominates the whole house, with even the number and size of the fire-irons indicating the status of each room.

John and Elizabeth lived in their allotted wings of the house, which enfold the royal apartments in the centre. From 1672 both John and Elizabeth lived their political and social lives to the full, having survived revolution, civil war, republic and Restoration. They were never behind in seizing the latest chance or pursuing the latest fashion, and Ham is a splendid statement of their achievement and of their taste.

5 The queen's bedchamber today (left) and a model of it as it was in 1680 (right).
It was not just the richness of the decor, but the way the furnishings were set out, that gave meaning to the room.

123. P. Lely, *George Villiers, Second Duke of Buckingham*, c. 1675. Oil on canvas, 30 × 25 in. (76.2 × 63.5 cm.). London, National Portrait Gallery.
The son of George Villiers, first Duke of Buckingham (the favourite of James I and Charles I), the second duke succeeded to the title in infancy (see Pl. 86). After the execution of Charles I he became in exile a close adviser to Charles II, but the duke's political principles were as uncertain then as they were to be in Restoration politics. Under Cromwell he married the daughter of Fairfax, a match which aroused suspicions about Fairfax's loyalty to the Protector. During the exclusion crisis Dryden's poem 'Absalom and Achitophel' portrayed him as Zimri: 'Stiff in opinions, always in the wrong; / Was everything by starts, and nothing long'.

secret Treaty of Dover in May 1670. Motivated by a desire for revenge and an ambition to destroy Dutch commercial power, and perhaps not unattracted by the financial incentives offered, Charles agreed to collaborate with Louis in an attack on the Dutch republic; but the most extraordinary aspect of the Treaty was the secret clause which committed Charles to declare himself a Catholic and introduce Roman Catholicism into England. His brother (and with no legitimate child yet born to Charles, still his heir) James, Duke of York, had been converted to Catholicism sometime in 1668 and in early 1669 Charles himself informed a small group of advisers that he, too, wished to declare himself a Catholic. His intention was communicated to Louis, from whom was requested the financial and military help considered necessary to quell the expected internal disorder at the revelation. If the conversion was genuine and Charles really intended to make the announcement, it showed an astonishing (and uncharacteristic) political naïvety; if it was merely a tactical device of diplomacy, it has never been satisfactorily explained. In either case, although nothing finally came of the clause, it afforded Louis a useful weapon against Charles if ever he chose to use it.

For the next two years, as Louis and Charles disagreed over the date of the first moves of the war, the royal ministers struggled to get the country's finances into a position to fight it. A recovery in trade, improvements in financial administration and a reduction in expenditure under the new Treasury Commission were beginning to have some effect on the royal debt, but in 1672 the Treasury became the victim of one of its own recent reforms. The strict commitment in the Treasury Order bill of 1667 to the repayment of loans to the government in the order in which they had been made had encouraged loans from small investors and increased the Treasury's credit-worthiness; but at the beginning of 1672, a year of heavy demands on the Exchequer for war preparations, it was calculated that the necessary repayments would eat away disposable revenue for the year to less than £400,000. The only solution to a financial nightmare seemed to be to suspend the repayments. Although this, the 'Stop of the Exchequer', released about £1.2 million for the war, it produced a crisis of confidence in the City, permanently damaged government credit and added to the fury of parliament when it next met in 1673.

This was not the only cause of public disquiet. As the war approached Charles wished to show Louis some progress toward his declaration of Catholicism. In March 1672 he issued his Declaration of Indulgence lifting the penal laws from Catholics and allowing Protestant nonconformists free exercise of their religion under licence. So blatant a use of the royal prerogative – effectively suspending all of the many acts which outlawed religious dissent – could not but deeply disturb those who saw statute law as the guarantee of English rights and freedoms, infuriate the Anglicans who had always been the greatest upholders of the regime, and arouse fears of Catholic infiltration of the court to support the increasingly persistent rumours of James's conversion. Charles postponed the announcement of his own conversion, however, and to Louis's relief the whole matter was silently dropped, as Charles had been using it as an excuse to delay the opening of hostilities. The war began two days after the publication of the Indulgence. French troops rapidly pushed deep into Dutch territory, but an English attempt to gain a quick profit was foiled by the failure of Sir Robert Holmes's attack on the returning Dutch Smyrna fleet. Indeed, English successes were even fewer in this war than in the last. At Sole Bay in May and at the Schoneveld and off the Texel in the following year, the Dutch had the better of the allied fleet.

A meeting of parliament had been avoided in 1672, ministers believing that resentment against the Indulgence and the French alliance would make it unmanageable; but at the beginning of 1673 the need for a fresh parliamentary supply to continue the war demanded its recall. To secure a small grant Charles was forced to cancel his Declaration of Indulgence and to accept a Test Act removing Catholics from office. The subsequent resignation of James as Lord Admiral amply confirmed his Catholicism. Towards the end of the session, agents of the Dutch and their allies mounted an impressive propaganda campaign against the war. In skilfully written pamphlets, widely disseminated, they suggested that the French alliance, the Indulgence and the presence of so many papists in high positions at court were simply the most visible elements of the endeavours of Charles's ministers to introduce into England the Catholic religion and a French-style absolutism.

The interpretation seemed deeply plausible to those predisposed to believe it and it was immensely and immediately successful, producing a popular outcry for peace. Under this pressure the fragile unity of the king's ministers broke up. Awareness of Clarendon's fate, easily sacrificed by the king to appease a Commons furious at the miscarriages of a disastrous war, had taught them the value of courting popularity in case of a loss of royal favour. Lord Ashley (now the Earl of Shaftesbury) sought immunity from parliamentary attack for his support of the war and the Indulgence by joining in the hue and cry after popery; Buckingham and Arlington hurled blame at each other. The government's financial straits forced a new meeting of parliament in the winter, but the violent onslaught of the session of 1673–4 struck against its religious and foreign policies and against James's conversion; no supply was given and England was forced to seal a separate peace with the Dutch in February 1674.

Danby and Anglican politics, 1673–1678

In the hope of regaining the confidence of the Anglican majority, Charles now decided to turn back to an Anglican policy and a staunchly Anglican minister, Sir Thomas Osborne. In July 1673 Osborne became Lord Treasurer; a year later he was created Earl of Danby. By the end of 1674 Buckingham and Shaftesbury had been removed from office and Arlington relegated to a political backwater. All three now dedicated themselves to ruining the new minister and his new policy. Danby encouraged the vigorous execution of the laws against nonconformity and Catholicism, and in 1675 tried to pass a bill which would in effect have completely excluded all Protestant dissenters from government office. But the confidence of parliament in the king and his ministers could not be reconstructed so easily. To strengthen the government's lamentable weakness in the House of Commons, Danby sought to create a more unified court 'party' in the House of Commons, partly through a system of payments to MPs from the excise revenue. Danby's 'court party' was the logical extension of the faction-building within the House of Commons in which most ministers had indulged since the Restoration. Royal poverty and the financial demands of war made control of the Commons ever more important and increasingly the pathway to political power. Danby's more comprehensive system produced some results; but it also had dangers, for it added to the concern of conservative country gentry for the survival of free parliaments. They continued to believe in a relationship between government and parliament based on trust, not on bribery and corruption: these techniques merely contributed to their growing alienation from Charles's court and government. Danby thus failed to quiet popular fears of absolutism, although by persecuting both Catholic and Protestant dissenters he provoked their alliance against his repressive Anglicanism and caused the issue of popery to be eclipsed in English politics as James joined in the attempts to remove him.

England's withdrawal from the war in 1675 had not ended it: Charles's nephew Prince William of Orange continued to lead the Dutch in his crusade against the expansionist aims of Louis XIV. Hoping to prevent Charles from succumbing to the pressures from parliament and public opinion to re-enter the war on the side of the Dutch, Louis had been supplying him with a small subsidy since 1675. Danby tried to reverse the alignment with France. In 1677 his success in securing the renewal of old taxes and the addition of some new revenue enabled him to wean the king away from Louis's subsidies. In November Charles permitted the marriage of William of Orange to James's eldest daughter Mary, the second-in-line to the English throne; and in December a treaty signed with the Dutch obliged England to join the war, if Louis refused to negotiate on terms acceptable to them. Louis did refuse, and Danby spent the winter in preparations. In the 1678 session of parliament he succeeded in obtaining supply

124. Titus Oates portrayed in a contemporary print.
Titus Oates, the son of an anabaptist clergyman who was expelled from the Cromwellian army in the 1650s but who became a zealous Anglican in the 1660s, was likewise unsettled in character. Here he is portrayed as the friend of England's liberties against popery, discovering the Pope writing to Jesuits to exhort them to take part in the popish plot. The Pope, his title of supremacy falling from his head, is warned by his ally the devil 'Friend, Oates is behind you'.

for the troops that he had raised and sent over to Holland, but his opponents found it easy to spread suspicion that the new forces were to be retained to strengthen the standing army. The session was also disturbed by the revival of the attacks on James after his reconciliation with Danby had ended his temporary alliance with the opposition. During the summer Danby's grand new foreign policy fell apart; the clamour for peace among the Dutch stopped the fighting before the English troops had joined it and the Treaty of Nimeguen ended the six-year-long war. The English government was left with an army, but not enough money to disband it and an addition to the floating debt of more than £750,000.

The Exclusion Crisis and the Tory Reaction, 1678–1685

As in 1667 and in 1673, a war produced the crisis which helped to destroy a tottering ministry. But in 1678 it was accompanied by a wave of anti-Catholic hysteria which threatened the destruction of more than just Danby. 'The Exclusion Crisis', as the events of 1678–81 became known, divided the nation, shattering the last fragments of illusory unity. Into the difficult circumstances of late 1678 – with Danby doing his best to prepare for a parliament that might relieve the crown of its acute financial embarrassment – broke the Popish Plot. The Plot had its origin in the vivid imagination of Titus Oates, an unsavoury ex-Anglican clergyman who had spent the past year or so training to be a Jesuit priest at the College of St Omer in northern France. Oates and his associates in autumn 1678 brought before the Privy Council evidence of a supposed violent Catholic plot to kill the king. Sceptical at first, the government was forced to take the story seriously when the magistrate who had first examined Oates, Sir Edmund Berry Godfrey, was discovered murdered. The most damaging evidence, though, was the chance discovery of a series of letters written by James's secretary, Coleman, indicating some vaguely treasonable contacts with France and a conspiracy to bring the Catholic religion into England. Coleman had acted on his own initiative, but rumour was bound to implicate James.

These sensational stories, widely publicized in pamphlets and broadsheets, seemed to confirm the unrefined fears of the early 1670s of Catholic cabals in high places aimed at subverting English religion and liberties. The result was an outburst of fury against the Catholic population. There were riotous demonstrations against the Pope, while inoffensive Catholic priests were ferreted out, tried and convicted on inadequate evidence and executed for treason. The government gave up hope of stemming the tide. When parliament met in October, Shaftesbury and the other enemies of Danby used the plot to try to destroy his recent alliance with James and, when this was unsuccessful, to destroy both of them. James's removal from court and influence was demanded, and it was revealed that early the same year Danby had conducted negotiations with the French foreign minister aimed at obtaining subsidies in return for a prorogation of parliament. Danby had acted reluctantly and on Charles's express orders; nevertheless, here was ample material for his impeachment.

Charles could not allow the impeachment of Danby, who possessed many more sensitive secrets than this, and he was forced to prorogue parliament. But he could not avoid another meeting for long: it was his only possible source of money since Louis XIV would scarcely intervene with new subsidies to save Danby, the architect of the anti-French policies of 1677–8. After a period of indecision, in early 1679 Charles struck a bargain with Danby's more moderate Presbyterian opponents: the Lord Treasurer's resignation and a new parliament in return for his immunity and fresh taxation. But in the elections which followed, the first test of national opinion since 1661, the tide against the court ran so strongly that the moderates could not hold to their promises. Even Charles's attempt to calm the situation and divide the opposition by taking many of its leaders, including Shaftesbury, into the Privy Council, and by sending James into temporary exile in Brussels, could not prevent Danby's impeachment, or the introduction of a bill into the Commons to exclude James from the throne. The king was forced to prorogue, then dissolve, the new parliament.

In the hot-house atmosphere of the crisis, the structure of politics was undergoing the beginnings of a transformation. The question of the exclusion of James split both Houses of Parliament. Diverse cabals and factions started to coalesce into two opposing 'parties'. Over one of these, the opponents of James, who were now becoming known as the 'Whigs', Shaftesbury was slowly coming to exercise his dominance. No one ever seems to have been able to understand Shaftesbury. His earlier changes of side during the civil war belied his consistency in opposition in the 1670s and 1680s. Even his enemies were puzzled whether to call him a turncoat or a single-minded fanatic. The satirist John Dryden resolved the paradox by calling him 'Restless, unfixt in Principles and Place; / In Power unpleas'd, impatient of Disgrace'. No one even seems to have known him particularly well: perhaps the only close friend he ever had was the philosopher John Locke, many of whose writings were produced in support of his policies. During the 1660s and early 1670s Shaftesbury had been a loyal servant of the king, as anxious as any of his ministers to maintain royal authority to its height. If his politics were motivated by a principle, it was his opposition to any alliance of Church and state, either in the repressive Anglicanism of Danby, or in the Catholic bigotry of James. But as his failure to dislodge James became evident, Shaftesbury seemed to his enemies to be bent on destroying the monarchy itself. Those who opposed the Whigs' attempt to exclude James were now becoming known as the 'Tories'. They claimed to be the party of conservatism, to stand by the ancient constitution and the hereditary monarchy, fearing that any attempt to meddle with these could only renew the chaos and conflict of the 1640s. Shaftesbury, with his briliant political brain, led the Whigs in the development of a party machine, but the Tories were quick to follow and soon both parties were adept at appealing to country opinion by pamphleteering, petitioning and electioneering, as well as at the organization of politics within parliament.

While secretly renewing negotiations with France, in summer 1678 Charles called new elections for another parliament. The results were little different to those of the spring. In the middle of them, Charles fell seriously ill. If he were to die, a coup by either Shaftesbury or Charles's ambitious illegitimate son, the young and popular but rather foolish Duke of Monmouth, was possible in order to seize the throne before James could return from exile to claim it. James hurried back to England and a touching reunion with his brother; although the king ordered him out of the country once more, his resolve to protect James's inheritance seemed to have been stiffened after his recovery. Shaftesbury was removed from the Council followed by many of his friends; Monmouth was exiled; and the new parliament was postponed. The Whigs pressed for it to meet, organizing petitions throughout the country and an extensive propaganda campaign. But in early 1680 there were signs of a growing Tory reaction. Whig pamphlets were answered by Tory ones, Whig petitions by Tory addresses. Tories accused Whigs of wanting to bring down the constitution and revive the anarchy of the civil war; Whigs told Tories they were either popishly affected or blind. The old divisions of the war, never suppressed, were handed down to a new generation as Whigs became identified with nonconformists, Presbyterians and ex-Cromwellians, and Tories with the Church of England and Cavalier royalism.

By August 1680 a meeting of parliament could be postponed no longer. The last of the temporary taxes of 1678 had run out and news from the little colony of Tangier seemed to indicate its imminent loss to a powerful Moorish army unless it was speedily relieved. But by the time parliament met in October, the Whigs had regained the upper hand. The knowledge that parliament would sit wrecked court solidarity, encouraging ministers to avoid impeachment and worse by making their peace with the Whigs. It was even believed that the only reason Charles called parliament was at last to give in to James's exclusion. Certainly

'Taking and Making Draughts of Sea Fights'

THE VAN DE VELDES AND THE ANGLO-DUTCH WARS

1 William Van de Velde the elder. *The Battle of Scheveningen, 10 August 1653.* Grisaille on panel, 44½ × 61½ in. (113.3 × 155.8 cm.). Greenwich, National Maritime Museum.
The English ship, the *Andrew*, is seen burning, and in the middle distance is Martin Tromp's flagship. He was killed and the Dutch withdrew, leaving the English badly mauled but claiming victory. It was the last battle of the First War, and Ven de Velde captures its drama.

2 Detail of *The Battle of Scheveningen.* William the elder portrays himself here sketching in his galliot in the left foreground of the picture.

On 10 August 1653 the Dutch artist William Van de Velde the elder was at sea in a galliot which was accompanying the war fleet of the United Provinces. He sat coolly sketching the Battle of Sheveningen, a bloody and decisive engagement in the First Dutch War (1652–54). These naval wars marked the full emergence of a new mode of conflict in which large purpose-built ships manoeuvred in line ahead and tried to control sea space and sea-going trade. Van de Velde was pioneering a new form of depiction, the detailed eyewitness account of a great event. It was war journalism. This development was led by Dutch artists who first studied, then meticulously recorded on canvas, their houses, their workaday pursuits, their fruit and flowers, their land and sky. Proximity to the sea and economic dependence on it led them to paint maritime subjects as well; and observation of things and places stimulated the recording of less material things such as light and atmosphere. But William's aim at the Battle of Sheveningen was to record precisely what happened at a battle which the English came to consider as decisive as that at Worcester two years earlier.

The fight was about trade, colonies and historic claims to status in the Channel. Many thought 'that the trade of the world is too small for us two, therefore one must down'. England seemed to have geographical advantages, better ships, better naval administration, more unified command and less dependence on vulnerable overseas trade and fishing than the Dutch. After the Restoration, court and city interests thought the next war would be a walk-over. Yet neither side could win it, and there were heavy losses on both sides. William was drawing at the first action of the war off Lowestoft on 13 June 1665, and again between 11 and 14 June at the famous Four Days' Battle when 8,000 men and 17 ships were lost by the English. His record is extensive and precise. Van de Velde was present, too, on 7 June 1672 at Southwold Bay, the opening action of the Third Dutch War.

William took up residence in England in 1672–73 and thereafter he drew his pictures on the English side. He had fled from the advancing French, from his wife's lawyers (they had separated in 1662) and from his mistress's husband. He brought with him his son, another William and also a successful marine painter. Father and son stayed until their deaths in 1693 and 1707 respectively. In England there was plenty of work

3 Attrib. M. Van Musscher, *William Van de Velde the younger in his Studio.* Oil on panel, 18¾ × 14½ in. (47.6 × 36.8 cm.). Greenwich, National Maritime Museum.

and there were very distinguished patrons. Maritime subjects were in fashion and with royal admirals at court the commissions and rewards soon flowed. Secured by £100 from Charles and £50 from the Duke of York, William the elder was at sea again at the First Battle of Schooneveld on 28 May 1673. Work for his royal patrons kept him totally occupied. Studios were provided at Greenwich for the pair where they prepared the Southwold pictures to become Mortlake tapestries. Charles valued the artists to the extent that he forbade William the elder to go to sea for the Texel engagement of August 1673, the last of all the battles. Father and son spent the rest of their careers in royal service, painting arrivals, embarkations and yachts, and establishing in their thriving workshop an indigenous tradition of marine painting in England.

As artists the two men presented a sharp contrast. The elder was essentially a draughtsman. He produced pen paintings or 'grisailles' in which he aimed at great accuracy in recording, and which drew on contemporary Dutch interest in light and optics. Four sources of light (back, front, diffused and directional) were achieved using some pale grey washes, but mostly by complex pen hatchings. The younger brought more bravura to his art. He sought to capture mood and atmosphere as well as accuracy. In place of hatching he employed thin, transparent layers of paint steadily built up on the canvas in an altogether more painterly manner. The achievement was one of sensation and tonal impact. In this he nicely complemented his father, adding colour and atmospherics while preserving accuracy and formal composition. His studio portrait, in which he displays his father's drawings at his own feet in due homage, is very fine. William the younger was comparable with the greatest of Dutch painters in combining naturalism with universal representations in paint of form, colour and environment. His paintings were not just concerned with an accurate record from nature, but also with a more intensely felt reality behind them.

The Van de Veldes were professionals, highly skilled illustrative journalists, yet typifying the contemporary search for scientific accuracy through looking and recording. That they achieved this accuracy by depicting a new form of European warfare is historically interesting, while the younger man's facility for making his pictures into lasting statements about man in his environment gives his work a timeless dimension.

4 (*above*) William Van de Velde the elder, *The Battle of Lowestoft, after the blowing up of the Eendracht, 13 June 1665*. Pencil and wash with pen and brown ink, $13\frac{3}{4} \times 19\frac{3}{4}$ in. (34.8 × 50.3 cm.). Greenwich, National Maritime Museum.
This, the first battle of the second war, was an English victory. William watched the Dutch flagship blow up. The viewpoint and high horizon indicate that this drawing was a design for a tapestry.

5 (*below*) William Van de Velde the younger, *The Golden Leeuw at the Battle of the Texel, 11 August 1783*. Oil on canvas, 59 × 118 in. (150 × 300 cm.). Greenwich, National Maritime Museum.
One of the finest of all sea battle paintings. Tromp's flagship is firing her port guns at the *Charles* in this last battle of the Wars, where the Dutch beat off the Anglo-French attack. William shows all his skills of colour and tone here.

125. *The Committee, or Popery in Masquerade.* Broadsheet. *In this cartoon – as in much political literature of 1679–82 – the battles of the civil war are fought again. The Whigs are portrayed here as heirs to the schismatical and rebellious Puritans of the 1640s and 1650s. Some of the most influential early histories of the civil war were first published as propaganda exercises during the exclusion crisis.*

he offered statutory guarantees against the subversion of the Protestant religious establishment by his popish successor: yet he stood fast by James's hereditary right. But again the Commons insisted on exclusion and refused to offer any supply. In its desperation the government could only call fresh elections in the hope that the extremism of Shaftesbury and the Whigs had alienated the country. The government, seriously worried that the new parliament might be supported by violent demonstrations of the turbulent London crowd, summoned it to Oxford instead of the capital. Nearly 4,000 troops were stationed in and around the two cities. But the assembly of 1681 was no more conciliatory than its recent predecessors. Again the king responded to the introduction of an exclusion bill in the Commons by dissolving parliament.

The crisis, though, was now easing. News arrived that Tangier had survived (just), and in March, Louis, finally worried that exclusion might succeed and put William of Orange on the throne in place of James, agreed to a small subsidy. At the same time the reforms of a new Treasury Commission, headed by Clarendon's son Lawrence Hyde, were beginning to have some effect; at last there were prospects of a sustained financial recovery. For once there was no need to call parliament and Charles could nurse the reaction of the Tories and hasten the death of the Whigs, who were now deprived of a parliament to keep up the pressure and excitement of the crisis. He struck them out of the lists of local officers, the deputy lieutenancies and commissions of the Peace; the charters granted to town and city corporations were recalled and exchanged for new ones, which allowed them less autonomy and which thrust Whigs from their places on governing bodies; the laws against Protestant nonconformists were enforced more vigorously than ever; and by some skilful, if blatant, rigging of electoral procedure in the City, the Tories seized control of London. Some Whigs were

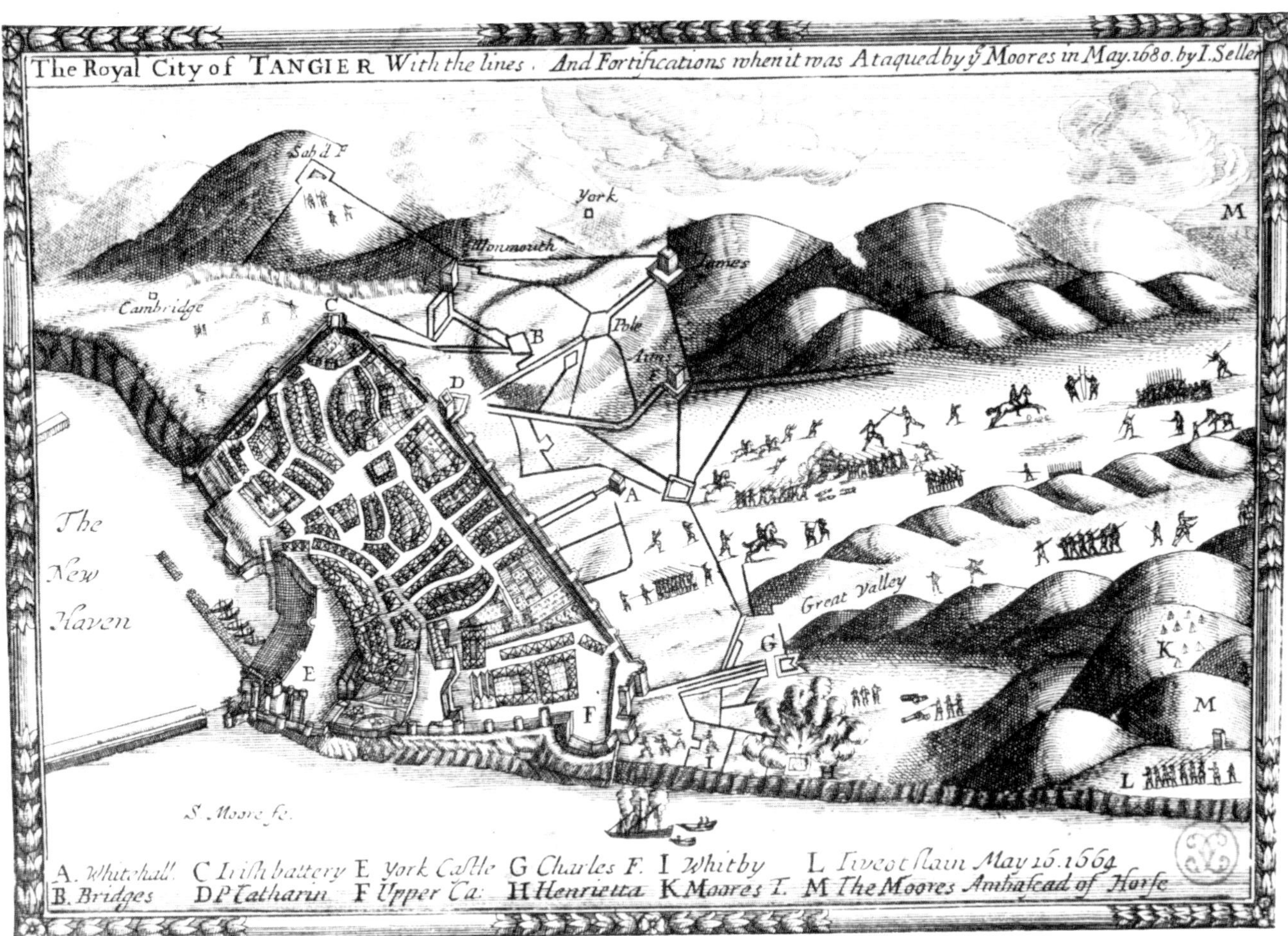

126. The Port of Tangier, 1680. Contemporary engraving. London, National Army Museum.
England gained Tangier from the marriage treaty with Portugal in 1661. But the port attracted little commercial capital, and like other English possessions overseas it became a dumping-ground for criminals. The threat to the garrison from the Moors in 1680, during the exclusion crisis, was seized upon by the Crown as a pretext for demanding money from parliament. The MP Sir William Jones remonstrated that 'Tangier is a place of great moment, but I take the preservation of religion to be far greater'. In 1683, after the government had vainly tried to sell the port to France or Portugal, the English abandoned it.

driven to more radical, even republican, solutions. A plot to kill the king discovered in 1683 was used by the government to smash the Whig leadership: certainly some of its members had dabbled in conspiracy, but the evidence was slight and the trials unscrupulously manipulated by the crown. Several of the conspirators were executed, including the youthful Lord William Russell and the political theorist Algernon Sidney. Shaftesbury had already fled, at the end of 1682, and died miserably in Holland a few weeks later.

Charles died, suddenly and unexpectedly, in February 1685. James made sure of his succession with what some thought was indecent haste; but his worry was needless. There were no demonstrations or uprisings against him and the country was quiet. Shaftesbury, by the enormous pressure that he had brought to bear on Charles and by the growing radicalism of his policies, had alienated many, until, to an increasingly large section of the nation, the threat to stability appeared to come as much from the Whigs as from the Catholics. The moderate gentry began to rally to James and the Tories. At first, wrote one man, 'I was so far in ignorance as to think that their great zeal was only bent against popery, whereas since it is plainly evident that too many of them had at that time designs in hand more wicked than their malice could invent to accuse the papists of'. But the crisis of 1678–81 had had a permanent effect on English politics: from a mixing of the old divisions of the war with a new issue, the exclusion of James from the throne, came the division of the politically active into the two opposing groups of Whig and Tory, the root of the two-party system of modern British politics.

James II and the 'Glorious Revolution', 1685–1689

One of Charles II's ministers, the Marquess of Halifax, wrote that he had an 'immoderate love of ease'. James, by contrast, had an immoderate sense of mission. James was never one to be forced into compromise by political opposition. Resistance to his own will was, for him, little short of rebellion. Unlike Charles, he was a faithful friend or an implacable enemy and expected of his ministers the same absolute loyalty he gave them. He was unwavering in his single ambition – the reconciliation of England to Rome. It seems unlikely, though, that James ever intended to effect the conversion of the nation to his own religion by force. On the contrary, he believed that once Roman Catholicism had taken root in the country its attractions would be so obvious (and the limitation of his favour to Catholics so powerful an argument for those ambitious for office) that Protestantism would speedily die a natural death. Indeed, he began his reign with assurances of his commitment to preserve the Church of England and he continued the alliance with the Tories of Charles's last years. His first ministers included men prominent in the years of the Tory reaction: Lawrence Hyde, now Earl of Rochester; Hyde's brother, the second Earl of Clarendon; the Marquess of Halifax; and the Earl of Sunderland. The elections James called soon after his accession produced a strongly Tory parliament, which quickly voted him the permanent revenues that had been enjoyed by his brother and additional taxes calculated to produce about £2.2 million over eight years.

This unusual generosity was in part the product of Tory enthusiasm for the symbol of their cause and in part a response to the threat to the country's stability presented by the landing of the Duke of Monmouth, Charles's illegitimate son, on the Dorset coast in June. Monmouth had never given up his own claim to the throne (or his insistence that his parents had been secretly married) and had spent 1680–3 assiduously cultivating popularity in the West Country. In 1685 he sought to capitalize on this in a bid to overthrow James. He recruited a respectably-sized army from among West Country artisans, Whigs and Dissenters and moved on Bristol. But government reaction was swift and its retribution terrible: Monmouth's army was shattered with ease at Sedgemoor by regular troops, and Lord Chief Justice Jeffreys was sent into the West on his 'Bloody Assize' to hunt down and hang or transport the rebels. Monmouth himself was captured and executed.

The defeat of Monmouth was taken by James as a sign of divine approbation of his plans, which he began to put more single-mindedly into execution. In the autumn he sent an embassy to the Pope. He kept the extra troops he had raised to reinforce the army during the rebellion and, ignoring his ministers' protests at his contravention of the 1673 Test Act, he granted commissions in the forces to Catholics. When parliament met again in November, he bitterly resented its objections to the commissions and to the army itself and rapidly prorogued it. He tried to prepare for a more tractable session of the same parliament by obtaining a legal ruling in favour of his power to dispense with the Test Act, a verdict secured by getting rid of judges who seemed liable to disagree. When Henry Compton, Bishop of London, refused to suspend one of the clergy of his diocese for preaching against popery, James set up a new Ecclesiastical Commission designed to bypass episcopal authority and improve central control of the Church, and used it to suspend Compton himself. In October 1686 James began to revise the commission's of the peace, introducing Catholics into local government.

In the winter of 1686–7 it became obvious even to James that the Tories were unwilling to repeal the Test Act or the penal laws against Catholics, which he had hoped would encourage conversions to his own religion: so he turned for support to the Dissenters and the Whigs. He dismissed some of his most devoted Tory ministers, including Rochester and Clarendon, and in April 1687 he issued a Declaration of Indulgence granting the free exercise of their religion to Catholic and Protestant nonconformists. Increasingly he became surrounded with Catholics as fanatical as himself. Sunderland, who in 1688 declared his conversion to Catholicism, survived and thrived in the ministry by his pliant conscience, but even this adept courtier and able politician could not preserve any sense of what was politically wise or feasible in a court dominated by a single purpose. James ordered a purge of Tory power in London and the city was returned to their opponents' hands. In July the Parliament of 1685 was finally dissolved, and in preparation for a new one James sent instructions into the counties for every JP and officer of the militia, who were either in a position to influence elections or the sort of men who might stand for election themselves, to be asked whether they would support the repeal of the Test Act and the penal laws. Those who refused were removed from office. In every county there was a rout of Anglican squires from the commissions of lieutenancy and the peace. They were replaced by Catholics, ex-Whigs, Dissenters, ex-parliamentarians and Cromwellians. The gentry, the traditional rulers of their counties, were displaced by men of lesser status and, to them, dubious background.

127. E. van Heemskerk, *Election in the Guildhall, Oxford, 1687.* Oil on canvas, 24 × 29 in. (60.8 × 73.6 cm.). Museum of Oxford, on loan from Oxford City Council.
The charter of the borough of Oxford was remodelled in 1684 to give the crown control over the corporation and to exclude its Whig opponents. Here a messenger of James II instructs the voters at Oxford in 1687.

James's attempt to force Catholics onto the universities, his ejection of the entire fellowship of Magdalen College, Oxford, when it resisted, and the trial of Archbishop Sancroft of Canterbury and six other bishops for their refusal to have the Declaration of Indulgence read from the pulpits of their dioceses, only outraged the Anglican establishment further. But while infuriating Anglicans and Tories, James gained only some of the Whigs and Dissenters. Many remained more suspicious of his Catholic plans and his increasingly arbitrary proceedings than willing to be beguiled by his tempting offers of liberty of conscience. The birth of a son to James's wife Mary in June 1688 brought the unwelcome prospect of the perpetuation of the Catholic regime and hastened a coalition of moderate Whigs and Dissenters with Tories against government policy. Uncooperative as they might be, Tories were unlikely to rebel: their whole philosophy was one of obedience to the Lord's anointed. Only foreign intervention, it seemed, could divert James from his resolution, and prominent men looked to William of Orange.

William had plenty of reason to become involved in English politics. Until the queen's unexpected pregnancy, his wife was heir presumptive to the throne and the prospect of her succession gave him some influence in England. Indeed, James had asked him to endorse the repeal of the Test Acts and penal laws, knowing that Catholic freedom could be made permanent after his own death only by William's agreement. William had little cause to encourage the king's Catholic plans and he refused. James was furious, but the birth of his son deprived William of much of his influence. For William this was deeply worrying, particularly because a

128. The arrest of Judge Jeffreys, 1688. Contemporary engraving. *Judge George Jeffreys, created Baron Jeffreys in 1685, occupied a special place in Whig demonology. Among the victims of the trials over which he presided were Algernon Sidney in 1683 and those of Monmouth's rebels who suffered under the 'bloody assizes' of 1685. In 1688, attempting to hide as the political tide turned, he was arrested in disguise at Wapping. He died in the Tower after petitioning for a pardon.*

crisis of French power in Germany in 1687–8 made renewed European conflict likely, and the coalition of an increasingly powerful France with England was a possibility which he had to prevent. Some Englishmen begged him to intervene; although while many prominent politicians had indulged in clandestine intrigues with William's envoys, only a few, including the Earl of Devonshire and the almost forgotten Earl of Danby, were prepared to go so far as to offer full cooperation in a rising against James. The Dutch States-General, however, with whom William had had many disagreements in the past, were well disposed to support intervention: James's angry recall of a few English regiments which had been in Dutch service since 1674 helped to fuel popular fears in Holland that the Anglo-French onslaught on the Dutch of 1672 might be repeated.

By the spring of 1688 it was clear that William was planning some sort of intervention in England. In fact he was preparing a full-scale invasion, but with such secrecy and skilful manipulation of rumour that for a long time his precise intentions were unclear. Louis was alarmed enough to offer James military and financial support; but by the time James needed it at the end of the summer, all his available forces were committed elsewhere. In November 1688 William's invasion fleet set sail to the accompaniment of a declaration that his purpose was to force a meeting of a 'free and lawful Parliament' for the reconciliation of the king and his people.

As the invasion became certain, James hastily tried to regain popular support by abandoning his most controversial policies. He removed the Catholics from the army; he restored men to the local offices of which he had earlier deprived them; he returned all the corporation charters surrendered since 1679; and he dissolved the Ecclesiastical Commission that had suspended Compton. But he continued to invite suspicion by his refusal to call a free parliament, or to promise the redress of other grievances once William had been defeated. Five days after sailing, William, with 12,000 troops, landed at Torbay. His invasion was hazardous, but his victory almost bloodless. James's fleet failed to intercept his and as William marched cautiously towards London, the English army (about twice as large as his own) fell apart through defections and desertions. James himself was tortured by indecision. He received little popular support, although the leaders of many of the provincial risings in William's favour were careful to insist that their object was neither rebellion nor the placing of William on the throne. Loyal Tories urged James to stay and summon parliament; he preferred to avoid the humiliation of surrender by flight to France. In doing so, he cut the ground from beneath his friends' feet. Those who wished to make William king were immeasurably strengthened by what they referred to as James's abdication, which spared them the need to make constitutionally more far-reaching claims to justify their coup. After fierce argument in the Convention Parliament called by the prince, at the beginning of February 1689 those Tories who had remained true to the principle of hereditary monarchy were defeated and the crown was offered jointly to William and his wife Mary, James's own daughter.

This was a result which Tories were reluctant to accept, but few were prepared to fight in James's defence: he had disobliged and ignored them too much for that. He had ridden roughshod over the ancient constitution, the Church of England and the pre-eminence of the traditionally powerful. While Tories were prepared to defend the idea of hereditary monarchy, they had little to offer in support of James himself. William owed much of his success to James's political arrogance, although he had also the skill to seize all the opportunities that James had thrown into his advancing path.

The Failure of the Post-Restoration Consensus

Instead of the revival of harmony and unity for which so many had hoped, the reigns of Charles II and James II had been periods of conflict and division. Their ministers' attempts to control parliamentary discussion by bribing MPs had raised alarm about the future of free parliaments. Their efforts effectively to annul parliamentary statutes by dispensation or suspension aroused fears for the survival of parliaments at all. Their armies, their French alliances and their Catholic inclinations made it seem that even the laws, the constitution and the religion of the country were under threat. Although neither made a secret of his admiration and envy of Louis XIV's power and splendour, there is little evidence that either seriously hoped to emulate them. Nevertheless, after a long period of weakness in the 1660s and 1670s when royal penury meant that parliament met almost every year, dominating politics and policy, in the 1680s the crown suddenly emerged with immense opportunities for absolutism. Financial stability had at last been achieved through the expansion of the permanent revenue in the last years of Charles's reign, rendering constant recourse to parliament unnecessary; a moderately-sized army provided defence against disturbance at home; Tory principles of non-resistance and the memory of the miseries of the civil war made serious rebellion unlikely in any case. In most European countries the seventeenth century had seen a trend towards royal power and the theories of the divine right of kings, which provided absolutism with its philosophical underpinnings. Some men feared that the same was happening at home.

If in 1660 optimists had hoped that the deep divisions of the civil war could be easily forgotten, they were sadly mistaken: the Act of Indemnity and Oblivion had failed to obliterate them, and the war's bitterness and hatred lived on to complicate politics and to affect a second generation during the exclusion crisis. For a while Whigs and Tories united in opposition to James's Catholic policies. But the alliance broke down even in the arguments over James's deposition, and the Whig-Tory split became central to English politics, a source of constant lamentation for men who decried the modern 'uncontrollable power of faction'.

'Never had king more glorious opportunities to have made himself, his people, and all Europe happy', wrote John Evelyn on Charles II's death. Evelyn's view of Charles's situation at the Restoration was over-optimistic, beset as the king was by the problems of a difficult inheritance. Yet his comment reflects the hope, joy and triumph of 1660. Twenty-eight years later, Charles and James by their misgovernment had shattered that promise. Englishmen's liberties, their religion and the ancient constitution could, it seemed to many of them, be preserved only by the deposition of the king.

CHAPTER SEVEN

Minds and Manners 1660–1688

The Court and the Courtiers

A few days before Charles II died, John Evelyn observed him at Whitehall: 'I can never forget the inexpressible luxury and profaneness, gaming, and all dissoluteness, and as it were total forgetfulness of God (it being Sunday evening) . . . the King sitting and toying with his concubines, Portsmouth, Cleveland, and Mazarine, etc., a French boy singing love-songs, in that glorious gallery, whilst about twenty of the great courtiers and other dissolute persons were at Basset round a large table, a bank of at least 2000 in gold before them.' In the estimation of Evelyn, who was an independent country gentleman with extremely varied interests, active and responsible in national affairs and a pious Anglican, the king had thoroughly dissipated the immense stock of goodwill with which he began his reign by his libertinism, his neglect of state business and his apparent indifference in matters of religion. Twenty-five years earlier Evelyn had watched Charles's triumphal entry into London 'with 20,000 horse and foot, brandishing their swords and shouting, with inexpressible joy; the ways strewed with flowers, the bells ringing, the streets hung with tapestry, fountains running with wine. . . . I stood in the Strand and beheld it, and blessed God'.

The easy morals of the court played their part in the alienation of the king and his circle from the generality of English people. Charles was a sexual virtuoso among English monarchs and his skills in performance remained remarkable to the end of his life. His reign was one of the few occasions in modern British history when royal mistresses were officially acknowledged by titles and pensions; women of some beauty and no repute became duchesses, royal bastards proliferated and grew up to be dukes, and the king's amours fuelled court gossip for twenty-five years. The contrast with his father's court could not have been more marked, for there Charles I and Henrietta Maria had encouraged a cult of platonic love that honoured their own relationship and spread an air of chivalrous refinement around them. Against that memory and even against the memory of Cromwell's affectionate family life, the seaminess of Charles's affairs showed to his disadvantage. His inclinations to love, thought Lord Halifax, had 'as little mixture of the seraphic part as ever man had'. Fondling his mistresses in the Privy Chamber or even in the public gallery, creeping back to Whitehall in the dawn, exchanging bawdy intimacies where he could be overheard were forms of behaviour that might be indulgently observed by courtiers, but they scandalized Englishmen of straiter morals who had been conditioned by a generation of Puritanism.

The king's character set the tone for the court, and on the whole the king's example and influence were pernicious. The Duke of York, a man of some sternness with an honourable military record gained in exile (a record that he extended in naval affairs after the Restoration), began to soften in this sybaritic world and to take on mistresses, behaviour which degraded his marriage to the daughter of the Earl of Clarendon. Many of the king's companions decayed around him, rotting in the luxurious atmosphere of the court. The Duke of Buckingham, a gifted man of sharp political skills with a talent for scientific as well as literary experiment, was the most spectacular casualty. In 1657 his marriage to the daughter of General Fairfax was seen as a tactical triumph and heartening evidence of the reconciliation that could occur between great royalist and parliamentarian families. Instead of capitalizing on this position at the Restoration to make himself the leader of the forces of moderation and enlightened compromise in national affairs, he threw himself into a career of accelerating debauchery that wasted his immense fortune and dissipated his political assets, so that at the end that censorious Whig, Bishop Burnet, could hold up his flawed character thus: 'He had no principles of religion, virtue, or friendship; no truth or honour, no

129. Morsellis Laroon, *Charles II as Patron of the Royal Society*, 1684. Oil on canvas, approx. 14 × 8 ft. (420 × 240 cm.). Horsham, Christ's Hospital.
Royal patronage was essential to the success of the Royal Society. A contemporary who knew Charles described him thus: 'He is somewhat taller than the middle stature of Englishmen; so exactly formed that the most curious eye cannot find any error in his shape. His face is rather grave than severe, which is very much softened whenever he speaks; his complexion is somewhat dark, but much enlightened by his eyes, which are quick and sparkling. . . . His hair, which he hath naturally in great plenty, is of a shining black, not frizzled, but so naturally curling into great rings that it is a very comely ornament. His motions are so easy and graceful that they do very much recommend his person whether he walks, dances, plays at pall mall, at tennis, or rides the great horse, which are his usual exercises.'

130. After J. Huysmans, *John Wilmot, Second Earl of Rochester*, *c.* 1665–70. Oil on canvas, 50 × 39 in. (127 × 99 cm.). London, National Portrait Gallery.

steadiness or conduct in him. . . . He could keep no secret, nor execute any design without spoiling it. Pleasure, and frolic, and extravagant diversion were indeed all he minded: by his eager pursuit of these he ruined one of the greatest estates in England, and perhaps one of the finest wits and finest personages that the world then knew.' He had, however, kept up his family's long history of damaging relationships with Stuart kings, for his reckless conduct added abundantly to the disreputable character of the court.

The Earl of Rochester's name is virtually synonymous with the rakishness of Charles's court, yet he had first gone there as a promising young politician and had distinguished himself as a volunteer in naval engagements with the Dutch. His civility was eroded by the irresistible pleasures of the court and by the excesses of his fast-living companions, whom he outperformed in most things that mattered to them – wit, sex and drinking. Adrift in a sea of alcohol for many years, he went under in 1680 at the age of 33, making last-minute gestures of repentance. The conduct of these noble roisterers may have been vastly entertaining to themselves, their friends and hangers-on, but outraged too many observers to be politically acceptable: Sir Charles Sedley and Lord Buckhurst, who preached naked from an alehouse balcony, did not wholly convert their London congregation; Buckingham, who killed the Earl of Shrewsbury in a duel for Shrewsbury's wife, did not help the reputation of the court. These rakes left a trail of accidental murders, violent beatings and careless rapes behind them and the king was disinclined to impose discipline or restraint. Pepys, noting with dismay in his diary in February 1669 that Rochester had struck the dramatist Killigrew in the king's presence and had received no reprimand, thought it was 'to the King's everlasting shame, to have so idle a rogue his companion'.

The zone of licence and frivolity soon spread to include the universities. A year after the Restoration, Anthony Wood at Oxford complained that scholars were no longer so attached to divinity and the humane authors: now 'their aim is not to live as students ought to do, viz. temperate, abstemious and plain and grave in the apparel; but to live like gents., to keep dogs and horses, to turn their studies and coalholes into places to receive bottles, to swash it in grey coats with swords by their sides'. A group of fellows of All Souls College was discovered trying to print an edition of Aretino's erotic postures on the University Press. Even so, the king's studies in this field made their activities look ineffectually amateur, as the birth of a royal bastard in Merton College in 1665 must have demonstrated. The court was then in residence at Oxford, taking refuge from the Great Plague, and Wood was not at all attracted by his close view of courtiers: 'though they were neat and gay in their apparel, yet they were very nasty and beastly, leaving at their departure their excrements in every corner, in chimneys, studies, coal-houses, cellars. Rude, rough, whoremongers; vain, empty, careless.'

Literature and the Arts

Vain, empty and careless these men may have been. Yet they produced a spirited literature to accompany their amours, jealousies and political intrigues. A buoyant wit and a lyric touch mark the love verses of Rochester, Buckingham, Dorset, Sedley and the rest – a remarkably high proportion of Restoration poets were titled men – but there is often a strain of obscenity that vitiates their art. Although these courtier poets were the heirs to the pre-war and civil war cavalier tradition of Lovelace, Suckling and Carew, the old nobleness of manner had been lost along with the speculative intellectual curiosity that had been characteristic of the mainstream of poetry from Donne to Marvell. All those earlier poets could be witty and flippant in love, changeable in affections and cynical or resigned in misfortune, but the Restoration writers lacked the generosity of spirit and the vision of an ideal love that gave such assurance and gallantry to the cavaliers.

Again, the character of the court must in some manner be responsible for the change. At the court of Charles I the cult of ideal love was a successfully maintained fiction, patronized by the royal couple. Poets, playwrights and artists had participated willingly in this cult (though they were often ready to laugh at it in private) because it provided an acceptable ethos for creative activity, it expressed the imaginative community of the court world and it encouraged an excellence of conduct and language appropriate to a refined courtly culture. By contrast, after the Restoration it was next to impossible to maintain an elevated or generous tone in the poetry of love when licentiousness was the norm at court and no decorative fictions were contrived to disguise it. Occasionally Rochester seems conscious of the futility of the lust that masquerades as love, the vanity of the pursuit of sexual and social pleasure in a world without honour or ideals, as in his poem 'Upon Nothing', in which he sourly praises the principle of negativity as the spirit of the age; or in his 'Satire against Mankind', which despondently comments on man's perversity in frustrating the finer qualities of his nature. The preacher at his funeral, noting that this last trait was prominent in Rochester's own character, lamented that he took 'as much pains to draw others [into vice] and to prevent the right ways of virtue, as the apostles and primitive saints did to save their own souls and them that heard them'. Perhaps Rochester's death-bed conversion was a late recognition of the need for values beyond the sensual.

Along with love poetry, religious poetry also went into decline in this period, both discouraged by the Restoration climate. Communicating one's spiritual experience in verse obviously became unfashionable after 1660, though this is not to suggest that the vivid, Bible-haunted imagination of seventeenth-century Englishmen suddenly faded; it is only an indication that the secular polite literary world of the Restoration was inhospitable to devotional poetry. Both the earlier Stuart kings had had a high respect for religious verse and it was assumed in their courtly circles and far beyond that gentlemen wrote social and religious verse as complementary aspects of a balanced character. The life of the spirit was then valued at every level of society and the wide circulation of devotional verse was an aid to Christian community among Anglicans, Puritans and Catholics alike. The manifest impiety of the upper reaches of Restoration society soon caused that tradition to lapse. The king again set the tone: 'His sense of religion was so very small that he did not so much as affect the hypocrite; but at prayers and sacraments let everyone, by his negligent behaviour, see how little he thought himself concerned in these matters.' That was Bishop Burnet's opinion, and most of the leading figures of society were equally neglectful of religion.

When, however, we encounter a gentleman of some piety, such as Evelyn, who was a committed Anglican, we find that there is now a preference for plain, firm sermons, for the public statement of a Christian's duty, and little evident interest in the intimate spiritual experiences that informed the poetry of previous generations. Moreover the shift in taste towards a clearer, more worldly form of expression discredited the complex, allusive, metaphor-dominated poetry, which earlier in the century had been so favourable to religious meditation: the works of Donne, Herbert and Vaughan had memorably expressed their sense of the harmony of the visible and invisible worlds. Given the notably cynical and profane character of the court and city circles that dominated the literary world in this period, it is hardly surprising that when religion is the subject of poetry, the mode tends to be satirical, with religion regarded as a branch of politics, as in Butler's *Hudibras*, Dryden's 'The Hind and the Panther' and Oldham's 'Satires Upon the Jesuits'. The great exception, the singular anomaly, is Milton.

The arts that benefited most from the king's return were music and drama, both of which received extensive royal patronage. Charles II's taste in music was for the French style. He maintained a large establishment at court to provide music while he dined, for dancing after dinner, for ceremonial receptions and for his private pleasure. In the Chapel Royal, which became the fashionable place of worship after the Restoration, he introduced, in imitation of Louis XIV's practice, an orchestra of 24 strings which played sinfonias between the anthems. They enlivened the service with their 'brisk and airy' melodies, which also contributed to the increasingly secular tone of Anglican devotion, and many conservative Anglicans felt the music was too fashionable to be spiritual, 'better suiting a playhouse than a church'. In fact the Chapel Royal gave employment to John Blow, Pelham Humphrey and later to Henry Purcell, who all worked in the buoyant new style and who extended their talents to the composition of music for the stage, just as the members of the Chapel orchestra were hired out to the theatres as the need for highly skilled performers increased and as more plays appeared that required incidental music.

During the Commonwealth, music had flourished in the home with singing and playing on the lute, virginals or viols; now music had no social boundaries. Churches recovered their organs and choirs, theatres provided musical entertainments, as did taverns at a more popular level. English musicians began composing for the fuller orchestra of strings, wind and brass that was becoming popular, again from French influence. The style of Lully was in vogue and French musicians found plenty of employment in London, while a few chosen figures, including Pelham Humphrey, were sent to France to learn the approved style at the source. The brilliance of these musical developments was one of the distinctive signs of the times, a response to the evident demand for greater pleasure in social life.

This desire for heightened pleasure showed itself clearly in the renewed splendour of costume that the Restoration encouraged. It would be unjust to imagine

131. Samuel Cooper, *James II as Duke of York*, 1661. Miniature. London, Victoria and Albert Museum.

132. A Lambeth Charles II blue-dash charger, 1662. *Charles II, in the third year of his reign, informally portrayed.*

133. Anon., *Observatory from Croom's Hill, Greenwich, c.* 1680.
Oil on canvas, 40 × 66 in. (101.5 × 167.5 cm.).
Greenwich National Maritime Museum.
On the top of the hill is Flamsteed House, built by royal command in 1675 for John Flamsteed, 'astronomical observator'. To its right is a 60 ft. telescope. In the background is the Queen's House, built for Henrietta Maria by Inigo Jones. The house to the far left was begun as a palace and later in the 1660s became a naval hospital.

that the dress of prominent families in Commonwealth times was subdued to Puritan shades of black and white – Sir Peter Lely's portraits of the 1650s show great richness of colour, and we might remark on the appearance in parliament in 1650 of Major-General Harrison, described by a contemporary as wearing 'a scarlet coat and cloak, both laden with gold and silver lace, and the coat so covered with clinquant [tinsel], that one scarcely could discern the ground' – but in general, soberness of costume was undoubtedly favoured. The Restoration opened the door to French fashions, particularly for men, who in this age quite surpassed women in variety of attire. Doublets and petticoat breeches abundantly beribboned were suddenly in vogue with rich lace cravats and broad feather-heaped hats. The austere Evelyn rushed into print vainly protesting against this trend in his *Tyrannus, or the Mode*, which gives some engaging glimpses of fashionable types: 'It was a fine silken thing which I spied walking the other day through Westminster Hall that had as much ribbon about him as would have plundered six shops and set up twenty country pedlars. All his body was dressed like a May-pole or Tom-o'-Bedlam's cap . . . and the colours were red, orange, and blue, of well gummed satin.'

Novelties of dress often ran the risk of absurdity, so it is not surprising to find Pepys apprehensive about the figure he cut when he first put on some new fashion; and in Restoration comedies the stylish affectations of rakes, fops and wits were an unfailing source of amusement; yet clearly there was a consuming interest in matters of costume. Here again, all eyes were on the king, who set the tone. Pepys noted with approval in October 1666 Charles's declaration in Council that he would set 'a fashion for clothes, which he will never alter. It will be a vest, I know not well how; but it is to teach the nobility thrift, and will do good'. The style referred to – a long, close-fitting waistcoat worn beneath an embroidered coat with knee-length breeches – did in fact become, with modifications, the standard type of gentlemen's apparel until well into the eighteenth century. As for women's costumes, the dominant fashion for dresses consisting of bodice and skirt in silk or satin continued from the 1630s until late in the century and was subject to fewer variations than male attire.

A notable vanity of the time was the periwig. Although wigs had been around for most of the century, the full-blown article appeared only in 1660 when the king and his courtiers introduced it from France; thereafter it rapidly became indispensable to a gentleman's attire. Pepys felt the social pressure to acquire one in May 1663: 'at Mr Jervas's, my old barber, I did try two or three borders and periwigs, meaning to wear one; and yet I have no stomach for it'; by November he was persuaded. Why this triumph of artifice over nature should have become so essential to men for so long, when it was attended by so many inconveniences of cleaning, powdering and setting, is one of the mysteries of social life. As one critic complained, it was difficult to have a meal without filling one's mouth with hairs. Yet the fashion prevailed and wigs were considered to bestow dignity and sexual attraction on their owners. Dryden, for example, described the flutter of combing that went on among gentlemen of quality in a playhouse when a new beauty entered:

But as when vizard mask appears in pit,
Straight every man, who thinks himself a wit
Perks up; and managing his comb with grace,
With his white wig sets off his nut-brown face.

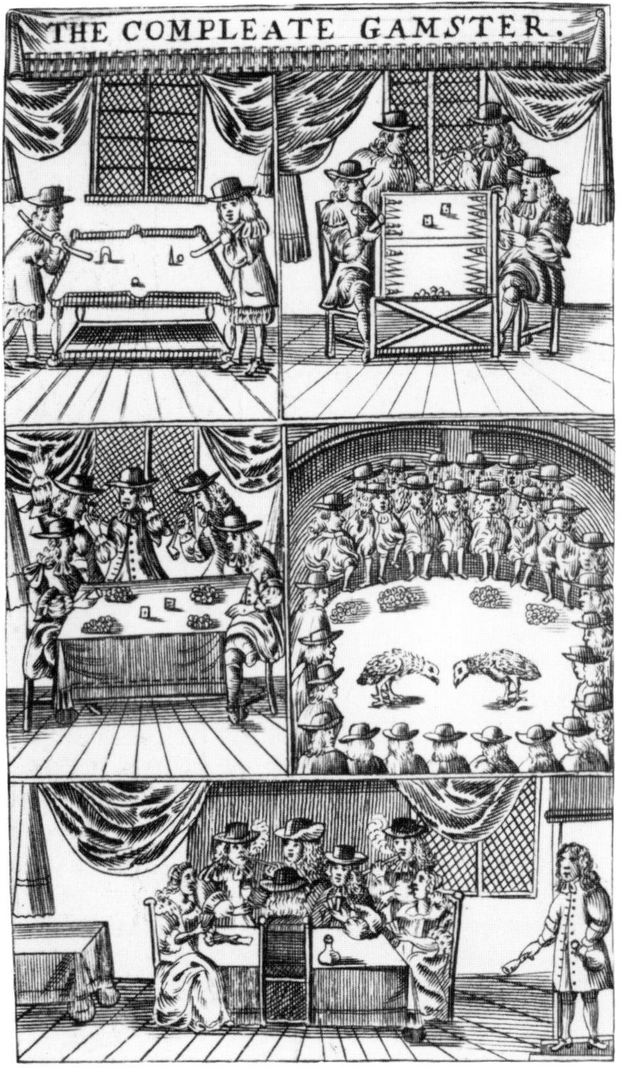

134. Attr. Charles Cotton, *The Compleate Gamster* (1680 edition). *This popular work was first published in 1674. Although the games and sports in which it offered instruction were not new, the anti-Puritan reaction of the Restoration period added to their followings. Puritans had, however, been less severe on cock-fighting (centre right) than on bear-baiting. The reputed author, Charles Cotton – poet, horticulturalist, angler and friend of Izaak Walton – had been a royalist in the Cromwellian period.*

The playhouse soon became the major cultural focus of Restoration society. The king and the Duke of York both loved drama, going frequently to the two London theatres where they were viewed and gossiped about by the courtiers and fashionable gentry who made up the audience. The reopening of the theatres in 1660 after nearly twenty years of closure brought in several innovations that added to their sociable appeal. Music had a much more prominent part in performances with incidental music being written for many plays, in the current French style at first, but later acquiring a more distinctive English character when Purcell began to compose for the theatre in the late 1670s. From time to time operas were produced, successors to the masques of the old Stuart court, but much broader in emotional and dramatic range and no longer exclusive to the court. Davenant, the author of the last Caroline masque, also wrote the first English opera, *The Siege of Rhodes*, first produced in a private performance in 1656 (see p. 135) and lavishly revived at the Restoration. This opera had recitative and arias by several composers to heighten the action, and its favourable reception prepared the way for the more imaginatively integrated works of John Blow and of Purcell, whose *Dido and Aeneas* (1689) was the most expressive invention of the time. Plays and operas all benefited from the illusionist scene paintings that gave opportunities to artists like Streeter, Fuller and later Thornhill to show their command of deceptive perspectives and splendid backdrops. The pleasures of the theatre were now enhanced by the presence of actresses: Pepys's enthralled reports still convey the spell they cast over their audiences, and to the more exalted spectators they offered an additional attraction as prospective mistresses.

In this sociable, expectant atmosphere the new comedies of manners – the theatre of Dryden, Wycherley, Etherege and their successor Congreve – caught the spirit of the age in all its vivacity and wit. Their vital adroitness captivates from the moment the curtain rises. Dryden thought that one of the great improvements of his time had been in the language of society and he pointed especially to the influence of the king in this respect, who had been reared in French courts during his formative years in exile: 'If any ask me whence it is that our conversation is so much refined, I must freely, and without flattery, ascribe it to the court, and in it, particularly to the king, whose example gives a law to it.' The Restoration playwrights made the most of the new style of conversation: the brisk, 'sparkish' exchanges between the wits, the tingling language of flirtation, the elegant observations on the beau monde, the arch asides – these gave vitality to the plays and it is their linguistic brilliance that makes them live today. They also transmit a wonderful sense of well-being, a delight in the present condition of society with its elegance of manners and expression, and its easy commerce between men and women. Although most of the principal characters seem vigorously indifferent to morality, the actions of the plays generally engage issues of some seriousness relating to the conduct of the affections in society. With the easy *mores* of Restoration London, the new generation had much more freedom to love where it pleased and to hazard the risks and pleasures of choice as it rejected the old system of marriages of convenience and interest. These comedies of new-style courtship still had marriage in view, but the routes there were more experimental than before.

Comedies shared the theatres with the heroic tragedies that enjoyed a remarkable vogue until the mid-1670s. Usually with a classical or an exotic setting, such as the India of Dryden's *Areng-Zebe* or the Africa of Settle's *Empress of Morocco*, these plays dramatized the conflicts of political allegiance or the rival claims of love and duty under a code of honour in a way that owed much to French precedent. But they tended to be strenuously over-written, flamboyant and grandiloquently inane, and one need only try to find some English play to compare with Corneille's tragedies to understand how ineffectual was the 'serious' drama of the Restoration. Buckingham's highly entertaining parody, *The Rehearsal* (1671), did much to deflate the pretensions of heroic drama, though it by no means killed off the genre – the prolonged popularity of which confirms that Restoration society did have a high idea of its historical importance and required a drama that would complement the heroic image it gave itself when in serious mood. However, the new tragic drama was pitched too high to have much genuine relevance to society, the prevailing character of which, with its licence and political jobbery, was too clearly at odds with the noble and elevated models that the theatre proposed.

135. A scene from Elkanah Settle's tragedy *The Empress of Morocco* at the Dorset Garden Theatre, 1673. Contemporary engraving.
The play, a great success, was one of the first productions of the Dorset Garden, the most magnificent theatre London had known; it boasted elaborate scenery and machinery, a Baroque proscenium arch, and an auditorium adorned with the busts of poets and with the royal arms (seen here). The Restoration stage was sumptuously respectable. In the hierarchically arranged seating the members were as much concerned to see each other as to witness the dramatic action, which had retreated from the open and projected stage of Shakespearean times behind the recently invented proscenium. This play answered to the taste for things north African after the occupation of Tangier (see p. 171), and to the interest in maritime expansion.

There was, then, a great deal of literary activity in court circles, but much of it has suffered, in the eyes of later generations, from too much levity or obscenity, from fading topicality and from a slightness of matter generally. In the earlier eighteenth century Alexander Pope was to look back dismissively at 'the mob of gentlemen who wrote with ease', and even in Restoration times some of the leading authors regretted the

136. Scenes from the Story of Abraham. Seventeenth-century embroidery.
New York, Metropolitan Museum of Art (gift of Irwin Untermyr).
Working in tent stitch, a seventeenth-century English needlewoman arranges material from three prints from Gerard de Vode's Thesaurus sacrarum historiarum Veteris Testamenti *(Antwerp, 1585). Needlework and embroidery were standard female occupations in seventeenth-century households.*

lack of substance in fashionable writing. 'Thinking itself is a kind of pain to a witty man,' Dryden complained to Rochester.

One has to look far beyond the fashionable courtly domain for the literary works of incontestable power. Both Milton and Bunyan were outsiders, sustained by the Puritan traditions that had been rejected by the new establishment. The appearance of *Paradise Lost* in 1667 was one of the most untimely events in English literary history. Its grand design of universal history and its imaginative colour, that owe much to Spenser and to Italian writers of epical romance, declare it to be a late work of Renaissance humanism; its theological scheme dealt with issues that had reached their height in the 1640s. In fact, *Paradise Lost* was published in the same year as Thomas Sprat's *The History of the Royal Society*, and Milton's cosmology with its attendant angels and devils coincides with Newton's early research into the mechanics of celestial motion that would be formulated in *Principia Mathematica. Paradise Lost* entered a literary world distracted by comedies of manners, bombastic tragedies, satires and amorous verse; it caused no great stir at first, but steadily attracted admiration. Milton himself was leading a secluded life during the years after the Restoration, for as one of the chief propagandists of the republic and justifier of Charles I's execution to European states he had much to fear from the new regime – indeed he seems narrowly to have escaped hanging in the brief purge of surviving regicides in 1660 through the intervention of his friend Andrew Marvell, who had made the transition to Restoration society more successfully.

Paradise Lost does of course have some engagement with contemporary society: some of the political strains in the poem show Milton assuring himself that even though the Puritan Revolution has failed, God's purposes remain ultimately favourable towards those strict Protestants who persevere in their faith. The complex theology of *Paradise Lost*, by which Milton 'justifies the ways of God to men', is only one component in the vast intellectual system of the epic, which incorporates theology, theodicy, ethics, aesthetics, politics and a

137. A carved limewood mirror of Charles II's reign.
Compare the carving by Grinling Gibbons (Pl. 146).

'Artisan Masons, Foreigners and Aliens'

CHRISTOPHER WREN AND THE STONE OF THE WINDRUSH VALLEY

1 A. Verrio, G. Kneller and J. Thornhill, *Sir Christopher Wren*. Oil on canvas, 92 × 70 in. (233.4 × 177.6 cm.). Oxford, Sheldonian Theatre.
Wren's wide-ranging genius is summarized in this portrait where his plan of St Paul's his celestial globe, his mathematical instruments and his telescope illustrate his accomplishments. He points to the skyline of Post-Great Fire London, which was largely his creation.

In May 1681 Christopher Wren visited Christopher Kempster at his quarry in Upton, a hamlet near Burford in Oxfordshire. The great man had come into the country on a mission of persuasion, to urge Kempster to build Tom Tower at Christ Church, Oxford. Wren recommended him as 'a very able man, modest, honest and treatable, and one that your masons will submit to work with because of his interests in the quarries at Burford, and therefore you will have the stone from him at first hand . . . Going now to the quarry, I persuaded him'. Wren thought highly of Kempster, and rightly so. Kempster had not only built around Oxford (see Abingdon Town Hall, Pl. 13), but also played a major part in the building of St Stephen Walbrook, St James Garlickhythe, St Mary Abchurch and St Mary Somerset, which are among Wren's best City churches. His skills were combined with his stone, the Burford stone from Kit's Quarry at Upton.

The Windrush Valley on the edge of the Cotswolds is one of the most beautiful stretches of country in England. Its villages, Sherborne, Windrush, the Barringtons, Taynton, Fulbrook, Swinbrook and its 'capital' Burford, are all exceptional because of their setting and because of their stone. These villages boast quarries of fine, easily worked and weather-resistant stone of astonishingly beautiful colour. Taynton stone was used to build Merton College Library, Oxford, Eton and St George's, Windsor, besides local churches; Burford stone built Wadham College, Oxford, and Windsor Castle; Barrington stone built many Oxford colleges. That these stones constitute the buildings of much post-Great Fire London is due largely to two families and their links with Wren: the Strongs of Taynton and the Kempsters of Upton.

Wren had used Barrington stone for his very first building in 1666, the Sheldonian Theatre in Oxford. As an Oxford don living amongst its colleges, he was well aware of the qualities of that stone. Taynton's fame and patronage went back to the time of Edward III at least. It is not surprising that Wren sought out masons and stone which he knew would serve his purposes for the new London. A close interest in the properties of stone and the skill of craftsmen came naturally to a man of such curiosity and scientific outlook. Yet to move a group of Oxfordshire masons into the City of London was not easy. The Masons' Company jealously guarded admission to its ranks, and 'foreigners' were discouraged. But the monopoly was difficult to maintain in an expanding city where masons were in short supply. The Great Fire of 1666 added to demand, and parliament enacted that 'foreigners' might work until the building was completed and might remain in the city if they undertook to work there for at least seven years. And what work there was to be done, and money to be earned! Between 1667 and 1675 buildings such as the Guildhall or the Monument offered rewards of £27,000. Fifty-two parish churches were to be rebuilt, and 17 or 18 contractors shared £150,000 between 1670 and 1690. On the most famous project of all, the new St Paul's, £257,000 was earned by 14 contractors between 1675 and 1700. No wonder Christopher Kempster could build himself a substantial house by his quarry in 1698.

None benefited more than the Strongs and the Kempsters from this new access for 'foreign' masons. Immediately after the fire, the Strongs began selling stone to London. Thomas Strong had met Wren when they worked on the extension to Trinity College, Oxford. In September 1670 he was made free of the Masons' Company and was joined by his brother John. So began a long and enriching link with London rebuilding, for the youngest brother Edward was at

2 Christopher Kempster's House, Burford, Oxford.
Kempster built this fine house near to his quarry in 1698.

work by 1680 and Thomas's son, another Edward, was made free in 1698 and was still working in 1712. St Stephen Walbrook, surely Wren's masterpiece, was largely the work of the Strongs, and Thomas senior was soon at work on St Benet's and St Austin's. He died in 1681. His brother Edward took over his contracts and added four more City churches in the 1680s. Soon the Strongs were major contractors at St Paul's, and 65 masons were on Edward's team there by 1695. Much of the choir, the east wall and the apse of the cathedral was done by Thomas, senior before his death, and though the Strongs were only one family of masons employed on the building, their record of more than 30 years' service was the longest.

Christopher Kempster, born in 1626, was a neighbour, contemporary and friend of Thomas Strong senior. He was selling his Burford stone in London by 1668 and was free of the Masons' Company in August 1670. Working with the Strongs on St Stephen Walbrook, he went on to build four other City churches. His brother William had joined him from the quarry in 1677 and his sons were in the business as well. Christopher Kempster senior was already 45 when he started in London and was still working in 1709 when he was over 80. From 1687 he was the principal contractor at St Paul's and built much of the dome and the new towers. William Kempster was responsible for most of the south-west tower where his skill as a mason is exemplified in the marvellous circular stairway, as is his sophistication as a carver in the Dean's door. These masons were not just foremen, they were quarrymen, craftsmen, artists and designers in their own right. They embodied a remarkable mixture of skills, producing and transporting the stone, building it up, and often carving it. They exemplified also the existence of provincial resources and entrepreneurial skills, imported to the metropolis. The sleepy Windrush valley, its quarries mostly grassed over now, provided the stone and the 'foreigners and aliens' to construct some of the finest urban buildings in the world.

3 The stairway in the south-west tower of St Paul's, *c.* 1705.

4 St Paul's Cathedral, engraving by William Hulsborough, 1713.
This view shows Queen Anne's statue newly erected to celebrate the Peace of Utrecht.

5 Interior of St Stephen Walbrook, London, 1672–87.
Arguably Wren's finest church, it seems perfectly to combine the centralized and longitudinal plans for worship.

138. P. Lely, *Henriette de Kéroualle, Duchess of Portsmouth*, 1670s. Oil on canvas, 50 × 40 in. (127 × 102 cm.). Wilton House, Wiltshire.
In 1670 this Breton lady accompanied Charles's sister, Henrietta Duchess of Orleans, to England at the time of the Anglo-French negotiations that led to the Treaty of Dover. Her presence made an immediate impression on the king and may have prolonged the treaty. She became maid of honour to the queen and, from that high vantage-point, began to exert a strong influence on English politics. She bore Charles a son (the first Duke of Richmond) in 1672, and was created Duchess of Portsmouth in 1673. According to Evelyn her splendid apartment at the end of the gallery at Whitehall was 'twice or thrice pulled down and rebuilt to satisfy her prodigal and expensive pleasures'.

139. P. Lely and studio, *Prince Rupert in Garter Robes*. Oil on canvas, $89\frac{1}{2} \times 51\frac{1}{2}$ in. (227.3 × 131 cm.). Private collection.
Son of the Elector Palatine and of Elizabeth of Bohemia, Rupert fought in the Thirty Years War in the 1630s and for his uncle Charles I in the 1640s. In Charles II's reign he fought in the second and third Anglo-Dutch naval wars, but his Restoration political career was restless and unfulfilled.

140. Anon., *John Milton, c.* 1629.
Oil on canvas, $23\frac{1}{2} \times 19$ in. (59.7×48.3 cm.). London National Portrait Gallery.
Between the youthful Milton of this portrait and the mature Milton who published Paradise Lost, Paradise Regained *and* Samson Agonistes *lay the Puritan Revolution. In the 1640s the poet, seeing God's purpose at work both in his own career and in the momentous events around him, laid aside the poetic ambitions that had already produced* Comus *and* Lycidas *to write radical political pamphlets – although few of them were widely read. By 1652 he was blind; and for a time in 1660 his services to the Puritan regimes (see p. 118) placed his life in danger from the restored monarchy. A man of extraordinary erudition and austere habits, he wrote long works on history and on logic and a profoundly heretical treatise,* De Doctrina Christiana. *But he took his divine vocation to be a poet – a Christian and English equivalent to Homer or Virgil, called to uplift his countrymen by his art and by his teaching.*

philosophy of history with a unified action that concerns the destiny of the individual and of mankind. The grandeur of that action and the extraordinary power and beauty of the poetry that carries it showed that the long dream of an epic in English had at last been fulfilled.

The Pilgrim's Progress also came from those religious convictions rejected by the Restoration Church settlement. After 1660 Bunyan was frequently restrained by the laws against Dissenters brought in during the early and mid-1660s, was twice imprisoned, and when freed continued to preach his baptist beliefs around the Bedfordshire circuit; his life has the character of a primitive saint upholding the true faith under persecution. Out of these experiences came a stream of writings, notably his spiritual autobiography *Grace Abounding* (1666) and *The Pilgrim's Progress* (1678). In clear, moving English, lit by the phrases and cadences of the Bible, Bunyan also justified the ways of God to man and described with such urgency and sincerity the ways by which men might find God that for some two hundred years *The Pilgrim's Progress* continued to be the plain man's pathway to heaven. When the bishops of the restored Anglican Church together with the politicians began the process of excluding Dissenters from national life and trying to suppress their activities, they scarcely understood the spiritual energies they were trying to control.

141. Frontispiece to John Bunyan, *The Pilgrim's Progress* (11th edition, 1688).
Twelve editions of The Pilgrim's Progress *appeared between 1678 and 1688.*

Science and the Royal Society

Yet literature in the Restoration period was not the principal theatre of intellectual display in society: the scientific community was at last large enough and sufficiently well-organized to develop its own arena of discourse. 'The truth is, a spirit of learning came in with the Restoration, and the laity and clergy were possessed with a generous ambition of surpassing one another in all kinds of knowledge. Mathematics and the new philosophy were in great esteem': these thoughts were expressed by that well-placed observer of the scene, Bishop Burnet, in his *History of his own Times*. Although Francis Bacon had laid out a comprehensive programme of scientific investigation early in the century and urged the experimental method as the best means of enquiry, progress had been slow in the years up to the civil war. Facilities for research barely existed and instruments were often rudimentary. When a breakthrough occurred, such as Harvey's discovery of the circulation of the blood in 1616, it took a long time to get into print (1628) and even then its implications were neglected.

During the Commonwealth the main centre of scientific activity had been at Oxford where John Wilkins, the Warden of Wadham College (and, incidentally, Cromwell's brother-in-law), encouraged experimental philosophy and worked with men such as Christopher Wren, William Petty and Robert Boyle on problems in mathematics, chemistry, optics and astronomy. With the Restoration and the subsequent concentration of intellectual, cultural and social life in London, the centre of activity shifted to Gresham College, which had been founded by the sixteenth-century London financier Sir Thomas Gresham and where many more investigators were able to participate. Moreover, in the years following the Restoration, scientific investigation became fashionable as a result of the king's interest, for he had a curious and enquiring mind. His patronage enabled the new group of gentleman scientists to call itself the Royal Society and from time to time the king or the Duke of York would attend the discussions and experiments. Charles even had an observatory and a laboratory installed at Whitehall for his own instruction. The king's support gave the Society valuable protection, for that, along with the distinguished membership which included several bishops, allowed it to operate without incurring the suspicion that experimental science was a subversive activity, impiously prying into the divine secrets of nature and liable to promote atheism. This is a much more positive aspect of the king's influence: his open, accessible nature and his curiosity made him an excellent patron

[50]

SECT. III.

De motu Corporum in Conicis Sectionibus excentricis.

Prop. XI. Prob. VI.

Revolvatur corpus in Ellipsi: Requiritur lex vis centripetæ tendentis ad umbilicum Ellipseos.

Eſto Ellipſeos ſuperioris umbilicus S. Agatur *SP* ſecans Ellipſeos tum diametrum *DK* in *E*, tum ordinatim applicatam *Qv* in *x*, & compleatur parallelogrammum *QxPR*. Patet *EP* æqualem eſſe ſemiaxi majori *AC*, eo quod acta ab altero Ellipſeos umbilico *H* linea *HI* ipſi *EC* parallela, (ob æquales *CS*, *CH*) æquentur *ES*, *EI*, adeo ut *EP* ſemiſumma ſit ipſarum *PS*, *PI*, id eſt (ob parallelas *HI*, *PR* & angulos æquales *IPR*, *HPZ*) ipſorum *PS*, *PH*, quæ conjunctim axem totum 2*AC* adæquant. Ad *SP* demittatur perpendicularis *QT*, & Ellipſeos latere recto principali (ſeu $\frac{2BC\ quad.}{AC}$) dicto *L*, erit *L*x*QR* ad *L*x*Pv* ut *QR* ad *Pv*; id eſt ut *PE* (ſeu *AC*) ad *PC*: & *L*x*Pv* ad *GvP* ut *L* ad *Gv*; &

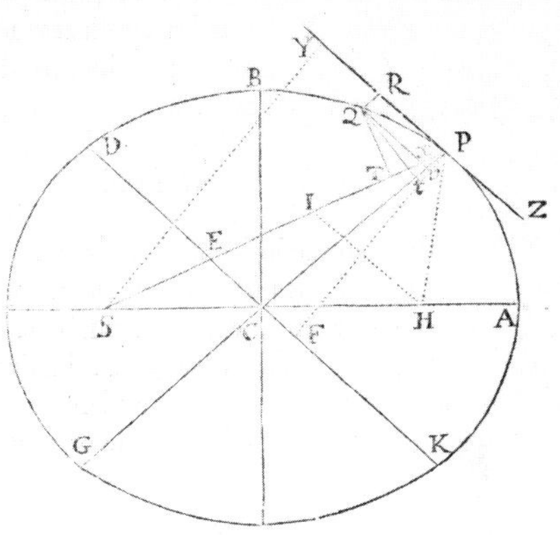

142. A page from Isaac Newton, *Philosophiae Naturalis Principia Mathematica* (1687).
On Newton's pages the revolutionary laws of motion were spelled out.

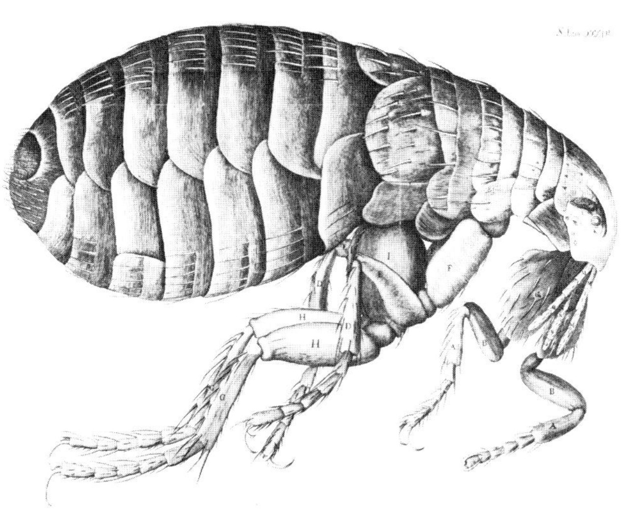

143. An illustration from Robert Hooke, *Micrographia* (1665).
A flea under the microscope.

of 'the philosophic assembly'. Evelyn, who was a founder of the Society, gives us a fair sense of the king's speculative mind in many conversations recorded in his diary: they talked about modern architecture and gardening styles, bees, tree plantations, smoke pollution in London, the planet Saturn, engraving, the invention of grenades made of glass. Charles deserved the central position he occupies in the frontispiece to Sprat's *History of the Royal Society* (1667), a book that was written primarily to promote understanding of the Society's ambitions and to defend the rational investigation of natural phenomena.

A well-justified optimism prevailed in these early years as members extended their enquiries into all manner of practical and theoretical subjects. A strong bias towards research of a practical value existed from the beginning, in line with the Baconian ideal that the 'new philosophy' should work for 'the relief of man's estate'. Evelyn himself contributed papers that were then published as books on the properties of trees, on soil improvement, on the development of the cider trade, on salads as an aid to health and longevity; he wrote a history of engraving and of coins and medals, and for long planned, but never completed, a history of trades. The great achievements of the Society were in chemistry and the physical sciences. Boyle settled chemical experiment on a rational basis and laid the foundations of the study of pneumatics, that is, the mechanical properties of air and gases, their density, elasticity and behaviour under pressure. He formulated, too, a corpuscular system of matter. Hooke studied combustion and cell tissue, pursued investigations into the nature of light and developed a theory of colours that preceded Newton's work in optics. Hooke was also the first practical meteorologist, designing the instruments and keeping the records necessary to document what he called 'A History of the Weather'. Nehemiah Grew did basic research on plant anatomy and John Ray on the classification of plants. The genius of Isaac Newton rose above these men: his *Principia Mathematica*, offered to the Society in 1687, contains the theory of gravitation and the laws of mechanics that made possible an integrated model of the universe only modified in our own century.

Mathematics was now becoming the indispensable auxiliary of scientific enquiry: its scope was enlarged by the development of logarithms and by Newton's invention of the calculus. The experimental activity of the time could not have gone forward without the invention of instruments that gave sufficiently accurate readings for profitable research and many of the basic scientific tools were created or improved within the ambit of the Royal Society: the microscope (whose functions were exquisitely described by Hooke in his *Micrographia* of 1665), the balance spring (another of Hooke's contributions), the thermometer, barometer and air pump. The Society even developed a bathysphere for experiments under water. A good deal of attention was paid to matters affecting shipping on account of the interests of the king and his brother in that direction. Schemes to establish correct longitude at sea, which involved the refinement of timekeeping methods, were insistently pursued. Sounder principles of shipbuilding were proposed: Sir William Petty (who had introduced the principles of land survey and measurement to aid the Cromwellian settlement of Ireland) devised a boat with a double bottom – aptly called 'The Experiment' – as well as 'a versatile keel that should be on hinges'; improved rigging was designed; gunnery at sea was made more accurate.

The strength of the Royal Society lay in its institutional nature. Because it met regularly, had paid officers and recorded its transactions, the Society was able to maintain a continuity in research and to encourage collaborative activity; it also provided a laboratory and equipment, rare facilities in seventeenth-century England. In these ways the organization of the Society overcame the difficulties that had impeded scientific work earlier in the century, when experiments were carried out in isolation without much discussion or comparison of results and when observations were often lost in the confusion of private papers, as had been the case for example with Francis Bacon. Moreover the Royal Society corresponded with country members and with foreign savants and academies, thus opening up the broad international approach to experimental work that has been a characteristic of the scientific community ever since. The scope of enquiry into the properties of nature was limitless: as the Secretary of the Society, Henry Oldenburg, wrote to John Winthrop, the Governor of Connecticut, in 1667, 'Sir, you will please to remember that we have taken to task the whole universe, and that we were obliged to do so by the nature of our design.'

Overall the intellectual forces of the Society were equal to this challenge, as the work of Newton shows. But not all research was illustrious: a number of early investigations were concerned with the truth of wonderful narrations or popular beliefs. For example a correspondent in Sumatra was asked if it was true that diamonds grew in mines and if there was a tree 'that shrinks down when one offers to pluck it up into the ground, and would quite shrink unless held very hard? And whether the same . . . hath a worm for its root?' So confused were facts and fables in the seventeenth century, and so scarce was available reliable evi-

144. Canaletto, *London from Somerset Gardens, looking towards London Bridge*, 1751.
Pen and brown ink and grey washes, $9\frac{1}{4} \times 29$ in. (23.4 × 73.8 cm.).
London, Courtauld Institute (Prince's Gate Collection).
Dating from the mid-eighteenth century, Canaletto's picture shows the completed Wren skyline and conveys a metropolis which has cast off its air of medievalism and provincialism.

dence, that much time was wasted on unprofitable enquiries of this kind. A certain portion of the membership thoroughly enjoyed this study of curiosities, for many gentlemen were more truly 'virtuosos' than scientists, though the line is hard to draw in this period. The mark of the virtuoso was a love of rareties, natural and artificial, which he would endeavour to accumulate in his cabinet of curiosities. Usually, too, he professed a connoisseurship in the arts and a knowledge of antiquities. Wonder and delight were his dominant emotions, and these pleasures frequently inhibited the growth of any systematic analysis of the causes or properties of his unusual possessions. Many of the Royal Society gentlemen had a touch of the virtuoso about them: Evelyn showed more interest in Mr. Ashmole's toad in amber than in Newton's theories, and John Aubrey recorded with unscientific relish how a dish of salads was chafed from seed to leafage in the course of a dinner party; he was content with the miracle and showed no curiosity about the process of germination.

As well as being a forum for discussion and experiment, the Royal Society also served as a kind of social club where the more searching and speculative minds of the time came together. It was relatively free from penetration by the court wits, who were inclined to make fun of what was going on at Gresham College (as in Shadwell's play, *The Virtuoso*, of 1676). The membership after the first few years fluctuated around the 200 mark, though the active members at any time composed well under half the total. With so many illustrious men at the centre of its affairs, election to the Society was highly desirable for gentlemen with intellectual pretensions and entry was not too difficult provided one had the right credentials or contacts. The sociable aspect of its life came to the fore in the discussions and gatherings that took place before and after the formal meetings, usually in the coffee houses that were a new amenity of the London scene.

The Physical Setting

Not only was the intellectual landscape of England changing, the physical setting was altering too. Leading members of the Royal Society also concerned themselves with improvements in architecture. Evelyn drew attention in several of his tracts to the messy, dilapidated state of London and its lack of modern buildings. Compared to Paris, London was still essentially a medieval city. There had been no construction of note during the unsettled years from 1640 to the Restoration, and Inigo Jones had died in 1652, leaving his pupil John Webb as the only professionally trained architect in the country to carry on the classical line that had been precariously established under the early Stuarts. Webb, however, designed little after the Restoration apart from the King Charles block at Greenwich. When Christopher Wren turned to architecture, he had to instruct himself, as did his fellow scientist Robert Hooke. Wren's primary career was in astronomy, culminating in his election as Savilean Professor at Oxford in 1661 before he was thirty. He maintained his work in astronomy, mathematics and geometry, but was encouraged by friends to give practical expression to his interest in architecture – initially by his uncle Matthew Wren, who asked him to design a chapel at Pembroke College, Cambridge, and then by his colleague at Oxford, Gilbert Sheldon, who wished to give the university a ceremonial theatre when he left to become Archbishop of Canterbury in 1663. The Sheldonian involved a good deal of archaeological

145. The Sheldonian Theatre, Oxford, 1663–9. Engraving by Loggan.
Wren's first architectural work, the theatre was designed for university ceremonies. Basing the plan on Serlio's pictures of the Theatre of Marcellus, he nevertheless succeeded in making the building both English and domestic in scale. The theatre was a feat of science as well as of art. Theories of roof construction were tested by the ceiling, which spans 70 by 80 feet and has no cross-beams. The design of the theatre was presented to the Royal Society.

reconstruction appropriate to an academic building, combining elements of various antique theatre designs. Wren borrowed with freedom and confidence, mixing styles and capping it all with a friendly cupola of the usual whimsical variety that gives so many seventeenth-century English structures a benign air which moderates the severity of their classical dress. Like most of Wren's later works the theatre is a practical building, designed with a clear eye to function, yet bestowing on that function a certain sober magnificence.

After the Great Fire of London in 1666 Wren faced the unique challenge of harmonizing the architectural character of the new City. It was King Charles's discerning eye that ensured that Wren got the chief commission to design the City churches. Charles was architecturally well-informed and ambitious, for he had seen in Paris the attractions of modern civic building and as early as 1664 he seems to have discussed with Wren plans for the modernization of Whitehall Palace. There would be many more royal projects during his reign. Within days of the Fire, three members of the Royal Society – Wren, Hooke and Evelyn – had presented the king with different schemes for rebuilding the City on formal, monumental lines; of these, the king preferred Wren's, but in the end none was carried out because of the refusal of many small landowners to cooperate. Wren turned this setback to his advantage, however, for his solutions to the problem of designing more than fifty churches in odd and often inconvenient sites were marvellously ingenious, and the domination of his towers over the City established him as the unrivalled architect of the age. Not merely do these towers signal the location of their churches and stand as landmarks, they also declare the exhilaration of Wren's creative mind in producing so many different forms united by a pleasure in solid geometry and a delight in recombining the elements of classical style with his own fanciful motifs. Inigo Jones had had no aerial ambition, but Wren restored to English architecture the medieval love of adorning the skyline with memorable towers and spires. He enjoyed a freedom of invention that Jones, with his pioneering correctness, never allowed himself; yet Wren did not have enough bravura of style to be described as a fully Baroque architect, for his work embodied a certain intellectual restraint, partly from personal inclination, partly in deference to the Anglican mode.

Paradoxically, the Great Fire did much to advance the decorative arts in England. Up to this time, buildings had relatively limited schemes of interior decoration because the applied arts and furniture design had not kept up with architectural advances. When Wren attained the dominant place in the commission for rebuilding, he determined to assemble teams of men who could create modern interiors compatible with his structures, with the aim of dispelling the notion that England always lagged a generation or two behind France and Italy in matters of design. St Paul's provided the focus for this activity, but all the parish churches and company halls benefited from the wide range of skills that Wren brought together. Throughout the 1670s his craftsmen developed an increasing mastery. The art of woodcarving reached incomparable heights

146. Grinling Gibbons, the choir stalls on the north side of St. Paul's Cathedral, 1696–8.
Gibbons's decorative Baroque woodcarving is famed for its fluency and for its finely captured detail. His work adorned palaces and country homes – Hampton Court and Petworth among them – as well as churches. These stalls are perhaps his finest work.

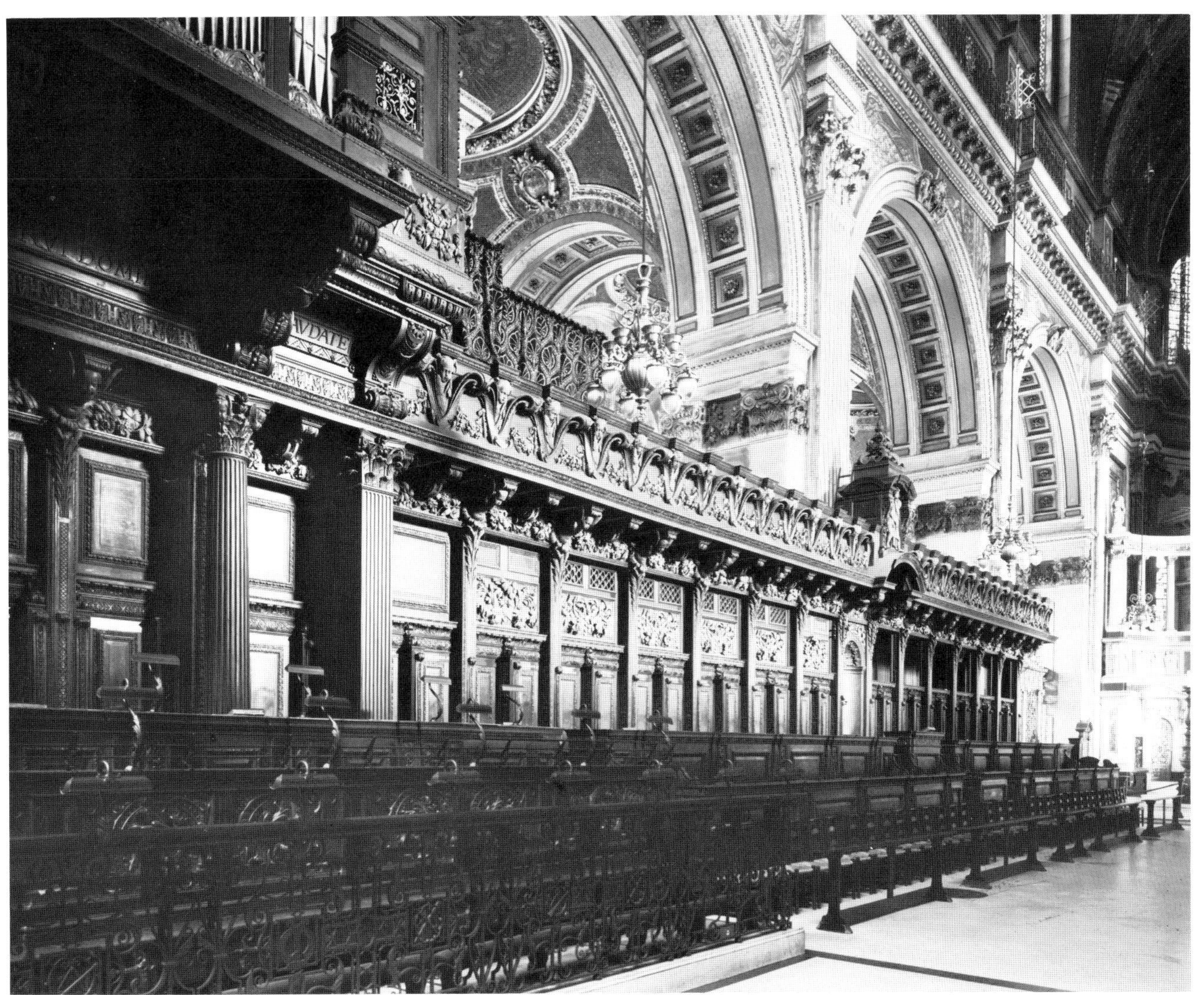

147. Jean Tijou, gates of the south aisle, St. Paul's Cathedral. *Tijou had a strong influence on the wrought ironwork for which late seventeenth- and early eighteenth-century England was famous. His* A New Book of Drawings *(1693), and his patronage of such pupils as Thomas Robinson and Robert Bakewell, brought Baroque ironwork to this country.*

with Grinling Gibbons, who apparently received his training in Holland, as his sensitive still-life motifs of fruit and flowers and birds would suggest; yet his associates Jonathan Maine and Edward Pierce, whose training had been in England, could almost match him in the imaginative handling of wood and stone. Jean Tijou from France executed marvels of wrought-iron work and effectively introduced into England a new craft, which soon became indispensible in churches and country houses. John Grove, Henry Doogood and, later, Edward Goudge applied their exuberant plasterwork to produce those richly encrusted ceilings so characteristic of Restoration interiors. As Wren moved on to projects for the royal palaces and as architects associated with him, such as Hawksmoor, Vanbrugh and Gibbs, later advanced to the design of great houses, they took with them their top London men who intermingled with provincial masters to create that broad tradition of craftsmanship that ran throughout the eighteenth century.

A most distinctive development was the fashion for decorative wall paintings in secular and religious buildings that came in with the Restoration. Its first exponents were Robert Streeter and Isaac Fuller, who had learned the art in France and Italy and who were greatly appreciated for their celestial fantasies. They were eclipsed by Antonio Verrio, who came to England about 1672 bringing the authentic Italian Baroque manner, followed by Laguerre from France a decade later. Both were eagerly patronized by the royal family and the leading aristocracy. Verrio specialized in mythological compositions that climbed all the way up the staircase wall and spread out along the ceilings of the state rooms, providing a heroic setting for his noble patrons. Nowhere is the aggressive confidence of the later Stuart aristocracy more strikingly felt than in the great new houses with their Baroque paintings celebrating the magnificence of their owners, for example at Ham House (see p. 162), Stowe, Cassiobury, Thoresby, Petworth or Chatsworth.

The monarchy, too, grew increasingly confident of its powers. During the 1670s and 1680s King Charles, envious of what Louis XIV had achieved, began to magnify his royal image by major additions or alterations to the palaces at Greenwich, Windsor, Hampton Court and Whitehall, and he commissioned Wren to build a new palace at Winchester. The paintings that Verrio executed for the remodelled interiors at Windsor show how Charles tried to project his reign as a succession of heroic achievements (when objectively it appears as a line of lost opportunities): the themes were the Restoration of the Monarchy symbolized by the Triumph of Charles, the Restoration of the Church of England, Charles in Glory (beyond the envious reach of plots), the Victories of his Arms, and the Four Continents paying homage to the King. King James II in his brief reign was happy to continue the process of aggrandizing royal authority through the arts, but he only got as far as having Verrio paint the Restoration of the Catholic Church in the chapel at Windsor before he lost his throne.

As is so often the case, it is a particular painter who fixes the image of a generation. The men and women of the Restoration submitted their fortunes to Sir Peter Lely, already at the head of his profession in 1660, who had modified the Van Dyckian manner to produce a slightly more sensuous, lingering evaluation of his subjects. The quicksilver refinement that Van Dyck gave to his sitters has dulled a little, the alertness of spirit more clouded by the flesh, but these changed qualities were appropriate to the age. Lely responded to the Restoration by adding greater luxuriousness to his style, as if to gratify the pleasure-seeking society that confided its affairs to him. One senses that Lely was sympathetic to the indulgent lives of his clientele: the sumptuous enveloping silks of his great ladies form the element of pleasure in which they lived, the flesh tints are applied to please those who believed in the goodness of the flesh and its restorative virtue. Whereas the treatment of the hands was often Van Dyck's way of suggesting the sensitivity or self-possession of his subjects, with Lely the modelling of the eye, 'the sleepy eye that spoke the melting soul', hints at the secret life of sensuous content. Even wives can look like mistresses when Lely paints them. Not all was softness and romance, however. Some of his male portraits speak of tenacious political careers and complacency in success: the wide disbelieving eyes of his royal figures – Charles II, the Duke of York, Prince Rupert – seem unable to imagine the virtue of other men. Few intellectuals and few churchmen sat for Lely, for he was not their sort of painter; but for those men and women who were satisfied with the present state of society and proud of their place in it, Lely was the right choice.

CHAPTER EIGHT

Revolution, War and Politics 1689–1714

The Consequences of Revolution

The most direct result of the Revolution of 1688 was a change of monarchs. It was more than 200 years since the true, hereditary successors had been excluded from the English throne; and for the great majority of Tories and Anglican clergy, with their belief in divine right, it was a trauma. Expectations that James II might bend to the *force majeure* of the Prince of Orange's army, call a 'free' parliament and submit to its terms were shattered by his flight to France in December. Hopes that his titular rights might still be preserved by the fiction of a regency, or that William might even act merely as consort to his wife, Princess Mary, proved equally vain. Whig votes in the 'Convention', called in January 1689, would have killed them even without William's own obduracy. But, decisively, the prince would accept nothing less than the crown itself, sharing the title but not its power with his wife – though her legal claims were manifestly superior. Tories were left with the meagre consolation that the parliament that offered them the throne deemed James II to have 'abdicated', and with the equally improbable myth that his baby son was an imposter, smuggled into the accouchement chamber in a curiously large warming pan.

James II's replacement by William III in February 1689 was one of the most decisive changes of monarch in England since the coming of the first William in 1066. Even on a personal level the change was dramatic. James II had been devotedly Catholic, blinkered and narrowly English in outlook. He was hostile to the pretensions of parliament, impatient of the restrictions that the law imposed on his powers. William, though James's nephew by blood, was anything but English in most ways. While he indulged his wife's Anglicanism, his personal sympathies lay with the starkly un-English Calvinism of the Dutch Reformed Church. His favourite friends were as foreign as his accent. His intelligence was acute and his tastes cosmopolitan. His political preoccupations were European, far removed from the average Englishman's insularity. He had no great love of representative institutions, but had learned to live with them in the United Provinces and accepted that he must do so in England.

William's motives for mounting his expedition in November 1688 had not been altruistic. He had devoted his life hitherto to resisting the ambitions of Louis XIV's France, and only his determination to enlist England's wealth and naval power in that struggle could have nerved him for such a high-risk venture. Within three months of his accession his new kingdom had indeed been drawn into the Nine Years' War, recently provoked by French aggressive designs on Germany. William was not without assistance from James II, whose invasion of Ireland in March 1689 hit the English in their most sensitive spot, and from Louis XIV, whose support for this invasion made England's subsequent involvement in the anti-French coalition easier to reconcile with her traditional interests. By the time the decisive battle of the Irish campaign was fought at the Boyne on 1 July 1690, it was widely accepted that only further pursuit of the war against France could protect the gains of 1688–9 in both religion and politics.

Few Englishmen can have imagined, however, when war against France was declared in May 1689, what a titanic struggle lay ahead. Since the fifteenth century, England's interventions in Continental wars had been episodic and, except in 1658, notable for inefficiency and ineffectiveness. But 'King William's War' lasted for over eight years until September 1697, and its sequel, the War of the Spanish Succession, absorbed Britain's wealth and energies for a further eleven (1702–13). These wars, and their effects on government and politics, were a recurring theme throughout the remainder of the Stuart period. But another and vital effect of the change of rulers in 1689 (a change in Scotland and Ireland as well as England), was the creation of a serious succession problem.

Mary II died childless in 1694. William did not remarry and his sister-in-law Anne's numerous and unsuccessful pregnancies are legendary; her only surviving child William, Duke of Gloucester, died in July 1700; and the Bill of Rights of 1689 had regulated the English succession no further than Anne and her children. To begin with, however, it was not so much the succession as the legitimacy and acceptability of

148. Grinling Gibbons, drawing for a monument for William III and Mary II. London, British Museum.

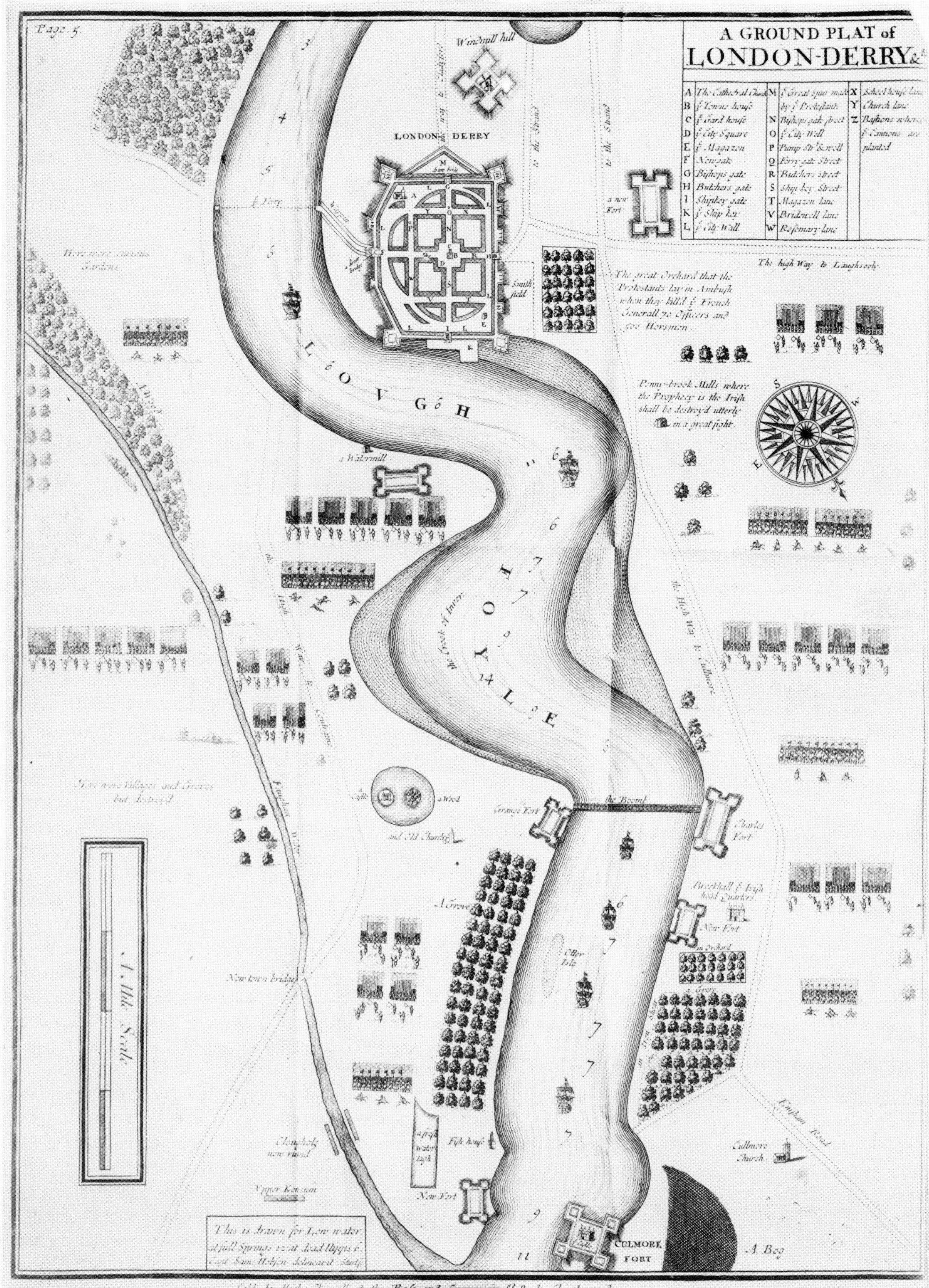
Page 5.
A GROUND PLAT of
LONDON-DERRY &c.
A The Cathedral Church
B ye Towne house
C ye Gard house
D ye City Square
E ye Magazen
F Newgate
G Bishops gate
H Butchers gate
I Shipkey gate
K ye Ship key
L ye City Wall
M ye Great Spur made by ye Protestants
N Bishops gate street
O ye City Well
P Pump Str. & well
Q Ferry gate Street
R Butchers street
S Ship key Street
T Magazen lane
V Bridewell lane
W Rosemary lane
X School house lane
Y Church lane
Z Bastions where ye Cannons are planted
Windmill hill
LONDON-DERRY
a new Fort
Smith field
The great Orchard that the Protestants lay in Ambush when they kill'd ye French Generall 70 Officers and 500 Horsmen.
The high Way to Laughsooly.
Here were curious Gardens
L O U G H
Penn-brook Mills where the Prophecy is the Irish shall be destroy'd utterly in a great fight.
a Watermill
F O Y L E
Here were Villages and Groves but destroy'd
a Wood
Grange Fort
the Boom
Charles Fort
and Old Church
A Grove
Brookhall & Irish head Quarters
New Fort
Otter Isle
New town bridge
A Mile Scale
Cloughole now ruin'd
Fish house
Cullmore Church
Enisham Road
New Fort
CULMORE FORT
A Bog
This is drawn for Low water
Sold by Rich. Chiswell at the Rose and Crown in St. Pauls Church yard.

150. Dutch School, *William III Landing at Brixham*, 1689.
Oil on canvas, 56½ × 90½ in. (143.5 × 229.9 cm.).
Windsor Castle, Royal Collection.
William's invasion in November 1688 was a high risk. Neither the safe landing of his army nor James II's subsequent loss of nerve and retreat could have been confidently predicted. William's fleet, driven back by a storm when it set out on 19 October, made a fresh start on 1 November, when the 'Protestant wind' began to blow. On the hazy morning of 5 November the expedition, aiming for Torbay in Devon, was dangerously carried too far to the west, towards Plymouth, where James had a garrison. Then, on that Protestant anniversary, providence appeared to intervene. The wind changed; the mist dispersed; and the fleet rode safely and in sunlight into Torbay. The expedition had supposed itself to be in grave danger from James's navy; but the royal fleet, under-equipped, divided in its allegiance and ignorant of William's destination, was trapped by the wind off the Thames estuary, and offered no resistance.

149 (opposite). Londonderry. Contemporary engraving, 'sold by Richard Chiswell at the Rose and Crown, St. Paul's churchyard'.
Control of Ireland was essential if William III was to overcome his enemies both in England and abroad. In 1689 Irish Catholics rose in defence of James II against their new Protestant masters in England. James landed in Ireland in March and rallied the Irish parliament to his cause. The Presbyterians of Ulster fled to Londonderry and Eniskillen, and at Londonderry survived in the summer the three-month siege by James's forces which is remembered in this print. The pro-William picture emphasizes the French backing for the Irish forces, recalls a 'prophecy' that at Londonderry 'the Irish shall be destroyed utterly in a great fight', and records the destruction of villages and gardens by the besiegers.

William III's own rule that was in question. Fortunately for him, Mary was personally popular – which he was not – and devoted to the Established Church. While she lived, hers was the main influence keeping Anglican Tories loyal (or resigned) to a regime which most of them privately regarded as illegitimate, even though only a tiny minority of English Protestant clergy and laymen followed William Sancroft, the Archbishop of Canterbury, in refusing to swear allegiance to it. The war was not going well in the early 1690s and, with serious invasion scares in 1690 and 1692, there were strong temptations for politicians to traffic with the Jacobite agents who plied between England and James II's exiled court at St Germains.

On the positive side the Revolution monarchy survived rebellions in both Scotland and Ireland: in Scotland with ease, though disaffection remained strong in the Highlands when the revolt was over (1689), but in Ireland with difficulty. The sympathies of the Irish Catholic majority were almost universally for James and at one time there were 100,000 rebels in arms in support of his invasion. Their failure in 1691 left the Anglican Protestant supremacy impregnably entrenched, creating its own long-term problems for the future of Anglo-Irish relations, but as the total quiescence of Ireland in 1715 and 1745 was to prove, drastically reducing the possibility of a future Stuart restoration through this door.

151. Attrib. Sir Godfrey Kneller, *Queen Anne*, *c.* 1690.
Oil on canvas, 92 × 56¼ in. (233.7 × 143 cm.).
London, National Portrait Gallery.
Born in 1665, daughter of James II and of Anne Hyde, and younger sister of Mary, Anne married George, Prince of Denmark, in 1683. Their many children all died young.

Confidence in the future of the Revolution monarchy was visibly growing in England in 1694 before the queen's sudden death revived the Jacobites' flagging hopes. By the winter of 1695–6 James and Louis were sufficiently confident of a supporting English rising to renew their invasion plans and this time to link them with a conspiracy to assassinate King William. Their confidence was almost certainly misplaced; but in any event, the uncovering of the Fenwick conspiracy in 1696 not only scotched the invasion but proved a turning-point in the reign. The revelation of a plot in which James II appeared to be implicated caused a revulsion against his cause. For the first time office-holders were expected to acknowledge William's title to the throne as 'rightful and lawful', and an 'Association', a solemn engagement to defend the king and his government sponsored by the Whigs in parliament as a touchstone of loyalty, was couched in similar terms.

Nevertheless, a question mark against the future of the Protestant Succession remained. Princess Anne's health was suspect and when her son died in 1700 further parliamentary provision for the succession became an urgent necessity. The Act of Settlement of 1701 accordingly established the Dowager Electress Sophia of Hanover, a grand-daughter of James I of England, as the legal heir after Anne. If Anne outlived her – by no means a certainty despite Sophia's 71 years – there was a healthy line of the Electress's descendants, headed by the Elector George Lewis, earmarked to follow. The Hanoverians were a respectable choice; and while they would never be acceptable to the strictest legitimists in the Tory party, the fact that the Settlement bill originated in a strongly Tory House of Commons seemed a good omen. Soon afterwards, when James II died, Louis XIV provocatively recognized his son (best known to history as the Old Pretender) as James III of England. When Anne came to the throne unexpectedly early, in March 1702 following a fatal riding accident to William, the whole country, apart from the most hard-bitten Jacobites, was united in acclaiming her. Most Tories, in fact, openly gloried in their 'Church of England Queen', and her accession certainly helped to reconcile them to the new war which broke out in May. In consequence Jacobitism was a low-key affair in England for the first eight to nine years of her reign.

Scotland, however, was a different story; and a combination of the union of crowns, a common frontier and a bitter war against Scotland's 'auld ally', France, now made Scottish attitudes to the succession a matter of the first importance to England. Anglo-Scottish relations had become very strained at times in the 1690s and James, so unpopular in Scotland while he was on the throne, seemed a more attractive figure, even south of the Highland Line, when draped in the mists of distance. So when the Scottish economy, already in enough difficulty, was threatened with further damage by a new war, and heavier taxation began to fall again on a country only recently recovered from a serious famine, the Edinburgh parliament elected in 1702 soon proved the most obstreperous since before the civil wars. Its anti-English measures seem to have been inspired more by defiance of Westminster or by factional calculations than by widespread sympathy with the Pretender, but English politicians could not afford to ignore their implications. Above all, the Act of Security (1703–4), which gave the Scottish parliament the right to make its own settlement of the succession on Anne's death, caused great alarm. A back-door for the Pretender and a French army had been pushed at least some way open.

To Lord Godolphin (Anne's Lord Treasurer) and to virtually every Whig at Westminster, a Union of the two parliaments seemed by 1705 the only solution to the Scottish problem. Without it anarchy threatened if the queen died suddenly at a time when most of the army was critically engaged abroad. From a mixture of motives, enough Scottish politicians were persuaded that the survival of Scottish legislative independence was undesirable, to enable the Union, negotiated in 1706, to pass in the Edinburgh as well as Westminster parliament in 1707. The Scots made no mean bargain. They were given fair representation in the new parliament of 'Great Britain'. They retained separate identity through their own legal system and their own established Presbyterian Kirk, and were granted full economic rights in England and in her colonies. But although time was to give the Union an air of inevitability, the partnership of 1707 was essentially experimental and in its early years precarious. An invasion attempt as early as 1708, though it ended in fiasco, showed that Union had not ended Franco-Jacobite hopes of regaining England through Scotland.

But in England, too, over the next few years Jacobite sympathies became more overt, justifing the prescience of the Whigs in pushing through a Regency Act in 1705, providing for a 'caretaker' administration to preside over the potentially dangerous interval between the queen's death and the arrival of the Hanoverian heir. Three factors initially caused the revival of English Jacobitism in 1709–10: war-weariness; High-Church hysteria provoked by the Whig impeachment of the clergyman Henry Sacheverell; and the general election of 1710. At this election, desire for peace and fears for the Church produced a Tory majority of unmanageable proportions – a majority almost as big a threat to the incoming Tory coalition under a wily arch-moderate, Robert Harley, as to the devastated Whigs. As backwoodsmen and parsons babbled in their cups of their dreams of a Stuart restoration after Anne, a substantial bloc of over fifty MPs organized themselves as a pressure group to try to bring that event about by peaceful means. Had these Jacobites not been so hamstrung until 1714 by restraining instructions from the Pretender, who misguidedly believed that Harley was secretly acting in his interests, they might have been a severe embarrassment from late 1711 onwards to a mostly non-Jacobite ministry. For it was then that general Tory unease about Hanover greatly increased because of a serious quarrel between the Elector, an advocate of 'No Peace without Spain', and the Harley ministry over the latter's secret negotiations with France. Later efforts to conciliate him, intensified after Sophia's death in May 1714, proved fruitless and Tory politicians became convinced that the first Hanoverian king would, to begin with, be ill-disposed towards them.

It was this situation, and the queen's near-fatal illness in December 1713, that brought the succession issue to the boil again in the last year of the reign. The Whigs took heart and launched a series of attacks on their opponents to which the charge of Jacobitism was central. The 'Hanoverian Tories' took fright, organized themselves in the 1714 parliament, and co-operated with the Whigs to try to pressurize a government whose intentions now seemed to them far from reassuring. A fierce struggle for power between Harley, now earl of Oxford, and the mercurial chief Secretary of State, Bolingbroke, intensified their anxieties: especially when Bolingbroke, who was as reckless as Oxford was cautious and was known to have cultivated close relations with the Jacobite MPs, began to look the likely winner. Some modern scholars question whether he seriously intended to gamble on a Jacobite coup, at least after the Pretender had rejected a final appeal to become a nominal Protestant. But the suddenness with which the queen's last illness and death followed the dismissal of Oxford made the question academic. Having pinned their faith for some years mainly on a political restoration through repeal of the Settlement Act, the Jacobites found the final crisis upon them on 1 August 1714 with their military plans less than half matured. Thus the first Hanoverian king, George I, was able to enjoy a year's peaceful occupancy of the throne, and his Whig adherents a firm entrenchment, before the Protestant Succession was seriously threatened by force of arms.

The 1688 Revolution did not merely change England's rulers and make the safeguarding of the new monarchy and the succession a dominant political concern until well into the Hanoverian period. It was also responsible for transforming England's system of government.

Many of the changes this involved were not immediately evident, so that it has been possible to argue that in itself the Revolution directly changed very little constitutionally. Certainly William III had no intention of presiding over the emasculation of the royal prerogative. Throughout his reign foreign policy remained

'And Taught the Doubtful Battle Where to Rage'

WITH MARLBOROUGH AT MALPLAQUET

By the Summer of 1709 the combatants in the War of the Spanish Succession were exhausted. A terrible winter had added to the suffering, and even John Churchill, Duke of Marlborough, who was the acknowledged generalissimo of the allies but who was losing the favour of Queen Anne, was talking secretly of peace. His Whig political allies however were demanding that Louis XIV drive his grandson from the Spanish throne, and realistic peace negotiations looked unlikely. There were many advocates of a final push in the coming 1709 campaign to drive the French from the Spanish Netherlands and open up the road to Paris.

The allies assembled 152 battalions and 245 squadrons by June to finish off the army of Marshall Villars, the 'last army of France', under strength and undernourished. Yet on 11 September, when Marlborough faced this army before the village of Malplaquet, he had to reflect on the appalling loss of life which had been brought about during the summer by the allied strategy of avoiding field battles and of limiting campaigns to sieges in the Low Countries and to chess-board manoeuvres. The heaviness of casualties was brought about by such innovations as the flint-lock musket and the socket-bayonet, and by the neglect by generals of Turenne's advice 'to make few sieges and fight plenty of battles; when you are master of the countryside, the villages will give us the towns'. Marlborough agreed and always sought decisive engagements, and so it was against his better judgement that he waged a war of attrition in the summer of 1709.

But in September, battle was about to be joined and the allies could look to Marlborough's high quality staff work, careful planning and battlefield control to win it for them. His battle tactics had been established in earlier campaigns. He liked to take the initiative on the field with aggressive and frequent probes against enemy lines. To do this he often drew up his forces unconventionally and combined infantry, cavalry and cannon in unusual groupings. When sufficient enemy forces had been drawn off from a selected point in the line, usually the centre, then troops which had been specially held back would break through. Once that was achieved, pursuit would follow to capture fresh territory. By

2 The Battle of Malplaquet. Tapestry in Blenheim Palace.
'A most murthering battle', said the Duke, who was subsequently dubbed 'the butcher' by his enemies. Allied losses were twice as many as the French. The tapestry gives some idea of the broken terrain which Villars used to such good effect.

1 Sir Godfrey Kneller, *John, First Duke of Marlborough and Colonel John Armstrong his Chief Engineer*, *c.* 1711. Oil on canvas, 93 × 78 in. (236 × 198 cm.). Blenheim Palace.
Sarah, Duchess of Marlborough regarded this likeness as one of the best of her husband.

now Villars, the leading French general, had grasped Marlborough's tactics and he was ready for them at Malplaquet. On strategic grounds, too, Villars was well pleased. The allies, against Marlborough's consistent advice, had failed to make the expected dash into Picardy which would have threatened Paris, and had instead become bogged down in the costly siege of Tournai, which ended on 5 September after 69 days. Villars had been given time to dispose and strengthen his army, while the Tournai garrison had won a moral victory. Villars had picked his ground and forced the action on his terms when the allies threatened Mons.

Malplaquet was a terrible site for a battle, but Villars used it well, disposing troops and concealed artillery in its woods and ravines. He expected Marlborough to launch his usual flanking attacks in an attempt to force a weakening of the strong French centre. Villars anyway had no intention of letting these troops be drawn off to strengthen the flanks. The site made such flanking attacks very difficult. Marlborough's one masterly improvisation here, of sending the troops from Tournai on an extreme right flanking movement through the woods, did not work.

As Villars anticipated the Allies began their probing attacks on his flanks, and on the Allied right the Imperial troops suffered heavy losses. On the left, things were worse, and the young Prince of Orange lost 5,000 men in half an hour. Attacks intended merely to probe became involved in attrition. The battle began at 8 a.m. and it was 11.45 a.m. before Villars decided to draw troops from his centre. He sent them to strengthen his left flank, which had been weakened by the sheer numerical superiority of the allies. Only then could Lord Orkney advance in the centre and take the redoubts there. Boufflers was still winning on the French right, but had to withdraw as his own left and centre were forced back. Villars was wounded too. The French retired in good order from the field at 3 p.m. The allies had sustained 25,000 casualties. They took few prisoners. Villars, in military defeat, had won a moral victory and as Marlborough acknowledged, 'The French have defended themselves better in this action than in any battle I have seen.' He was unable to give pursuit and could do no more than occupy Tournai and Mons, 'two towns which did not belong to France', as he said. French frontiers were intact, and the allies in general and Marlborough in particular faced dire political consequences.

4 The Siege of Tournai, 1709. Engraving by P. Mortier.
Instead of choosing an advance on Ypres and the Picardy routes into France, the Allies besieged Tournai from June to September. The Allies lost 5,340 men in the siege.

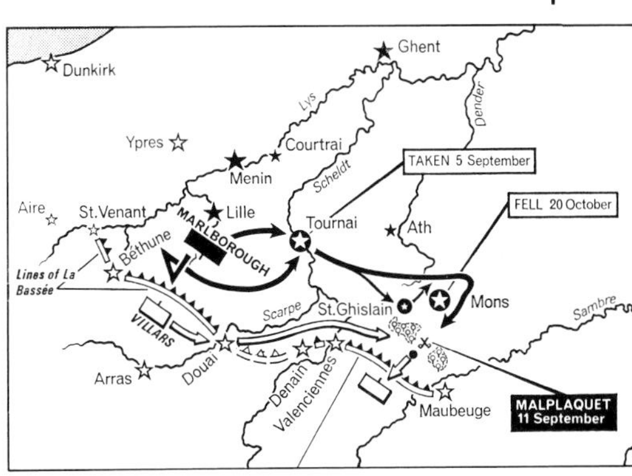

5 Map of the Campaign of 1709, from R. Chandler, *Marlborough as Military Commander*, Batsford, 1979, p. 249.
At the start of the 1709 campaigning season Marlborough had favoured a bold advance into Picardy, but more cautious counsels prevailed and Malplaquet cost the French little ground.

3 Marshal-General Claude-Louis-Hector, Duc de Villars. Engraving by E. Desrochers.
Villars persuaded Louis that a pitched battle could be fought in 1709. He had grasped Marlborough's tactical method. Only lack of numbers forced his withdrawal at Malplaquet.

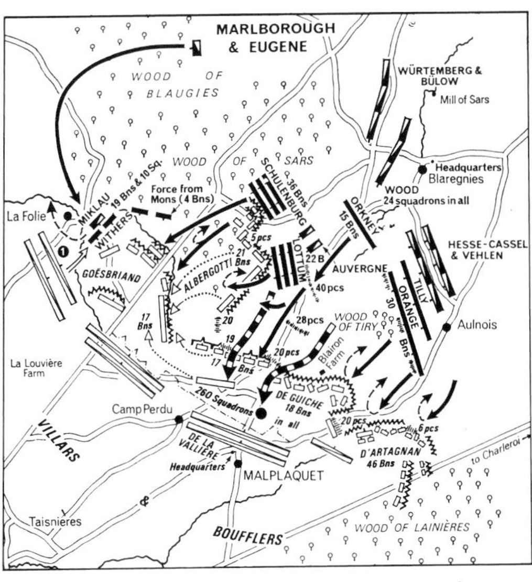

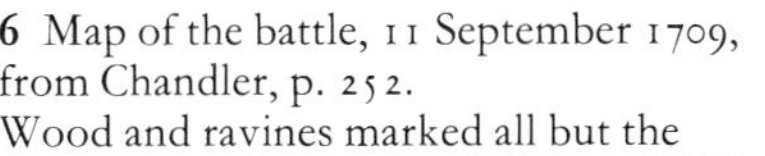

6 Map of the battle, 11 September 1709, from Chandler, p. 252.
Wood and ravines marked all but the central ground of the battlefield and Villars thus had strong flanks out of all proportion to his numbers. He disposed his artillery with particular effectiveness against the allies on his right.

under his sole control; he vetoed important bills and he chose his advisers without formal restriction. It is true, too, that the very different way England was governed by the last year of his reign, compared with James II's final year, stemmed in good measure from the country's involvement down to 1697 in an unprecedentedly demanding war.

Two notable examples are finance and the role of the Cabinet. William's war demolished the system of public finance, which had been the root cause of so much seventeenth-century constitutional tension, and compelled its replacement. It made the anachronistic distinction between ordinary and extraordinary revenue totally irrelevant and ultimately forced the separation of civil expenditure from the cost of maintaining the army and navy through the Civil List Act (1698); parliament assumed permanent responsibility, in peace as well as war, for financing the armed services. Just as annual sessions had been imperative since 1689 for raising the many 'extraordinary' impositions needed to finance the war, after 1698 parliament simply had to meet every year if only to vote the armed services budget – and in particular the new Land Tax, which remained the staple direct tax from 1693 to 1798. By contrast, the new 'Civil List', from which the Crown was to defray the expenses of the Royal Household and the bureaucracy, was fixed initially by parliament but was guaranteed to each monarch for life. The novel system of public credit evolved in 1693–4 to raise loans for the war – which, because of its permanence, historians have dubbed 'the Financial Revolution' – had equally important constitutional implications. By voting duties for 99 years to fund the first long-term loan in 1693 and by underwriting the incorporation of a state bank, the Bank of England, parliament became the guarantor for the present and the future of the new 'National Debt': in effect, the underwriter of the crown itself. As for the origins of the modern Cabinet, these can be traced directly back to William's decision to have a body of ministers meeting regularly to advise Queen Mary on policy matters during his soldiering on the Continent.

However, this is only one side of the coin. On the other side must be set, for one thing, the central constitutional document of the Revolution Settlement, the Bill of Rights (1689). This was not dramatic in its provisions, for it embodied a Declaration of Rights, presented to William and Mary along with the crown, which had been much watered down for fear William would refuse both; but its statements of constitutional principle were, even so, not negligible. Hence William's grudging assent to the Bill of Rights itself, which (among many other restrictions of the powers which James II had wielded) declared illegal the use of the royal prerogative to suspend the operation of laws (which James had employed, for example, in his Declarations of Indulgence); effectively killed off the monarch's dispensing power, too; and illegalized the keeping of a standing army in peacetime without parliamentary sanction. Historians have differed over whether the Declaration was or was not 'an implied contract'. But radical Whig members of the Convention clearly intended it, and some explicitly referred to it, as such. Secondly, it is not always appreciated how many of the articles or principles unwillingly jettisoned from the Declaration of Rights were later carried into law, usually to the king's dissatisfaction. Important instances were the requirement that the monarch should call a general election at least every three years (1694); the string of Place Acts and clauses which excluded several thousand crown office-holders from the Commons (1694–1706); the reform of the treason laws (1698); and the liberating of the judiciary from arbitrary royal interference (1701). This last was one of many new and stringent limitations on the royal prerogative incorporated in the Act of Settlement. Most of them were not to apply until Anne's death and some never came into force at all. They were nevertheless another sign of parliament's belief that it was fully entitled to restrict the royal prerogative.

It was no coincidence that the 1701 Act of Settlement contained the first ever statutory constraint on royal freedom of action in foreign policy. William's practice during the war of taking diplomatic decisions without consulting ministers, let alone informing parliament, grew increasingly unacceptable after 1697. Eventually his negotiation of two Partition Treaties with France in 1698 and 1700 with the aim of carving up the Spanish Empire in the interests of future peace caused such a parliamentary and public storm in 1701 that they put an end, for good, to the tradition of secret royal diplomacy practised in England since the 1660s. After William's death and the succession of a more feeble and more insular monarch, the practical restraints on the conduct of foreign policy by the crown and its ministers inevitably increased, especially as parliament sat not only annually but often for five or six months in a year.

The twelve years of Queen Anne's reign, in fact, were crucial in enabling the full constitutional harvest of the Glorious Revolution to be gathered in. Though only 37 she was already so 'unwieldy and lame' that at her coronation she was carried into Westminster Abbey and had much ado to struggle down the aisle to the throne. Her husband, Prince George of Denmark, a kindly but monumentally dull man, was incapable of giving her intelligent advice and support;

and her own understanding was at best second-rate. Unlike William, therefore, she badly needed a leading minister to take on most of her burdens and it is in Anne's reign that the office of 'Prime Minister' began to develop, though the term was never used officially. Godolphin, from 1702 to 1710, and Oxford (also Lord Treasurer) from 1711 to 1714 were the first politicians to whom the term could reasonably be applied. Anne also needed a Cabinet far more than her predecessor had, to co-ordinate the war effort and diplomacy; and a small Cabinet committee of working ministers, meeting twice a week in Whitehall, to prepare business and map out policy at the highest level.

On the other hand, Anne was no cipher. She took a serious view of her functions as monarch. She religiously attended the Sunday meetings of the full Cabinet of 12–14 members. Statesmen who neglected to win Anne over to any desired line of policy, or bullied her into ministerial appointments she disliked, usually had cause to regret it; and where appointments in her beloved Church were concerned, she could be tenacious in the extreme. Another prerogative, that of dissolving parliament, she used with devastating effect against the Whigs in 1710.

Parliament's now regular and essential role in the government of the realm; the (on average) biennial re-election of its Lower House throughout the 21 years after the 1694 Act; and the growth and mobilization of the electorate in response to this frenetic activity all ensured the continuance into the post-Revolution era of the party divisions – Whig versus Tory – which had begun to dominate English politics in the late 1670s. One of the most important sources of division between the parties after the Revolution was the two wars that William III set in train and the radically new relationship with Europe that these involved for England. Without some knowledge of the progress and scale of these wars, their strategy and diplomacy, it is not possible to understand fully the course of domestic politics or the effects which parties had in changing the membership and policies of the various administrations of 1689–1714.

The Wars Against France

In 1686 William had already formed the anti-French coalition to which, after May 1689, he was able to devote English men, money and ships. The League of Augsburg consisted of the Emperor Leopold I, the Kings of Spain and Sweden, the Duke of Savoy and several German princes, including the powerful electors of Bavaria and Brandenburg. When Louis XIV's dreaded armies invaded and brutally ravaged the

152. After Sir Godfrey Kneller, *Sidney Godolphin*, *c.* 1705. Oil on canvas, $35\frac{1}{2} \times 27\frac{1}{2}$ in. (90.2 × 70 cm.). London, National Portrait Gallery.
Godolphin first attained high office in 1684, when he was made a baron. Although heading the Treasury from 1690 to 1696, he retained sympathy for the cause of James II, whom in 1688 he had supported to the last. He was Lord High Treasurer, and Marlborough's intimate ally, from 1702 until 1710, when the queen dismissed him.

Rhenish Palatinate in the autumn of 1688, it was not to be expected that all these states would act with resolution and unanimity. But during the winter the Dutch and the Emperor went to war and William played a key role in negotiating with them and the other Augsburg powers to constitute the first Grand Alliance.

What Europe later knew as 'the Nine Years' War' (1688–97) was in England often, and understandably, called 'King William's War'. Its initial aims were William's own – his long-standing objectives of protecting the Netherlands from France and restricting French expansion elsewhere in order to maintain a balance of power in Europe. But of course the questions of defending the Revolution settlement of the crown, quelling the Irish rebellion and protecting English trade from a maritime rival now more potent than the Dutch soon changed its purely continental character.

The strategy of the war, too, was essentially William's. And while it did envisage a positive role for the Anglo-Dutch navies against French lines of commerce and supply, its main thrust, distressingly for his English subjects, was on land. For William believed that only if Louis's armies were broken would he cease to be a continuing threat to the rest of Europe. Hence the annual campaigns in Flanders, in which pitched battles were few and much of the military resources of both sides was absorbed by lengthy sieges of fortified towns. They led in the event to a war of attrition which neither side won, although the French would most probably have done so if they had not been engaged on so many fronts. William was his own commander-in-chief and his campaigns showed none of the brilliance later displayed by Marlborough. The pitched battles generally favoured the French – Neerwinden (1693) so decisively that only William's durability and the great resources he was able to draw on enabled his army to recover from that savage mauling. And just as on the battlefield William was outfought and outmanoeuvred by Marshall Luxemburg, so in siege warfare he could never rival the genius of Vauban. Fortunately for the allies, Luxemburg died in January 1695 and Villeroi proved a mediocre replacement; the French faced a serious financial and economic crisis, aggravated by two dreadful harvest failures; and William's persistence was rewarded with the recapture of Namur, which forced Louis's Flanders army to pull back its line to its position of 1691. Stalemate ensued and encouraged both sides to make the Peace of Ryswick in September 1697.

Contributing to the deadlock was the equally indecisive course of the war at sea after 1689. The near-defeat of the English fleet at Beachy Head in June 1690 led to an invasion scare; and although this was balanced by Russell's victory at La Hogue in May 1692, serious damage was inflicted by the French navy on the Levant Company's valuable Smyrna convoy in 1693. However, there were two things on the credit side for England: all French invasion plans were frustrated; and from 1694 to 1696 the presence of an English fleet in the Mediterranean gave valuable protection to English commerce and support to the allied cause in southern Europe – a pointer to the future. After 1692 no major naval engagement took place: the French kept their battle fleet largely in port and concentrated on attacking British commerce to great effect, mostly by privateering. The official Admiralty estimate of numbers of merchant ships lost was 4,000. Not until the closing years of the Spanish Succession War was an efficient British convoy system developed, capable of preventing that destruction of commerce that proved so profitable to the French, and only then was Britain's superiority in ships and seamen turned into wholly effective command of the seas.

King William's War was a war like no other before it. By 1694 the allied armies numbered more than 300,000 men, of whom some 70,000 were in English pay (though not all of them of English or Scottish birth). The annual cost for England of the war on land alone was about £2.7 million. Yet at the same time she built up between 1689 and 1697 the largest navy in the world in terms both of numbers of ships and fire-power. All this absorbed sums of money undreamed of when the war began. They were raised partly, of course, through loans; though the new long-term 'funded' loans, so critical to the success of the next war from 1702 to 1713, made a psychological rather than a substantial contribution in the 1690s. But the bulk

153. George St. Lo, *England's Safety*, a tract of 1693.
The title-page of this pamphlet, written by a naval captain, is one of the first illustrations of seamen's uniforms. St. Lo appeals for a strengthening of England's naval resources.

came from taxation. Customs rates soared. Excises were extended to many commodities other than liquors. Above all, the Land Tax was utterly indispensable. Eventually it raised £2 million a year like clockwork; and despite its obvious flaws and inequities, it survived through the next century as perhaps the clearest indication that after the Revolution the English propertied classes were at last willing to shoulder their fiscal responsibilities and recognize that liberty, property and the Protestant Succession had to be paid for – and were worth paying for.

The struggle for these prized legacies of the Revolution Settlement was very far from being over when King William's War ended in 1697. The Peace of Ryswick settled little. France did abandon the Rhineland territories whose occupation had started the war and handed back a string of Netherlands fortresses to Spain – confident that the fortresses could be recaptured at any time. William's place on the English throne was at last recognized by Louis; though this recognition was shown to be worthless four years later. All the signatories of the 1697 treaty were aware that no permanent stable peace was possible until the main European problem had been settled – what was to happen to the vast Spanish Empire when its ruler, the childless and witless Charles II, should die. In the seventeenth century Spain had suffered severe military and economic decline. Yet it retained an empire that comprised mainland Spain itself, the Spanish Netherlands, much of Italy and the whole of explored Central and South America apart from Brazil. The great fear was that France would gobble up most if not all of it, unless its destination could be decided by prior agreement. Until that could be done any peace in Europe would inevitably be precarious. But even if Spain and her dominions were to pass entirely to the other main claimant family, the Habsburgs, a serious threat to the balance of power and therefore to peace would be created. William's ultimate legacy to England was to make this a matter of concern to Tories as well as Whigs; but of more immediate concern to her was her highly profitable trade with Old Spain and the Mediterranean, her illicit but lucrative trade with Spanish America and the prospect of having the Southern Netherlands controlled by a great power hostile to the Protestant Succession.

We saw earlier how William tried to avert these threats by negotiation with France. He was realist enough to know that no settlement of this explosive problem had any chance of permanence without Louis's assent. A second Partition Treaty in 1700, which left all Spain's possessions except those in Italy to the Habsburg Archduke Charles, was necessary because the Bavarian beneficiary of the first treaty died. But the publication of Charles II's Will on his death in October 1700 and Louis's prompt decision to accept its terms, so acquiring the entire inheritance for his grandson Philip of Anjou, destroyed three years of patient diplomacy. After the frustrations and massive expense of the Nine Years' War it was not easy to persuade either parliament or public opinion that English interests again demanded war. But Louis's reckless acts of provocation in the Indies and in the Low Countries removed all other options, and the last straw, his recognition of the Pretender, came *after* William's second Grand Alliance had already been constructed (September 1701). Within two months of William's death England was once more at war and paymaster of the great new confederation which he had formed. It again included Austria and the United Provinces and contained virtually every important state in Germany except Bavaria.

England's conduct of the Spanish Succession War and much of her diplomacy down to 1710 were controlled by Anne's Captain-General, John Churchill, raised to the dukedom of Marlborough in December 1702. He and his wife Sarah had been the princess's closest friends for many years before she came to the throne, and after a long estrangement from William III he had returned to play a prominent part in negotiating the Grand Alliance treaty. The task of raising the necessary funds to pay for the war was in the hands of his friend Lord Godolphin, a Tory by background, but long regarded as the quintessential man of business, 'never in the way [as Charles II once said of him] or out of the way'. Neither Marlborough nor Godolphin, in fact, was a committed party man; and with the aim of ensuring a secure parliamentary majority to sustain a war that surpassed even its predecessor in scale, they together 'managed' all Queen Anne's ministries, of whatever complexion, down to 1710.

From the early 1690s the precise role England should play in these wars was a matter of fierce dispute. Most Whigs came in time to accept William III's conviction that France could only be defeated by means of full-scale land warfare with England playing the role of a 'principal' in a continental coalition; and after 1702 they continued to support both a 'Williamite' foreign policy and war strategy under Marlborough. The majority of Tories, on the other hand, concluded from the experiences of 1691–6 that it was impossible to defeat the mighty French state on land. Wary, too, of any policies that seemed likely to entangle their country permanently in Continental dynastic politics, they preferred a more limited commitment based on sea power with England content to be an 'auxiliary' in any alliance. Marlborough and Godolphin recognized the value of naval strength and of limited combined operations, but they held firm to William's priority of major land campaigns. Not only that, they considerably extended their range when, as the price of enticing Portugal out of her French alliance in 1703, they agreed that England would assist in ejecting by force the Bourbon Philip V from Spain and putting the Habsburg Archduke Charles on the throne. 'No Peace without Spain' was henceforth a cardinal point in Whig war policy, and in less than three years a large British army was involved in heavy fighting in Spain and Portugal.

In Italy heavy English subsidies kept the Duke of Savoy's army in the field to co-operate with Austria's best general, Prince Eugene. In the north-east sector the war followed a course very different from that in the 1690s. The key to the difference was, simply, Marlborough. The duke combined supreme gifts as a strategist with organizing ability and a diplomatic flair rarely found in any soldier in any age. Even Marlborough at first found frustration in the Netherlands; but the bold French decision to strike towards Vienna in 1704 in an attempt to eliminate Austria from the war gave him his chance. His epic six-week march to the Danube with 40,000 troops to join the imperial forces under Eugene astonished Europe almost as much as the devastation of Tallard's army at Blenheim which followed it. Blenheim saved Vienna, liberated the Empire, made Marlborough the most admired and feared soldier in Europe, and reconciled even Tory squires for a few years to paying four shillings in the pound in Land Tax to keep over 100,000 troops in arms. Further military triumphs at Ramillies in 1706 and Oudenarde in 1708 proved that what genius could achieve in Germany it could accomplish even in the fortress-studded north-eastern theatre; and given more co-operation from the Dutch, especially in 1706, it might have enabled Marlborough to strike deep into France and capture Paris while the French were still reeling. But the Spanish campaigns were proving a serious drain on manpower and money, and after the allied forces were heavily defeated at Almanza in 1707 it looked increasingly unlikely that the archduke (des-

154. *The Surrender of Marshall Tallard.* Tapestry in Blenheim Palace, Oxfordshire.
This tapestry adorned Blenheim Palace, the house built to celebrate Marlborough's triumphs. The captured French general Tallard, here surrendering at the battle of Blenheim on 2 August 1704, was held as a prisoner of war at Nottingham.

pite a brief tenancy of Madrid when he was crowned Charles III) would ever be able to supplant Philip V. Meanwhile the war at sea saw some allied successes. For example, Rooke's victory at Malaga (1704) did much to consolidate the earlier capture of Gibraltar, and the seizure of Minorca in 1708 confirmed Britain's naval stranglehold on the Mediterranean. On the other hand, merchant shipping losses remained heavy until the reforms at the Admiralty undertaken by the Whigs from 1708 to 1710.

In 1709 Louis sued for peace. His kingdom was bankrupt, its economy in ruins. Owing to Whig intransigence, negotiations broke down over the question of No Peace without Spain. Britain demanded that Louis must not only acknowledge Charles III as King, but must actually be responsible for expelling Philip V. So France fought on, with the redoubtable Villars in command in the north-east; and Marlborough's last major field victory, at Malplaquet on French soil, presented the public with so grievous a casualty list that pressure for peace, already present among Tories, mounted swiftly in Britain. Queen Anne herself, now estranged from the Duchess of Marlborough, was its most crucial convert. In 1710 there was a fierce reaction against Godolphin and the Whigs; Anne dismissed the Treasurer and pieced together a predominantly Tory ministry under Harley that was pledged to a negotiated peace; and the swing of opinion to the Tories was spectacularly confirmed in the October general election.

The new government lost little time in initiating secret unilateral negotiations with France. Marlborough's wings were rapidly clipped, although with limited resources he still managed in 1711 to penetrate the vaunted 'Ne plus ultra' lines at Bouchain after a brilliant feint. But this could not prevent his dismissal in December on a trumped-up charge of corruption. There followed in May 1712 the infamous 'Restraining Orders' to his successor Ormonde, calculated to isolate the Dutch and the Imperialists militarily as the clandestine negotiations had done diplomatically. Franco-British preliminaries had been concluded back in the autumn of 1711 and with Britain, the paymaster of the Alliance, so obviously determined on a negotiated peace, and a general conference in progress at Utrecht since January 1712, there was little her allies could do to carry on the struggle without her. At length in April 1713 the Dutch and other allies – though not quite yet the Emperor – had no option but to agree to a general peace at Utrecht. The 1713 treaties did not achieve the Whig aim of putting a Habsburg on the Spanish throne. But the death of the Emperor Joseph (April 1711) and his replacement by the archduke had made this objective politically undesirable as well as militarily unrealistic. The balance of power was better served by the confirmation of Philip V now that he had become a good Spaniard. Otherwise Britain achieved all her war aims and substantial gains besides – recognition of the Protestant Succession, a coveted legal entrée into the Spanish South American market, Minorca and Gibraltar as permanent naval bases in the Mediterranean, St Kitts in the West Indies and her first foothold in French Canada. Nor were the interests of her allies wholly neglected, thanks to Harley's resolve to control the negotiations himself and to resist the extremism of his firebrand colleague Henry St John. The Dutch got a better Barrier in the Low Countries than they had feared after their defeat at Denain (1712) and the Emperor acquired for Austria considerable areas of former Spanish territory in Italy as well as the Spanish Netherlands.

155. The Treaty of Utrecht, 1713. Contemporary engraving. *The treaty, signed by Britain, France and the Dutch, was to be the foundation of eighteenth-century European diplomacy. France and the Empire made a separate peace in 1714.*

In fact the Utrecht Settlement, though it left Britain with the invidious reputation of *Perfide Albion*, proved to be no mean achievement. Given the stipulation on top of the territorial redistribution that the crowns of France and Spain were never to be united, Oxford was not far wide of the mark when he claimed four years later that it had left 'the balance of Europe . . . upon a better foot than it has been for an hundred years past'. There was irony but no coincidence in the fact that the Whigs, who had vehemently attacked the making of the settlement when in opposition, were to spend so much effort in office over the next three decades trying to preserve the rough equilibrium it had created.

'The New and Glorious Pile of Chatsworth'

CHATSWORTH AND WILLIAM, FOURTH EARL AND FIRST DUKE OF DEVONSHIRE

1 The South Front by Talman.
Echoing Roman models, the design owes much to Bernini's third plan for the river front of the Louvre.

Coming over the moors from Chesterfield and seeing Chatsworth below the hill by the Derwent, a traveller in 1681 described it as 'a bright diamond . . . set in a vile socket of ignoble jet'. In 1697 Celia Fiennes found the 'vile socket' unchanged, but the 'bright diamond' glowed with a new lustre thanks to the remodelled south front designed by William Talman, 'a revolutionary design for an English country house' (Lees-Milne).

Talman had helped refurbish Burleigh House for Lord Exeter, the brother-in-law of William Cavendish, fourth Earl of Devonshire. Devonshire was attracted by Talman's architectural ideas which, like the earl's own taste, derived from France. The earl was well-equipped to select an architect and indeed to be one himself. Educated abroad during the Interregnum, heir to great wealth and acres, he had learned continental ways. Steeped in the classics, he was a life-long reader of Tacitus with an interest in political ideas. During his exile and education he developed a love-hate relationship with all things French, including their poetry, drama, architecture and politics. He developed his fiery temper there as well, and his brawls were part of European gossip.

Though a Restoration rake (he always remained a great womanizer) Devonshire was England's most consistent aristocratic spokesman for Protestantism, parliamentary rights and popular liberties, and was one of the seven signatories of the letter inviting William of Orange to England in 1688. Though lacking political *gravitas*, he was consistent in his beliefs that Protestantism was a check on arbitrary government, that parliaments should be held regularly, that property was sacred and that tyrants should be disobeyed. The rebuilding of Chatsworth was a statement of a European classical culture based on Roman models and on a stock of classical mythology and imagery. This ideal took the form of a Baroque palace in the Derbyshire countryside. The building was complex and cosmopolitan, the setting provincial. The architecture and décor proclaimed that political power and standards were to be found not only in the fleeting fashions of the court, where governments came and went, but also amongst a cultured, leisured, senatorial class of Whig landowners. These men were to keep the nation's conscience and, from their broad acres, defend its rights. Chatsworth's Baroque style was made, not to serve absolutism like its counterparts on the continent, but to assert Whig ideas of liberty. Architecturally the house was an English Versailles, but politically it opposed everything Louis XIV represented.

2 Sir Godfrey Kneller, *William Cavendish, fourth Earl and first Duke of Devonshire,* n.d. Oil on canvas, $84\frac{1}{2} \times 55$ in. (215×140 cm.). Chatsworth House, Devonshire Collection.

Devonshire, increasingly absent from court after James II's accession, began the remodelling of Chatsworth in that year. In 1685 his feud with Colonel Culpepper landed him in prison. His plea that parliamentary privilege protected him from gaol was overruled and a vindictive fine of £30,000 was imposed, though he never paid it. The earl walked out of prison, returned to Chatsworth and began to re-read Tacitus – a favourite author of critics of absolute monarchy in the sixteenth and seventeenth centuries – on the tyranny of the Emperor Domitian. Then he summoned Talman to turn his own aesthetic enthusiasms into political statements. By the time of the Revolution of 1688 the south front was completed.

Devonshire's admiration for French art, but not for French politics, was seen in the expanding schemes at Chatsworth which followed the Revolution. European artists such as Verrio, Laguerre and Tijou worked on the building with English craftsmen. In the chapel (1689–93), statues of Faith and Justice adjoin Biblical stories on the walls and ceiling. The scenes allude to correct conduct in public life and suggest a Whig political scheme in a Baroque idiom. The appearance of a unified design is misleading, for the building developed piecemeal. In the 1690s, while the south front was being decorated, the east wing was rebuilt, the hall was pulled down and rebuilt, an ingenious cantilevered staircase was installed and the north-east tower was first re-leaded and then demolished. By that time the irascible and changeable earl, who became a duke in 1694, had quarrelled with Talman. They were to part company amidst recriminations on both sides.

Talman's work, though, was evident in the creation of the magnificent state rooms on the first floor of the south front in the years to 1696. Celia Fiennes noticed how these rooms opened up 'quite through the house a visto' enhanced by huge mirrors. These rooms, in imitation of Hampton Court, Kensington and Versailles, brought

3 Anon., *Chatsworth, Bird's-eye View from the South-east, c.*1707–11. Oil on canvas, $114\frac{1}{2} \times 124\frac{1}{2}$ in. (290 × 316 cm.). Private collection.

metropolitan politics into the provinces. Ostensibly designed for royal visits, which never occurred, the rooms were really expressions of Devonshire's dukedom and his role as King of Derbyshire. Hierarchy and etiquette were frozen both in the plan of the state rooms and in the decor, which stressed the power and glory of the Cavendishes in such schemes as Laguerre's *Apollo and Phaeton* in the withdrawing chamber and *Diana as Moon Goddess* in the bedchamber.

The duke's last work was on the west front after 1699. It was his own design based on the Marly Pavilion of 1633 by Mansart. The wing was completed by 1706 with ten water closets, also to the Duke's design. During the last two years of his life the west wing was decorated by the young English painter James Thornhill. His *Fall of Phaeton*, which was placed on the staircase, and the *Sabine Room* were a fitting climax to the work. Only the north wing remained to be rebuilt, and the young Thomas Archer was called in to design it. Devonshire did not survive long enough to quarrel with him. The duke's Chatsworth patronage had provided opportunities for a whole cluster of Baroque artists in England. No building better embodies the culture and the politics of England's Whig aristocracy.

4 (below left) The Sabine Room in the West Front painted by James Thornhill. This is perhaps the best Baroque interior in England.

5 The Chapel.
The painting is by Laguerre and his assistant Ricard.

Domestic Politics under William III

Britain could never have waged war for twenty years and emerged successfully if her governments had not been able to count, by and large, on support from the political nation. Keeping this support, however, involved forging an effective working partnership between the crown – the monarch and the executive – and a parliament meeting regularly and for long sessions; and this proved far from easy. Indeed, post-Revolution parliaments posed unique problems in this respect, partly through their inescapable presence, but mainly because of the political atmosphere in which they almost invariably met. The mounting ferocity of party politics (a ferocity fuelled by frequent general elections) has already been alluded to; and its implications were all-pervasive. But there was also an important complicating factor: the cross-currents of court-country issues that eddied across the mainstream of Whig-Tory conflict, especially powerfully in the early and late 1690s. Campaigns against the presence of office-holders in the Commons and against corruption in high places figured prominently at these times, bringing together country Whigs and country Tories in a shared distrust of the executive – though impermanently and in no sense as a *party*. The same issues were resurrected occasionally and in a much lower key under Anne. But it was only for three years after the Peace of Ryswick, when these normal country bugbears were reinforced by an old emotive issue – the maintenance of a standing army in peacetime – and by a new source of alarm, the influence of the king's foreign favourites, that the higher loyalties of men who were pre-eminently Whigs or Tories were fairly consistently overridden by allegiance either to the country or to the court.

It would have been astonishing if the Revolution of 1688 had left the principles of the first Whigs and Tories of the Exclusion period wholly intact. The Whigs began life as a party of opposition; after 1689 they became competitors for the favour of the new king, their 'Great Deliverer'. Similarly, Tory priorities could not have been unaffected once their traditional dedication to the crown had been battered by the excesses of James II and an unpalatable settlement in 1689. Just as these experiences bred in many backbench Tories 'country' attitudes which would have been alien to their predecessors, so a new generation of Whig leaders, largely aristocratic, grew less enthusiastic after 1694 about further limiting the prerogative. They grew cooler, too, towards theories which – like the idea developed by Shaftesbury's friend John Locke under Charles II of an 'original contract' between king and people – implied that true sovereignty lay with the subject or that kings could legally be deposed if they ruled tyrannically. Nonetheless, the Whigs as a body stood for the Revolution Settlement of 1689–94 and with complete unanimity, as of old, for a Protestant Succession; whereas, although few Tories openly repudiated the Revolution, they were unhappy over its disturbance of the hereditary principle and their ambivalence over the Hanoverian succession finally developed into deep division.

Of the wholly new issues which polarized the parties after 1688, the wars and the even wider question of Britain's present and future relationship with Europe were by far the biggest. But arguably the most contentious area of dispute between the partisans, especially after Convocation began noisily parading High Church grievances in 1701, was the traditional area of religion. The Tories, the party of 'the landed interest', continued to regard themselves as 'the Church Party' too. Their old antipathy to Puritan 'fanatics' made them grudging, or downright hostile, to the Toleration – the freedom of worship granted by law in 1689 to Protestant nonconformists; and they deplored the latter's new device of 'occasional conformity', that is, occasionally taking communion in an Anglican church to circumvent the Anglican sacramental tests for office-holders and town councillors. The Whigs on the other hand, though mostly Anglicans, did have powerful support from Dissenters in the trading and 'monied' interests; they were hostile to High Church extremism and strongly for the Toleration, of which occasional conformity seemed to them a legitimate extension.

Under William III, when the experience of having two parties contending for office was at first completely novel and when both these parties were still experiencing the shock waves from the Revolution as well as a resurgence of the 'country' ideal, ministerial stability seemed for most of the time almost impossible to achieve. Yet William was also trapped in a dilemma of his own making. He came to the throne with a crude and imperfect knowledge of the political divisions afflicting his new kingdom, and the concept of party remained to him an evil to be, at best, tolerated and whenever possible ignored. His one guiding rule as he lurched from one patched-up ministry to another was not to become the prisoner of either Whigs or Tories. The former, as William's most consistent supporters in and before 1688 and the majority party in the Convention House of Commons, expected to receive their full reward after February 1689. When the king's first ministry turned out to be an inchoate mixture of men from both parties, many Whigs grew truculent. 'We have made you king', William was roundly told by his

Whig Comptroller, Tom Wharton, '. . . what occasion can you have for knaves to serve you?' The king recognized the Whig party's greater loyalty but thought it (wrongly) to be riddled with republicanism and (rightly) too inexperienced in the work of government. It took some four years for a group of younger Whigs to come to the fore who were not only fervent in support of the war but had the ability and unanimity to provide the government with its sinews. This group had as its core the four gifted men who were later to be called 'the Junto': Wharton, a formidable parliamentarian and supreme electioneer; John Somers, a lawyer of lofty intellect; Charles Montagu (later created Lord Halifax), a master of finance; and Admiral Russell, later Earl of Orford. In Anne's reign they recruited a fifth member, Charles Spencer, Earl of Sunderland.

Disillusionment with the Whigs was the main reason for William's decision to call another parliament in 1690. There were significant Tory gains at this election and for the next three years the king reshuffled the ministerial pack on several occasions, not breaking with the Whigs entirely, but allowing Tories a growing sway in his new Cabinet Council. Although suspicious of Tory loyalty, he banked much on the proved administrative competence of men such as Carmarthen, Daniel Finch (the lugubrious, staunchly Anglican Earl of Nottingham), and at the Treasury, Godolphin. But the strong influence of Carmarthen (the former Danby) savoured too much of old-style court management and corruption for numerous backbench Tories as well as Whigs to stomach, and one group of apostles of 'pure' Whiggery, led by Paul Foley and Robert Harley, embarked in 1691 on the road that eventually led them to complete separation from their own court-soiled party colleagues. Ironically it was administrative failures, especially in conducting the war at sea, as well as ineffectual Commons' management that caused the king to change the balance of his government decisively in favour of the Whigs, the party most prepared to support the war on his own terms. Between March 1693 and May 1694, with the bringing of Shrewsbury (a hero of 1688 and the Junto's patron), Trenchard and Russell into the Cabinet and the promotion of Somers to Lord Keeper and Montagu to Chancellor of the Exchequer, the foundations were laid for the nearest thing to a party-dominated ministry that William's reign was to see. These foundations were to be cemented by the election of 1695, by the discovery of the Assassination Plot and by Montagu's appointment as First Lord of the Treasury (1696). William still stood in theory by the principle of 'mixed government' and, for example, refused to dismiss the Tory Carmarthen. Yet it was undoubtedly the parliamentary skill and the financial

156. Sir Godfrey Kneller, *John Lord Somers*, 1700–10.
Oil on canvas, 36 × 28 in. (91.4 × 71 cm.).
London, National Portrait Gallery.
John Lord Somers, the son of a Worcestershire attorney, took part in the Whig opposition during the exclusion crisis, and became a leader of the Whig 'junto' in the 1690s. Having literary and historical as well as political interests, he was a friend and patron of Addison, Steele and Congreve. Kneller, a native of Lubeck who came to England in 1675, quickly became a leading painter of portraits in England.

and administrative achievements (among them a major currency reform and the creation of a state bank) of the new Junto and of Shrewsbury that enabled William to make an honourable peace in 1697.

That peace, however, marked for the Whig leaders the beginning of the downward slope. The election of 1698 added to their difficulties with the new 'country' House of Commons refusing, to the king's disgust, to vote him more than a derisory standing army. Harley, not the ministry, effectively controlled this House; and one by one between 1698 and 1700 all the Whig chiefs except Wharton left, or were removed from, office. William had until now managed to deny high office to the most intransigent High Church extremists; but late in 1700, to save the legislature from paralysis and himself

157. Sir Godfrey Kneller, *Robert Harley, First Earl of Oxford*, 1714. Oil on canvas, 96 × 58½ in. (243.8 × 148.6 cm.). London, National Portrait Gallery.
Harley belonged to a Herefordshire gentry family which had been prominent in the parliamentary cause during the civil war, and he retained something of the family's Puritanism. He acquired a great library of manuscripts, now in the British Library.

from complete humiliation at a time of gathering international storm clouds, he made a deal with Godolphin and with the unlikely alliance of the leading Tory zealot, Lawrence Hyde, Earl of Rochester and Robert Harley. The consequences were seen when the ministry was reconstructed with the balance tilted plainly towards the Tories, when parliament was dissolved and when Convocation was recalled. Harley refused office, but became Speaker in the new parliament – the most Tory of the reign – elected in January 1701. The king had performed his side of the bargain but was soon of the opinion that he had got a poor return for it. The new Commons majority, seemingly unimpressed by the Spanish crisis, indulged in such diversions as attacking the second Partition Treaty, impeaching Bentinck and three Junto lords for their alleged (and imaginary) responsibility for it, and delaying the Bill of Settlement after festooning it with clauses that were an implicit indictment of many features of William's own rule. Only the staunchness of the Whigs in the Lords and the rallying of the Country Whig dissidents to their leaders in the Commons brought parliament to its senses before the autumn.

The lesson was not lost on the king. With a new war imminent, he took the advice of Somers and dissolved parliament again after only one session. But although Godolphin and some other Tories lost office, William's reign ended as it had begun with a makeshift left-of-centre coalition government uneasily in charge of his affairs. The big difference was that by March 1702 the political nation was split far more comprehensively along Whig-Tory lines than at any time in the previous 15 years.

Politics under Anne

This was the situation Anne inherited, along with the certainty of war, when she came to the throne. And for a year or two it seemed that this self-avowed friend 'to the interests . . . of the Church of England' was intent on ending William's policy of 'balancing parties' in the government. So many Tories – and High Tories at that, such as Nottingham and the arrogant West-country magnate, Sir Edward Seymour – were brought back into office early in the reign that even Marlborough and Godolphin thought she had gone too far. The country did not appear to agree, since the Tories swept the popular constituencies in the 1702 election. But 'the duumvirs' knew they had to manage the House of Lords, where Whiggery was still strong, as well as the Commons; and it would be hard to do that, keep harmony between the Houses and ensure the moderate domestic policies which they saw as vital to a successful war effort while the Whig party was allowed only a token presence in the Cabinet. About the unsettled parliamentary outlook they proved only too right. But about Queen Anne herself they need not have worried. She was wholly convinced of the justice of the war and anxious that Marlborough should be given every support in waging it his way. Moreover, however strong her natural inclination towards 'the Church party', she heartily disliked factious and immoderate politicians on either side. She showed this early when her trouble-making uncle, Rochester, resigned in a huff in 1703 and she coolly accepted his resignation. Her priorities are best illustrated in the parliament of 1702–5 by the saga of the three Occasional Conformity bills, prompted by Nottingham and introduced by the High Tory commoners in successive sessions. Anne firmly supported the first and most penal bill, because she thought the practice of occasional conformity hypocritical and its discouragement necessary for the Church's security. But as opposition built up in the Lords, which blocked the first measure and threw out the second, she gradually came round to the view of her managers that these measures were not politic in wartime, since they caused parliamentary acrimony,

AN

ARGUMENT,

Shewing, that a

Standing Army

Is inconſiſtent with

A Free Government, and abſolutely deſtructive to the Conſtitution of the Engliſh Monarchy.

Cervus Equum pugna melior communibus herbis
Pellebat, donec minor in certamine longo
Imploravit opes hominis frænumq; recepit.
Sed poſtquam victor violens diſceſſit ab hoſte,
Non Equitem dorſo, non frænum depulit ore.
Horat. Epiſt. 10.

LONDON;
Printed in the Year 1697.

158. A pamphlet of 1697 against standing armies, title-page. *This anonymous pamplet was probably compiled by the Whig writers Walter Moyle and John Trenchard, perhaps with the help of the deist John Toland. William III's decision to maintain a permanent army after the Peace of Ryswick in 1697 aroused fears among the gentry backbenchers in parliament not only of high taxation but of tyranny – fears on which Robert Harley skilfully played as he built up the 'country party' in the Commons in 1697–9. The pamphlet was part of a violent political and literary controversy in which, as in the arguments of 1679–82, the history of the Puritan Revolution was re-lived and the memory of Oliver Cromwell's standing army evoked. In the standing army controversy the publicists who opposed the retention of William's forces saw a chance to propagate more far-reaching republican views, and organized the printing or reprinting of the writings of the civil war republicans John Milton, Algernon Sidney, James Harrington, Henry Nevile and Edmund Ludlow.*

delayed the voting of revenue and put the financial support of the wealthy City Dissenters in jeopardy. And when, in November 1704, the Commons attempted to railroad the third bill through the Lords by the crude and irresponsible device of 'tacking' it to the Land Tax bill and defying the Upper House to throw out the whole, she applauded her ministers' successful attempts, made together with Harleyites and Whigs, to thwart the extremists.

The Tack was a mark of the High Tories' growing desperation, for earlier in the year Nottingham, Seymour and Jersey, who had been involved in several fierce Cabinet wrangles over war strategy, had tried to use political blackmail on the queen to force the few remaining Whigs out of high office, only to find that she preferred to part with them instead. It was the Harleyites, not the Whigs, who immediately profited, with Speaker Harley becoming Secretary for the North and his brilliant young disciple Henry St John, Secretary at War; but Marlborough and Godolphin knew that without a reasonable quid pro quo the Whigs, despite the encouragement of Blenheim, would not maintain indefinitely their invaluable enthusiasm for the war. At the 1705 election they gained back much ground; and once the Junto had tasted blood with the appointment of two Whigs to Cabinet office either side of the election, they were soon in full cry. The years 1705–10 are in some ways the most instructive, politically, in the whole period from 1689 to 1714, for they reveal the full logic of the existence of two parties in a parliamentary system being finally worked out in the queen's government. Four groups of players act out the drama: first, the Lords of the Junto, intent on achieving, bit by bit, a complete monopoly of power and using it to wage uncompromising war in Flanders and Spain; second, the duumvirs, anxious at first to hold the Whigs to their pound of flesh, but as pragmatists compelled to recognize that the war could not be successfully carried on year after exhausting year without ultimately conceding one-party government; third, the queen, deploring 'the merciless men of both parties' and using every delaying tactic she could think of to stave off the advance of 'the five tyrannising lords'; fourth, Harley and his friends, encouraging the queen and seeking some moderate alternative prescription for her ministry more favourable to the Tories.

These middle years of the reign have their turning-point in 1708, which saw the fall of the Harleyites, a new election yielding a clear Whig majority and, in the autumn, the death of Prince George, which for a time weakened the queen's will to fight. Before Harley's fall it was still possible to preserve some semblance of coalition government. Moreover it was a government with

160. 'A Happy Outcome for the Church of England and Queen Anne'. Contemporary painted fan.
In this Tory and High Church portrayal, the eye of providence (a persistent feature of seventeenth-century cartoons) protects the queen and the Church – represented by St. Paul's – while Dr Sacheverell, surrounded by loyal bishops, stands firm against the evils of popery and Dissent.

many successes to its credit, for example the Regency Act, Ramillies and the Union, to prove that, given just the right balance of parliamentary forces, coalitions could for a while work well. By November 1708, however, Anne had been forced to readmit both Somers and Wharton to high office; and with Sunderland already a Secretary of State and Orford returning to the Admiralty a year later, the entire Cabinet had become Whig by 1709, save Marlborough and Godolphin, whom the political world now regarded as Whigs in all but name. But although full of ability and experience, Britain's first true party government proved relatively short-lilved. The Whigs in 1709–10 made two serious mistakes of policy. They failed to catch the changing mood of the country towards the war, incurring the odium of being the party in power when the Hague peace talks failed and the 'butcher's bill' of Malplaquet was presented. And by the decision to impeach an Anglican clergyman for 'high crimes and misdemeanours' they contrived to confirm the latent fears of many Englishmen that the Church was in danger under a Whig supremacy. Dr Henry Sacheverell was impeached in December 1709 for printing an explosive sermon preached in St Paul's, appropriately on Gunpowder Day, in which he had claimed that both Church and state were 'in peril from false brethren' (that is, Whigs), and had seemed to challenge the legality of the 1688 Revolution and of the whole consequent settlement, including, of course, the Toleration. After a full-dress trial before the House of Lords in March 1710, conducted in an atmosphere of enormous public excitement verging on hysteria, the doctor was found guilty but escaped with a derisory sentence. Queen Anne had little sympathy for Sacheverell, whom she rightly recognized as a bombastic and egocentric troublemaker. But she did share the apprehensions of her subjects about danger to the Church as well as their distaste for the continuing slaughter of the war; and these views, together with her stored-up resentment of the past four years, made her a willing ally of Harley in accomplishing the most celebrated political *renversement* of the eighteenth century. By the autumn of 1710, in a few short months, a strong Whig ministry had been dismantled, Harley himself had become *de facto* first minister and a tactical dissolution of parliament had resulted in a Tory victory of landslide proportions.

159 (opposite). Peter Tillemans, *Queen Anne in the House of Lords*, 1708–14. Oil on canvas, 55 × 48½ in. (139.7 × 122.2 cm.). Royal Collection.
Tillemans's painting shows the House of Lords as it was reconstructed within the old medieval walls by Inigo Jones in the 1620s. The Armada tapestries on the walls were retained. Jones's plaster barrel vault was painted in trompe-l'oeil *with imitation coffering.*

161. *London's Happiness in Four Loyal Members*, a broadside of 1710. *In the parliamentary elections for the City of London in October 1710, party animosities reached a new pitch. This print celebrates the Tory triumph which had brought the election of four candidates friendly to the High Church interest and opposed to the mercantile lobby represented by the Bank of England. When the results were known 'the bells fell a ringing for joy as the Church men would have pulled the steeples down. The city was illuminated with candles and bonfires and there was such a mob running to and fro – huzzaing and rejoicing that the like had hardly been seen upon any occasion'. The mob broke windows and stopped and rifled the coaches of suspected Whigs and Dissenters – although the frenzy did not reach the level of the Sacheverell riots seven months earlier.*

There is evidence that Harley underestimated the strength of the pro-Sacheverell fever among the voters and found himself confronting a House of Commons more extreme in its Toryism than he had bargained for. Certainly, his original ministry seemed designed to implement that 'moderating scheme' he had long advocated to the queen. The Harley administration of 1710–14 is often referred to as 'the last Tory ministry of the eighteenth century'. Yet it is worth noticing that its chief engineer, soon after becoming Earl of Oxford and Lord Treasurer (May 1711), was pilloried in a Commons address for his 'wild and unwarrantable schemes of balancing parties'. In point of fact a ministry that began life as a mixture of Harleyite Tories, High Tories and court Whigs had become entirely Tory at Cabinet level by July 1711, except for Harley's ally, the renegade Duke of Shrewsbury, and overwhelmingly Tory at all levels by June 1712; and Harley would have moved still faster in this direction had the queen herself not been so enamoured of the ideal of a 'mixed ministry'. But he and Anne were in entire accord on the overriding objective of the government, the making of peace. Nothing must be allowed to stand in its way, or obstruct the voting of one more year's war budget to demonstrate to the French, during negotiations, that Britain still meant business. Unfortunately, though the rampant High Tories in the Commons fully shared the desire for peace they were equally intent on carrying through all their most cherished partisan and country measures at home, including a vendetta against the former ministry; and by February 1711, 150 malcontents had organized themselves into the October Club, which gave the ministry almost as much trouble as it gave the Whigs during the first session of the 1710–13 parliament. Oxford pulled through, helped by public sympathy after an attempt on his life in March, but one of the prices he had to pay was tension between him and his old friend, St John – the first beginnings of the great quarrel which was ultimately to play a crucial part in destroying the ministry and crippling the Tory party.

St John, piqued by his exclusion from the early peace talks, was also temperamentally ill-equipped to move at Harley's cautious pace and in sympathy with many Octobrist demands: only by eradicating every remaining Whig from office 'down to the meanest', he urged, could Toryism be secured. Nevertheless he lost this first round; and Oxford was able to lay the peace preliminaries before parliament when it met again in December 1711. When the House of Lords, which had been kept reasonably co-operative in the previous session, then threatened a crisis by voting against 'peace without Spain', Oxford persuaded the queen to take the startling step of creating a dozen peers *en bloc* to restore the ministry's control of the House. He moved equally firmly to forestall any possible recurrence of Tory parliamentary unrest while the Utrecht bargaining was in progress. The dismissal of Marlborough, the commitment of Walpole to the Tower by a Commons' vote and a promise to complete the purge of Whig placemen at the session's end all worked wonders. So, gratuitously, did the Junto; their rather disreputable compact with Lord Nottingham (who had surprisingly declared against the peace) allowed a mild Occasional Conformity bill to be revived and pass into law.

All thereafter went serenely for the government until parliament was prorogued. More and more Whigs became reconciled to the inevitability of the peace and the only two matters that caused Oxford anxiety during the long recess down to the conclusion of the Utrecht treaties in April 1713 were the protracted course of the negotiations themselves and a row in the Cabinet which took his breach with St John (now Lord Bolingbroke) a stage nearer the open. The Tories were duly grateful for the peace when it finally arrived; but as the short 1713 session soon showed, it also released them from their inhibitions. The ministry ran into unexpected shoals. Most serious, the Commerce Treaty, which was an essential part of the Utrecht agreements, giving the French 'most favoured nation' status, was wrecked in the Commons. Eighty Tories joined the Whigs in opposing it, and though some did so under economic pressure from constituents, at least as many were expressing anxiety about prospects for the Hanoverian succession in the light of the new relationship with France. The Junto had already begun a propaganda campaign aimed at persuading public opinion that Harley's ministry was planning to sell out to the Jacobites. Nevertheless Oxford emerged from a ministerial reshuffle that summer with his own position and that of his allies strengthened, and Bolingbroke's hopes of displacing him seemed vain.

But the Joker in the political pack of Anne's reign had always been the queen; and so it proved again. Late in 1713 relations between her and the Treasurer, so long the latter's greatest asset, began to sour. Oxford's strange behaviour in staying away from Windsor during Anne's critical illness over Christmas – apparently to calm public nerves and preserve confidence in the City – made matters worse. The queen was now listening to bedchamber promptings from a new favourite, Abigail Masham. Bolingbroke cultivated Masham and his star began to rise again. When the new parliament, elected the previous autumn, met in 1714, the succession was the issue in the forefront of everyone's mind. Divisions between Jacobite and Hanoverian Tories boiled to the surface. The ministry's control of the Lords, secure since January 1712, began to waver as more Tory peers joined Nottingham in opposition; and in April the government survived a vote of confidence there so narrowly that Wharton was able to taunt Oxford with being only 'saved by his dozen'. Bolingbroke promoted the passage of a Schism bill through both Houses to the horror of the Dissenters: partly to rally the Tory troops, partly to cause maximum embarrassment to Oxford, the ex-Puritan. The Treasurer escaped the trap with his usual deft parliamentary footwork and counter-attacked his rival by intriguing with the Whigs against him.

This was the act of a desperate man, however. When Anne intervened in July to prorogue parliament, as the Whig hounds were closing on Bolingbroke in an enquiry into his conduct of trade negotiations with Spain, Oxford's days were numbered. But so, too, as Fate decreed, were those of the ailing queen and with them the hopes and ambitions of 'the Man of Mercury'. From her deathbed, only four days after she finally steeled herself to dismiss the Treasurer, Anne handed the white staff not to the expectant Bolingbroke but to the moderate Shrewsbury, a pro-Hanoverian who still retained some credit with his old friends, the Whigs. Yet with his party in such disarray it is very doubtful whether, even as Treasurer, Bolingbroke would have dared to interfere with the machinery set up under the Regency Act to deal with such an emergency. A Regency Council partly composed of Hanover's own nominees duly took over executive power from the old ministry and kept the country calm until King George I set foot in his new kingdom. The Whigs revelled in the prospect of the Promised Land, which but a few months before had seemed impossibly remote. Bolingbroke surveyed the wreckage of his own career and grieved (prematurely as events proved) for the death of the Tory party. But Oxford could at least face his certain persecution with grounds for satisfaction as well as with the tranquillity of his Christian faith. For in a career that had exactly spanned the years 1689–1714, he had helped to guide Stuart England to five of its greatest achievements: limited, constitutional monarchy; a secure Protestant Succession; the Union with Scotland; the triumphs of the country's greatest war; and, not least, the peace that confirmed beyond question Britain's new standing as a great power, not only in Europe but in the wider world of commerce and colonies beyond.

CHAPTER NINE

The Augustan Age 1689–1714

The Church in Danger

Their country's emergence as a great power, together with the knowledge that the benefits of 'the late happy Revolution' had been secured in the process, had bred by 1714 a great self-confidence in the English. The contrast between the national mood of this time and that of, for instance, the period from 1665 to 1667 during the second Dutch War, was remarkable. The post-Revolution generation was an intensely self-aware one, proud of its achievements. Subsequent generations were to look back on Anne's reign in particular as England's Augustan age – and not merely in a literary and cultural sense. We shall glance shortly at some of the more prominent of its non-military and non-political achievements and at the characteristic features and *moeurs* that reflect the distinctive values, as well as prosperity, of the age, and were an intrinsic part of its legacy to posterity.

It would be quite wrong, however, to imagine that success and self-confidence induced universal complacency. Far from it. Nineteen years of warfare brought their share of disasters as well as triumphs and involved such a heavy cost in human suffering and family hardships that Bolingbroke spoke for the majority of his countrymen when he 'heartily wish[ed] our children's children may never see their like again'. The idea that such visitations were divine punishments for the sins of a backsliding people was still surprisingly widespread half a century after the Puritan Revolution. Some trends in their society caused deep concern among post-Revolution Englishmen. The sheer ferocity of party conflict seemed terrifying at times: indeed, from the queen downwards many sincere Christians thought it a national sin. But it was the moral and religious climate of the day which aroused most alarm. Whether the decline of public morality, at least in the higher orders of society, was any worse in William III's England than it had been under the influence of a libidinous court in Charles II's reign is much to be doubted. What changed was the level and strength of the outcry against it and against the irreligion associated with it. After the 'great deliverance' from Popery and arbitrary power in 1688 – a miraculous instance of Divine Providence – how could England remain so ungratefully reprobate? A notable feature of the post-Revolution decades was the commitment of laymen to the fight against heathenism and low moral standards. But naturally, it was from those professionally involved in the saving of souls that the loudest cries of consternation and the most insistent calls for remedies were heard.

Clergymen of all denominations under William and Anne were frequently disturbed by how little they themselves seemed able to achieve. Two serious setbacks in the years following the Revolution especially oppressed them. The first was the Toleration Act of 1689, which for the first time allowed freedom of worship, under licence (though not equality of civil rights), to all *Protestant* Dissenters, apart from the unenforceable stipulation that they must accept the doctrine of the Trinity. The act had one effect that neither Anglican nor nonconformist divines foresaw. The former expected defections from their flocks to the Dissenters (though, even so, they were taken aback by the sheer volume of applications soon pouring in for licensing places of non-Anglican worship). A bigger shock was the general decline in formal religious attendance. Archdeacons were soon anxiously reporting to their bishops that thousands of ordinary parishioners were laying hold of the new freedom to worship outside their parish churches in order to thumb their noses at church and meeting-house alike. The Church courts, whose revival in the 1680s had already been checked by James II in the Catholic cause, were powerless to act as enforcers; and the effectiveness of their other functions, not least their capacity to deter and discipline moral offenders, declined in consequence. A much heavier blow was to follow in 1695, however, with the end of effective press censorship.

Since 1662 the Licensing Act had enabled the Church to exercise pre-publication control over printed matter. When parliament allowed this Act to lapse in William's reign, clergymen of all persuasions were appalled at the consequences. A stream of literature purveying all manner of heterodox, irreligious or scandalous opinions flooded the London book market and rapidly overflowed into the provinces. 'What vast loads of filth, of all kinds, are to be seen up and down in heaps amongst us', exclaimed John Harris to the fashionable

162. Sylvester Brounower, *John Locke*, *c.* 1685.
Pencil drawing, $4\frac{3}{8} \times 3\frac{3}{8}$ in. (11.1 × 8.6 cm).
London, National Portrait Gallery.
Like Newton, Locke made a powerful and lasting impact on European intellectual life, above all perhaps in his Essay concerning Humane Understanding *(1690). Physician and friend to the first Earl of Shaftesbury, he probably wrote his* Two Treatises of Government *as a statement of the radical Whig case during the exclusion crisis. After Shaftesbury's defeat he fled to Holland, to return only in 1689. He published major works on education, on religious toleration and on the currency.*

auditors of his Boyle Lecture in 1697. The effects were obvious to Charles Trimnell when he preached before the Commons ten years later against the 'vice and irreligion that, like a pestilence . . . now rages among us'. Anxiety and anger at licentious attacks on religious and moral authority and on the very foundations of belief were not confined to one clerical party. Trimnell and Harris were Low Churchmen. But the dynamic Francis Atterbury, leading the High Church demand for the recall of Convocation in the late 1690s, had sounded the alarm bells louder than any against a situation in which 'such an open looseness in men's principles and practices and such a settled contempt of religion and the priesthood have prevailed everywhere; when heresies of all kinds, when scepticism, Deism and atheism itself overrun us like a deluge'.

Under the last two Stuarts not only the Established Church but all the Christian churches saw themselves as locked in a great struggle for men's minds as well as for their moral well-being and their souls. None of the intellectual challenges which Atterbury highlighted were strictly new. The rationalism which professed to be sceptical about all elements of 'revelation' in religion and which sought to reduce Christian doctrine to terms that the least subtle mentality could grasp had unquestionably been stimulated by the major scientific advances of post-Restoration England and the empirical philosophy underlying them (see Chapter Seven). But it found its supreme expression in 1695 with John Locke's *The Reasonableness of Christianity*. So it was, too, with Socinianism, the more radical of the two heresies (Arianism was the other) that undermined the central Christian doctrines of the Trinity and infiltrated both Anglican and Presbyterian clergy after the Revolution. John Evelyn had observed its influence stirring, 'deny[ing] the Godhead of Christ', in the last years of the Commonwealth. But it was the mass distribution of

Christianity not Mysterious:

OR, A

TREATISE

Shewing,

That there is nothing in the GOSPEL Contrary to

REASON,

Nor ABOVE it:

And that no Christian Doctrine can be properly call'd

A MYSTERY.

By *JOHN TOLAND.*

The Second Edition Enlarg'd.

We need not desire a better Evidence that any Man is in the wrong, than to hear him declare against Reason, and thereby to acknowledg that Reason is against him. **Archbishop Tillotson.**

LONDON,

Printed for *Sam. Buckley* at the Dolphin over against St. *Dunstans* Church in *Fleetstreet*. MDCXCVI.

163. John Toland, *Christianity not Mysterious* (1696), title-page.
A young Irishman with a rare capacity for self-advertisement, Toland came to London in the 1690s and outraged his contemporaries both by his religious and by his political radicalism. He applied the claims of 'reason' not only – as earlier seventeenth-century writers had done – to Church history and to patristic theology but to the gospels themselves. His book was presented by the grand jury of Middlesex and in 1697 was publicly burnt in Dublin. John Locke, whose The Reasonableness of Christianity *had appeared in 1695 and whose views had much in common with Toland's, was careful to distance himself from Toland's provocative bluntness.*

Socinian tracts by the London merchant Thomas Firmin in the 1690s which gave these views wide currency. Deism, which has been defined as 'that belief which stripped religion of all but a remote Creator who had left a mechanical universe to its own devices', had its English origins as far back as the 1620s. But inspired by a perverted version of Isaac Newton's world-view, it first achieved extraordinary influence over the minds of Englishmen of birth and education in the 1690s, with the writings of Charles Blount and John Toland's sensational *Christianity not Mysterious*.

One reason why the clergy often felt that they were losing the battle against both infidelism and immorality was their consciousness of having, as an order, declined sharply in public respect since the Revolution. Anticlericalism was rife – largely among the Whigs, but not exclusively so – being compounded partly of outright hostility, partly of 'settled contempt', partly of amused indifference. It was to some extent provoked by the economics of the Established Church, which were bizarre and indefensible. The gulf between wealthy and poor clergy in the Protestant Church of England had been a scandal since the sixteenth century; and for almost 20 years after the Revolution the lot of the thousands of parsons on or below the clerical poverty line, unable to keep up appearances or to buy books, worsened owing to war taxation. More serious in its effects on lay opinion was that 'prostitution of oaths' whereby 95 per cent of Anglican clergy had contrived to preserve their livings in 1689–90 at the expense of those Divine Right principles they had been trumpeting just a few years earlier. Most damaging of all were their own divisions, hardening about 1700 into 'formed parties' of High and Low Churchmen, and the massive diversion of time and energies away from their spiritual mission which these divisions involved. The obsession of the High Church majority with the danger from post-Toleration Dissent was a prime cause of both division and distraction: all the more tragic because Anglican fears can be seen in retrospect to have been so exaggerated. Certainly the main nonconformist sects – Presbyterians, Independents and Quakers, though not perhaps the Baptists – did grow progressively in numbers and in visible presence for at least two decades after the 1689 'Indulgence'. (This was in sharp contrast with the Catholic community, still officially subject to the old penal laws, which remained fairly static and with few exceptions politically quiescent). Yet even at peak strength around 1715, of some 1900 congregations and, at most, 450,000 'hearers', nonconformists still represented under ten per cent of the population; and with problems enough of their own (inter-sectarian and doctrinal) the heirs of the Puritans were never in a position to contemplate any 'take-over-bid' for the loyalties of the faithful at large. Nor were they equipped to campaign successfully against paganism among the urban poor. English Christians presented an unedifying spectacle of discord at a time when the Faith itself had rarely stood in greater peril.

Most harmful of all to the public image of the churches was the unprecedented degree of political activity in which their own dissensions involved them. It was bad enough for the clergy – even many former Puritan clergy – to allow deists and sceptics virtually to dictate the ground on which their ideological battles would be fought and thereby appear to accept that Christian belief *was* a thing of the mind rather than of the spirit and the heart. But if that was unwise, it was sheer folly for them to engage themselves so blatantly in the struggle between the secular parties – High Churchmen allying with Tories, and Low Churchmen and Dissenters with Whigs – in the hope that they could advance their causes or defend their interests in parliament. For example, the main reason for the mounting anticlericalism of the Whigs under the last two Stuarts and their subsequent determination to muzzle the Anglican clergy after 1714 was undoubtedly the open politicking of the High-Church parsons in the Tory interest in the eleven general elections of this period, and especially in those held after 1700.

And yet despite its many self-inflicted wounds and other adverse circumstances outside its control, such as lay patronage and lay ownership of tithes ('impropriations'), the Church of England did make tangible progress in the fight against worldliness, doubt, ignorance and unbelief. In fact, by comparison with the demoralized, stultified condition of English Christianity by the early years of George II's reign, Anne's reign provided devout Anglicans with some heartening evidence of religious revival. The glare of the political spotlight may have caused distraction, but certainly not indifference. Parliamentary action could be divisive (as with the Occasional Conformity bills), or simply ineffectual (for instance, the Blasphemy Act of 1697); but it did contribute significantly to relieving the poverty and increasing the self-respect of the lower clergy, most notably through Queen Anne's Bounty Act (1704), which allocated revenue that came to the crown from the Church to increase poorer ministers' stipends. Furthermore the Church still had vigorous leadership, taking heart from the impeccable spiritual and moral example of the queen herself. Prelates such as Archbishop Tenison and Bishops Burnet, Wake, Nicolson and Lloyd proved that it was possible to combine political activism with a high standard of professional oversight and pastoral care. Regular

164. The Friends' Meeting House at Jordans, Chalfont St. Giles, Buckinghamshire.
The meeting house (now restored) was built in 1688 in an area which had a long tradition of religious nonconformity, and where Quakers had survived persecution under Charles II. James II's policy of wooing the Quakers by toleration enabled the house to be built, and after the Toleration Act of 1689 Quaker numbers grew. By 1688 much of the revolutionary fervour of the early Quakers had been lost. William Penn and other prominent early Quakers were buried near the house.

visitations by bishops to their dioceses led to a strong emphasis on frequent communions and a great increase in catechizing and confirming the young. Church attendance temporarily revived, as can be seen from the galleries added to many town churches, and new churches began to be built – some, like St Philip's, Birmingham, of great beauty – in under-provided provincial towns as well as in London. Except for the increase in election riots there was a very low incidence of popular disorder under the last two Stuarts in comparison with the first half of the seventeenth century or the mid-eighteenth: food rioting, for example, was astonishingly rare, despite many poor harvests. Demographic stability and higher real wages (see Chapter One) played an important part in this trend. But the degree of social control that the clergy could still exercise over 'the poorer sort' should not be discounted. Neither was it entirely coincidental that although the second worst London riot of the eighteenth century occurred in 1710, it did so during the trial of the High Church zealot, Dr Sacheverell. The thousands who rampaged through the streets, sacking meeting-houses and attempting unsuccessfully to storm the Whig-Dissenting stronghold of the Bank of England, did so in protest against 'the Church in Danger'.

The Sacheverell riots, admittedly, can hardly be considered as manifestations of lay piety. But the same cannot be said of the evident willingness of many better-off lay Anglicans – and Dissenters – to join their clergy in the work of moral reformation and spiritual regeneration. The first of scores of 'Societies for the Reformation of Manners', which brought common law actions against moral offenders, was founded in 1691. Eight years later Bishop Fowler expansively conceded that 'our whole bench have never done the 40th part of that service . . . to our Church that those Church of England laymen have done'. The progress of the Queen Anne Bounty scheme depended as much on private beneficence as on state aid: it was not found wanting. Even more striking was the role of private lay philanthropy in the biggest Anglican success story of the early eighteenth century, the charity school

'Come Ye Sons of Art Away'

HENRY PURCELL AND MARY II

1 Attrib. J. Closterman, *Henry Purcell.* Chalk drawing 15 × 11¼ in, (38.1 × 28.6 cm.). London, National Portrait Gallery.

2 Peter Hoadley, *William and Mary.* Miniature, oil on board, 2½ × 2 in. (6.1 × 5.2 cm.). Amsterdam, Rijksmuseum.

A queen and a composer must rarely have had the same funeral music. Yet when Henry Purcell (1658–95) was buried in November 1695, his funeral music was the same that was used eight months before at the obsequies of his last royal patron, Mary II. This music was part of the large output by Purcell, who was 'esteemed', as John Evelyn said, 'the best composer of any Englishman hitherto'.

But Purcell was a consumptive. The illness ran in the family and he died young, leaving behind him a large and varied output of Church and chamber music, of odes and celebratory song cycles, and of music for the stage. He was man and boy a product of the Chapel Royal, the most professional group of musicians in seventeenth-century England, where his brother Daniel sang alongside him with the 12 boy choristers and where his uncle Thomas was one of the 32 Gentlemen of the Chapel. Anglicanism and royal patronage were the foundations of seventeenth-century musical achievement in England. The standards of the Chapel were maintained by the long service of its Gentlemen, among them John Harding, who sang at James I's funeral and who died in 1684. Such men enabled the musical tradition to survive even through the Interregnum.

Composers in Restoration England created and performed for Church, stage, music room and court. Their professional world was joined with the literary one of Shadwell, Tate and Dryden, who provided many of the 'libretti' for the music. Posterity has mostly judged the music to be better than the words, but the cross-fertilization was important. Purcell's march in Queen Mary's funeral music was originally written for Shadwell's play *The Libertine*, which was an adaptation from a French *Don Juan*; such adaptations were common.

Some people were shocked when Charles II had violins modelled on Louis XIV's 'vingt-quatre violins du roi' in the Chapel Royal, 'after the French fantastical light way, better suiting a tavern or playhouse'. Purcell's music made full use of them, although with less prominence after 1688 when his royal patrons had more austere tastes – a musical tactical retreat which dismayed some hearers who thought the result 'clog'd somewhat of an English vein'. Purcell was always adaptable. From the 'French style' he could move quickly to the Italian one, and in 1683 he described a work of his as 'a just imitation of the most famed of Italian masters . . . to bring the seriousness and gravity of that sort of music into vogue and reputation'. Purcell was Composer in Ordinary to Charles II, as well as composer for the royal violins from 1677 and Keeper of the Royal Instruments from 1683. After his work for James II's coronation he became a member of the King's Private Music as a keyboard player. Purcell's professionalism and variety of talents gave him the top job of composing the music for William and Mary's coronation in 1689. The Revolution had not destroyed good music.

Odes and welcome songs offered Purcell the best publicity for his work, being performed for royal entrances into London or birthday celebrations. These works had to make a quick and pompous impact and displayed contrasts of voices and instruments; with John Blow, Purcell almost created this form from 1680 onwards. The odes, though later elaborated, took the basic form of a 'French' overture, usually for strings and a vocal solo, which was then taken up by the chorus. The singing was interrupted by a canzona or symphony followed by more solos and duets, which were again taken up for the finale by the full chorus. Purcell wrote six birthday odes for Queen Mary before he finally composed her funeral music.

3 Tulip vase designed by Daniel Marot for Mary's Water Gallery at Hampton Court, 1694. London, Victoria & Albert Museum. Mary's tastes were homely, but she was a discriminating collector of porcelain, and liked displaying her collection to visitors.

4 Mary's Lying in State, a contemporary engraving.
Mourning for Mary was lavish in both England and Holland. £5,000 was spent on the funeral.

Mary had a difficult life. Born of a political marriage which went sour – between James II and Clarendon's daughter Anne – her own marriage had consigned her to a mansion in the Hague. She remained childless and was torn between loyalty to her husband and some residual love for her father. Her husband deserted her for the battlefield and for his Dutch male companions, and her father was exiled and embittered. Imbued with a simple Protestantism, Mary could not understand the High Church views of her sister Anne. She felt guilty because she enjoyed a game of cards. Yet she was not without dignity and taste. She beautified Hampton Court and created Kensington Palace. Her liking for gardening and china was in keeping with her domestic image. Purcell's Birthday Ode for 1694 (her last birthday), 'Come ye Sons of Art Away', seems rather too grand for her. The libretto addressed to William, 'her daring hero in the field' (who left for the battlefield on her birthday), is weakly pompous: 'The day that such a blessing gave/No common festival should be.' Its sentiment is banal: 'While Maria's royal seat best instructs you how to pray/Hourly from her own conversing with the Eternal Throne.' But the music is masterly.

Purcell might almost have known that Mary's funeral music would serve as his own. He set it to the Biblical texts 'Man that is born of woman', 'In the midst of life we are in death', and 'Thou knowest Lord the secrets of our hearts'. Mary had died 'full of spots' on 28 December 1694. She left a paper requesting no embalming, lying-in-state or expensive funeral. The instructions were found too late and she endured all three, unlucky to the end. The funeral was held on 5 March 1695, with Purcell's last major work fitting the splendour of the occasion. His 'seriousness and gravity' are everywhere present in vocal settings reminiscent of Monteverdi; individual lines force themselves into the four-part settings as in an opera. Versatile and adaptable to the end, Purcell's polyphony remains English to the last, as English as his queen.

5 The manuscript of Purcell's 'Come ye sons of Art Away', composed for New Year's Day, 1694. London, Royal College of Music.
Purcell's music, duly recognized in his lifetime, influenced the next great composer working in England, Handel.

movement. The Society for the Promotion of Christian Knowledge (SPCK), which co-ordinated the movement, set it the clear objective of establishing schools which would arm the children of the poor with basic literacy and basic Christian principles as a shield against Ignorance and the Devil (the two being hand-in-glove). By 1729 the Society had 132 schools in London and 1419 provincial schools on its books. The SPCK (1699) was one of the two great Anglican voluntary societies founded at the turn of the century: as well as promoting formal education it also encouraged parish libraries and the publication and widespread distribution of inexpensive religious literature. And while the SPCK combatted heathenism at home, the Society for the Propagation of the Gospel (1702) took on a similar role in the colonies.

Christian laymen also fought as support troops, if not in the front line, in the more sophisticated struggle for the minds of educated society. An outstanding example was the endowment of the Boyle Lectures (1692–1714), established under the will of the most distinguished chemist of Restoration England as a means of vindicating the Faith against its many contemporary enemies. They provided a platform for deploying some of the Church's most able intellects, led by the dazzling young Richard Bentley, against the 'Forces of Darkness' – libertines, deists, heretics and the whole 'atheistical host'. Although deism was not vanquished until the 1730s, it had been thrown on to the defensive by 1714, while the Socinians (within the Anglican Church, at least) were by then in full retreat. And it is not without significance that one of those who could claim posthumous credit for these achievements was the scientist Robert Boyle. Whatever the eventual implications of the English Scientific Revolution for Christianity, nearly all its heroic figures in these early decades were committed believers. Few were more committed than Isaac Newton. Ironically, while deists and sceptics exulted in Newton's demonstration of the amazing power of the human intellect to interpret the universe, the *Principia* and its theory of gravity seemed to the Anglican avant-garde the sharpest God-sent intellectual weapon their Church had ever possessed: the 'clockwork universe' supplying irrefutable evidence of the existence of a divine clockmaker. Like his friend John Locke, who became the other guru of the eighteenth-century Church of Reason, the master had demonstrated not the reasonableness of doubt, still less of unbelief, but the *Reasonableness of Christianity*.

165. Fighting in the Coffee-House after the Trial of Sacheverell. Contemporary print.
The passions roused by the Sacheverell affair reached even the coffee-houses.

Minds, Men and Manners

Although Leibniz might have demurred, Augustan England could fairly boast in Newton and Locke the two greatest intellectual giants of the day. The French *philosophes* later looked back on them with reverence as the founding fathers of the European Enlightenment. In seven astounding years after the Revolution of 1688 Locke published classic treatises on political thought, educational theory, religious toleration and metaphysics, as well as theology (see also p. 257). His *Essay concerning Humane Understanding* (1690) alone would have guaranteed him an enduring reputation; and the influence of his philosophical genius is discernible in the work of his pupil, the third Earl of Shaftesbury (grandson of the Whig leader of Charles II's reign), whose *Characteristics of Men, Manners, Opinions* (1711) became a European landmark in the field of moral philosophy. Like Locke, who found time to involve himself closely in currency reform and the Board of Trade, Newton applied his supreme gifts to

166. John Worlidge, *Systema Agriculturae* (1675 edition).
John Worlidge of Hampshire compiled in this book the first comprehensive treatise on husbandry, and so brought together much scattered information published during and after the Interregnum. First printed in 1669, the work enjoyed widespread popularity in the later Stuart period, and was republished in 1675, 1681, 1687 and 1716. The neatly ordered gardens and trees, the trim hedges and the afforestation indicate what a systematically run farm might look like, and suggest the agricultural advances brought by the age of the Scientific Revolution.

practical affairs as Master of the Mint from 1699 to 1727. But he continued his work as a physicist and mathematician until the publication of his *Optics* (1704), and presided over the Royal Society for 25 years until his death. The Society itself enjoyed a new halcyon period from the late 1690s, not least because much was being done by its scientific Fellows to carry forward and broaden the achievements of the pre-Revolution period. For example, Flamsteed and Halley (of comet fame) were unequalled anywhere as astronomers, and through them the Royal Observatory at Greenwich became an important centre of research associated with the Royal Society. Fellows of the Society in this period made notable advances, too, in medical and pharmaceutical research through Hans Sloane, William Hillary and William Cockburn, discoverer of a specific for dysentery.

From its earliest years, the Royal Society had been interested in the practical application of innovation and invention to economic development. Its Agricultural Committee continued to spread the gospel of 'improvement'; and it must take some credit for the fact that over its 25 years Stuart England saw the later seventeenth-century agrarian revolution carried a further unspectacular stage forward. Although Jethro Tull invented the first successful seed-drill on his Berkshire farm about 1701, agricultural progress came more from experimental practice and propaganda than from 'technology': arguably the most important figure on the scene was not a farmer or landowner, but an apothecary, John Houghton, F.R.S., whose *Letters for the Improvement of Husbandry and Trade* (1691–1702) kept his numerous readers abreast of new methods.

The years of the wars against Louis XIV were important in preparing Britain for her emergence late in the eighteenth century as the world's first industrial nation. That this was so in spite of dislocation of markets was a tribute to general entrepreneurial enterprise rather than to individual genius. But two highly important technical breakthroughs do date from the early years of the eighteenth century: the application by Thomas Newcomen of steam power to a pumping engine for use in mines; and the discovery by a Quaker ironmaster, Abraham Darby, of the priceless secret of how to utilize coal – in the form of coke – in blast furnaces in order to yield workable iron. Since late Tudor times the English had been heavily indebted to foreign immigrants for transmitting new industrial techniques and after 1688 this was still true of some new luxury manufactures: high-quality pottery (the Elers brothers), glass (Le Blanc) and fine paper (Portal). On the other hand, home-grown talent was responsible for most of the engineering work that benefited the late Stuart economy. 'The ingenious Mr Sorrocold' was much in demand in the north for his water-engines, for bringing the first piped water into towns as well as for industrial use: powering the great Lombe silk mill at Derby in the 1720s was to be his *tour de force*. Thomas Steers was a pioneer of the science of commercial wet-

LXII.

95

Alii Atria magnas sedes & capacissimas dictas tradunt: unde Atria licinia & atrium libertatis. LYCHNI] Græce Armene usus est; ne vile aliquid intro ferret. A Lychno autem lucerna dicta est. unde et brevis est Lucilio et Persio Disposita pinguem nebulam uomuere lucerna. HORAT Ungor Olivo Non quo fraudatis immundis nacta lucernis. Si enim aliud diceretur non staret versus.

According to OGILBYS Version into English.

After the Feast was ended all took down
Thy mighty Goblets place and Bacchus crown
The ample palace rung with noyses mixt
And shineing Lamps to golden roofs were fixt
Bright Torches vanquish the dark nights fires.

The next day being Thursday July 24. 84. his Grace the Duke of Beaufort rested and spent in veiwing the lands and various works and Machines of the Lead & Colemines belonging to Sr Roger Mostyn. among which his Grace and select company took a Survey of the engine which I have above exhibited all which Wheels and Pinions being once again repeated, viz. 2 Water-Wheels the under to receive the water which comes from ye upper by a large trough or Canal &c forme a Machine to dreyn water from this Colework, by the Sea side at the foot of a very high Cliff or Rock

LEAD MINES, the soyle about them is short and crumbling of a clay like colour in some places almost of a bright yellow in others darker, they abound with Oker and Umber, which burnt in a crucible or melting pot turns to red and is sold as such. These Mines have silver but so little it seems the play is not worth the candle Sr Roger Mostyn onely raiseth lead. Concerning the Veins of the Mines the flakey and shining is sayd to be best for Silver, the glittering and sparkling is next but the white crusted with Oker is best for lead this last the Workers of the Mine call Caus-Teeth is very weighty and resembles a Yellowish enammell and is soonest melted into perfect Lead, so more dock building at Rotherhithe and Liverpool. And men like William Bailey and John Hore were hard at work on the many river navigation schemes of the period especially essential to the textile and coal trades: widening and deepening channels and anticipating later canal-builders by making navigable 'cuts', as at Exeter and Neath, and installing locks.

The inventiveness of the age is reflected in very different ways from these, however. The unprecedented demands of war finance and the joint-stock euphoria of the first half of William III's reign together gave birth to the ingenious schemes advanced by 'projectors'. The Bank of England was the brain-child of the most original of them, William Paterson, though it needed Montagu's political drive to make it a reality; Paterson later devised the blueprints for Walpole's 'Sinking Fund' to reduce the National Debt, just as John Blunt, of the Sword Blade Company, hatched the scheme carried through by Harley in 1711 to incorporate the South Sea Company to deal with the pressing problem of the floating debt. The French wars were won in the back-rooms of finance and government as well as on the battlefields and on the seas. And in those rooms the exotic figures of the projectors rubbed shoulders with men of less fertile ideas but equally vital gifts. Some of the master-craftsmen of the new civil service deserve in their own unobtrusive way to rank with the most influential figures of their day: men such as William Lowndes, Secretary of the Treasury through many changes of ministry from 1695 to 1724, and Pepys's heirs at the Admiralty and Navy Office, Josias Burchett and Charles Sergison.

A society – and an economy – at war; a society in religious crisis; a society divided by 'the rage of party': all these descriptions can be validly applied to Stuart England in the years 1689–1714. And yet they exclude much that is most significant about that society. Any historian's gallery of great Augustans must, for example, include Congreve, Defoe, Addison, Steele, Swift, Pope and Gay, even if the greatest achievements of some – *Gulliver's Travels, Robinson Crusoe, The Dunciad* – were after 1714. Augustan England, by definition, was quintessentially a great age of Letters. The same gallery must surely find room, too, for Sir Christopher Wren (still active in Anne's day) and for Talman, Vanbrugh, Hawksmoor, Gibbs and Campbell. For this is the very heart of England's Baroque Age in architecture. A survey of the social scene is inevitably selective; but it will serve to highlight some of the features of Augustan society which are most distinctive and inter-related: its basic prosperity; its development of that passion for 'consumption' and especially the emulative and luxury consumption that distinguishes eighteenth- from seventeenth-century England; its growing and socially broadening sophistication and 'taste'; its cultivation and increasing commercialization of leisure; and its innate 'sociability'. The trend towards secularism and heightened aesthetic awareness (see Chapter Seven) laid a profound mark on the generation that followed. But that generation exhibited less cultural exclusiveness than its predecessor and placed greater emphasis on social refinement (as in the reaction against vulgarity in the theatre) and on native tradition.

In spite of amost 20 years of war taxation, England was a much more prosperous country in 1714 than she had been at the Restoration. Whatever the causes – and most economic historians would place the trade boom of 1674–88 at or near the head of the list – few would dispute this fact. By looking at ways in which surplus wealth was used, we can better understand something of the values of the society that generated it. While economic investment remained vital, the *social* application of wealth often vied for priority. A high proportion of the surplus was invested in social status and its symbols, or in the pursuit of social aspirations.

What Neil McKendrick has called the eighteenth-century 'Consumer Revolution' was already under way by 1714; and Defoe, for one, observed that it was no respecter of social rank. Writing during Goerge I's reign, he complained of that appetite for emulation which impelled even 'mean' tradesmen to 'have their parlours set off with the tea-table and . . . the silver coffee-pot', and 'the burghers' wives of Horsham' to deck themselves in silk gowns. More remarkable was the amount of money devoted to a joyous indulgence of artistic and aesthetic tastes, rare in England in the first 60 years of the seventeenth century, but now, with the decline of the Puritan ethic, an accepted form of self-expression among the well-to-do. It is nowhere more clearly displayed than in the ornate but still glorious interiors of late seventeenth and early eighteenth-century houses – both large and not-so-large: their decorated ceilings, their panelling and their plasterwork. 'The middling sort' were not to be denied their share: indeed one provincial apothecary modelled the painted ceilings of his Derby town house on those

167. A late seventeenth-century wheel-pumping engine of Sir Roger Mostyn, from T. Dingley, *The Account of the Official Progress . . . Henry Duke of Beaufort*, ed. R. W. Banks (1888).
Sir Roger Mostyn, baronet, was a gentleman of Flintshire who ruined his estate by his contributions to the royalist cause in the civil war but who by 1684 had dramatically improved his fortunes through the profits of lead and coal mines worked by his large engines. In that year he was able to give 'a very great and noble entertainment' at his house for the Duke of Beaufort, from the record of whose official progress through Wales this illustration survives. The patronage of landowners was vital to the development of science and technology.

168. Winslow Hall, Buckinghamshire.
The house, perhaps designed by Wren, was built in 1700 for William Lowndes, Secretary to the Treasury, whose family had been settled in the Buckinghamshire village of Winslow since the early sixteenth century. Much concerned with plans for reform of the coinage and for innovative public funding, he grew rich from his services to the Treasury but retained a reputation for honesty. The house brought the architectural tastes of the capital to the countryside, much as the Tatler *conveyed the intellectual and social values of London to the provinces.*

of Chatsworth itself. But, of course, the great 'temples' to the Augustan aristocratic ideal offered most scope for the genius of the master-decorators of the day, such as Thornhill, Verrio and Laguerre, and to a host of other craftsmen. Rooms of beauty called for fashionable, elegant furniture to enhance them. The great decades of English furniture-making began in George II's reign. But although in 1689 Louis Quatorze was most sought-after by the wealthy, the war years saw English native craftsmen striving to satisfy the ambitions of home consumers – for comfort as well as appearance. Not only London craftsmen either: by 1714 the elder Chippendale was already making his name in Worcester.

Love of display, however, as well as aesthetic appreciation and higher standards of comfort, influenced many in their acquisition of costly furniture. Up to a point it was part of the collecting mania that gripped Augustan England. Among the aristocracy and upper gentry fine paintings, porcelain and statuary were the principal obsessions. William III brought many Old Masters with him from Holland and the fashion rapidly caught on. One contemporary was to recall in the 1720s 'how all Europe has been rummaged, as we may say, for pictures to bring over hither, where, for twenty years, they yielded the purchasers – such as collected them for sale – immense profit'. Meanwhile the Continent had been combed for Delft ware; and even Asia too, by a few fanatics, for fine porcelain. As early as 1697 Celia Fiennes found a rich tradesman in Bury St Edmunds who had two rooms 'full of china'. And indeed by 1714 'the humour . . . of furnishing houses with china ware' was widely indulged as far down as the professional and business ranks – to the prejudice, it was said, of many a family budget.

Perhaps the most surprising feature of the domestic face of England at a time of two seemingly exhausting wars was the extent to which it was being rebuilt. Far from diminishing, the building activity of the post-Restoration years appears to have redoubled in intensity after the Revolution. In the countryside the surviving evidence in almost every county is astonishing, in view of the insistent groans of the landed interest about taxation. Farms, parsonage houses and small manor houses all tell the same story, as well as the new or

169. Pool Bank Farm, Crosthwaite, Westmorland.
A substantial farmhouse of the later seventeenth century.

170 (opposite). Ashburnham House, Westminster, the staircase and cupola.
The most elegant town house of the late seventeenth century to survive in London, Ashburnham House was the London residence of a rising gentry family of Sussex, the Ashburnhams.

171. Blenheim Palace, Woodstock, Oxfordshire, from the south-east.
One of the most imposing Baroque palaces of Europe, Blenheim was built for the Duke of Marlborough by Queen Anne's command after the victory of Blenheim in 1704. Vanbrugh, the architect, would recall that 'When the Queen declared she would build a house in Woodstock Park for the Duke of Marlborough, and that she meant it in memory of the great services he had done her and the nation, I found it the opinion of all people and parties, that although the building was to be calculated for and adapted to a private habitation, yet it ought at the same time to be considered both a royal and a national monument, and care taken in the design that it might have the qualities proper to such a monument, viz. beauty, magnificence and duration.'

remodelled mansions of the established squirearchy, like the Kynastons of Shropshire, the Twisdens of Kent or the Sebrights of Hertfordshire and the opulent residences built by incoming merchants and lawyers. The late W. G. Hoskins placed 'the great rebuilding' of rural England between 1575 and 1625, but Mr. Machin suggests that the peak may have come nearer 1700 than 1600. The author of the *Complete English Tradesman* may not have been far wrong, therefore, when he wrote in 1727 that 'we see more new houses at this time in England, built within twenty to forty years, than were built in England in two hundred years before'.

The itch to build certainly took hold of the aristocracy with a vengeance, particularly after 1697. Chatsworth, begun just before the Revolution by the first Duke of Devonshire (see p. 212), blazed the Baroque trail in England, setting new standards in grandeur, scale and magnificence; and after the Peace of Ryswick that trail became a broad highway. Blenheim Palace, built for the Marlboroughs, cost the nation a quarter of a million pounds. Private purses, however, not the Exchequer, paid for such splendid piles as Lord Nottingham's home at Burley, Carlisle's at Castle Howard, Somerset's at Petworth, Shrewsbury's at Heythrop, Strafford's at Wentworth and many more that were begun, and sometimes completed, before 1714. But while travellers and sightseers in the provinces occasionally gaped in awe at these monuments to aristocratic self-esteem and the grandiose vision of their architects, they were much more aware of the pervasive residential revolution going on contemporaneously in many English towns. The Great Fire of London and the smaller conflagrations which destroyed Northampton in the 1670s and much of Warwick in the 1690s finally sealed the fate of the late-medieval and Tudor urban building-style with its lath and timber and higgledy-piggledy informality. Safer building materials became the priority and order the watchword of the new age. In numerous provincial towns uniform rows or terraces – and here and there, squares – of brick and stone houses were springing up: houses with flush façades and, in all the better-class streets, elegant doorways, large and evenly-spaced sash windows, and spacious, airy interiors.

In contrast with the great Baroque houses and especially their more extravagant features, which owed much to continental models, the greater severity and classicism of the new town-building was both more indigenous and essentially more expressive of Augustan taste. *Its* model was London. The conventions adopted in the rebuilding of the inner City after the Fire and subsequently in the thrusting western suburbs were eagerly taken up by the provinces: in Bristol, for example; in Preston, which was nicknamed 'Little London'; and in Nottingham, which so enchanted Celia Fiennes when she visited it in 1697 (see p. 42).

Late Stuart towns, led of course by the great trendsetter, London, were not only the country's main engines of consumption but the indispensable centres for two of Augustan England's most absorbing activities – the enjoyment and commercial exploitation of leisure. Sport, of course, was a partial exception: fox-hunting, obviously; and cricket, too, catching on rapidly in the south-east, but still mostly played on rural commons or landed estates. The surging popularity of horse-racing on the other hand – by 1714 there were around 100 recognized courses – was already finding its main outlets, outside Newmarket, in the big shire-town meetings like those at Nottingham and York, or in smaller 'gentry towns' such as Beverley.

These were heady years for the theatre, the years of Congreve's and Farquahar's greatness. They were memorable years, too, more so even than those before 1688, for the lover of good music, expertly performed. In both fields London naturally set the fashions, but she exported some, at least, to the main cities and towns of the provinces. In a period when spontaneous music-making was giving ground to a new professionalism, Londoners alone (and their visitors) could enjoy Italian opera, which took the city by storm during Queen Anne's reign, or the pleasure-gardens and permanent theatres where professional orchestras entertained strollers and theatre-goers. But London's new music clubs and societies quickly produced many provincial

172. Francis Barlow, *Windsor Races, 24 August 1684*, 1687. Engraving.
The engraving is of 'the last horse race run before Charles the Second'. Charles's interest in horse-racing boosted the sport, which grew alongside the more traditional activity of hunting. Race-meetings were often used for political consultations, and for that reason the Cromwellian regime, nervous of royalist conspiracy, had tended to suppress them.

Not antient Rome, with her Olimpick Game,
By wch she did achive so great a Fame,
When o'r the Circus the bright Chariots whirld,
Surprising with delight the Gazing world,
Coud ere compaire to Englands nobler Chace,
When Swift as lightning or the winged Race

The generous Beast out-strips ye wind,
And leaves the wondering Croud behind.

In this Debate Monarchs their Umpirage boast,
And even an Empire's wealth is won & lost:
The noble Bruites with Emulation fir'd,
Scorning by Managers to be inspir'd,
As if they understood their Betters will,
They show wth pride their eager force, & skill,

And without aid of Spur, or reine,
They cutt ye air, & scoure ye plaine.

To future times may these illustrious Sports
Be only the divertisments of Courts,
Since the best man, best Iudge, & best of Kings,
Whose President the best Example brings:
When ere his God-like mind unbent from care
To all his pleasures this he woud prefer;

So Gods of old did not disdaine
The rural pastimes of the plaine.

And Dorsett ever celibrated be,
For this last honour which ariv'd to thee,
Blest for thy Prospect, all august and gay,
Blest for the memory of this glorious day
The last great Race the Royal Hero view'd
O Dorsett to thy much lov'd plains he ow'd.

For this alon a lasting name
Records thee in the Book of Fame.

'. . . The Wearing Out of Ignorance, Passion and Prejudice'

THE *TATLER* AND *THE SPECTATOR*

Dr Johnson remarked that 'before the Tatlers and Spectators . . . England had no masters of common life . . . to reform either the smugness of neglect or the impertinence of incivility'. The first issue of the *Tatler* by Richard Steele, appeared on 12 April 1709, and that of *The Spectator*, by Steele and Joseph Addison, in March 1711. These publications made journalism a form of literature and were the ancestors of magazines and the novel.

Nothing is published successfully without a readership. The civil war period when government control of the press broke down created a vituperative, dangerous, widely-read journalism; and although the genre was curbed by the re-imposition of censorship under Cromwell and again at the Restoration, the licensing laws lapsed in 1695. The essential environment of the new journalism was London, with its relatively high literacy rate and with the excitement of politics and of society. In 1652 the first coffee-house was opened in London and by 1663 there were 80 of them. They joined more than 1,500 alehouses, inns and eating houses in the city. The huge catering trade introduced tea, chocolate and coffee alongside the popular alcoholic drinks. On all this fluid floated the gossip of London.

1 A Coffee-House. Engraving, *c.* 1705. This all-male company is smoking, gossiping and conducting business over coffee.

Coffee was described as 'useless since it serveth neither for nourishment nor debauchery'. But for the businessman wanting to keep a clear head at the Exchange, coffee taken in convivial male company was ideal. Business was transacted and formal bargains were fixed informally over coffee. Business and gossip were inevitably joined by politics, and many politicians and civil servants enjoyed the coffee-houses and taverns as well. With talk came print; landlords became the middlemen who would link writers with their reading public. By Anne's reign there were 500 coffee-houses in the capital patronized by a large readership eager for newspapers, pamphlets, posters and advertisements as they arrived hot from the presses. Soon journalism reached the provinces, where it stimulated trade in drink, advertising, printing, transport and the postal services. The writers themselves made money: Addison and Steele sold half their rights in the subscription copies of *The Spectator* in 1714 for £600. The writer had no need of individual patrons, and with economic independence acquired independence of mind and outlook as well.

In 1709 Steele was 39 and a well-known coffee-house figure. An amiable Englishman from Ireland trying to make good, he had found only spasmodic patronage and had not been very successful either in the army, in the theatre, in his two marriages, or as a Whig politician. But his wide experience in all these enabled him to seize his chance in journalism. At first his *Tatler* resembled any other newspaper, such as the *London Gazette* or the *Momus Ridens*. Its first 64 issues were published on Tuesdays, Thursdays and Saturdays in order to catch the mail coaches for the provinces. But thereafter a change took place. More permanent-looking periodicals began appearing such as *The Gentleman's Journal*. They catered for more specialized interests and were addressed to a provincial as well as to a London readership. Steele built on their success. So competent was he in pinpointing his audience's interests that soon his readers were submitting their own contributions to his periodical. This was a new sort of literary involvement. It was not only London clubmen, but provincial bankers, doctors, lawyers, and above all women who

THE

LUCUBRATIONS

OF

Iſaac Bickerſtaff Eſq;

VOL. I.

Οὐ χρὴ παννύχιον εὕδειν βουληφόρον ἄνδρα. Homer.

LONDON,

Printed: And ſold by *John Morphew*, near *Stationers-Hall*. MDCCX.

2 Title-page of the first bound edition of the *Tatler* under the pseudonym Isaac Bickerstaff (1710).
Each issue of the *Tatler* consisted of a single sheet, printed in double columns on both sides of the paper. It was usually 1,600 to 1,900 words, but could be crammed to contain up to 3,000. It cost 1d., though the first four numbers were free.

3 Sir Godfrey Kneller, *Richard Steele*, 1711. Oil on canvas, 36 × 28 in. (91.4 × 71.1 cm.). London, National Portrait Gallery.
Both essayists were members of the Kit-cat Club of Whig worthies, and this is Steele's portrait done for the Club. He produced *The Tatler* under the name Isaac Bickerstaff, an allusion to Swift's contemporary satire on almanack writers.

filled the subscription lists for *The Tatler* and then for *The Spectator*. This trend helped the formation of a unified national outlook.

The content of *The Tatler* was new. Avoiding mere gossip and political in-fighting, Steele wrote about manners and morality. He showed men and women in their daily lives working out a code of correct conduct for private and public life. He invited readers to laugh at mistakes and foibles, but he also suggested that proper behaviour lay in a golden mean. This was the morality of the cultured, temperate, leisured English gentleman. Steele wore his morality lightly, even playfully, but never hypocritically.

Joseph Addison, son of a dean, was an Oxford don and a more successful Whig politician than Steele; his was the graver personality. He was a poet, a widely travelled and intelligent man with a pious streak and a respect for the moderate and temperate in all things. In 1710 the fall of the Whig Junto left Addison without employment. In March 1711 he joined in literary partnership with Steele and with him produced *The Spectator*. The new journal extended the initiatives and innovations of its predecessor. In tone and content it left the tavern and the coffee-table for the morning tea-table, the desk and the provincial armchair. Fictional stock-types were introduced, the best known of them being the lovable Tory squire, Sir Roger de Coverley.

The England of Addison and Steele was an England graver in mood than the extravagant, brash society of the Restoration period. As Europe's banker and as leader of the Grand Coalition against France, England was once more a nation with a mission. The country expected its gentry and its professional classes to set a moral example. The satire of Addison and Steele cleared the ground, stated an agenda for moral concern, and contributed to the ensuing debate. Such matters as the role of women ('Ill natured Husband', *Tatler* no. 149 and 'Love Letters', *Tatler* no. 30), and sexual conventions ('Seduction', *Spectator* no. 182 and 'Poor and Public Whores', *Spectator*, no. 266) were openly discussed. Items on family life introduced a strain of thoughtful sentimentality and common sense. Only rarely were politics mentioned directly (in spite of the authors' Whig commitments). Addison and Steele correctly gauged that a serious satire of sentiment, with a content which combined specific description with general conclusions, would be marketable on its own. The essays were seen by their readers as philosophical. As Addison said, he and Steele 'brought philosophy out of the closets and libraries, schools and colleges, to dwell in clubs and assemblies, at tea-tables and in coffee-houses'.

Mr. SPECTATOR,

'I Have loſt ſo much Time already, that I deſire, upon the Receipt hereof, you would ſit down 'immediately and give me your Anſwer. I would 'know of you whether a Pretender of mine really 'loves me. As well as I can I will deſcribe his 'Manners. When he ſees me he is always talking 'of Conſtancy, but vouchſafes to viſit me but once 'a Fortnight, and then is always in haſte to be gone. 'When I am ſick, I hear, he ſays he is mightily 'concerned, but neither comes nor ſends, becauſe, 'as he tells his Acquaintance with a Sigh, he does 'not care to let me know all the Power I have 'over him, and how impoſſible it is for him to live 'without me. When he leaves the Town he writes 'once in ſix Weeks, deſires to hear from me, com'plains of the Torment of Abſence, ſpeaks of Flames, 'Tortures, Languiſhings and Extaſies. He has the 'Cant of an impatient Lover, but keeps the Pace 'of a Lukewarm one. You know I muſt not go 'faſter than he does, and to move at this rate is as 'tedious as counting a great Clock. But you are 'to know he is rich, and my Mother ſays, As he 'is ſlow he is ſure; He will love me long, if he 'love me little: But I appeal to you whether he 'loves at all

Your Neglected

Humble Servant,

Lydia Novell.

'*All theſe Fellows who have Mony are extream*'*ly ſawcy and cold, Pray Sir, tell them of it.*

4 An extract from *The Spectator*, Friday 10 August 1711.
This letter illustrates the emergence of a new readership for papers like *The Spectator*. A female reader tells the editor about her courtship problems, a good example of the concern for 'minds and manners' in the journal.

5 Sir Godfrey Kneller, *Joseph Addison*, before 1717. Oil on canvas, 36 × 28 in. (91.4 × 71.1 cm.). London, National Portrait Gallery.
Another Kneller portrait for the Kit-cat Club. Addison was briefly Secretary of State after 1714.

imitators; and while cathedrals began to house concerts, inns like the Greyhound at Norwich were also pressed into service, just as they were in the capital. Towns could cater for the socializing instincts as well as the cultural appetites of their inhabitants and their neighbouring gentry. The golden age of that most decorous of late Stuart and Georgian social institutions, the provincial assembly, began around 1700. Bowling greens, like those at Bedford and Newcastle, and town walks (some specially laid out, as in Preston and Shrewsbury) were the out-of-door counterparts in social terms of the assemblies, though without all the attractions of London's parks and pleasure gardens. In one small group of towns, the spa towns, leisure was beginning to be cultivated as nowhere else. 'Taking the waters' had been for some years before 1688 a vogue prescription among a section of the medical fraternity. Queen Anne's visit to Bath in 1702 made it socially compelling also, and Bath itself, with Epsom and Tunbridge Wells, 'where a lady . . . may as soon shipwreck her character as in any place in England', were the first places to develop methodically their facilities in response to demand. By 1714 Scarborough was beginning to follow.

Three other institutions that especially illuminate the social mores of Augustan England are the town square, the coffee-house and the periodical. More than any new aspect of the residential habitat of the early eighteenth-century Englishman, it was the fashionable square, built round a common garden or paved area, which best summed up, at once, the prosperity, the civilized taste and the sociable instincts of the 'pseudo-gentry' of the towns. Where London pointed the way with Red Lion, Bloomsbury and St James's Squares, Bristol, Manchester and Birmingham quickly followed – demonstrating in the process how congenially merchants, professionals and the leisured genteel could coexist in Queen Anne's England. If the square was an integrator, the coffee-house was a leveller. Already (by 1688) the favourite social haunt of London males above labourers' rank, coffee-houses continued to grow in popularity to such an extent that there were about 650 in the capital by 1714. And while some had a special clientele (Will's, for instance, catering for literary men, Old Man's for soldiers), many gave shopkeepers the opportunity to rub shoulders with peers.

By the reign of Anne, the habit of attending coffee-houses had spread to almost all the larger provincial towns and with it the habit of reading the periodicals and newspapers that were so distinctive a feature of the early eighteenth century (see p. 236). Defoe sent 100 copies of each edition of his *Review* to Norwich alone. On Thursday 24 May 1711, Swift devoted his *Examiner*

173. The Baths at Bath. Engraving by J. Johnson, 1672.
The health-giving properties of Bath's waters set the town on the path to prosperity. The town of Spa, near Liège, visited by innumerable ailing Englishmen in the seventeenth century, gave its name to the taking of waters;

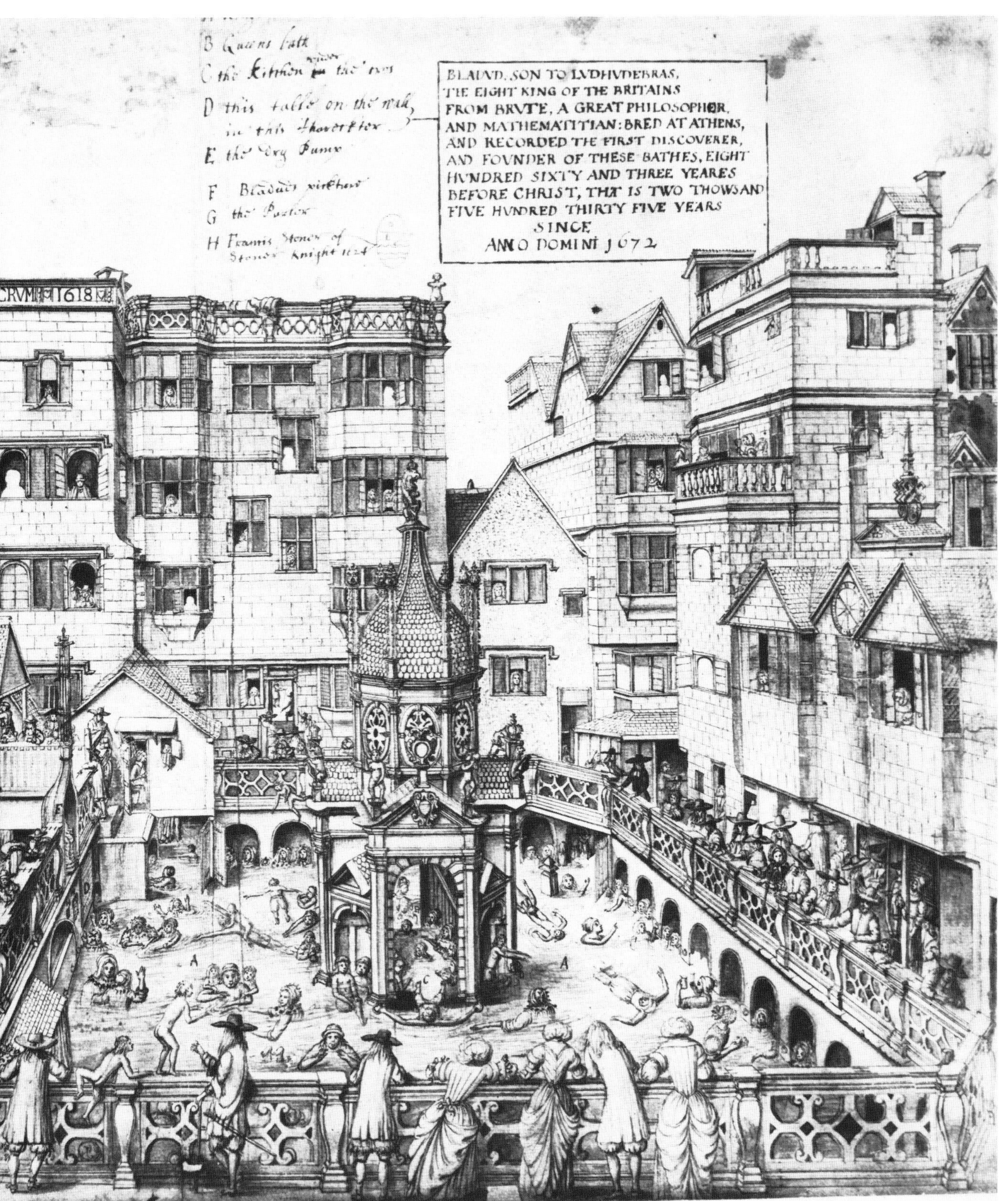

but when the Thirty Years War made the journey there difficult, England began to look to her own resources. By 1663 there was a 'Spa' at Knaresborough in Yorkshire.

to the problems of the Church of England. That same evening his opinions would be dissected by fellow clergy at Truby's and by scholars at the Grecian coffee-house. By Saturday they could be perused in a reading room in Bath or a parlour in Stamford's resplendent Bull Inn, athwart the Great North Road. By Sunday a High Church parson in Yorkshire would reconvene his flock after evening service at the vicarage, 'where he first reads over the paper, and then comments upon the text; and all week after carries it about with him'. Thus the best periodicals could bridge the narrowing cultural divides between London and the provinces, or between educated (and sometimes not-so-educated) townsmen and countrymen. In their content, distribution and readership can be seen a microcosm of the controversies and values, characteristic social conventions, and something of the cohesion as well as the divisions, that were an important part of England's hallmark at the close of the Stuart age.

174. W. Westley, 'The North Prospect of the Square of Birmingham', 1732. Engraving.
The Square, built as a select residential area, was begun about 1700, and several houses were built in Anne's reign. Birmingham experienced increases of wealth and population in the later seventeenth century, thanks largely to the development of its metal industry.

175 (opposite). J. H. Brandon, *William III*, *c.* 1699. Oil on canvas, $33\frac{1}{4} \times 27\frac{3}{4}$ in. (84.5 × 70.5 cm.). Castle Amerongen, Apeldoorn, The Netherlands.

IE MAIN TIENDRAY

CHAPTER TEN

The English at Home

Family and Household

Writers of the seventeenth century often referred to the family as a 'little Commonwealth', a microcosm of the paternalist state. In it, a benevolent but authoritarian father played the role of king, ruling his wife, his children and his servants for the greater glory of God and of that greater Commonwealth of England in which the family was the smallest and most fundamental unit. Perhaps reality often tarnished this ideal, but there is no doubt that the nature of the family and the household needs to be understood if the society to which they belonged is to be fully comprehended.

Apart from the fact that it often contained servants, the typical English family of the seventeenth century was similar in its structure to the family of the late twentieth century. That is to say, it was a nuclear family comprised of parents and children who lived in their own household quite separately from the kin of either husband or wife. It was even unusual for aged parents to live with their married children, though that was probably due to low life expectancy as much as to social custom. This physical separation from the wider family of the kin, which was common in northern and western Europe but unusual elsewhere in the world, has been seen as an important factor in explaining the spirit of individualism that is such a fundamental feature of Western European culture. It is also clear that separate family formation had considerable economic significance. Each new family formed a new economic unit, an independent farm or workshop or a source of labour for others. It also formed a new unit of consumption which would require its own furniture, bedding and cooking equipment.

The typical Stuart family was quite a small unit, not as small as a modern family, but much smaller than one might expect in the absence of modern techniques of birth control. Household listings demonstrate that the typical family of the poor contained no more than four or five people. The families of the middling and upper ranks of society were rather larger, and considerably

176. *The Cholmondeley Sisters, c.* 1600–10.
Oil on wood, 35 × 68 in. (89 × 172.7 cm.). London, Tate Gallery.
An inscription on the painting suggests that the sisters were born on the same day, married on the same day, and gave birth on the same day.

larger if one counts servants as members of the family as contemporaries usually did. However, even these privileged groups in society shared in a trend for small families to get even smaller as the Stuart period progresses, a development probably of considerable importance in explaining the undoubted rise in material prosperity.

One factor that helps to explain these basic features of the family is the age at which people married. Great emphasis was placed by contemporaries on marrying late rather than early in order to improve the chances of acquiring sufficient economic competence to support and raise a family. Such advice seems generally to have been followed and the average age at marriage for the great majority of people of both sexes was in their mid or late twenties. Late marriage might be occasioned by the need to wait to inherit a farm or a workshop. But even without such expectations, late marriage made very good sense. It meant that savings could be accumulated to finance a small business or at least to furnish a house, and perhaps even more important it was the most effective means of limiting the size of one's family. The average age at the time of marriage rose throughout the period and demographers have suggested that this was a collective response to the hard times during the first half of the century. Such a motivation cannot be proved, but whatever the reason a later marriage certainly meant that there were likely to be fewer children and a smaller family and provided the basis for a better standard of living. The fact that there were quite considerable variations between classes in the age of women at marriage tends to support this hypothesis. Men in the upper and middling ranks of society, who had less need to fear a large family, tended to marry brides much younger than themselves and much younger on average than the brides of the great majority of the population. The brides of better-off men tended to be in their late teens or early twenties, one good reason why families were larger in these ranks of society than amongst the poor.

The age at marriage was a matter of social custom, economic constraint or individual choice. The other major factor that tended to restrict family size was seen as the hand of God. In the absence of contraception, one would expect mothers to give birth about once in every two years with the intervals becoming longer at the end of the child-bearing years some time in their late thirties or early forties. This is certainly the pattern that demographic studies have revealed and it was the typical experience of married women to undergo five, six, seven or more pregnancies despite their late age of marriage. However, the poor diet and health of the mothers themselves meant that many of these

177. Margaret Cavendish, *Natures Pictures* (1656), frontispiece. *Margaret Cavendish, wife and biographer of the royalist general the Duke of Newcastle, wrote poems, plays and philosophical treatises. She 'kept a great many young ladies about her person, who occasionally wrote what she dictated. Some of them slept in a room contiguous to that in which her grace lay, and were ready, at the call of her bell, to rise any hour of the night to write down her conceptions lest they should escape her memory.' Perhaps those are the ladies here practising the growing art of conversation with her.*

pregnancies were never brought to term, while the children that were born were subject to such appallingly high levels of infant and child mortality that in many places it took two live births to produce one adult. Rates of infant and child mortality actually got worse in the course of this period, mainly through the impact of new diseases such as smallpox, or new strains of old diseases such as influenza. This grim harvest of small children, together with the high age at marriage, meant that the typical family rarely had more than three children alive at the same time, while families with one, two or no children at all were very common.

178. James Thornhill, *The Triumph of Peace and Liberty*, *c.* 1708. Part of the ceiling of the Painted Hall, Royal Naval College, Greenwich.
Thornhill, of a Dorset family and the grandson of a Cromwellian colonel, is best known for his Greenwich paintings, which were commissioned by Queen Anne. William, with Mary beside him, tramples arbitrary power, while peace, piety and other virtues attend him. Above, Hercules and Minerva destroy the vices. Thornhill was also employed in many country houses and, in spite of Wren's opposition, decorated the dome of St. Paul's with paintings illustrating the life of St. Paul.

179 (opposite). Burghley House, Lincolnshire, the Heaven Room, painted by Antonio Verrio, 1695/6.
Verrio, born in southern Italy, learned his art as a decorative painter in Naples and in France. Charles II brought him to England to re-establish the tapestry works at Mortlake that had been suspended during the civil wars; and although that enterprise failed, Verrio found favour with Charles. He retained the crown's favour under James II but after the Revolution declined all appointments under William III, until in 1695 his patron the Earl of Exeter induced him to accept an important commission for a series of decorative paintings at Hampton Court. About the same time he produced for Exeter the series represented here.

180. John Souch, *Sir Thomas Aston at the Deathbed of his Wife*, 1635. Oil on canvas, 78 × 107 in. (198 × 271.5 cm.).
Manchester City Art Galleries.
An allegorical presentation of life and death in a gentry family of Cheshire. The family arms are at the top. On Sir Thomas's left, beyond the symbol of death in his hand, is his wife, Magdalene, daughter of Sir John Poulteney. She died on 2 June 1635; the painting is dated 30 September. At the foot of the bed is her living self. On Sir Thomas's right, holding a navigational or surveying instrument, stands his son Thomas, the only survivor among the four children of the marriage; he died in 1637. The tablecloth is a painted cotton cloth from Masulapatan, bearing a lute and a globe. In 1639 Sir Thomas took as his second wife the heiress of Sir Henry Willoughby; she produced the only male child to survive him. Sir Thomas was a leading royalist in his county during the civil war, and died of war wounds in 1645. He was admired for his integrity and learning. The painter, John Souch, lived in Chester.

Death struck adults in their prime as well as children. It was fairly unusual for both parents to be alive when their children reached adulthood. Second and subsequent marriages were therefore common, with the result that step-parents, single parent families and complex families containing the children of several different unions were probably even more common in the seventeenth century than in the twentieth century, the difference being that death rather than divorce caused the break-up of families. Divorce was virtually impossible in Stuart society. Many couples separated, formally or informally, but neither partner could remarry while the former partner was alive. Choice of partner was there-

fore 'till death do us part', as the marriage service enjoined.

Those girls and boys who did survive the illnesses of childhood were not likely to spend very long at home. Schooling was either intermittent or non-existent for the majority of the English population and few parents below the middling ranks in society could afford to keep a child in idleness much beyond the age of ten; then it was time for the child to work (see p. 45). Some found work in their parents' homes, helping on the farm or assisting with the knitting, spinning, weaving and other manufacturing tasks which provided an increasing proportion of the population with a living. The majority of children, however, left their own homes and spent the next fifteen or so years before marriage in the home of their employer as a servant or perhaps as an apprentice.

Service took many forms in Stuart England. All families of the middling rank and above, and even many artisan families, employed at least one (normally female) domestic servant. Many employed several, while the largest households of the aristocracy might have a staff of forty or fifty. Nearly all farmers, except the very smallest, employed living-in farm servants and most tradesmen and manufacturers took on apprentices who would also live in their masters' households, as would many of their journeymen who had completed their apprenticeship. Servants of one sort or another were a majority of all people in the age-groups between the early teens and the mid-twenties and it is this ubiquity of service which provides the strongest contrast between the household structure of Stuart England and that of the later twentieth century. Servants rarely stayed with one master for long unless they had been formally apprenticed. Many changed masters almost every year, moving from village to village, picking up a variety of skills and saving a part of their miniscule wage in preparation for that day when they could leave the world of service, marry and set up a household of their own. The end of service could mean a considerable fall in their standard of living, since servants in farm families or in the homes of the middling and upper ranks of society were likely to be much better fed and housed than were the married members of the working population.

Some boys and girls went into service with families whose social status was similar to their own, and in this respect service was a valuable means of balancing the labour requirements of different families. A farmer with several children, for instance, might keep some of them at home to work on his own farm, but send others out into service with farmers whose children were too young or too old or too few to satisfy his

181. The Fettiplace Monument, Swinbrook Church, Oxfordshire. Marble and alabaster.
The tomb was built in 1686 by Edmund Fettiplace to bear the memorials to himself and his two predecessors. The monument was designed by the Oxford sculptor William Bird.

needs for labour. However, most children went into service with families of higher wealth and status, a fact that probably helped the dissemination of new ideas and tastes downwards from the gentry and middling ranks to the poorer majority of the population. This aspect of service also helped to ensure that the households of the wealthy were larger than those of the poor; so did the fact that the daughters of the middling to upper families generally stayed at home until they married, and that the sons of those families enjoyed a longer full-time education than the children of the poor. This education might be at a boarding-school, which would

182. A Charles II coromandel lacquer cabinet on a giltwood stand.
This piece reflects the growing trade, wealth and sophistication of later seventeenth-century England. The cabinet was imported from China, while the stand was made in England, in a style that reflects the strong influence of the French Baroque.

183. The year-going spring clock made by Thomas Tompion for George III, *c.* 1695–1700. London, British Museum.
This celebrated clock is the masterpiece by the greatest English clockmaker of the seventeenth century. Born in Bedfordshire, Tompion came to London in 1671, where he met the scientist Robert Hooke, and he was soon trying out Hooke's ideas for improvement in horology. Tompion gained royal commissions through the sponsorship of Hooke, who recorded in his diary his discussion with Charles II about the performance of a watch by Tompion incorporating a then revolutionary spring balance. William III's clock is of veneered ebony with silver mounts.

'Wheatley in the Valley. Cuddesdon on the Hill'

A RURAL PARISH AND ITS TOWNSHIPS

1 Cuddesdon Parish Church, south-west view, engraving of 1823.
The church originally served six townships but was left 'stranded' in one of the smaller villages of the parish and was largely taken over by the resident bishop of Oxford.

Cuddesdon in Oxfordshire stands on a hill in an old ecclesiastical parish of the same name. The parish was a large one in a varied landscape (see map). It contained within its boundaries five active villages and hamlets which had very different histories. These differences led to tensions between the villages and especially between Cuddesdon township and that of Wheatley in the valley below. Cuddesdon, the mother village of the parish, can be described as a 'closed' one: that is, its social, economic and political life was dominated by a lord whose presence imposed some restrictions on its development. Wheatley was a growing, 'open' village untroubled by a lord and having plenty of scope for the exercise of initiative by its inhabitants. This contrast was reflected in an ecclesiastical squabble in the late 1620s and early 1630s.

One of Cuddesdon's disadvantages in its fight to preserve its historic dignity as the village with the parish church was that its population was small. Only nine substantial farmers paid the 1665 Hearth Tax; and by enclosing most of their farming land, they had left little scope for initiative, expansion or immigration into the township and had consolidated its 'closed' status. Two other features further consolidated it: the manor, the ancient estate of Cuddesdon, which was the subject of much dispute and litigation between various claimants until the 1690s, dominated the land and its tenancies; and from 1632 the bishops of Oxford settled in the village, and built themselves a palace there which further cramped the style of village life. Cuddesdon became a shrinking settlement. It looked with envy at the other townships in the parish, such as Denton and Chippinghurst to the south, which had more settled lordships often with long-established tenants in the manor houses and a more balanced agricultural organization; Denton, for instance, had 15 householders paying Hearth Tax. But Wheatley provided the sharpest contrast.

Unlike the squire-ridden settlements of Holton, Waterperry and Cuddesdon, Wheatley was an 'open' village where property was subdivided among a thriving and growing population. The explanation for this lay in the roads: the traveller from Oxford to London had to traverse high ground through or near Wheatley, where the Thame had to be forded or bridged. Likewise, those travelling towards Worcester or south Wales avoided the drop into the Thames valley at Oxford, kept to the higher ground and passed through or near Wheatley. The servicing of this traffic by the village pubs and inns generated economic diversity unknown in the rest of the parish. Wheatley did not have the manorial conflicts and burdens of Cuddesdon. Its medieval manorial lords were distinguished but absent; its subsequent ones were both absent and undistinguished. In 1590 the inhabitants declared that 'they had never heard of a manor'. When the Archdales became resident lords in the early seventeenth century, they were not a gentle family but prosperous farmers from Denton in the parish. Sebastian Smythe bought Wheatley manor and added it to his Cuddesdon manor in 1682, but neither he nor his successors lived in Wheatley Manor House.

Wheatley was thriving and populous, and had more than 283 communicants in 1612. There were 31 cottages newly built in 1581 and in 1625 there were 77 houses on the High Street and Crown Road. There was encroachment on the waste, an indication of a population and building boom. A large population brought diverse agriculture, and a mixture of closed and open fields held off restrictive enclosures. Even in 1813 there were 920 acres still not enclosed. In the seventeenth century there were many sheep and a variety of agricultural products, which fostered a healthier and more flexible economy than those of the neighbouring villages. Quarrying for stone and clay was long-established and there were at least five large inns at work by the end of the century. This variety produced a more sophisticated local government than was found in the other townships. Wheatley had a well-established and well-administered system of Overseers of the Poor who acted as local government officers in all walks of village life. Appointed by the Justices of the Peace, their job demanded hard work and expert local knowledge. They relieved hardship, disposed of local charities and collected local taxes. There was also provision for diverse social services. Shrouds were handed out in the typhus epidemic of 1643, and for Elizabeth Kerbie in 1649 there was a pair of shoes valued at 2s. 8d. Abraham Archdale's £15 in 1647 helped clothe the needy and also local rents raised from Richard Munt for using 'part of the twi-

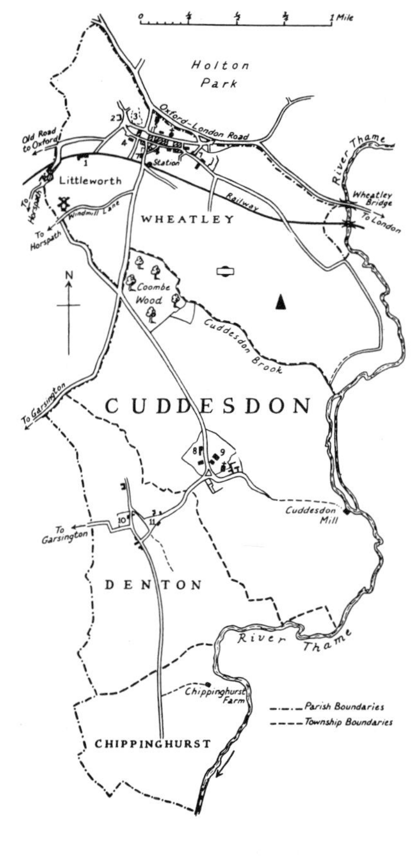

2 Map of ancient parish of Cuddesdon (from the Victoria County History, vol. 5). The ground rises steeply on all sides except the east, while Cuddesdon Brook, and heavy afforestation in the past, marked a natural boundary between Wheatley and Cuddesdon townships.

gyard'. Rates were levied on the community as well. Thomas Symes and Greyland Page, both members of the village elite, were Overseers from 1639 to 1646. Symes paid for five hearths in 1665. Social and political life was controlled by families such as these, not by the lord.

Wheatley's clash with Cuddesdon arose over the chapel at Wheatley and its relationship to the parish church at Cuddesdon. There had been a chapel in Wheatley since at least the fifteenth century; the villagers paid a curate to take services for them and elected their own chapel wardens. These established communal freedoms were resented by Cuddesdon. In 1629 Wheatley defended the right to elect a churchwarden to its chapel 'without any interposing meddling or challenging any right or interest in the said election by the Vicar of Cuddesdon ... or by the parishoners ... of Cuddesdon or Denton'. In 1632 there was a proposal to consecrate a chapel. This may have been the old one, but was more probably a new one. The proposal underlined Wheatley's needs of worship, which were not properly satisfied by dependence on a church two miles away in another village. The plan was hotly opposed in Cuddesdon village where there were protests against 'the inconveniences which are likely to grow to the church, the vicar and inhabitants ... by the consecration of the chapel of Wheatley without saving and reserving of the ancient right, immunities, usages and customs due to the said church and vicar'. The mother village protested in vain, and the junior but stronger village won its point.

3 The 'King and Queen', Wheatley. This is one of the inns which brought Wheatley most of its distinctive prosperity.

4 Cuddesdon Palace before it was destroyed in 1644. Eighteenth-century engraving, based on an earlier drawing. This substantial dwelling was destroyed during the civil war when there was much local military activity.

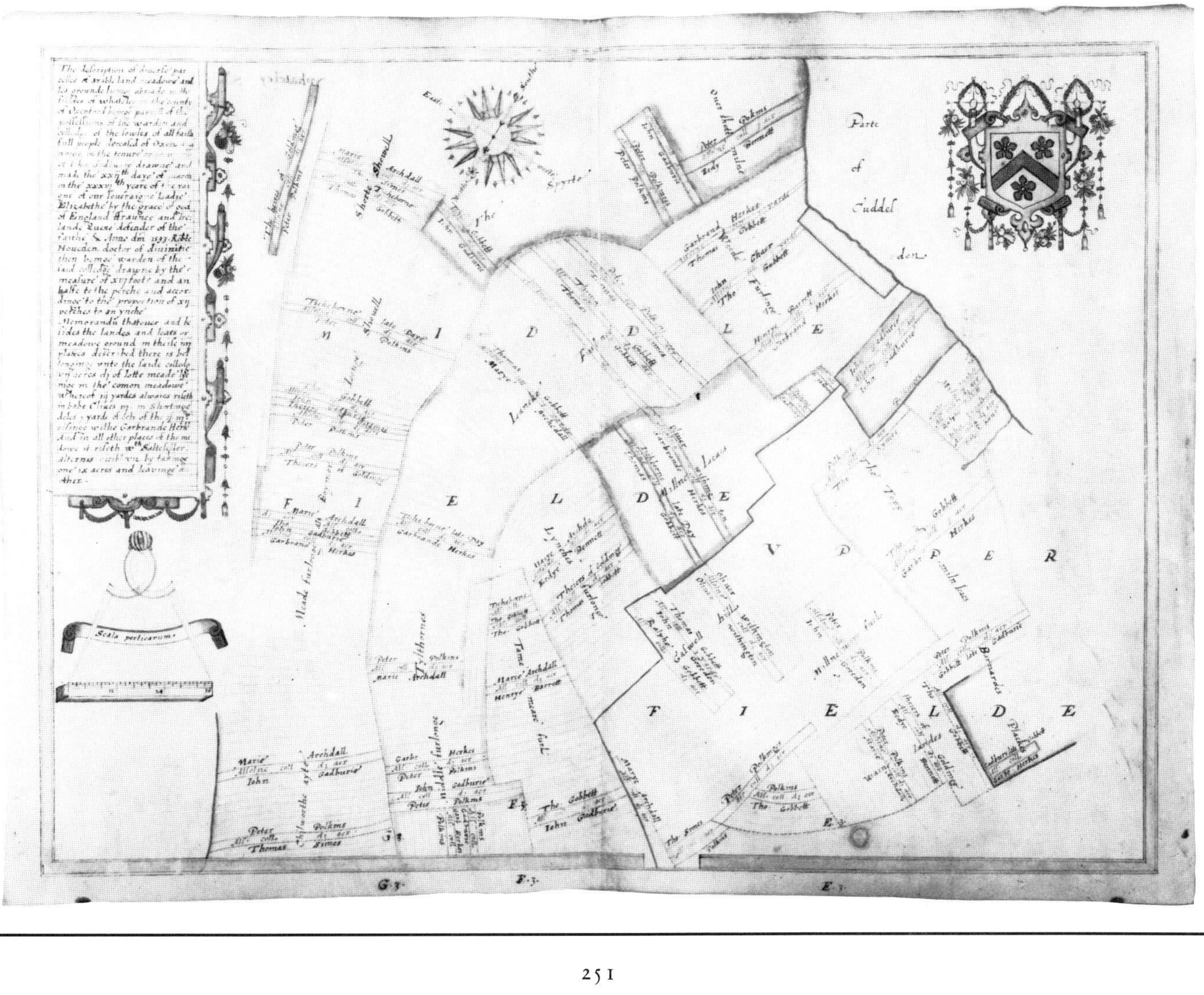

5 Map of the Fields of Wheatley (Lye, Middle and Upper Fields, 1593–4). Oxford, All Soul's College.

PREVIOUS PAGES

184. Topiary garden, Levens Hall, Cumbria.
The topiary garden was laid out c. *1700 by Guillaume Beaumont for Colonel James Graham. Yet the tide of fashion was turning against the seventeenth-century love of artificial gardens in favour of a closer proximity to nature. In 1712 the* Spectator *hinted at the new taste by complaining that 'our British gardens . . . instead of humouring nature, love to deviate from it as much as possible. Our trees rise in cones, globes and pyramids. We see the marks of the scissors upon every plant and bush . . .'*

185. J. Siberechts, *Bifrons Park, Kent, c.* 1705–10 (but perhaps earlier). Oil on canvas, 34½ × 52¼ in. (86.8 × 132.5 cm.). New Haven. Conn., Yale Center for British Art, Paul Mellon Collection.
*The house, which changed owners a number of times in the later Stuart period, took its name from its two fronts (*bis fronts*), and was notable for its garden statuary (visible here). Patrixbourne church is nearby.*

186. Matthias Reed, *View of Whitehaven*, 1738.
Oil on canvas, 42 × 72in. (106.7 × 183 cm.).
Whitehaven Museum and Art Gallery.
Unlike many new or expanding towns in the later seventeenth century, the colliery town of Whitehaven experienced planned growth. The growth was guided by the owner of the colliery, Sir John Lowther, who fulfilled his declared aim of 'building a regular town', and created the harbour.

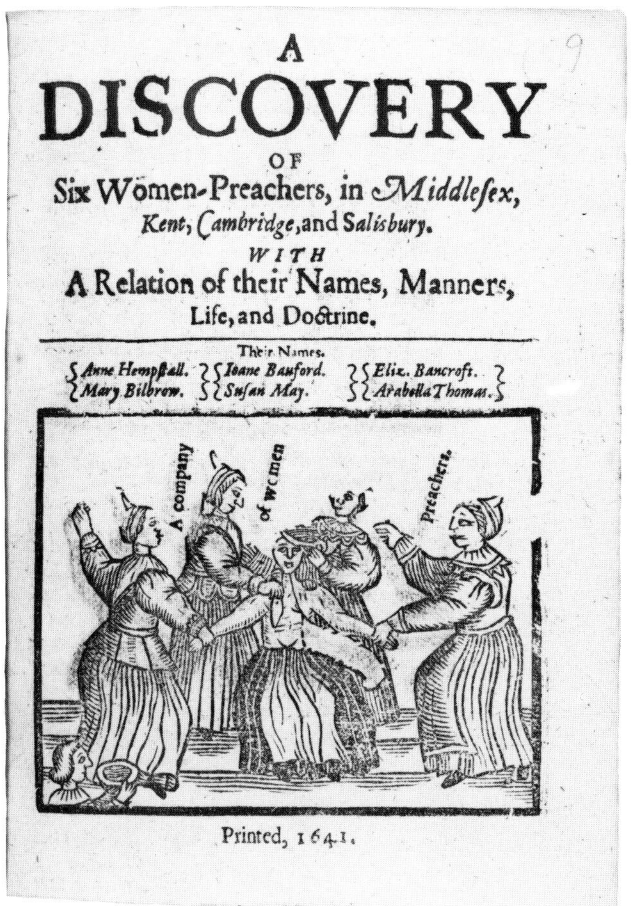

A
DISCOVERY
OF
Six Women-Preachers, in Middlesex, Kent, Cambridge, and Salisbury.
WITH
A Relation of their Names, Manners, Life, and Doctrine.

Their Names.
Anne Hempstall. Mary Bilbrow. Ioane Bauford. Susan May. Eliz. Bancroft. Arabella Thomas.

A company of women Preachers.

Printed, 1641.

187. *A Discovery of Six Women Preachers*, a pamphlet of 1641.
Although such pamphlets as this may tell us more about people's fears than about the events purportedly described, there were women preaching regularly in London by 1641. The upheavals of the Puritan Revolution produced a spate of women preachers and prophetesses, and the civil war sects created a novel forum for female self-expression.

also of course take them away from home; but otherwise these boys were likely to stay at home until they were 16 or 17, which was the normal age to begin a professional or commercial apprenticeship or go to university.

Love and Marriage

Contemporaries often complained of the lewd behaviour of their servants, but it seems that they were doing them an injustice. Though not a certainty, all evidence suggests that girls in particular were remarkably chaste and became even more chaste as this period continued. Indeed, it seems probable that the vast majority delayed their sexual initiation until their mid-twenties and that their first sexual partner was either already their husband or likely to become their husband fairly soon, quite often after they had proved their fertility by becoming pregnant. The evidence for such an assertion is the high age at marriage, the absence of effective contraception, the low level of illegitimacy (which was getting even lower), and the fact that pregnant women, who were interrogated by parish authorities worried by the thought of having to raise a bastard on the rates, nearly always turned out to have been well into their twenties before they lost their virginity. Such behaviour suggests that the sex drive is not quite the constant that some people brought up in the modern, more liberal world think it is, and that it can be contained by the norms of a society which sees good reason to do so.

The choice of a marriage partner was a fundamental decision that was likely to make a great deal of difference to the individual's chances in life. Historians have tended to discuss the factors governing this decision in terms of a conflict between parents and children – parents wishing to arrange marriages and the children often being unhappy with the particular arrangement. Conflict probably did occur quite often in circumstances where parents had property that they intended to bequeath to their children or that would pass on to them at marriage. Family strategy might well have clashed with the inclination of the children and there are well-documented examples of children being disinherited for failing to observe their parents' wishes. However, for a number of reasons it would be wrong to exaggerate such conflicts.

There is good evidence that society generally accepted that children had the right of veto on their parents' choice of spouse and that such a right became stronger towards the end of the Stuart period. It is also clear that in most cases there was unlikely to be great disagreement, since both parents and children tended to put material considerations above those of love; it was a common viewpoint that 'property begets affection' and that love should follow marriage rather than precede it. The dowry or portion of a young unmarried woman rather than her good looks or other qualities was likely to be the main subject of discussion both by young men and their fathers. Girls might have suffered more than boys in respect of choice of partner, though again it is easy to exaggerate. The wills of middle-class Londoners show that they normally provided their daughters with a legacy to be paid at marriage. They rarely made such a legacy conditional on the surviving mother's consent to the daughter's marriage partner; when they did, they normally only stipulated that a girl marrying without consent should not receive her legacy until she reached the age of 24.

Parental influence was likely to be of even less significance amongst that majority of the population that had little or no expectation of gaining property through marriage. Neither the law nor the Church required parental consent for the great majority who married over the age of 21. This did not mean that adult children might not ask for their parents' consent out of custom or respect, but low expectation of life meant that many, probably most, parents would not have been alive to give that consent even if their children wanted it. With both generations marrying in their late twenties, parents were likely to be nearly 60 before their eldest children got married and not many people reached the age of 60 in this world of high mortality. Finally, the institution of service meant that many children of the poor would have almost forgotten the parental home that they had left some fifteen years or more before marriage, a home that was probably some distance from the village or town in which they finally chose their spouse. This choice was more likely to be based on romantic inclination and sexual experiment than the choice made by those in the middling ranks of society, but it was still a choice heavily influenced by economic considerations. Both husband and wife could expect to work and work hard at this social level and it would seem probable that it was for their economic and domestic skills rather than good looks that they chose each other.

What can be said about the state of matrimony itself at this time? This is difficult and poorly documented territory, but it is possible to make a few points. First, there was no equality before the law, nor indeed in any other respect, between husband and wife. 'Women . . . so soon as they are married are wholly at the will and disposition of the husband,' wrote Edward Chamberlayne, the author of a popular guide to English society which went through several editions in the second half of the seventeenth century. 'They can own no goods, not even their clothes.' A wife was a chattel who had no control over the disposition of her dowry or of her children. She could make no contract since she had no full legal personality. Her status was indeed more that of a higher-ranking servant than of an equal and her duty was to obey her husband. All this is in very strong contrast to the position of the widow. She had clear legal rights to a portion, normally a third, of her former husband's property, was a full legal person and indeed played a fundamental role in English society as the head of a sizeable minority of all households. Such a satisfactory independence was, however, reserved for the widows of the prosperous. The widows of the poor just got poorer, since a woman's wage was rarely sufficient to maintain a family in any comfort if at all.

[13]

This Lordſhip which *Adam* by Command had over the whole World, and by Right deſcending from him the *Patriarchs* did enjoy, was as large and ample as the Abſoluteſt Dominion of any *Monarch* which hath been ſince the Creation: For Dominion of Life and Death, we find that *Judah* the Father pronounced Sentence of Death againſt *Thamar* his Daughter-in-law, for playing the Harlot; *Bring her forth* (ſaith he) *that ſhe may be burnt.* Touching War, we ſee that *Abraham* commanded an Army of 318 Souldiers of his own Family. And *Eſau* met his Brother *Jacob* with 400 Men at Arms. For matter of Peace, *Abraham* made a League with *Abimilech*, and ratify'd the Articles with an Oath. Theſe Acts of Judging in *Capital Crimes*, of making *War*, and concluding *Peace*, are the chiefeſt Marks of *Sovereignty* that are found in any *Monarch.*

(5) Not only until the *Flood*, but after it, this *Patriarchal Power* did continue, as the very Name *Patriarch* doth in part prove. The three Sons of *Noah* had the whole World divided amongſt them

188. A page from Sir Robert Filmer, *Patriarcha* (1680).
The success of Filmer's book reveals deeply-held feelings both about the family and about politics. Written under Charles I, the work was circulated widely in manuscript but was published only posthumously, in 1680, as a high Tory contribution to the arguments of the exclusion crisis. Filmer's premises were conventional enough: kingship had grown up from the association of families, and the function of kings was analogous to that of fathers. He put those premises to novel and startling use. First, he maintained that just as heads of families enjoyed the right of undisputed obedience from their members, so kings could exact comparable submission from their subjects. Secondly, he argued that the powers which God had bestowed on Adam, the first father-king, had descended to the Stuarts. The Whig reaction against Filmer produced two famous books, John Locke's Two Treatises of Government *and Algernon Sidney's* Discourses concerning Government. *Locke protested that 'there was never so much glib nonsense put together in well sounding English' as in Filmer's writings. In Locke's and Sidney's eyes the authority of kings derived from, and was limited by, the rights which the people had invested in them.*

189. The Bradford Cup, a wine cup of 1634, maker's mark HS with a star below, 1634.
The initials W.B. are those of William Bradford, one of the Pilgrim Fathers, who sailed to New England on the Speedwell *in 1620 and was elected governor of the colony in 1621. In 1606 he had belonged to a 'Brownist' or 'separatist' congregation on the Yorkshire-Nottinghamshire border, whose members, unlike most Puritans, could not bring themselves to worship within the Church of England. After a spell of imprisonment for his nonconformity he emigrated to Holland, where there was greater freedom of worship. In 1620 he was a moving spirit in the departure of the pilgrims, who had been granted a patent by the Privy Council for a strip of land in New England, and in whose ranks separatists were well represented. In 1629 another patent entitled the colonists to implement laws which they had designed according to the 'ancient platform of God's law' and the laws of England. A learned man with literary tastes, Bradford's strength of personality gave stability to the early colony.*

The legal subjection of women does not necessarily mean that they were unhappy or that marriage was a bleak and loveless state. Indeed, a contemporary proverb claimed that England was 'the paradise of women', despite the inequality of wives. This may merely be an example of seventeenth-century male chauvinism, or it may reflect the fact that women were treated even worse elsewhere. 'Such is the good nature of Englishmen towards their wives', wrote Chamberlayne, echoing a popular proverb, 'that if there were a bridge over into England . . . it is thought all the women in Europe would run hither.' It is difficult to judge the truth of such comments. The conduct books which provided guides to social behaviour made it clear that the husband was the senior partner; but they also emphasized love and mutual respect as the basis of marriage and surviving diaries and correspondence show that this was not just a pious wish.

Many husbands and wives certainly did love and respect each other in Stuart England. One school of historians, led by Lawrence Stone, even suggests that they were loving each other more as the period continued, and that, especially amongst the gentry and the urban bourgeoisie, something approaching the modern ideal of a companionate marriage based on affection was developing with a corresponding decline in the subordination of the wife to the husband. This is an attractive thesis and is supported by a certain amount of contemporary comment. It is, however, impossible either to sustain or refute it in detail and indeed it seems doubtful whether it is possible to generalize about love in marriage at all in this way. It would be a bold man or woman who claimed to be able to prove whether marital love had increased or decreased in the twentieth century, despite the arrival of the 'modern marriage', and it is clearly even more difficult to make such assertions about the married life of ancestors three centuries ago.

Parents and Children

The same school of historians who herald the arrival of the affectionate bourgeois marriage during the reigns of the later Stuarts see a fundamental change in attitudes towards children at the same time; though such a thesis requires the deployment of an argument which makes the previous treatment of children quite incredibly harsh and cruel. Children, it is said, had not been thought of as children, but as miniature adults or servants subject to the unloving authority of their parents. They were not loved because parents were not prepared to invest emotion in a child who might so easily die. They were beaten unmercifully, both to ensure the discipline of the household and to instil a realization of their basic sinful nature, bring them to a state of repentance and save their souls. But some time in the late seventeenth century, according to this view, things began to change, at least in the homes of the gentry and of the middle classes. Parents began to love their children more and to beat them less. Kindness, encouragement and tenderness began to appear in children's lives and a reasoned rebuke replaced the harsh word and the rod as the means of correction.

Much emphasis is placed by such writers on the publication of John Locke's *Thoughts on Education* in 1693. This work is seen both as a reflection of changing attitudes and as an immense influence on subsequent generations of parents. Locke stressed that children should be trained early and put in awe of their parents, but emphasized esteem and disgrace as reward and punishment, with beating reserved only for cases of extreme stubbornness or rebellion. He also recommended a fairly rugged regime on the grounds that if the child is once used to hardship, hardship will never hurt. 'Plenty of open air, exercise and sleep', he suggested. 'Plain diet, no wine or strong drink, not too warm clothing, especially the head and feet kept cold, and the feet often exposed to wet.' Locke's book is certainly interesting and contains many sound ideas, but there is no way of telling how many people followed his advice, nor indeed any advice offered by other writers of the period. Modern studies show that parents do not slavishly follow the recommendations of baby books and it is doubtful if seventeenth-century parents were any different.

The analysis of sentiment is a popular subject for contemporary historians but by its very nature it is one fraught with considerable difficulty. All that is really known is what a few, mainly middle and upper class people wrote in their diaries, letters or autobiographies and it is not a certainty that they were even telling the truth. Again, it may be the expression of sentiment rather than sentiment itself that was changing. The growth of literacy and of a vernacular literature were important factors in the development of the expression of sentiment: people learned different forms of address and different and more effective ways of describing their emotions, and this can possibly lead historians to believe that their relationships and emotions had changed.

The most recent work on attitudes to children in the Stuart period suggests that previous writers have exaggerated the cruelty and indifference of parents who are now seen as relatively caring and loving people, with only some bad exceptions that have been pin-pointed by writers wanting to paint a bleak picture. The lives

'Well Furnished with all Sorts of Provisions'

LIFE IN SEVENTEENTH-CENTURY TEWKESBURY, GLOUCESTERSHIRE

1 Page at the start of the Tewkesbury entry in Smith's 'Names & Surnames of all the able and sufficient Men in body fit for his Majesty's Service in the Wars, within the County of Gloucester, 1608'. Gloucestershire County Record Office. Smith came from North Nibley and served Lord Berkeley, the Lord Lieutenant of Gloucestershire, in 1608. The first few lines read as follows:
'"The Burrowe of Tewkesbury: Whereoff
John Geast mercer 1.
Nicholas Weaver pedlar 2. p.
James Bridges servant to Nicholas wever. 2.
Thomas Collens haberdasher. 2. p.
Richard Wever pewterer. 2. p. sub.

Thomas Wetherle 1.	Servants of the
Rowland Heath 1.	said Richard Wever."'

The abbreviations of numbers and letters alongside the names indicate the man's age range and military potential. Thus 1. = 'to bee about twenty'; 2. = 'to be about fforty'; p. = 'to bee of the tallest stature fitt to make a pykeman'.

John Smith, a lawyer for the aristocratic Berkeley family in Gloucestershire, left an especially detailed muster-roll for that county of 1608, and in it a valuable document for social and economic history. The roll enumerates the able-bodied men thought capable of fighting for the county should the need arise; ages and trades are listed as well. Smith's nineteenth-century editor, bearing in mind that most of those listed were fairly humble, remarked that few readers 'would really feel gratified by meeting with an ancestor among them'. Yet these rolls give a strikingly real picture of communities in the county.

In Tewkesbury, the second largest town in Gloucestershire, Smith counted 453 able-bodied men. There were probably about 2,000 adults in the town by the late seventeenth century. It was a lively town near the confluence of the Rivers Severn and Avon, both navigable though the latter only from the 1630s. It was a natural road junction as well. There was a wide economic base for the town: land and sea met on Tewkesbury's quays and the settlement was almost surrounded by waterways (liable to flood) which stretched around the old Abbey precinct. The town looked, and still looks, attractive, with its half-timbering and side entrances off its alleyways. But Tewkesbury's spacious prosperity and its status as a regional centre are best understood from its riversides: it had four bridges, and ferries plied across the Severn.

2 Lilley's Alley, Tewkesbury. Characteristic of the cramped streets were the alleyways and courts where the entrances to the buildings were to be found.

Economic strength was reflected in a municipal independence which was no doubt good for business. The Charter of 1575 was reissued and enlarged in 1605, and again in 1610 when the manorial rights were purchased by the Corporation from the crown. The town had its own gaol, school and justices of the peace. But there were limits to the borough's independence. As in most seventeenth-century towns, the favour of local landowning families was important. Tewkesbury's MPs were usually chosen not from the townsmen, but from neighbouring families such as the Hickes.

The muster-roll illustrates the economic variety of a town where trade and industry matched the surrounding rich agriculture. There was farming due east in Oldbury Field and extensive pasturage for the livestock was still kept by the burgesses. Market gardening and tobacco-growing (a novelty) flourished, both activities threatened only by the growth of nearby Evesham and by moral objections to tobacco. But there were few farmers in the town. George Mann of Barton Street was the only husbandman mustered, although there were seven listed as yeomen. The carrying of grain rather than its cultivation was important, and Tewkesbury was not a prominent milling centre. The four Avon mills which it did boast were owned by the neighbouring gentry family, the Pophams. No miller was mustered by Smith.

Thomas Lowe of High Street was one of 31 'mariners' mustered; others included Richard Cotton of Church Street, one of four 'trowmen' (boatmen operating on the Severn) in that street alone. The three carriers may well have been rivermen as well. It is said that nearly half the down-river cargoes from Gloucester went in Tewkesbury boats. There was boat-building, and coals were shipped into the quays. Tewkesbury mariners were found in Irish ports. This was an international as well as an estuary trade and the cargoes were varied. Grain and malt were predominant, followed by stockings, chairs and candles. There was a salty tang about the town.

The Wednesday and Saturday markets on the streets traded in grain, cattle, wool and yarns. Four industries stand out in the muster-roll: clothing, leather, malt and woodworking. The cloth and clothing trades employed 74 men, including 27 tailors and eight weavers, and 16 tailors lived in Church Street alone. The dominance of the leather trade was personified by George Crump of High Street, one of nine glovers out of 18 mustered in that street. There were 28 shoemakers and 12 tanners. Low-lying Barton Street was less populous, but it still had three of the 14 maltsters and six of the 12 coopers. There were 12 other joiners and carpenters, and 19 men were in the metal trades as pewterers and cutlers.

Industrial breadth made for economic and social stability, and was sustained by extensive service trades in Tewkesbury. John Geast, a High Street mercer, was one of 12 in a community which boasted five haberdashers, four milliners, a stationer, a scrivener and a schoolmaster, George Alcott. In the pubs, citizens were served by 19 innkeepers, tapsters and tipplers; there were also 13 in the malt trade as well as the brewer, Thomas Whore of Church Street. Some used the services of William Coke the parchment-maker, though fewer would have used the obsolescent skills of William Milles and Henry Little, who made bows and arrows.

Social liveliness marked the community, too, for the churchwardens hired out players' 'gear' and amateur dramatics raised money for church funds. The citizens' religion was a serious-minded one. They did not willingly pay for it, for in spite of their sumptuous parish church (the old abbey) the priest was paid only £10 per year. Endowments from citizens such as Thomas Poulton, from such local peers as Viscount Campden and from the crown provided extra preachers and sermons. Incumbents and 'lecturers' (privately financed preachers) quarrelled over money. The Tewkesbury clergy seem to have been of Low Church and Puritan sensibilities. One of them was John Geree, who admired Charles I but was distinctly evangelical and opposed episcopacy. Another was Richard Cooper, who in the 1650s was a congregationalist, or 'Independent'.

It took the Industrial Revolution to bring substantial changes to Tewkesbury, a town disparagingly described by Daniel Defoe in 1705 as 'a quiet trading, drunken town, a Whig baily and all well'. The smaller towns carried limited political weight in seventeenth-century England. Tewkesbury was in many ways typical of them, exhibiting some variety but also an unchanging pattern of life.

4 Mythe Road and John's Bridge.
The confluence of roads and waterways made Tewkesbury a natural market centre.

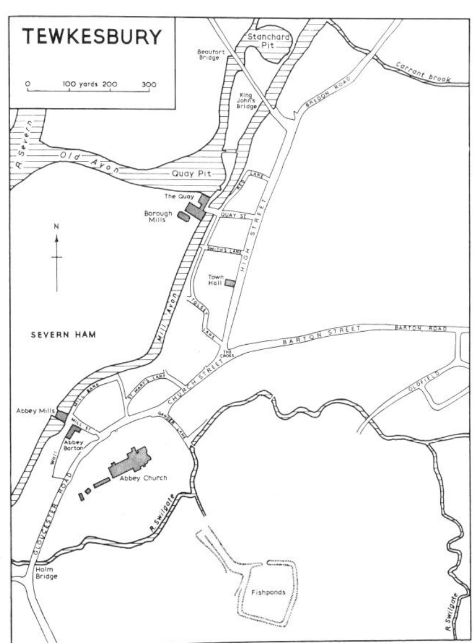

3 Map of Tewkesbury, adapted from the map in the Victoria County History of Gloucestershire, Vol. 8.
Waterways – two rivers and several lesser brooks – determined much of Tewkesbury's shape and history. The town was an inland port.

5 A view from the Quay in 1804.
Detail from a pen and wash drawing, Tewkesbury Town Hall.
This later picture still gives a good idea of the busy port area as it must have looked in the seventeenth century as well.

190. Flemish school, *The Thames at Richmond*, *c.* 1620.
Oil on canvas, 60 × 120 in. (152 × 304 cm.).
Cambridge, Fitzwilliam Museum.
The Surrey and Middlesex banks of the Thames, the settings for splendid royal and noble houses, also provided employment and leisure for simple people. A pedlar, a carter and boatmen are at work, while morris-dancers are viewed with interest by the better off.

of children did not improve very much, but then they were not so very bad before. However, in one important respect the two schools of historical thought are agreed: both emphasize the undoubted decline in religious sensibility and enthusiasm towards the end of the Stuart period. This led to a decline in parental emphasis on a child's chances of salvation and a greater concern with secular ambitions for a child's future. In particular, the decline in the belief in original sin and the growing belief in the innocence of childhood had an important influence on the treatment of children. Even the most kindly parent might accept the famous epigram of the seventeenth-century American Puritan Cotton Mather, 'better whipt than damn'd', if they believed that the death of a child might take him straight to hell. In fact, as a recent study of seventeenth-century diaries has shown, such a belief often led to an almost unbearable conflict in the minds of parents, torn as they were between their love for their children and their sense that it was their duty to punish them for their own good. However, the same study shows that affection usually overcame duty in this respect with the result that diary entries are often heavily laden with guilt.

House and Home

It is not absolutely certain that the nature of marriage and the treatment of children changed very much in the course of the Stuart age; what certainly did change – as is easy to prove from the contents of houses that are listed in inventories – was the material conditions in which husbands and wives lived and in which they brought up their children. It is quite possible that historians have mistaken a growth in material comfort, literacy and self-confidence for a growth in family love. It is also quite possible, of course, that comfort, like property, begets affection.

One interesting change, which can be discerned from the living conditions, was a growth in the desire for privacy. From the late sixteenth century the open-plan, single-floor house, which was typical of medieval England, became increasingly a house with two or more floors, each with a number of separate rooms with spe-

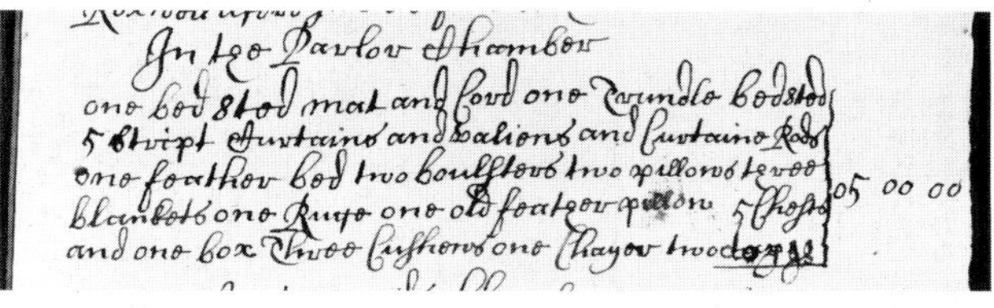

191. Inventory of John Coush of Roxwell, Essex, 14 June 1694.
Essex County Record Office.
Probate inventories provide some of our most detailed and intimate insights into family life. The goods in Coush's parlour chamber – bedding, curtains and furniture – are valued at £5.

cialized functions. By the late seventeenth century the typical London home of a member of the middle classes had a bedroom for each member of the family and separate bedrooms in the garrets for servants, a dining room, a parlour, a kitchen and a pantry or buttery. Some houses had nurseries, studies, withdrawing rooms and even billiard rooms as well. Privacy in the new homes of Stuart England, particularly in bedrooms, was ensured by the simultaneous development of the corridor so that access was no longer through another room. This subdivision of houses was not confined to the middling and upper classes. M. J. Power's study of East London housing in the later seventeenth century shows that in this very working-class area of London the density of occupation was generally below one person per room, and even rural labourers had

193 (above). Cottage at Great Casterton, Leicestershire.
This humbler seventeenth-century dwelling was built in an area of plentiful stone. Beyond the door would have been a screen, and beyond it the fireplace. In the round projection to the right would have been a bread-oven.

192 (below). Crossways Farm, Abinger Hammer, Surrey.
A fine vernacular farmhouse of the late seventeenth century. The gabled two-storeyed porch, the brick cornices and the relieving arches indicate prosperity. There are substantial surrounding farm buildings.

three or more rooms in their humble cottages by 1650. To say why privacy developed in this way is only speculation, though it seems clear that it must have made life more comfortable and have enabled people to develop more intimate personal and sexual relations if they so wished.

The growth of comfort went far beyond the simple development of privacy. Indeed, the bleak and poorly furnished homes of the sixteenth century, in which there were no glass windows and the smoke from a central fireplace trickled out through holes in the roof, had been totally transformed by the end of the seventeenth century. This can perhaps best be illustrated by looking at the homes of the London bourgeoisie, a prosperous group whose example was eagerly followed elsewhere in the country by those who could afford it. They lived in solid homes built almost entirely of brick and tile, which had replaced the filthy, rat-infested houses of thatch, lath and plaster that had burned down in the Great Fire of 1666. They had glass windows in every room, many of them fitted with shutters and white cotton curtains, while the sash-window that is so typical of the modern London house was being introduced in the 1680s and 1690s. Nearly every room had its own brick-built, coal-burning fireplace, each complete with a wide range of brass andirons, pokers, tongs and the like. In the 1680s the fashion developed for marble or tiled surrounds to the fire with a mantelpiece above, which was almost inevitably covered with 'toys' and ornaments.

The master and mistress and many of their children slept in four-poster beds, complete with feather mattresses, blankets, sheets of the finest linen, embroidered counterpanes and hung around with curtains, which were increasingly made of silk or cotton. There were textiles everywhere; tapestries or wool, silk or cotton hangings on the walls or on a hanging rail across the door; table or dresser 'carpets' on top of every flat surface; carpets on the floor, often imported from India and Persia. In the same period the beginning of that excellence in cabinet-making and furniture design developed which was to reach its full glory in the eighteenth century. Chairs, in particular, were transformed from the uncomfortable objects of the Jacobean period into something that was a real pleasure to sit on – elegant to look at, designed to fit the human body and increasingly upholstered – an 'easy chair' as the new fashion of the 1690s was called.

The improvements were not just a matter of better furniture and upholstery. Houses were filled with a profusion of desirable objects intended to satisfy the acquisitive instincts of an increasingly material culture. The looking-glass for instance, which had been a very small and very luxurious object in Elizabethan times, had become much bigger and could be found in nearly every room. Even the maids had their own looking-glasses and their own feather-beds. Meanwhile technological progress had enabled very large mirrors to be set up in the main living rooms, either as pier-glasses between the windows or as chimney-glasses over the fire, and these mirrors could reflect an increasing amount of candlelight from the much wider range of candlesticks, sconces and even chandeliers that were being installed. Most houses would have at least one pendulum clock and, by the reign of Queen Anne, perhaps a barometer as well. Most would have a considerable number of pictures and prints in the hall, on the stairs and in the main rooms; some had 40 or 50 as well as a large number of books, ornaments, statues and a wide range of small objects made of metal, ivory or alabaster and known collectively as toys. Each home would also have its collection of silver plate, pewter, brass, glass and (increasingly) china articles for the dining-room and the kitchen.

Overall it would hardly be an exaggeration to say that although tastes and fashions were to change, the well-furnished house of the reign of Queen Anne could compare in comfort and amenities to anything that would follow until gas-lighting and the bathroom transformed the English house in the nineteenth century. All this was a huge change from the Jacobean home and reflected not only an increase in prosperity but a real change in world-view by the men and women of the middling and upper ranks of English society. Such a change in taste was also, of course, a vital factor in creating the demand that provided employment for that much larger proportion of the English population whose homes, though improved, remained humble and fairly sparsely furnished.

Food, Drink and Health

Changes in material culture were also seen in what the English people ate and drank. The diet of the poor reflected their changing standard of living, which was at a very low ebb in the first half of the Stuart period, but which improved considerably after 1650 (see Chapter One). The poor of Jacobean and Caroline England seem to have eaten virtually no meat at all, relying almost entirely on poor quality bread, cheese, onions and thin gruel with a very occasional piece of bacon and all washed down with water or weak beer. The rise in real wages and the development of agriculture meant that conditions had improved considerably by the time that Gregory King was writing at the end of the seventeenth century. He estimated that the poorest quarter of the population ate meat once a week, normally on Sundays, and that the next poorest quarter ate meat twice a week. By the 1720s diet-sheets for institutions occupied by the poor (such as hospitals and workhouses) indicate that meat was eaten three or even four days each week. It is to be suspected that the meat eaten by the poor was not of a very high quality, but to eat meat at all was an enormous improvement over the hungry days before the civil war. Diets were also improved by an increasing consumption of bread made of wheat rather than rye or barley and a much wider availability of fruit and vegetables, with the potato just beginning to make a mark in the diet of the poor of northern England. It is also clear that the poor were drinking more and stronger beer by the end of the seventeenth century and were acquiring that taste for cheap gin that was to cause considerable moral concern in the 1720s and 1730s.

For anyone even moderately well off, the range of food and drink available changed enormously. Much more meat was being produced by the farmers and contemporary comment suggests that this was eaten in huge quantities. Agricultural change had indeed proved a veritable cornucopia with orchards and market-gardens growing in numbers and their produce in variety, and new crops being sown in the old arable fields. The growth and increased geographical spread of foreign trade had also greatly increased the range of imported food and drink, which now brought in olive oil, oranges and lemons and dried fruits for pies and puddings from the Mediterranean, spices from India and the East, exotic commodities such as mangoes, caviar and vanilla, and wines from all over Europe and the Atlantic Islands.

Four changes in particular stand out – the growth of the tobacco habit from virtually nothing to an almost universal usage by all classes during the reign of Queen Anne; the vast increase in sugar consumption; the development of a taste for hot drinks (first coffee and chocolate and then tea) from the 1650s onwards; and finally the emergence of an apparently almost insatiable taste for ever-stronger drinks. Experiments in eating went with the new raw materials available, as shown by the increase in the output of printed cookery books, the appearance of such French dishes as the ragout and the fricassée and the opening of the first French restaurants in London during the reign of Charles II.

The Queen-like Closet,
OR
RICH CABINET:
Stored with all manner of
RARE RECEIPTS
FOR
Preserving, Candying, and Cookery.
Very Pleasant and Beneficial to all
Ingenious Persons of the *Female Sex.*
To which is added,
A SUPPLEMENT,
PRESENTED
To all Ingenious LADIES,
and GENTLEWOMEN.
By *Hannah Wolley.*
The Fourth EDITION.
LONDON,
Printed for *R. Chiswel* at the *Rose* and *Crown* in St. *Paul's Church-yard,* and *T. Sawbridge* at the *Three Flowers-de-luce* in *Little Britain,* 1681.

194 (above). Hannah Woolley, *The Queen-Like Closet* (1681), frontispiece and title-page.
An unusual glimpse of life in the kitchen. Woolley, a prolific writer, produced not only such practical works as this but arguments for the better education of women and for the greater respect and independence that it might bring them.

195. *The Smoaking Age. Engraving of 1617.*
James I's attack on tobacco-smoking failed to hinder the spread of the habit. Tobacco contributed significantly to the development of Virginia, of Maryland, of Barbados and of other Caribbean colonial settlements.

The Vertue and Operation of this Balſame.

THat this *Balſame* may bee vſed to the health and profit of the buyers, it muſt bee alwaies kept cloſe, and the veſſell wherein it is, muſt be very wel ſtopt, or elſe it will conſume and waſte away.

Any perſon which hath his ſight beginning to faile him, let him continually ſmell vnto this *Balſame*, and hee ſhall be holpen, and his ſight ſhall be preſerued.

Neyther any olde or young folke that haue a ſtinking breath, ſo that the ſtinke come from the ſtomacke, but it helpeth, if it be receiued euery morning faſting, ſixe drops with a ſpoonefull of wine the ſpace of fourteene daies, and faſt two houres after they haue taken it.

Sixe drops of this *Balſame* put into a Fiſtel euery day the ſpace of twenty dayes, healeth and ſtoppeth the Fiſtel: alſo it healeth all wounds old or new, laid vnto them twice a day according to the quantitie of the wound.

196. Compounding and distilling a balsam.
Part of an early seventeenth-century broadside.
London, Society of Antiquaries.
The deficiencies of seventeenth-century medicine left plentiful scope for the purveyors of cure-all medicines. This advertisement for a balsam 'made by N.P. Master of Arts and Minister of God's word' gives nothing away about the ingredients of the cure, but confidently recommends it to sufferers from (among other ailments) bad eyesight, bad breath, loss of appetite, loss of memory, bruises, sores, swellings and the palsey. The balsam is also presented as an antidote to poison.

It also seems, from diaries and other contemporary comment, that it increasingly became the custom to eat out at the home of a friend or neighbour and that a person's reputation might well be enhanced by the 'good table' he could offer his guests. The dinner party thus replaced the old tradition of hospitality to the poor and to travellers, a tradition as much in decline as charity itself.

197. An apothecary's shop. Engraving by W. Faithorne.

Although Stuart Englishmen may have experienced an increasing range of comforts, they also knew pain and did not have the medicines and anaesthetics to control it, a fact that may help to explain the growing attractions of tobacco and strong drink. Indeed, Professor Holmes has suggested that Englishmen, or rather prosperous Englishmen, were demonstrating a decreasing tolerance of pain from about 1660 onwards. The beneficiaries of this decline in stoicism were the medical practitioners and particularly the apothecaries who grew rapidly in numbers and raised their status to become accepted as family doctors by the reign of Queen Anne. There was no revolution in medicine during the Stuart period, though there were some improvements, especially in the skills of surgeons, and some new cures, such as Jesuit's bark (quinine) for fever and improved compounds of mercury for syphilis. However, most medicine remained the matter of purges, vomits and bloodletting that it had been for centuries.

The apothecary-doctors played their part in this traditional medicine, but their main strength lay in their pharmaceutical skills, which enabled them to prescribe and supply an increasing range of exotic drugs to their customers in the shop or to those patients whom they saw at their bedsides. It has been estimated that the import of drugs was twenty-five times higher in 1700 than in 1600, and an increasing proportion of these drugs were painkillers and particularly opiates. The apothecaries sold the new drugs as powders, pills and especially cordials. Since the latter were often a mixture of opiates and alcohol, it is not altogether surprising that their patients felt better and the apothecaries got rich. Such drugs and cordials were expensive and so not available to the poor, who continued to rely on a wide range of old herbal remedies and on tobacco and cheap gin to alleviate their pains and to calm their nerves.

Thus, for all the improvements, Stuart England remained a country of great contrasts between town and country, rich and poor, men and women. Some of these contrasts sharpened over the period, especially that between rich and poor. It was also, however, an age in which material progress and the slow march of comfort benefited almost everyone at all levels of society. Inequality, ignorance, disease, pain, hunger, poverty and filth remained, but for all that there is no doubt that England was a much better place to live in at the death of Queen Anne than it had been at the accession of James I.

Epilogue

Amidst and between the great political upheavals of Stuart England, the nation increased in power, wealth and reputation. Her army and navy grew and triumphed; Scotland, Ireland and the American colonies were harnessed to England's interests; new overseas markets combined with commercial and agricultural diversification at home to bring greater material resources and security; scientific and philosophical accomplishment earned the country unprecedented respect among thinkers on the Continent.

Military and economic exploits were tangible gains. Intellectual and cultural change was a more perplexing experience. The seventeenth century divorced reason from imagination, and turned a poetic civilization into a prosaic one. Under Elizabeth and the early Stuarts, a Sidney or a Spenser or a Jonson could believe that rulers had serious lessons to learn from literary or classical myths, and rulers seemed ready to believe them. Myth persisted in political literature after 1660, but it was now more easily distinguished from fact; it continued to flatter rulers, but not to awe them. The chivalric ideals which had been so earnestly projected in Elizabethan culture survived in the harder-headed Restoration world only as objects of parody. The ideal of literary inspiration, so treasured and so fruitful in the age of John Donne and the early Stuart metaphysical poets, was discredited by the consequences of religious inspiration in the Puritan Revolution. After 1660 Dryden's classicism and rhymed couplets reduced the world to order; the Royal Society enjoined a plain, utilitarian, unambiguous prose; and the Stuart period, which began with the flights of Jacobean verse drama, ended with the smaller ambitions of Addison and Defoe.

Literature yielded the heavens to the telescope; and speculation yielded precedence to observation. Portrait painters were among the foremost observers, even if this golden age of portraiture was mainly the achievement of imported artists. Diarists and biographers, their numbers growing rapidly, were observers too. Puritans, observing their own souls, made contributions to these genres, but the great literary observers, Pepys and John Aubrey, flourished after the defeat of Puritanism; they guided their readers beyond the writer into the world around him. Aubrey's varied interests included archaeology, another area where observation advanced.

Was this more realistic and more observant society also a more secular one? The suggestion is initially persuasive. By the end of the period men turned a little less quickly to God's providence, a little more readily to human and natural causes, to explain the events around them. Intricate theological systems, predestinarianism among them, had lost much of their appeal, making way for a greater confidence in the freedom of man's will and in his ability to influence the world around him. The arrival of toleration, grudging and limited as it was, acknowledged a diversity of beliefs which in some quarters bred relativism and even scepticism.

Yet changes of mentality are rarely fast and rarely straightforward. In times of stress men of the late Stuart period surprise us, and perhaps surprised themselves, by the depth of their providentialist and theological assumptions. James II and William of Orange, confronting each other in 1688, were as certain that their cause was God's cause as Charles I and Oliver Cromwell had been forty years before. The chronology and the meaning of the Bible remained the greatest intellectual challenge man could meet; nothing was more important to Sir Isaac Newton than the correct interpretation of the Book of Revelation. Men studied the universe not to free it from God but to understand the heavenly design behind it. In spite of the intellectual achievements of the period, religious belief retained a strong grip on thought and instinct at the end of the Stuart age, in the politics of which it had been so convulsive a force.

Suggestions for Further Reading

The most rewarding approach to the seventeenth century is through the writers of the time. There are good modern editions of most of the leading imaginative authors. The historian is especially well served by editions of Pepys's *Diary* (ed. R. Latham and W. Matthews), of Clarendon's *History* (ed. W. D. Macray), of Aubrey's *Lives* (ed. A. Clark, or the abbreviated edition by O. L. Dick), and of the writings of perhaps the most perfect writer of seventeenth-century English prose, Sir Thomas Browne (ed. G. Keynes).

The reader wishing to explore further some of the themes and subjects of this book should find help among the following.

ROBERT ASHTON,
The English Civil War (1978).
An account of the origins and course of the conflicts of the 1640s.

GERALD AYLMER,
The Levellers in the English Revolution (1975).
A succinct survey, with documents.

J. C. BECKETT,
The Making of Modern Ireland (1966).
Brief but unrivalled.

G. V. BENNETT,
The Tory Crisis in Church and State 1688–1730 (1975).
A biography of Francis Atterbury, but also an introduction to the relationship between religion and politics in the period.

JOHN BOSSY,
The English Catholic Community 1570–1850 (1975).
A major study, although sometimes a difficult one.

CHRISTOPHER CLAY,
Economic Expansion and Social Change: England 1500–1700 (2 vols., 1984).
A lucid, comprehensive, up-to-date survey of the economic history of the period.

PATRICK COLLINSON,
The Religion of Protestants (1982).
One of the works in which Collinson has revised our understanding of Puritanism.

BARRY COWARD,
The Stuart Age (1980).
The best textbook of the period 1603–1714.

PETER EARLE,
Monmouth's Rebels (1977).
A vivid account of the rising of 1685.

ANTHONY FLETCHER,
A County Community in Peace and War: Sussex 1600–1660 (1975).
A comprehensive account of the relationship between central and local events.

EDWARD GREGG,
Queen Anne (1980).
A substantial biography.

CHRISTOPHER HILL,
The World Turned Upside Down (1972).
A characteristically learned and characteristically provocative study of the religious radicals of the Puritan Revolution.

DEREK HIRST,
The Representative of the People? (1975).
A study of the early seventeenth-century electorate.

CLIVE HOLMES,
The Eastern Association in the English Civil War (1974).
Sets the military conflict against its social and administrative background.

GEOFFREY HOLMES,
Augustan England: Professions, Status and Society 1680–1830 (1982).
One of the books in which Holmes has transformed our knowledge of the later Stuart period.

RALPH HOULBROOKE,
The English Family 1450–1700 (1984).
The essential introduction to its subject.

MICHAEL HUNTER,
Science and Society in Restoration England (1981).
Again, the best introduction.

RONALD HUTTON,
The Restoration (1985).
A vivid recreation of the years 1658–67.

J. P. KENYON,
The Popish Plot (1972).
Combines analysis with a colourful narrative.

ROGER LOCKYER,
Buckingham (1981).
A major biography, enjoyably written.

J. S. MORRILL,
The Revolt of the Provinces (1976).
An influential reassessment of the 1640s.

GRAHAM PARRY,
The Golden Age Restored.
A compelling account of the culture and literature of the early Stuart court.

J. H. PLUMB,
The Growth of Political Stability (1967).
Charts new directions for the study of later Stuart politics.

J. G. A. POCOCK,
The Ancient Constitution and the Feudal Law (1957).
A demanding, classic work on the political assumptions of seventeenth-century Englishmen.

CONRAD RUSSELL (ed.),
The Origins of the English Civil War (1973).
An important collection of essays edited by a historian whose work has redrawn the map of early Stuart political history.

KEVIN SHARPE,
Sir Robert Cotton (1979).
A study of an early seventeenth-century antiquarian which shows the interaction of politics and ideas.

T. C. SMOUT,
A History of the Scottish People 1560–1830 (1969).
The best introduction.

MARGARET SPUFFORD,
Contrasting Communities (1974).
A remarkable recreation of village life in Cambridgeshire.

LAWRENCE STONE,
The Crisis of the Aristocracy 1558–1640 (1965).
Although neither the central argument nor the statistical evidence presented in this large book has carried general conviction, it is a storehouse of valuable information. There is an abbreviated version.

KEITH THOMAS,
Religion and the Decline of Magic (1971).
A monumental account of popular (and unpopular) belief in England between 1500 and 1700.

HUGH TREVOR-ROPER,
Religion, The Reformation and Social Change (1967).
The most incisive and most elegant contribution to the period since the Great War, this collection of essays sets English events against their British and European backgrounds, and explores the interactions of political, social and religious developments.

CHARLES WILSON,
Profit and Power (1957).
A study of the Anglo-Dutch wars.

AUSTIN WOOLRYCH,
Commonwealth to Protectorate (1982).
A detailed account of the politics of 1653.

BLAIR WORDEN,
The Rump Parliament 1648–1653 (1974).
A study of parliamentary politics.

KEITH WRIGHTSON,
English Society 1580–1680 (1982).
A clear and vigorous introduction to the social history of the period.

PETER YOUNG AND RICHARD HOLMES,
The English Civil War (1972).
A history of the battles from 1642 to 1651.

For fuller bibliographical introductions see G. Davies and M. Keeler, *Bibliography of British History: Stuart Period, 1603–1714* (1970); J. S. Morrill, *Seventeenth-Century Britain 1603–1714* (1980); and the *Annual Bulletin of British and Irish History*, published by the Royal Historical Society. B.W.

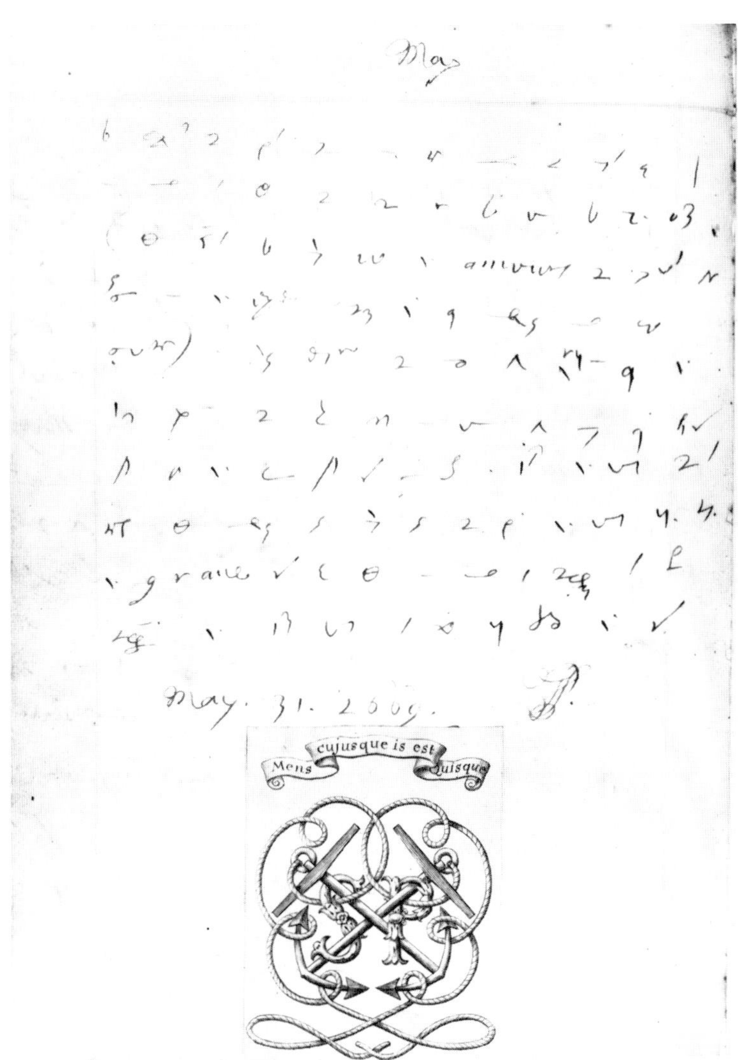

198. The last page of Samuel Pepys's Diary, 31 May 1669.
Pepys kept his diary from the closing months of the Interregnum until 1669. He used a system of shorthand invented earlier in the century by Thomas Shelton. In the mistaken belief that he was losing his sight, Pepys concluded, 'And so I betake myself to that course of ending the diary which is almost as much as to see myself go into my grave – for which, and all the discomforts that will accompany my being blind, the good God prepare me!' Yet to his contemporaries Pepys was known not for his diary, which was kept secret, but as an energetic and reforming naval administrator, as a bibliophile, and as a man of wide cultural and intellectual tastes. He composed music, became President of the Royal Society in 1684, and was made Secretary of the Admiralty in 1686.

Index

Numbers in *italic* refer to the plates and captions